365
DAILY

DEVOTIONS FROM
FAVORITE HYMNS

*Inspiration from the
Songs of the Church*

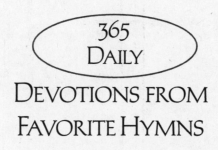

365 DAILY
DEVOTIONS FROM FAVORITE HYMNS

*Inspiration from the
Songs of the Church*

Daniel Partner

BARBOUR
PUBLISHING

Published by Barbour Publishing, Inc., P.O. Box 719, Uhrichsville, Ohio 44683
www.barbourbooks.com

Our mission is to publish and distribute inspirational products offering exceptional value and biblical encouragement to the masses.

Member of the
Evangelical Christian
Publishers Association

Printed in the United States of America.

For my son

If I take the wings of the morning,
and dwell in the uttermost parts of the sea;
Even there shall thy hand lead me,
and thy right hand shall hold me.
PSALM 139:9–10

INTRODUCTION: The Word of God's Grace

The apostle Paul began his epistles with a salutation that I wish to borrow as this book begins: "Grace be to you and peace from God the Father, and from our Lord Jesus Christ" (Galatians 1:3). I love this greeting because it reveals the Father's point of view toward those who are in Christ. These words, *grace* and *peace*, describe the two ends of the one thing that overshadows everything that exists in the universe: that is, God's love.

The physical creation consists of certain basic chemical elements such as hydrogen, nitrogen, and oxygen. All who believe in Christ are a new creation, composed of essential spiritual elements—the most important of which are grace and peace. As believers inhabit the sacred scriptures (as I hope you will while reading this book), the light of God's grace shines in their hearts. That grace is the aggregate of the blessings God has bestowed upon us. As we enjoy those blessings, their sum total is peace. In other words, grace is love in action; peace is the fruit of love's action.

This grace (the Father's goodwill and bounty in Christ toward his children) and this peace (the contentment and gladness experienced by those who rest in Christ) do not appear out of nowhere. The cross is the channel of God's grace. The death of our Lord Jesus Christ brought into human experience deliverance from sin, self, and the present evil age. The heart that opens but a crack to receive this blessing suddenly finds peace within itself, with God, and with others. What's more, it becomes the beneficiary of every spiritual blessing among the celestials, in Christ (Ephesians 1:3).

Scripture urges us to teach and admonish each other "in psalms and hymns and spiritual songs, singing with grace in [our] hearts to the Lord" (Colossians 3:16). Therefore, for centuries believers have been recording in song the overflow of love for God from their hearts. Now, we possess a tremendously rich heritage of hymns that describe God's love and the grace and peace that are ours in Christ.

This book is a selection of verses from some of these inspiring hymns. Each verse describes something of God's benefits toward us and our experience of it, and is accompanied by a few paragraphs of my observations that focus light from the scriptures on these sacred themes. Please read these selections with a copy of the Bible at hand. Here is a year's worth of daily readings, so there is no need to hurry. Be at leisure to look up and thoughtfully consider the scriptural references that accompany each reading. In them, you will find the word of God's grace, which will build you up and give you the enjoyment of your portion among the saints (Acts 20:32).

DANIEL PARTNER

O Word of God incarnate, O wisdom from on high,
O truth unchanged, unchanging, O light of our dark sky:
We praise you for the radiance that from the hallowed page,
A lantern to our footsteps, shines on from age to age.

WILLIAM W. HOW (1823–1897)
O WORD OF GOD INCARNATE

THE REVELATION OF GOD

Since God desires to be known and loved, he gave us the Word, which is the means of creation and the medium of his revelation (John 1:3, 14; Hebrews 1:2). We human beings are unique among the creatures on earth because we are capable of receiving that revelation. The Hebrew scriptures begin with the speaking of God in creation and continue as the record of God's revelation. In those ancient days, God spoke "at sundry times and in divers manners. . .unto the fathers by the prophets" (1:1). The people knew God through the Word, though he himself was hidden from sight.

The Gospel of John was originally addressed to Jewish believers in Jesus Christ, the descendants of those entrusted with the oracles of God (Romans 3:2). It begins with the Word because its readers were accustomed to that method of God's revelation (John 1:1–2). The Word that was from the beginning became flesh and dwelt among them, exhibiting the hidden God. That is to say, God spoke in the Son (1:14; Hebrews 1:2–3).

It is our privilege to hold in our hands the sacred scriptures, mankind's most precious possession (Romans 10:6–8). They alone convey God's light, life, and love to us. As we consider them, let us consent to the wholesome words of our Lord Jesus Christ, hold fast the form of the apostle's sound words, and delight in their revelation of God (1 Timothy 6:3; 2 Timothy 1:13).

In the beginning was the Word, and the Word was with God, and the Word was God. The same was in the beginning with God. All things were made by him; and without him was not any thing made that was made. . . . And the Word was made flesh, and dwelt among us.

JOHN 1:1–3, 14

The Church from you, our Savior, received the gift divine,
And still that light is lifted over all the earth to shine.
It is the sacred vessel where gems of truth are stored;
It is the heaven drawn picture of Christ, the living Word.

WILLIAM W. HOW (1823–1897)
O WORD OF GOD INCARNATE

THE LAMP AND THE LIGHT

To anyone who may ask, "What is truth?" Jesus Christ answers, "I am the truth." Furthermore, the sacred scriptures are given as the testimony concerning him (John 14:6; 5:39). They, too, are truth, God's unique method of revealing his Son to humanity (17:17). In their inanimate words, we see Jesus Christ, the living truth. This is why we must let the written Word be our spiritual tutor.

Although light is essential to life, it must have a lamp to contain and project it. Destroy the lamp and its light is extinguished. The two are merged to the point that it is hard to know where the gold of the lamp and the glory of the light divide. Christ is the light, the written Word is the lamp (8:12; Psalm 119:105). Let us remember that all God's works are perfect; therefore we can expect perfection in his Word. It is as perfect as the truth it conveys, and that truth is Jesus Christ.

The prophet Hosea spoke for God, saying, "My people are destroyed for lack of knowledge" (Hosea 4:6). If believers are in a low, fleshly condition, that is the reason. However, we are assured, "Ye shall know the truth, and the truth shall make you free" (John 8:32) and are encouraged to "desire the sincere milk of the word, that ye may grow thereby" (1 Peter 2:2). Truth is the foundation and source of our conduct, and our life is the outcome of scriptural truth received and obeyed. As a farmer grows wheat by sowing seed, so we can lead a holy life through the knowledge of God's Word.

> *If so be that ye have heard him, and have been taught by him,*
> *as the truth is in Jesus. . .be renewed in the spirit of your mind.*
> EPHESIANS 4:21, 23

The scripture is a banner before God's host unfurled;
It is a shining beacon above the darkling world.
It is the chart and compass that over life's surging tide,
Mid mists and rocks and quicksands, to you, O Christ, will guide.

WILLIAM W. HOW (1823–1897)
O WORD OF GOD INCARNATE

THE OPERATION OF THE WORD OF GOD

The Word of God has always operated and always will. The gospel is presently God's power in our lives (Romans 1:16), yet the beginning of Genesis displays the power of the Word, as well. There it causes tremendous results: light, atmosphere, flowing waters, lush growth, luminaries in the sky, living and moving creatures, and humanity. In fact, all came into being through the Word (John 1:3).

Words were the way God first communicated with mankind. God was presented to Israel by the speaking in the burning bush, the voice from Mount Sinai, the words of the prophets. These words pointed toward God and revealed him. Then the Word became flesh and dwelt among us (v. 14). Jesus Christ personified the process of revealing God to his creatures through words. The book of Revelation calls him the Alpha and Omega; the A and the Z (Revelation 1:8). Just as words are composed of the letters of an alphabet, Christ is God's Word personified—the revelation and explanation of God (Hebrews 1:1–2).

God's words, first known in the power of creation, now manifest their power in saving human beings. This very day it pleases God "by the foolishness of preaching to save them that believe" (1 Corinthians 1:21). The gospel of the grace of God is composed of simple words. Faith comes by hearing those words (Romans 10:17). When people hear the gospel of salvation and believe, they are sealed with the promised Holy Spirit (Ephesians 1:13). That gospel tells us that the day will come when our mortal bodies will put on immortality. Then these words will be fulfilled:

Death is swallowed up in victory.
1 CORINTHIANS 15:54

By the cross of Jesus standing,
Love our straitened souls expanding,
Taste we now the peace and grace!
Health from yonder tree is flowing,
Heav'nly light is on it glowing,
From the blessed sufferer's face.

HORATIUS BONAR (1808–1889)
BY THE CROSS OF JESUS STANDING

A CURSED TREE AND A TREE OF LIFE

Have you ever wondered how God could righteously judge Jesus Christ, the one Man who was truly righteous? Here's how this was possible:

The law says, "Cursed is every one that hangeth on a tree" (Galatians 3:13). Men executed Jesus Christ by hanging him on a cross, so despite his perfection, he innocently violated Deuteronomy 21:22–23. This caused the agony and the darkness of the beloved Son's separation from his Father. From that cursed tree flows the vibrant health of peace and grace to the human race.

The word *tree* in the above verse is not the Greek word that indicates a living tree. It is a word that can be translated "wood" or "log," that is, a dead tree or a pole. The cross on which Jesus died may not have had a cross piece at all, and so was a simple pole. But what a pole that was! The death it caused brought in a resurrection that brings life to everyone who believes.

This wooden pole is reminiscent of the tree of life whose leaves cure the nations (Revelation 22:2). Again, the word *tree* in Revelation 22:2 is the word for dead wood. So, the tree of life points back to the dead tree on which Christ died. This means that even in the far future, the inhabitants of the new earth will find health in the death and resurrection of Jesus Christ.

In the midst of the street of it, and on either side of the river, was there the tree of life, which bare twelve manner of fruits, and yielded her fruit every month: and the leaves of the tree were for the healing of the nations.
REVELATION 22:2

O boundless salvation! deep ocean of love,
O fullness of mercy, Christ brought from above,
The whole world redeeming, so rich and so free,
Now flowing for all men, now flowing for all men,
Now flowing for all men, come, roll over me!

WILLIAM BOOTH (1829–1912)
BOUNDLESS SALVATION

THE JUST SHALL LIVE BY FAITH

William Booth, the British evangelist and founder of the Salvation Army, saw the way of salvation as a free river flowing over all mankind. Indeed, the gospel is God's power for salvation to all who believe (Romans 1:16). Nothing can take its place. No other power in the universe can turn people to God. Yes, substitute methods have been devised to sanitize sinners and correct society through impassioned sermons, emotional excitement, political action, and much hard work. All this cannot save a man or make a woman right before God. Only the gospel, with no additions or apologies, can do this (5:18).

The gospel gives humanity God's righteousness (3:22), assuring us that "the just shall live by faith" (1:17). The prophet Habakkuk proclaimed this unconditional promise at a time when the law had failed and Israel nearly vanished in apostasy (Habakkuk 2:4). Now that foundational description of faith belongs to the whole world (Romans 1:17; Galatians 2:16; 3:11; Hebrews 10:38).

God chose faith as the means to convey his righteousness to us because no effort is involved in believing an honest man, to say nothing of the Almighty God. Nor is faith a commodity that can be purchased. What a relief it is to know that even faith is "not of yourselves: it is the gift of God" (Ephesians 2:8).

I am not ashamed of the gospel of Christ: for it is the power of God unto salvation to every one that believeth; to the Jew first, and also to the Greek. For therein is the righteousness of God revealed from faith to faith: as it is written, The just shall live by faith.
ROMANS 1:16–17

*I hear the Savior say, "Thy strength indeed is small;
Child of weakness, watch and pray, Find in Me thine all in all."*

ELVINA M. HALL (1822–1889)
JESUS PAID IT ALL

ALL IS OF GOD

To say that our strength is small, as Elvina Hall states in her hymn, is to put it mildly. We are children of weakness incapable of loving God. Yet God wants to be loved by us, so he pours his own love into our hearts (Romans 5:5). This love is seen in Christ's death for us when we had no strength (v. 6). It may seem astonishing, but God had to recommend his love to mankind. This was done when Christ died for us while we were still sinners (v. 8). We were God's enemies, totally undeserving of this favor (v. 10), yet because of the death of the Son, we are at peace with God and dwelling in his love. This supreme expression of grace is founded on the fact that nothing exists in us naturally that appeals to God's affections. This reflects the basic truth of divine revelation that "all things are of God" (2 Corinthians 5:18; see Romans 11:36; 1 Corinthians 11:12).

Let's consider how offensive men were at Golgotha. The crime committed there was unquestionably man's greatest offense. How did God respond? He met sin with grace and evil with good. Instead of pouring out the wrath that man deserves, he appeals for peace (2 Corinthians 5:20). That peace was secured by the death that Christ endured at the hands of hateful men. The gospel of peace is permanently founded upon that death. We must not overlook the fact that we were not reconciled to God the moment we surrendered to the gospel. Long before this, when we were still God's enemies, "we were reconciled to God by the death of his Son" (Romans 5:10). God did all the work through Christ. The death of God's Son is the solitary and sufficient cause of our salvation.

*For when we were yet without strength,
in due time Christ died for the ungodly.*
ROMANS 5:6

He has come, the Christ of God,
Left for us his glad abode;
Stooping from his throne of bliss
To this darksome wilderness.

HORATIUS BONAR (1808–1889)
HE HAS COME, THE CHRIST OF GOD

THE HUMILIATION AND EXALTATION OF CHRIST

The coming of God's Son to be a man is vividly told in the Gospels from an earthly point of view. The celestial complement to this story is seen in Philippians 2:6–11. These verses portray the enormous sweep of Christ's service and suffering. They take in the entire universe and all the ages from the beginning to the consummation.

Being in the form of God, Christ was above the heavens (v. 6). But when he descended to the curse of the cross, he voluntarily sank from the highest to the lowest place in the universe. *Jesus* is the Son's name in that earthly humiliation. His exaltation reverses this journey. Eventually, every tongue will declare that Jesus is Lord for the glory of God the Father (vv. 9–11). Then the lowest shall be the highest. However, this won't be complete until every heart is subdued at the end of the age (1 Corinthians 15:28).

Ever since Christ's resurrection, God has been engaged in the exaltation of the Son. Even now, many celestial powers submit to him (1 Peter 3:22). When our Lord returns, the earth will be added to his sphere of influence. Finally, the whole universe will be reconciled to God by the blood of his cross (Colossians 1:20).

Who, being in the form of God, thought it not robbery to be equal with God: but made himself of no reputation, and took upon him the form of a servant, and was made in the likeness of men: and being found in fashion as a man, he humbled himself, and became obedient unto death, even the death of the cross.
PHILIPPIANS 2:6–8

Crowds are behind thee, crowds are before, Life in a single moment thou canst restore. Only to touch thee, spotless and pure, Only to touch thy garment, faith brings the cure.

FANNY J. CROSBY (1820–1915)
ONLY THY GARMENT'S HEM

THE TOUCH OF FAITH, PART 1

The woman with the hemorrhage gives us a wonderful example of working faith (Mark 5:25–34). She sought a cure for her illness for twelve years and went to many physicians seeking relief, but she'd only gotten worse. All her money had been spent on doctors' services, so in addition to being very sick, she was bankrupt.

One day, she reached the limit of her endurance. This was the same time Jairus pleaded for Jesus to heal his daughter of a deadly sickness (vv. 22–24). The woman must have realized there was power within the Lord if he could cure by a simple touch. By touching any part of him, she too would be healed. Acting in faith, she joined the crowd that thronged around him. She forced her way through. "If I may touch but his clothes," she said in her heart, "I shall be whole" (v. 28). She reached between those who pressed upon Jesus, touched the edge of his cloak, and was immediately healed.

Jesus knew at once that power had gone out of him through a touch of faith. He stopped in the midst of the crowd and asked, "Who touched my clothes?" (v. 30). The woman came toward him fearfully. She lay down at his feet and told him the truth. The crowd hushed, and Jesus listened to her story of suffering and weakness and of her faith in his power to save her. He responded in his characteristically gracious manner, "Daughter, thy faith hath made thee whole; go in peace, and be whole of thy plague" (v. 34).

Others had touched him, but only this poor, suffering woman blended her act with faith and so made contact with the only source of salvation in the universe.

The word preached did not profit them, not being mixed with faith in them that heard it.
HEBREWS 4:2

Only thy garment's hem, Lord, I implore;
Only thy garment's hem life will restore;
Only a touch will bring joy to my soul;
Let me but touch thy garment, I shall be whole.

FANNY J. CROSBY (1820–1915)
ONLY THY GARMENT'S HEM

THE TOUCH OF FAITH, PART 2

What is this faith that worked such wonders for the ailing woman in Mark 5? It is a blend of two components: (1) an assurance, or assumption, and (2) a conviction (Hebrews 11:1 NRSV). The woman assumed the Lord was able to heal her and was convinced that a simple touch would accomplish this.

A man or a woman is capable of nothing more spiritual and righteous than to have faith in Christ founded on scriptural truth. This is powerful because it focuses a person's entire attention on God. The scriptures describe our one hope, or expectation (Ephesians 4:4). Faith assumes that this expectation is fact. The scriptures also thoroughly explain God's operation (1:11). Faith is convinced that, though this operation is unseen, it is real. Faith makes the invisible things of God into living realities. It transforms the Word of God into glorious facts, and it is the vital force that links the human spirit with the Spirit of God. Power went out of the Lord because the woman's spirit of faith made contact with the Lord's Spirit, and he immediately responded. That power was not like electricity or the flow of a river. It was the divine response to the woman's faith.

Faith can bring healing, subject to the will of God. However, our infirmity may be essential in our journey to glory. This was certainly true for Paul (2 Corinthians 12:7–10). Like his, our prayer in faith is directed to the most powerful source of healing there is. It will certainly receive a response, although this response may be the assurance that our condition is a part of God's purpose, accompanied by the gift of grace to endure it.

Faith is the assurance of things hoped for, the conviction of things not seen.
HEBREWS 11:1 NRSV

January 10

Years I spent in vanity and pride,
Caring not my Lord was crucified,
Knowing not it was for me he died on Calvary.

WILLIAM R. NEWELL (1868–1956)
AT CALVARY

OUR STATE OF AFFAIRS

Before Jesus' resurrection, the only people who could relate to God were those born as Israelites. Only the Jews were God's children. God's glory was among them; the promises and covenants were theirs; only they were given God's law and the privilege of serving God. The patriarchs were Israel's and, most gloriously, Christ came out of Israel (Romans 9:4–5). Therefore, our state of affairs was bleak from top to bottom: We were without Christ and alienated from Israel. We had no promises, no covenants, no hope, and no God (Ephesians 2:12).

If we had lived when Jesus personally ministered to Israel, we would have had no part in what he offered them. He said, "I am not sent but unto the lost sheep of the house of Israel" (Matthew 15:24). At best, our part would have been scraps of his ministry under Israel's table (vv. 26–27). But Israel rejected the kingdom of the heavens and crucified their Messiah. Though Israel's apostasy is temporary, because of it we have been given all the riches of the gospel (Romans 11:12).

Many of us spent years without Christ in vanity and pride, caring nothing about him. Yet, now, nothing comes between God and us because we are saved by grace through faith (Ephesians 2:8).

> *At that time ye were without Christ, being aliens from the commonwealth of Israel, and strangers from the covenants of promise, having no hope, and without God in the world: But now in Christ Jesus ye who sometimes were far off are made nigh by the blood of Christ.*
> EPHESIANS 2:12–13

Soon shall the trump of God
Give out the welcome sound,
That shakes death's silent chamber walls,
And breaks the turf-sealed ground.

HORATIUS BONAR (1808–1889)
SOON SHALL THE TRUMP OF GOD

OUR HEAVENLY DESTINY

When he wrote 1 Corinthians 15, the apostle Paul uncovered a secret never before told. It is expressed in one word: *change* (see v. 51). It points us to our heavenly destiny revealed in the epistle to the Ephesians (1:3, 20; 2:6; 3:10).

Like Adam's body, our bodies are earthy (1 Corinthians 15:49). Therefore, they must be changed before they can be celestial (v. 48). This change will come in an instant when the Lord descends from heaven with God's trumpet (1 Thessalonians 4:16–17). As the last note of that trumpet sounds, both the living and the dead will be changed.

Why is this change accomplished? According to the prophets, dominion over the earth is given to the nation of Israel. However, rule over the heavenly places belongs to the Church, Christ's body (Ephesians 2:6–7; 3:10). Between the two, the entire universe is brought under divine government (1:21–23). We are given a celestial body so we can function for God in the heavenly places (1 Corinthians 15:48–49).

So, Christ's body, the Church, is called the fullness of the one who fills all in all (v. 28). Only Israel fulfills the divine purpose here on earth. The Church's function is to fulfill God's purpose in the rest of the universe.

Behold, I shew you a mystery; We shall not all sleep, but we shall all be changed, in a moment, in the twinkling of an eye, at the last trump: for the trumpet shall sound, and the dead shall be raised incorruptible, and we shall be changed. For this corruptible must put on incorruption, and this mortal must put on immortality.
1 CORINTHIANS 15:51–53

Yes, for me, for me he careth
With a brother's tender care;
Yes with me, with me he shareth
Every burden, every fear.
Yes, o'er me, o'er me he watcheth,
Ceaseless watcheth, night and day;
Yes, e'en me, e'en me he snatcheth
From the perils of the way.

HORATIUS BONAR (1808–1889)
YES, FOR ME HE CARETH

WORRY AND GOD'S WILL

Scripture describes the development of believers' experience in relationship to worry. This experience changes as God's grace becomes more fully known.

The words of Matthew 6:25–34 are encouraging, yet the relief they offer is conditional. To find relief we must first do something: seek the kingdom of God and its righteousness (v. 33). Similarly, Peter's advice to the dispersed Jewish believers requires that they cast their care upon God "for he careth for you" (1 Peter 5:7). Here, the burden of worry is again eased by the worrier's effort in the casting of cares upon God, though the requirement is somewhat less than in Matthew.

In contrast, Philippians 4:6 doesn't give us something to do. Rather, we do less: "Do not worry about anything" (NRSV). How is this possible? Grace assures us that God is guiding all things to the divine goal (Ephesians 1:11). Our heart's desire is to see God's goal accomplished. This is neither hindered nor advanced by our worrying. When we present our requests to God, we agree with God's will no matter how our prayers are answered. Then we enter into an inexplicable peace that guards our hearts and minds from further worries (Philippians 4:6–7). Though this is difficult to explain, it is easily known through prayer.

Do not worry about anything, but in everything by prayer and
supplication with thanksgiving let your requests be made known to God.
And the peace of God, which surpasses all understanding,
will guard your hearts and your minds in Christ Jesus.
PHILIPPIANS 4:6–7 NRSV

> *Blest be the tie that binds*
> *Our hearts in Christian love;*
> *The fellowship of kindred minds*
> *Is like to that above.*

JOHN FAWCETT (1740–1817)
BLEST BE THE TIE THAT BINDS

THE MOTIVE FOR BROTHERLY LOVE

The Lord's final act before submitting to the cross was to pray for his disciples: "Father, I will that they also, whom thou hast given me, be with me where I am; that they may behold my glory, which thou hast given me: for thou lovedst me before the foundation of the world" (John 17:24).

The disciples were the Father's gift to the Son. Jesus Christ valued them, for their own sakes and because the Father had given them to him. Here we see how human lives are woven into the love between God and Christ. This thought gives us cause for great comfort: Our lives are bound up in the Father's love for the Son.

Earlier in the Lord's ministry, people had murmured and misunderstood him. Finally, many of his disciples deserted him (John 6:66). But this didn't seem to matter. He told them that "God chooses those who were coming to me" (v. 65). Just as we might choose a gift for a loved one, so believers are chosen as gifts in love from the Father to the Son. Could there be a stronger underpinning for our fellowship in brotherly love (1 Thessalonians 4:9)? The tie that binds our hearts in Christian love is the love of the Father for the Son.

But as touching brotherly love ye need not that I write unto you: for ye yourselves are taught of God to love one another. And indeed ye do it toward all the brethren which are in all Macedonia: but we beseech you, brethren, that ye increase more and more.
1 THESSALONIANS 4:9–10

I love to steal awhile away
From every cumbering care,
And spend the hours of closing day
In humble, grateful prayer.

PHOEBE H. BROWN (1783–1861)
I LOVE TO STEAL AWHILE AWAY

OUR LORD'S PRAYERS, PART 1

Like Phoebe Brown, it seems Jesus Christ also loved to steal away to spend hours in prayer. We know he arose early, while it was still night, and prayed in an isolated place (Mark 1:35). He once prayed all night seeking his Father's will in the choice of the Twelve (Luke 6:12–13).

The scripture doesn't often tell what the Son prayed about. At one time, we know he gave thanks to the Lord of heaven and earth (Matthew 11:25–26). This prayer reveals Christ's submission to his Father's ways, even though they may not match his wishes. He acknowledges his Father's delight in hiding the truth from wise and intelligent people. This was a time of intense rejection for the Lord Jesus. According to the prophet Isaiah, such rejection was the story of his life (Isaiah 53:3). Yet, instead of praying against this, our Lord thanked God for it.

Can't we see in this prayer the true heart of our Savior? It is expressed in these words: "Not my will, but thine, be done" (Luke 22:42). We must not think it was easy for him to pray in this way. Christ's sufferings were not his will; they were the will of his Father. In Gethsemane, his struggle was so great that he sweated as he prayed, and sweat dropped like blood on the ground (v. 44).

From the dawn of creation, Christ delighted in God's will. He gladly emptied himself of the divine form and took the form of a slave and the likeness of humanity (Philippians 2:6–8). We find no prayer of his related to this. But, when facing the death of the cross, he fell on his face and struggled to align his will with the Father's.

And he. . .fell on his face, and prayed, saying, O my Father, if it be possible,
let this cup pass from me: nevertheless not as I will, but as thou wilt.
MATTHEW 26:39

I love to think on mercies past,
And future good implore,
And all my cares and sorrows cast
On God, whom I adore.

PHOEBE H. BROWN (1783–1861)
I LOVE TO STEAL AWHILE AWAY

OUR LORD'S PRAYERS, PART 2

The Lord's prayer in John 17 gives glimpses of the Son's relationship with his Father. Could his joy in this relationship be the reason why he often stole away to be alone in prayer? He was with the Father in glory before the world was (v. 5). His Father loved him before the world's foundation (v. 24). What a contrast between this and his life with sinning, corrupted, and dying humanity! He was the life, but they refused his words of life (John 11:25; 6:66–68). They begged for loaves and fishes but would not believe that he was the bread of life from heaven (6:34–35).

Our souls are the means by which we experience this life. Consider this while reading the following words: "Therefore doth my Father love me, because I lay down my life, that I might take it again" (10:17). The Greek word here translated "life" is *psuche* and is better translated "soul." The soul Christ laid down was his only earthly means of enjoying fellowship with his Father. Each time he slipped away from the commotion of the crowds for a time of prayer, he again tasted a little of the divine intimacy he knew before he humbled himself to become a man (Philippians 2:6–7). Yet he laid down his soul and endured separation from God during those agonizing hours of darkness on Golgotha. Then he uttered his last earthly prayer: "My God, my God, why hast thou forsaken me?" (Mark 15:34).

But that was not our Lord's last prayer. He knows our infirmities and is at his Father's right hand, his accustomed place of glory. There he is now, pleading for our sakes (Romans 8:34).

It is Christ that died, yea rather, that is risen again, who is even at the right hand of God, who also maketh intercession for us.
ROMANS 8:34

January 16

I love by faith to take a view
Of brighter scenes in heaven;
The prospect doth my strength renew,
While here by tempests driven.

PHOEBE H. BROWN (1783–1861)
I LOVE TO STEAL AWHILE AWAY

THE PATTERN OF SCRIPTURAL PRAYER

Two prayers deeply involve us in God's plan for the ages. One is found in Ephesians 1:17–19, the other in Ephesians 3:14–19. These can entirely engage our times of prayer.

For example, instead of physical strength, the prayer in Ephesians 3 seeks strength for the inner man. Instead of one's own home, this prayer asks that Christ may have a home in one's heart and that the roots of the soul be founded in God's love. While we pray for one thing—our home or our health—the Lord needs something else. As Jesus once said, "Foxes have holes, and birds of the air have nests; but the Son of Man has nowhere to lay his head" (Luke 9:58 NRSV).

If we were to use Ephesians 3 as a prayer, we would travel the breadth and length and depth and height of God's plan for the ages. The problems of loneliness and lovelessness are solved by this prayer's petition for the knowledge of the "love of Christ, which passeth knowledge." While we do need material possessions, these do not satisfy our souls. So, this prayer asks that you would be "filled with all the fulness of God."

These verses are our pattern of "humble, grateful prayer."

That the God of our Lord Jesus Christ, the Father of glory, may give unto you the spirit of wisdom and revelation in the knowledge of him: the eyes of your understanding being enlightened; that ye may know what is the hope of his calling, and what the riches of the glory of his inheritance in the saints, and what is the exceeding greatness of his power to us-ward who believe, according to the working of his mighty power.
EPHESIANS 1:17–19

> As shadows cast by cloud and sun flit o'er the summer grass,
> So, in Thy sight, Almighty One, earth's generations pass.
> And as the years, an endless host, come swiftly pressing on,
> The brightest names that earth can boast just glisten and are gone.

WILLIAM CULLEN BRYANT (1794–1878)
AS SHADOWS CAST BY CLOUD AND SUN

ALL FLESH IS LIKE GRASS

It is both ironic and encouraging that these words come from the pen of William Cullen Bryant, who was esteemed—along with Henry Wadsworth Longfellow and Ralph Waldo Emerson—as a leading American poet. Born in Massachusetts, where he practiced law, Bryant moved to New York City and became editor of the *New York Evening Post*, which was instrumental in the formation of the Republican Party in 1856 and the election of Abraham Lincoln to the presidency. He was also a founder of the New York Medical College.

The irony is that Bryant was a leading light of mid-nineteenth-century American literary and political life, yet now his name is hardly known. It glistened and was gone, as he said it would. The encouragement is that he knew his name would pass away with all the generations and that one name will prevail (Philippians 2:9–10). The following is the other verse from his hymn:

> Yet doth the star of Bethlehem shed a luster pure and sweet;
> And still it leads, as once it led, to the Messiah's feet.
> O Father, may that holy star grow every year more bright,
> And send its glorious beams afar to fill the world with light.

The voice said, Cry. And he said, What shall I cry? All flesh is grass, and all the goodliness thereof is as the flower of the field: the grass withereth, the flower fadeth: because the spirit of the LORD bloweth upon it: surely the people is grass. The grass withereth, the flower fadeth: but the word of our God shall stand for ever.

ISAIAH 40:6–8

A safe stronghold our God is still,
A trusty shield and weapon;
He'll help us clear from all the ill
That hath us now o'ertaken.
The ancient prince of hell
Hath risen with purpose fell;
Strong mail of craft and power
He weareth in this hour;
On earth is not his fellow.

MARTIN LUTHER (1483–1546)
A MIGHTY FORTRESS IS OUR GOD

THE PREPARATION OF THE GOSPEL OF PEACE

Here on earth, we must not enter into conflict with other people—with flesh and blood no matter how they combat us (Ephesians 6:12). The armor that God has given us is only useful as we grapple with wicked spirits in the celestial realms (v. 11). The people who may oppose us are innocent antagonists used by those spiritual forces. We must look beyond the human instruments to the real adversary in the spirit world.

What then is the best way to interact with the people of this world, either friends or foes? We must be imitators of God who is entirely at peace with the world and does not reckon their offenses against them (Ephesians 5:1; 2 Corinthians 5:19). This is seen in the one item of the armor of God that touches the earth: the shoes that scripture describes as the preparation of the gospel of peace (Ephesians 6:15). It cannot be said enough: God is presently at peace with humanity. This is why he is called the God of peace (Romans 15:33; 16:20). Therefore, our approach to all people is in peace. As it is written, "How beautiful are the feet of them that preach the gospel of peace" (10:15). Such a gospel brings God's peace, even to the innocent human tools of the spirit powers that direct human affairs.

Now the Lord of peace himself give you peace always by all means.
The Lord be with you all.
2 THESSALONIANS 3:16

Be thou my vision, O Lord of my heart;
Naught be all else to me, save that thou art
Thou my best thought, by day or by night,
Waking or sleeping, thy presence my light.

ATTRIBUTED TO DALLAN FORGAILL (EIGHTH CENTURY)
BE THOU MY VISION
TRANSLATED BY MARY ELIZABETH BYRNE (1880–1931)

LIVING IN THE LORD'S PRESENCE

The writer of this hymn longs to see the Lord. Like all believers, he wants a vision of Christ that will fill his thoughts day and night. That is to say, he desires to live in the light of the Lord's presence. Practically speaking, Christ is now absent. Our longing to live in his presence leads us to yearn for his return when he will be truly present.

The Greek word translated "coming" is *parousia*, which can be literally translated "beside-being," and sometimes appears in our translations as the word *presence*. The Thessalonian believers were looking for the Lord's presence, so the apostle prayed for them like this: "And the Lord make you to increase and abound in love one toward another, and toward all men, even as we do toward you: To the end he may establish your hearts unblameable in holiness before God, even our Father, at the coming [presence] of our Lord Jesus Christ with all his saints" (1 Thessalonians 3:12–13).

We modern believers benefit from this prayer. In it we see not only the expectation of our Lord's future presence, but the motive for living a holy life today. This springs from the overflow of love to our fellow saints and to all other people, as well. It also looks forward to the glorious presence of the Lord. His presence is not a sensation of something invisible in our lives today. If Christ were not absent, we would not long for him. When Christ comes with all his saints, he will be actually near and known. He will be wonderfully present.

And the very God of peace sanctify you wholly; and. . .your whole spirit and soul and body be preserved blameless unto the coming of our Lord Jesus Christ.
1 THESSALONIANS 5:23

Riches I heed not, nor man's empty praise,
Thou mine inheritance, now and always;
Thou and thou only, first in my heart,
High King of heaven, my treasure thou art.

ATTRIBUTED TO DALLAN FORGAILL (EIGHTH CENTURY)
BE THOU MY VISION
TRANSLATED BY MARY ELIZABETH BYRNE (1880–1931)

OUR INHERITANCE IN CHRIST

In reality, all we have is in Christ. This is why Colossians says, "Ye are complete in him," and then goes on to tell of our great legacy in three words: death, burial, and resurrection (2:10–12). These three words describe the entire gospel concerning Jesus Christ and his believers (1 Corinthians 15:1–4). This is our rich inheritance.

When Christ died, we died also. This truth is repeated many times in Paul's epistles. It means we are dead to our sins and the flesh that attempts to buy God's approval with good behavior (Colossians 2:11). This idea is described elsewhere like this: "Knowing this, that our old man is crucified with him, that the body of sin might be destroyed, that henceforth we should not serve sin. For he that is dead is freed from sin" (Romans 6:6–7).

Christ's entombment is the verification of this death. When Jesus died, everyone involved knew he had been buried. Spiritually speaking, all believers were in Christ in that tomb (Romans 6:4; Colossians 2:12).

Most gloriously, we were made alive together in him (Colossians 2:12). In resurrection, we are seated with him among the heavenlies (Ephesians 2:6). Today we enjoy this status in spirit and set our "affection on things above, not on things on the earth" (Colossians 3:2). The splendid day will come when we will actually receive our allotment in the celestials and walk in the good works that he has prepared for us there (Ephesians 1:3, 11; 2:10).

Know ye not, that so many of us as were baptized into Jesus Christ were
baptized into his death? Therefore we are buried with him by baptism into
death: that like as Christ was raised up from the dead by the glory of the
Father, even so we also should walk in newness of life.
ROMANS 6:3–4

High King of heaven, my victory won,
May I reach heaven's joys, O bright heaven's sun!
Heart of my own heart, whatever befall,
Still be my vision, O ruler of all.

ATTRIBUTED TO DALLAN FORGAILL (EIGHTH CENTURY)
BE THOU MY VISION
TRANSLATED BY MARY ELIZABETH BYRNE (1880–1931)

ALL BELIEVERS WILL BE RESURRECTED

Will the writer of this hymn inherit the joys of heaven? He needn't worry. Christ guarantees a heavenly citizenship that is secured not by our worthiness, but by his (Philippians 3:20). This is evident in the earliest of Paul's letters, in which he wrote, "For the Lord himself shall descend from heaven. . .and the dead in Christ shall rise first" (1 Thessalonians 4:16).

Who were the dead in Christ in ancient Thessalonica? The saints there had been believers for hardly more than a year when they received their first letter from the apostle Paul. No wonder their faith was deficient (3:10). The epistle to the Romans, which thoroughly describes the gospel, was not written until six years later. Nine years later, Ephesians, the pinnacle of the gospel, saw the light of day. The Thessalonians knew little or nothing about what the apostle wrote in those letters, yet they were told they would be resurrected with those who belong to Christ at his coming (4:16; 1 Corinthians 15:23).

Our destiny is not dependent on ourselves. A child is not disinherited because he is immature, even if he is heir to a throne. It may be easy to think that immature believers like those in Thessalonica are not fit for the glory that will be revealed in them. The truth is, none of us are. To think otherwise exposes a boastful heart and darkens the grace of God that we are called to display (Ephesians 2:7–9).

Then we which are alive and remain shall be caught up together with them in the clouds, to meet the Lord in the air: and so shall we ever be with the Lord. Wherefore comfort one another with these words.
1 THESSALONIANS 4:17–18

We walk by faith, and not by sight;
No gracious words we hear
From him who spake as man ne'er spake;
But we believe him near.

HENRY ALFORD (1810–1871)
WE WALK BY FAITH

THE LIFE OF FAITH, PART 1

"The Spirit speaketh expressly, that in the latter times some shall depart from the faith" (1 Timothy 4:1). These words sober us because only believers can fall away from the faith. But these people do not slip away to believe in nothing. Instead, they give heed to deceiving spirits and the teachings of demons (v. 1).

Satan often operates by means of power, signs, and false miracles because he is an angel of light and his ministers are ministers of righteousness (2 Corinthians 11:14–15; 2 Thessalonians 2:9;). So let us not imagine that all miracles are from God. After all, we read of signs and wonders in the book of Revelation, but these are attributed to the beast. While it is performing miracles, God's saints suffer and are persecuted (Revelation 13:13–14).

In contrast with satanic operations, God's administration is in faith (1 Timothy 1:4). This is one of the chief features of the present era. According to Hebrews 11:1, faith is a conviction about matters that are not being observed. Second Corinthians 5:7 makes this practical when it says that we walk by faith and not by sight. These verses draw a contrast between faith and that which we can observe outwardly. Let us take this instruction and base our life on that which is not yet seen (Romans 8:24–25).

> *[We] who have the first fruits of the Spirit, groan inwardly while we wait*
> *for adoption, the redemption of our bodies. For in hope we were saved.*
> *Now hope that is seen is not hope. For who hopes for what is seen?*
> *But if we hope for what we do not see, we wait for it with patience.*
> ROMANS 8:23–25 NRSV

We may not touch his hands and side,
Nor follow where he trod;
But in his promise we rejoice,
And cry, "My Lord and God!"

HENRY ALFORD (1810–1871)
WE WALK BY FAITH

THE LIFE OF FAITH, PART 2

God has always given his saints gifts to help them along the way. Today we have three—faith, hope, and love (1 Corinthians 13:13). Other gifts have faded and passed away (v. 8), but these three mark the transcendent path that the King James Version calls "a more excellent way" (12:31).

Let us consider the first of these—faith. It is true that perceptible things like signs, visions, and miraculous ways of speaking once accompanied God's revelation. But today God's truth is known by faith. This is a splendid gift. After all, not everyone is able to believe the Word. We accept it only because God's Spirit operates within us, enlightening our hearts to the truth (Ephesians 1:18). We are blessed to accept what God says, but not because we can prove it by means of our eyes or ears. The reasoning, philosophy, and logic of our intellect are useless to explain it. It is by faith that we understand God's revelation. Therefore, faith is the ruling principle that will last until the next age begins.

God's ways of righteousness and peace are insignificant to the inhabitants of today's world. God's Word, which we love, is infertile in the modern mind. God's people are few and divided. But we believers must always remember this: We walk by faith, not by sight (2 Corinthians 5:7). God gives us the truth of the gospel and the faith to believe it, enabling us to live sanely, justly, and devoutly as we await the coming of the glory of the great God and our Savior Jesus Christ (Titus 2:13).

Holding faith, and a good conscience; which some having put away
concerning faith have made shipwreck...
1 TIMOTHY 1:19

Help then, O Lord, our unbelief;
And may our faith abound,
To call on thee when thou art near,
And seek where thou art found.

HENRY ALFORD (1810–1871)
WE WALK BY FAITH

THE LIFE OF FAITH, PART 3

When God established his covenant with Israel at Sinai, the people were made aware of his presence by physical evidence. The mountain shook and was engulfed with smoke. A voice spoke like a trumpet (Exodus 19:18–19). The law was written in stone.

In contrast to this, Israel's new covenant with God will be spiritual. Its law will be in the inward parts, written in human hearts (Jeremiah 31:31–34). Although Paul did not minister this covenant to Israel, he called his gospel a new covenant of the spirit because it also tells of things that cannot be proven by experiential evidence (2 Corinthians 3:6). He ministers things that are inward and unseen. This is why we look at the things that cannot be observed and walk by faith, not by sight (4:16–18; 5:7).

Is there a way to prove that all was created in the Son of God's love, that all things are held together in him, or that all are reconciled through the blood of his cross (Colossians 1:16–17, 20)? The faith is not like an eighth-grade science fair with demonstrations that prove there will be a new heaven and a new earth or that God will be all in all (1 Corinthians 15:28; Revelation 21:1). These and many other matters of the faith defy what is obvious to our senses and will never be verified by objective proof until they occur.

True, the Spirit supports our faith as the foretaste of these things. For this, we give thanks. But this is intensely subjective (Ephesians 1:14). So what do we say to people who do not share our understanding of the truth? To them we must say,

I know whom I have believed, and am persuaded that he is able
to keep that which I have committed unto him against that day.
2 TIMOTHY 1:12

That, when our life of faith is done,
In realms of clearer light
We may behold thee as thou art,
With full and endless sight.

HENRY ALFORD (1810–1871)
WE WALK BY FAITH

THE LIFE OF FAITH, PART 4

How do we know God's Word is true? Is its trustworthiness absolutely supported by archaeological or geological evidence? Should we search for signs in the events of history to prove its veracity? Perhaps an analysis of the structure and style of biblical writings will demonstrate their perfection. Events such as wars and famines cause us to consider passages like Revelation 17. We may wish to reread John's message from Patmos in light of the growing global economy. But we must not rely on such matters to confirm our confidence in the sacred scriptures. Even if events in the Middle East do not match prophecy during our lifetimes, we still believe those prophecies will be fulfilled. Why? It is because God has graciously granted us faith (Philippians 1:29).

It is our privilege to believe that God's Word is true. For example, Paul tells us that perilous times will come (2 Timothy 3:1–9). However, this prediction should not be used to test the trueness of the Word. This verse was written so we will continue to follow Paul in his teaching, motive, purpose, faith, patience, love, endurance, persecutions, and sufferings (vv. 10–11). No matter what happens in our lifetimes, perilous or not, we will believe that the scriptures are inspired and that God is operating all for our good (v. 16; Romans 8:28).

Why? It is because we have been given faith to believe. This faith is one of the three remaining spiritual gifts in this era (1 Corinthians 12:1, 31; 13:13). From a human point of view, it is a small thing, but when we center that faith on the gospel of the grace of God, its value is limitless.

For unto you it is given in the behalf of Christ, not only to believe on him, but also to suffer for his sake.
PHILIPPIANS 1:29

I know my faith is founded on Jesus Christ, my God and Lord;
And this my faith confessing, unmoved I stand upon his Word.
Man's reason cannot fathom the truth of God profound;
Who trusts her subtle wisdom relies on shifting ground.
God's Word is all sufficient, it makes divinely sure,
And trusting in its wisdom, my faith shall rest secure.

ERDMANN NEUMEISTER (1671–1756)
I KNOW MY FAITH IS FOUNDED

THE LIFE OF FAITH, PART 5

Throughout the Hebrew scriptures we find statements similar to this: "I make thee sick in smiting thee, in making thee desolate because of thy sins" (Micah 6:13). However, we should not quote such wrathful verses to describe God's present attitude, because he is at peace with the world until the end of this age (2 Corinthians 5:18–19). Yes, all around us we can see that humanity is given over to uncleanness, dishonorable passions, and a disqualified mind (Romans 1:24–32). There is a reason for this: The sad condition of humanity disciplines and drives us to seek God. This leads to the enjoyment of life in the gift of God's Son (5:18).

We rejoice that one day all creation will be brought into the freedom of the children of God (8:21). This outlook of joy and peace in the midst of a depraved world is a believer's privilege because the effects of God's wrath are easy to see, but the effects of Christ's cross are almost imperceptible.

Why do we see the cross? This is because the revelation of the gospel is out of Christ's faith and for our faith, so that "the just shall live by faith" (1:17). This saying is not only a promise for the future, but is also a description of our present privilege to daily live by faith in the good news of the salvation accomplished because of the perfection of Jesus Christ that enabled him to become the perfect sacrifice.

Knowing that a man is not justified by the works of the law,
but by the faith of Jesus Christ, even we have believed in Jesus Christ,
that we might be justified by the faith of Christ.
GALATIANS 2:16 (SEE ALSO ROMANS 3:22; GALATIANS 2:20; PHILIPPIANS 3:9)

When Abraham and Sarah had promised them a son,
They were surprised and knew not what to say;
But they knew what God had promised he was able to perform:
And the pow'r of God is just the same today.

FREDERICK A. GRAVES (1856–1957)
THE POWER OF GOD

THE LIFE OF FAITH, PART 6

Abraham was fully assured that God was able to do all that he promised to do, so scripture calls Abraham "the father of all them that believe" (Romans 4:11, 20–21). Whereas God spoke directly to the patriarch, he conveys the glorious gospel to us through the scriptures. Therefore, Abraham had much more evidence of the truth than we do. He heard God speak directly and saw proof of the Lord's faithfulness. We read the gospel's message of righteousness and stand in faith alone with no perceptible evidence.

Abraham was first on the path of faith, and we follow in his footsteps like children with a father (Galatians 3:7). The gospel we believe differs in many ways from the promises to Abraham, but in Romans 4 we find some similarities.

For example, like Abraham, we believe that God gives life to the dead (Romans 4:17). For the father of faith, this involved the ability to bring forth a son. For us, it means that Jesus Christ was raised from the dead for our justification (v. 25). We have no visible sign that God raised Jesus from among the dead, and there is no outward evidence to support the scripture's message of justification. But, together with the Father of all who believe, we have been given faith to believe that God is able to achieve what he has declared in the scriptures.

Even as Abraham believed God, and it was accounted to him for
righteousness. Know ye therefore that they which are of faith, the same are
the children of Abraham.
GALATIANS 3:6–7

In thee alone, O Christ, my Lord,
My hope on earth remaineth;
I know thou wilt thine aid afford,
Naught else my soul sustaineth.

JOHANNES SCHNEESING (D. 1567)
IN THEE ALONE, O CHRIST, MY LORD
TRANSLATED BY ARTHUR T. RUSSELL (1806–1874)

THE LIFE OF FAITH, PART 7

Suppose a person has faith enough to fill an ocean. If he believes in someone other than Jesus Christ, will he be saved (Acts 4:12)? Yet someone with a mere droplet of faith will be instantly delivered when she believes in the Lord Jesus. How much faith in Christ did Saul, the Church's destroyer, have in his heart as he traveled along the road to Damascus? I daresay, not much. Yet he was delivered from so great a death and received so great a salvation (2 Corinthians 1:10; Hebrews 2:3).

From beginning to end, salvation is entirely the work of God in Christ. There is no room in it for human works, fleshly boasting, or anything else. Even our faith is God's gift (1 Corinthians 1:26–31; Ephesians 2:8).

Christ has the preeminence in all things (Colossians 1:18). Yet everyone except those who understand the truth of the gospel thinks that Christ needs help when it comes to salvation. Therefore, the British author, artist, and social critic John Ruskin (1819–1900) observed, "The reason that preaching is commonly so ineffective is that it more often calls on men to work for God than to behold God working for men."

The key to a life of faith is not in the amount of faith a person might have, but the sufficiency of the one in whom that faith is placed. It is selfish to ask, "Do I rely enough on Christ?" The question is, "Is Christ Jesus enough for me to rely on?" Faith is the means to an end, not the end itself. The end is God through Christ Jesus.

As it is written, "Let the one who boasts, boast in the Lord."
1 CORINTHIANS 1:31 NRSV

> *O Father, haste the promised hour, When at his feet shall lie*
> *All rule, authority, and power, Beneath the ample sky;*
> *When he shall reign from pole to pole, The Lord of every human soul.*

WILLIAM CULLEN BRYANT (1794–1878)
O NORTH WITH ALL THY VALES OF GREEN

THE CONSUMMATION OF THE AGES

William Cullen Bryant prays for the hour when all rule, authority, and power—that is, all government—will lie at God's feet. When will this happen?

Government is a method of coping with evil. Today there are many styles of government in the world. In the coming age, Christ's kingdom will cover the earth. Even the new heaven and new earth have a throne—a government of God and the Lamb (Revelation 22:3). Government is not necessary when evil is entirely banished. Therefore, the promised hour that Bryant prays for comes after the record of Revelation 21 and 22.

Here is a description of the world's future according to scripture: The reign of Christ that begins in the thousand-year kingdom (Revelation 20:4) and extends through the age of the new heaven and new earth (21:3) is so favorable that it brings the universe to a state of perfection (1 Corinthians 15:24–28). Then all need of governmental restraints disappears because the universe has been purged of all evil—all enemies. Death becomes inoperative (v. 26), all believers are made alive in Christ (v. 22), and God becomes all in all (v. 28). This promised hour is the end of the biblical record.

Today, God is all in Christ Jesus. God will be all in the saints when we are made alive at Christ's coming (v. 23). God will be all in all when death is abolished (v. 28). This is the consummation of the ages (v. 24)—the conclusion of God's purpose.

Then cometh the end, when he shall have delivered up the kingdom to God, even the Father; when he shall have put down all rule and all authority and power. . . . And when all things shall be subdued unto him. . .that God may be all in all. . .
1 CORINTHIANS 15:24, 28

Soldiers of Christ, arise,
And put your armor on,
Strong in the strength which God supplies
Through his eternal Son.

CHARLES WESLEY (1707–1788)
SOLDIERS OF CHRIST, ARISE

THE WHOLE ARMOR OF GOD

We need not worry about spiritual warfare, because we are completely protected by the armor of God. However, let's be sure that not a single piece of it is missing by receiving every part as described in Ephesians 6:13–20.

Just like a soldier's physical armor, the effectiveness of this armor depends on its completeness. Also, there is a certain order to its parts in this portion of scripture. The instructions are given to us in a complete package and a divine sequence.

This is similar to the prayer in Colossians 1:9–11, which is a guide to prayer for power according to the might of God's glory (v. 11). Its requests are presented as a whole in a certain order. We should not pick out one plea over another if we wish to know such power. It is the same with the armor of God. We are not free to choose only a favorite part, or one we think is most important. We are safe in the celestial conflict when we carry out simple scriptural instructions.

The armor invigorates us in the might of God's strength (Ephesians 6:10). This has a threefold support: our cooperation, his operation, and prayer and petition. We cooperate by remaining in the truth (v. 14), by our walk in righteousness (v. 14), by our readiness with the gospel of peace (v. 15), and by holding to faith (v. 16). God operates through the helmet of salvation and the sword of the Spirit (v. 17). Prayer and petition are carried out on every occasion, with vigilance and perseverance, for all the saints (v. 18). This is the way we are invigorated in the Lord and in the might of his strength (v. 10).

Wherefore take unto you the whole armour of God, that ye may be able to withstand in the evil day, and having done all, to stand.
EPHESIANS 6:13

Fear not, O little flock, the foe
Who madly seeks your overthrow;
Dread not his rage and power:
What though your courage sometimes faints?
His seeming triumph o'er God's saints
Lasts but a little hour.

JOHANN M. ALTENBURG (1584–1640)
FEAR NOT, O LITTLE FLOCK

THE WORD OF GOD AND THE LAST DAYS

Many seekers of the Lord become discouraged by negative experiences they have had while meeting with other Christians. They see what Johann Altenberg describes as the foe's seeming triumph over God's saints. This is caused by the departure from truth that began in Paul's time and has, with a few exceptions, become worse with each succeeding century. This is why we should prize the apostle's last epistle. Second Timothy describes the Church's apostasy (3:1–5) and answers this question: How shall we serve God in such perilous times?

Second Timothy tells us that the inspired scriptures are the one great need in the last days (3:16–17). Its central subject is the encouragement to Timothy to be an unashamed worker who correctly divides the Word of truth, assigning each truth its proper place. If misplaced and misapplied, scriptural truth becomes error (2:15–18). Each of its chapters hinges upon an exhortation about the Word of God beginning with the directive to "hold fast the form of sound words, which thou hast heard of me" (1:13). The exact terms and phrases of scripture are entirely sufficient to describe God's truth. The epistle closes with the charge to proclaim the word with all patience (4:2).

As Johann Altenberg says in his hymn, the enemy only seems to have triumphed. However, we know that the solid foundation of God still stands, and that every moment we spend handling the Word of God profits us, perfects us, and outfits us for every good work (3:15–17).

The foundation of God standeth sure, having this seal, The Lord knoweth them that are his. And, Let every one that nameth the name of Christ depart from iniquity.
2 TIMOTHY 2:19

Great God of wonders! All thy ways
Are matchless, godlike and divine;
But the fair glories of thy grace
More godlike and unrivaled shine.

SAMUEL DAVIES (1723–1761)
GREAT GOD OF WONDERS

THE TRANSCENDENCE OF GOD'S GRACE

With a believer's eyes, we look around us and within ourselves and see the matchless ways of God. But we must look at grace to truly see God.

The disobedience of Adam caused all mankind to be made sinners (Romans 5:19). Our society and our religions cope with this sin through law various codes that attempt to restrain transgression. However, austere legal threats do not hinder the sinner. In fact, "the law entered, that the offence might abound" (v. 20). In other words, law causes more sin. "But where sin abounded, grace did much more abound" (v. 20). The logical question that follows this surprising statement is, "Shall we continue in sin, that grace may abound?" (6:1). God forbid.

In God's grace, the obedience of Jesus Christ conveys righteousness to believers through no effort of their own (5:19). When first reading this, one's mind may make an error in logic and imagine that this gives license to sin. But the actual effect of grace is exactly the opposite. Grace, not law, deters us from sinning. It trains us to live acceptably in God's sight in this evil age (Titus 2:11–12). It softens the heart, attracts the will, and provides the power to put its principles into practice. Grace reveals God.

> *That in the ages to come he might shew the exceeding riches*
> *of his grace in his kindness toward us through Christ Jesus.*
> *For by grace are ye saved through faith; and that not of yourselves:*
> *it is the gift of God: not of works, lest any man should boast.*
> EPHESIANS 2:7–9

When peace, like a river, attendeth my way,
When sorrows like sea billows roll;
Whatever my lot, thou hast taught me to say,
It is well, it is well with my soul.

HORATIO G. SPAFFORD (1828–1888)
IT IS WELL WITH MY SOUL

THE TRANSCENDENCE OF GOD'S LOVE

Two opposed images representing peace and sorrow appear in this hymn—a flowing river and a raging sea. Both may be our lot from time to time. However, our place in God's heart isn't controlled by the conditions of our life. Treasure or scarcity, bad health or fitness, camaraderie or loneliness—none indicate God's care for us or lack thereof.

What was the right time for Christ to die? Scripture says it was "when we were yet without strength" (Romans 5:6). When did Christ display God's love? It was "while we were yet sinners" (v. 8). What we are, what we do, what may befall us in this life does not affect God's love for us.

Consider a young man named Eutychus. Late at night, Paul was speaking to the church in Troas when one of his listeners, Eutychus, fell asleep on a windowsill (Acts 20:4–9). Eutychus couldn't hold his attention on the things of God even when the apostle to the nations described them! Many people are still uninterested in what Paul has to say. The sleeping Eutychus fell three stories to the ground and was killed (v. 9). Did he deserve this because he was not attracted to the truth? No. God's love transcends all that we may or may not do. God gave the sleepy, disinterested young man life again, and all was well with his soul (vv. 10–12).

And there sat in a window a certain young man named Eutychus, being
fallen into a deep sleep: and as Paul was long preaching, he sunk down
with sleep, and fell down from the third loft, and was taken up dead. And
Paul went down, and fell on him, and embracing him said, Trouble not
yourselves; for his life is in him. . . . And they brought the young man alive,
and were not a little comforted.
ACTS 20:9–10, 12

Lord, at this closing hour,
Establish every heart
Upon thy word of truth and power,
To keep us when we part.

ELEAZOR T. FITCH (1791–1871)
LORD, AT THIS CLOSING HOUR

RIGHTLY DIVIDING THE WORD OF TRUTH

What is the meaning of the phrase "rightly dividing the word of truth" (2 Timothy 2:15)? This phrase comes with an explanation. Hymenaeus and Philetus believed in the resurrection, but they misplaced it in the past while it actually occurs in the future (vv. 17–18). A person who rightly divides the Word of truth carefully places God's truths in their appropriate positions in the past, present, or future. Otherwise, as the example teaches, truth becomes error and subverts people's faith. Certain truths belong to Israel while others belong to the body of Christ. These should be divided, not mixed. When we rightly divide them, we can easily understand the truth.

Here is an example: The second epistle to Timothy was written five to ten years after the first one, sometime between AD 62 and 67. Then, although God's solid foundation still stood (2:19), the pillar of the truth had changed into a great house full of all sorts of vessels, some of which were dishonorable (1 Timothy 3:15; 2 Timothy 2:20; see also 1:15; 3:5). This occurred in part because Jewish believers, fleeing persecution, flooded the Gentile churches. Some among them did not understand that the Gentile believers were not required to keep the Jewish law. These people didn't rightly divide the Word of truth. The law once had its place in God's plan, but they misplaced it and created an error called "another gospel" (Galatians 1:6–7; 3:1–3).

The foolproof way to avoid teachings that do not belong in this era of God's grace is to take seriously the apostle's admonishment:

> *Hold fast the form of sound words, which thou hast heard of me,*
> *in faith and love which is in Christ Jesus.*
> 2 TIMOTHY 1:13

Come, thou soul-transforming Spirit,
Bless the sower and the seed;
Let each heart thy grace inherit;
Raise the weak, the hungry feed;
From the gospel, now supply thy people's need.

JONATHAN EVANS (1749–1809)
COME, THOU SOUL-TRANSFORMING SPIRIT

THE TRANSFORMED LIFE

Imagine you're a first-century believer in Rome reading a letter that has recently arrived from the apostle Paul. It reveals to you the gospel of God (Romans 1:1). You see magnificent truths concerning the conduct of mankind (1:18–3:20), the justification of believers (3:21–4:25), our reconciliation with God (5:1–8:30), God's supremacy (8:31–9:29), the justification of Israel (9:30–10:21), and the conciliation of Israel (11:1–36). In other words, your understanding of God and man has been revolutionized and renewed by the truth of the gospel. Then you come upon the word *therefore*, a logical link between two statements. This word is found in Romans 12:1–2, which is a key moment in the divine revelation: "I beseech you therefore, brethren. . .be ye transformed by the renewing of your mind."

When the Lord called Paul, he said, "I have appeared to you for this purpose, to appoint you to serve and testify to the things in which you have seen me and to those in which I will appear to you" (Acts 26:16 NRSV). This means that Paul had a unique task to perform in God's purpose. The book of Romans is essential to that task. The apostle knew that its gospel would meet all people's needs. So he begged the believers to allow the truth of its gospel to renew the spirit of their minds to revamp their attitude toward themselves and the world and as a result, transform their manner of living. This is why, at the crucial moment of Romans 12:1–2, we learn that believers can, through such transformed lives, prove the reality of the perfect will of God.

With this understanding, let us continue the renewal of our minds through daily reading, study, and prayer in the Word of God.

Be renewed in the spirit of your mind.
EPHESIANS 4:23

The heav'ns declare thy glory, Lord,
In every star thy wisdom shines
But when our eyes behold thy Word,
We read thy name in fairer lines.

ISAAC WATTS (1674–1748)
THE HEAVENS DECLARE THY GLORY

THE WORD OF GOD IS NOT BOUND

There is no higher profession for those who love God than to center their minds on the scriptures. There we experience the pattern of sound words and the teaching that is in harmony with godliness (1 Timothy 6:3; 2 Timothy 1:13;). Then, if for some reason we suffer evil as a malefactor, just like ancient believers did, we will find endurance, because the Word of God is not bound (2 Timothy 2:9–10).

Nothing but the God-inspired scriptures can outfit a person for good works (3:16–17). They are sufficient equipment for godly men and women in these perilous times (v. 1). If one will scrape away a bit of the surface of this world's artifice, it will be seen that everything else has failed and fallen into ruin. The Word of God is our only resort. Yes, it is true that many people who do not yet believe perform good works. But they are not acquainted with the sacred scriptures and so are not wise for salvation that is in Christ Jesus (v. 15). All else besides this salvation, no matter how beneficial and necessary it may be, will ultimately fall to pieces.

We live in the era when people "shall turn away their ears from the truth, and shall be turned unto fables" (4:4). Despite this, let us "preach the word; be instant in season, out of season; reprove, rebuke, exhort with all long suffering and doctrine" (v. 2), and greet each other with encouraging, scriptural words: "The Lord be with your spirit. Grace be with you" (4:22 NRSV).

All scripture is given by inspiration of God, and is profitable for doctrine,
for reproof, for correction, for instruction in righteousness: that the man of
God may be perfect, thoroughly furnished unto all good works.
2 TIMOTHY 3:16–17

*Amazing grace! How sweet the sound
That saved a wretch like me!
I once was lost, but now am found;
Was blind, but now I see.*

JOHN NEWTON (1725–1807)
AMAZING GRACE

THE CHIEF SINNER

The past wretchedness of many believers far exceeds that of John Newton, the former captain of a slave ship. Yet everyone's experience with grace follows the pattern of the chief of all sinners: the apostle Paul.

Why is this righteous Pharisee the greatest sinner? It is because he persecuted God's Church, threatening its very existence (1 Corinthians 15:9). He madly endeavored to do all in his power against Christ and his believers (Acts 9:1–2). He endorsed the murder of Stephen and seems to have led the persecution that emptied Jerusalem of all disciples except the apostles (8:1–2).

The case of this furious murderer is the pattern of God's present way of grace (1 Timothy 1:16). As Paul traveled to Damascus with authority to deport believers to Jerusalem for trial, he had no thought of reforming his ways. Yet he suddenly found himself to be a believer in Jesus Christ—him whom he wished to destroy just a moment before (Acts 9:5–6). That is grace. Nothing in this man's heart or conduct made him deserving of God's favor. He was worthy of a dreadful destiny. Instead, he was transformed into God's brilliant advocate of grace. The truth he brought is enshrined in our hearts: "By grace are ye saved through faith; and that not of yourselves: it is the gift of God" (Ephesians 2:8).

This is a faithful saying, and worthy of all acceptation, that Christ Jesus came into the world to save sinners; of whom I am chief. Howbeit for this cause I obtained mercy, that in me first Jesus Christ might shew forth all longsuffering, for a pattern to them which should hereafter believe on him to life everlasting.
1 TIMOTHY 1:15–16

A few more years shall roll,
A few more seasons come,
And we shall be with those that rest
Asleep within the tomb;
Then, O my Lord, prepare
My soul for that great day.

HORATIUS BONAR (1808–1889)
A FEW MORE YEARS SHALL ROLL

A LIFE IN RESURRECTION

Why is a believer in Christ different from everyone else? Scripture answers quite simply: Everyone else has no hope (1 Thessalonians 4:13). They have no idea what to expect in the future, especially after death. We, however, possess the glorious expectation of resurrection on the great day mentioned in Horatius Bonar's hymn. In fact, our life is all about resurrection: Christ's resurrection in the past, our spiritual resurrection in the present, and the bodily resurrection in the future.

We enjoy reading about Jesus Christ in the Gospels, but it is significant that Paul never calls attention to Jesus' earthly life. Concerning this, he says that Jesus was exclusively the servant of Israel attempting to prepare the chosen nation for the promised kingdom (Romans 15:8). Because Israel rejected him, her kingdom will have to wait.

Meanwhile, we were brought into God's plan. This occurred after Jesus' resurrection (Acts 14:27). So our relationship with Christ Jesus is entirely in resurrection. Presently, we are spiritually alive together in Christ. In him, we are raised and seated among the celestials (Ephesians 2:5–6). We now live in harmony with this truth, joyfully expecting the great day when all those who are Christ's will attain to the actual, bodily resurrection (1 Corinthians 15:21–23).

> *For since by man came death, by man came also the resurrection*
> *of the dead. For as in Adam all die, even so in Christ shall*
> *all be made alive. But every man in his own order: Christ the*
> *firstfruits; afterward they that are Christ's at his coming.*
> 1 CORINTHIANS 15:21–23

There is a green hill far away,
Outside a city wall,
Where the dear Lord was crucified,
Who died to save us all.

Cecil F. Alexander (1818–1895)
There Is a Green Hill Far Away

The Faithful Saying

Here is the sum of the gospel: The Son of God was made flesh and dwelt among us for the salvation of sinners (John 1:14; Romans 5:8). This is so simple that people find it either hard to believe or too good to be true. However, we prize a faithful saying, "worthy of all acceptation, that Christ Jesus came into the world to save sinners; of whom I am chief" (1 Timothy 1:15).

This faithful saying makes three statements: (1) Christ Jesus came into the world—the prophecies concerning his coming are fulfilled (Genesis 3:15). (2) He came to save sinners—those too weak to help themselves (Romans 5:6). (3) Blasphemers and persecutors like Paul are the chief sinners (1 Timothy 1:15). Notice that, by God's grace, the major blaspheming sinner was not inferior to the chief apostles (2 Corinthians 11:5). Indeed, Peter, the leader of the Twelve, found some things in Paul's writings hard to understand (2 Peter 3:16). Paul's experience displays Christ's patience to all who would thereafter believe (1 Timothy 1:16).

These true and faithful words deserve to be received and believed by all people. Jesus Christ can save the chief of sinners. So, as Cecil Alexander says, he can save us all (1 Corinthians 15:22).

And I thank Christ Jesus our Lord, who hath enabled me, for that he counted me faithful, putting me into the ministry; who was before a blasphemer, and a persecutor, and injurious: but I obtained mercy, because I did it ignorantly in unbelief. And the grace of our Lord was exceeding abundant with faith and love which is in Christ Jesus.
1 Timothy 1:12–14

Behold the Savior of mankind
Nailed to the shameful tree!
How vast the love that him inclined
To bleed and die for thee!

SAMUEL WESLEY (1662–1735)
BEHOLD THE SAVIOR OF MANKIND

BOASTING IN THE CROSS OF CHRIST

The description of the gospel at the beginning of 1 Corinthians 15 seems very simplistic: "that Christ died for our sins according to the scriptures; and that he was buried, and that he rose again the third day according to the scriptures" (vv. 3–4). Yet this is all we need to understand. It unlocks the meaning of the scriptures and solves the puzzle of the spiritual life.

Notice how the gospel's three steps—death, burial, and resurrection—are made personal for us in Romans 6: "Know ye not, that so many of us as were baptized into Jesus Christ were baptized into his death? Therefore we are buried with him by baptism into death: that like as Christ was raised up from the dead. . .even so we also should walk in newness of life" (vv. 3–4). These wonderful verses inform us that the gospel is not only about Christ—his death, burial, and resurrection—it also tells of our present death and life in him.

The vital matters of our spiritual life are based on this truth. For example, we all must live in this world. We do this in the light of Christ's death and resurrection, boasting "in the cross of our Lord Jesus Christ, by whom the world is crucified unto me, and I unto the world" (Galatians 6:14). We also live among our brothers and sisters in Christ. The cross is supremely applicable in this aspect of our lives. Here we follow the apostle who told the saints, "I determined not to know any thing among you, save Jesus Christ, and him crucified" (1 Corinthians 2:2).

> *I am crucified with Christ: nevertheless I live; yet not I, but*
> *Christ liveth in me: and the life which I now live in the flesh I live*
> *by the faith of the Son of God, who loved me, and gave himself for me.*
> GALATIANS 2:20

I know not when the Lord will come,
Or at what hour he may appear,
Whether at midnight or at morn,
Or at what season of the year.
I only know that he is near,
And that his voice I soon shall hear.

HORATIUS BONAR (1808–1889)
HE IS NEAR

WE WILL BE LIKE HIM

Horatius Bonar was confident that he would hear the Lord's call when he comes. He surely believed what we all must believe: "God hath not appointed us to wrath, but to obtain salvation by our Lord Jesus Christ" (1 Thessalonians 5:9). This truth is also found in 1 Corinthians 15, where we see that both living and dead believers will be given celestial, spiritual, incorruptible bodies at Christ's return (vv. 40, 44, 51, 53). Without such a body, no one can meet the Lord in the air (1 Thessalonians 4:16–17).

The Philippians were told of this marvelous hope in a different way: Our bodies of humiliation will be transfigured to conform to Christ's glorious body (Philippians 3:21). We can get an idea of what that body is like by recalling that the sight of it blinded Paul when he saw the Lord on the road to Damascus (Acts 9:3, 8, 18).

Our bodies will be transformed when the Lord descends from heaven (1 Thessalonians 4:16). This will happen "in a moment, in the twinkling of an eye, at the last trump: for the trumpet shall sound, and the dead shall be raised incorruptible, and we shall be changed. For this corruptible must put on incorruption, and this mortal must put on immortality" (1 Corinthians 15:52–53). What a glorious expectation! Our bodies will not be like Christ's was before his resurrection. We won't even be like he was before he returned to his Father. We will be like him as he is now—in glorious ascension.

For our conversation is in heaven; from whence also we look for the Saviour, the Lord Jesus Christ: Who shall change our vile body, that it may be fashioned like unto his glorious body.
PHILIPPIANS 3:20–21

All glory, laud and honor, to thee, Redeemer, King,
To whom the lips of children made sweet hosannas ring.
Thou art the King of Israel, thou David's royal Son,
Who in the Lord's name comest, the King and blessed one!

THEODULPH OF ORLEANS (ABOUT 760–821)
ALL GLORY, LAUD, AND HONOR
TRANSLATED BY JOHN M. NEALE (1818–1866)

THE SECRET OF ISRAEL'S BLINDNESS

As Jesus approaches Jerusalem for the last time, the lowly people who live outside the walls shout, "Hosanna to the Son of David: Blessed is he that cometh in the name of the Lord" (Matthew 21:9). But when he passes through the gates and encounters the citizens of the exalted city, they ask, "Who is this?" (v. 10). The best answer they can get is, "This is. . .the prophet" (v. 11). The elite of Israel were oblivious to the fact that their Messiah had come to them. This seems incredible until we consult scripture.

The prophet Isaiah tells of God's blinding and deafening of Israel (Isaiah 6:9–10). This prophecy is referenced more than any other—in all four of the Gospels, Acts, and Romans. God's blinding of the chosen nation is proof that God operates all things according to the counsel of his will (Ephesians 1:11). All things, even spiritual blindness, are out of God, through God, and for God (Romans 11:36).

Is there a greater sin than the murder of Jesus Christ? No. Yet this was done in the specific counsel and foreknowledge of God (Acts 2:23). So we must always remember this great secret: "Blindness in part is happened to Israel, until the fulness of the Gentiles be come in" (Romans 11:25). But this does not mean that God has abandoned his chosen people. We can rejoice in knowing that, when the full complement of the nations comes in, "all Israel shall be saved" (v. 26).

> *Jesus of Nazareth, a man approved of God among*
> *you by miracles and wonders and signs. . .being*
> *delivered by the determinate counsel and foreknowledge of God,*
> *ye have taken, and by wicked hands have crucified and slain.*
> ACTS 2:22–23

> *The head that once was crowned with thorns*
> *Is crowned with glory now;*
> *A royal diadem adorns*
> *The mighty victor's brow.*
>
> THOMAS KELLY (1769–1855)
> THE HEAD THAT ONCE WAS CROWNED

THE INAUGURATION OF THE KING OF KINGS

Roman soldiers scorned Jesus Christ by making him a mock monarch. They gave him a purple robe, a thorny crown, a flimsy reed for a scepter, and derisive praise (Matthew 27:27–30). Someday our Lord's bleeding brow will wear many diadems (Revelation 19:1), but the status that all those crowns give does not cause our hearts to love him as much as does his wreath of thorns.

The humiliating ceremony in Herod's court is actually the inauguration of the King of kings and Lord of lords. Here's why: Jesus Christ could not have assumed the supreme place in the universe unless he had descended to the depths of humiliation (Philippians 2:6–11). Suffering and shame are the divine preliminaries to joy and honor.

Pilate marveled that, in the midst of this humiliation, Jesus didn't answer Israel's priests (Matthew 26:62–63). It didn't matter if Jesus answered or not; the priests had never had ears for his words. Still, if they had considered the words of their own prophet, they would have known their Messiah by his silence: "He was oppressed, and he was afflicted, yet he opened not his mouth: he is brought as a lamb to the slaughter, and as a sheep before her shearers is dumb, so he openeth not his mouth" (Isaiah 53:7).

Today there is a great clamor among Christians to wear the crown of political power in our country. Let us be wise to remember that "the disciple is not above his master, nor the servant above his lord," (Matthew 10:24), and that our Lord's kingdom is not of this world (John 18:36).

It is a faithful saying: For if we be dead with him, we shall also live with him: if we suffer, we shall also reign with him.
2 TIMOTHY 2:11–12

Christ Jesus lay in death's strong bands,
For our offenses given;
But now at God's right hand he stands,
And brings us life from heaven.
Wherefore let us joyful be,
And sing to God right thankfully
Loud songs of alleluia! alleluia!

MARTIN LUTHER (1483–1546)
CHRIST JESUS LAY IN DEATH'S STRONG BANDS

CHRIST IS OUR LIFE

Here is an interesting bit of spiritual information: You died and your life is hidden with Christ in God (Colossians 3:3). These eleven words tell all about our spiritual life, echoing the basic truth of Romans 6:3–4: In God's eyes, we died in Christ and now are alive in him. Therefore, all we have is in Christ, and as Luther's hymn says, he is with God and brings us life from heaven. But more than *bringing* us life, Christ *is* our life and we are saved in his life (Colossians 3:4; Romans 5:10). We are complete in him who is the head of every authority in the universe (Colossians 2:10).

Our spiritual life is summarized in three words: *death*, *burial*, and *resurrection*. These describe our life in Christ. Two Jewish rites illustrate this. Circumcision is the cutting off of the flesh of the male sex organ. It signifies death, which cuts off all flesh (v. 11). Baptism pictures burial and resurrection (v. 12). Christ is our life, and he was cut off in death, so we need not be circumcised. Plus, we were baptized long ago in Christ's burial. What's more, in his resurrection, we are raised from the dead (v. 13). Physical, religious rites are not necessary, though they do no harm. The only thing a person must have to live a complete spiritual life is faith in God's operation in Christ's death, burial, and resurrection (1 Corinthians 15:2–4).

And ye are complete in him. . . . In whom also ye are circumcised with the circumcision made without hands, in putting off the body of the sins of the flesh by the circumcision of Christ: buried with him in baptism, wherein also ye are risen with him through the faith of the operation of God, who hath raised him from the dead.
COLOSSIANS 2:10–12

Let us love and sing and wonder, Let us praise the Savior's name!
He has hushed the law's loud thunder,
He has quenched Mount Sinai's flame.
He has washed us with his blood, He has brought us nigh to God.

JOHN NEWTON (1725–1807)
LET US LOVE AND SING AND WONDER

LAW VS. GRACE

How appropriate that the author of "Amazing Grace" would offer praise for our freedom from the law. Only God's grace brings us salvation. Nothing we do qualifies us for this. Still, from the beginning of the gospel, law has stained the purity of grace.

At first, only Jews believed in Jesus Christ (Acts 11:19). They had been keeping the law of Moses for many generations and continued in this tradition. But God wanted non-Jews to receive the gospel, too. Peter, who first brought a Gentile into the faith, knew God didn't expect people from the nations to keep the Jewish law (Acts 15:7–11). But not all Jewish believers understood this. So a conflict arose between faith and law, grace and works.

Mount Sinai's flame began to singe Gentile believers when false brethren from Jerusalem told believers in Antioch that they had to keep the law in order to be saved (v. 1). This was a perversion of the truth and is still today. Our behavior, no matter how right or scriptural, cannot qualify us for God's salvation or benefit our growth in the faith.

John Newton poetically expressed the message of Galatians when he wrote that Christ has hushed the law's loud thunder and quenched Mount Sinai's flame. All the saints should be well versed in the blistering manifesto against the mixing of grace and law that occurs in the book of Galatians.

O foolish Galatians, who hath bewitched you, that ye should not obey the truth, before whose eyes Jesus Christ hath been evidently set forth, crucified among you? This only would I learn of you, Received ye the Spirit by the works of the law, or by the hearing of faith? Are ye so foolish? having begun in the Spirit, are ye now made perfect by the flesh?
GALATIANS 3:1–3

Creator Spirit, by whose aid
The world's foundations first were laid,
Come, visit every pious mind;
Come, pour thy joys on humankind;
From sin and sorrow set us free;
And make thy temples worthy thee.

AMBROSE OF MILAN (ST. AMBROSE, 340–397)
CREATOR SPIRIT, BY WHOSE AID

THE EVIDENCE OF GOD IN CREATION

With the eyes of faith and the help of scripture, believers like Ambrose of Milan marvel at the power and wisdom of God displayed in creation. Billions of people, however, can't see God's attributes in nature. This is because they don't acknowledge God as God or glorify and thank him, so their hearts are darkened (Romans 1:19–21). Still, we shouldn't expect much of those who don't yet believe. After all, a natural man by definition is not spiritual and cannot receive the things of the Spirit "for they are foolishness unto him. . .because they are spiritually discerned" (1 Corinthians 2:14).

Although the natural man can't understand the things of God, scripture does not say that human nature is corrupt. The understanding of the heart, however, is darkened (Ephesians 4:18; Romans 1:21). This is why people violate their nature (v. 26). They are under the sway of "the prince of the power of the air, the spirit that now worketh in the children of disobedience" (Ephesians 2:2) The scriptures actually say that if people pay attention to their nature, they can do right (Romans 2:14; 1 Corinthians 11:14).

Believers delight to see God's attributes in the creation. Likewise, we know that humanity was created in God's image (Genesis 1:27). Therefore, let's look for evidence of this truth in our neighbors who haven't believed and pray for them. It is God's purpose to cause those who bear the image of the earthy to one day bear the image of the heavenly, and he has the power to accomplish this (1 Corinthians 15:49).

> *But God, who is rich in mercy, for his great love wherewith*
> *he loved us, even when we were dead in sins, hath quickened*
> *us together with Christ, (by grace ye are saved).*
> EPHESIANS 2:4–5

Come, let us rise with Christ our head
And seek the things above,
By the almighty Spirit led
And filled with faith and love.

CHARLES WESLEY (1707–1788)
COME, LET US RISE WITH CHRIST

OUR CELESTIAL DESTINY

The idea that people go to heaven is not mentioned in scripture until it is introduced in Paul's epistles. Although many believers look forward to participating in the earthly kingdom with Israel, our future citizenship is actually in heaven (Philippians 3:20). So Colossians 3:1 exhorts us to "seek those things which are above, where Christ sitteth on the right hand of God." Figuratively speaking, we are now seated in heavenly places (Ephesians 2:6). This will be a reality in the ages to come when God will show the universe "the exceeding riches of his grace in his kindness toward us through Christ Jesus" (v. 7).

The Bible is mainly concerned with events on the earth. But, again in Paul's epistles, it also reveals that God's kingdom will extend to the entire universe. For example, we can look forward to "the dispensation of the fullness of times [when God will] gather together in one all things in Christ, both which are in heaven, and which are on earth" (Ephesians 1:10). At that time, all things will be under the Lord's feet and he will be "head over all things to the church" (v. 22). This is why Christ will transfigure the body of our humiliation and make it like his glorious body (Philippians 3:21). We will need such bodies to take our places in his celestial kingdom (2 Timothy 4:18).

But our citizenship is in heaven, and it is from there that we are expecting
a Savior, the Lord Jesus Christ. He will transform the body of our
humiliation that it may be conformed to the body of his glory, by the power
that also enables him to make all things subject to himself.
PHILIPPIANS 3:20–21 NRSV

Prayer is the soul's sincere desire,
Unuttered or expressed;
The motion of a hidden fire
That trembles in the breast.

JAMES MONTGOMERY (1771–1854)
PRAYER IS THE SOUL'S SINCERE DESIRE

PRAYER ACCORDING TO GOD'S WILL

When Jesus Christ lived in Galilee, he ministered to Israel, confirming the promises made to the Jewish patriarchs (Romans 15:8). But things changed. The four Gospels tell how Israel refused the Messiah and his kingdom. Then Christ was crucified and resurrected. The book of Acts shows Israel refusing the kingdom again. This time it was offered by the apostles. So God temporarily set aside the chosen nation, brought the gospel directly to other nations, and inaugurated the present administration of grace (Romans 11:15; Acts 28:28; Ephesians 3:2).

When Jesus ministered, he gave his disciples a sample prayer, telling them, "Pray then in this way" (Matthew 6:9 NRSV). In other words, those disciples knew exactly how to pray. In contrast, both our experience and the testimony of scripture tell us that we don't know what to pray for, so we are dependent on the Spirit's groaning to convey our prayers to God (Romans 8:26). This shows our complete dependence on divine grace and is an example of God's way during his administration of grace.

In the midst of our inarticulate prayers, the Sprit prays in harmony with God's will, so everything cooperates for our welfare. No matter how things appear, God loved us long ago and has made us a vital part in the grand purpose of the ages (v. 28). He fixed our glorious destiny from the beginning, before we could have any part in that decision. This destiny is higher than our highest dreams; it is nothing less than conformity to the image of the Son (v. 29). Even more, it puts the Son in the highest station, because he cannot be firstborn without us, his many brothers and sisters (v. 29). Thus, we participate in his glorification.

For whom he did foreknow, he also did predestinate to be conformed to the
image of his Son, that he might be the firstborn among many brethren.
ROMANS 8:29

At the name of Jesus bowing,
Falling prostrate at his feet,
Claim his vict'ry over evil
And the enemy defeat.

LYDIA BAXTER (1809–1874)
PRECIOUS NAME

A BELIEVER'S PRAYERFUL POSTURE

Lydia Baxter mentions our bowing at the name of Jesus. From this posture, we make requests and offer thanks to the Lord. For example, the man who asked healing for his epileptic son did so on his knees (Matthew 17:14–15). The leper knelt down as he sought cleansing (Mark 1:40). Peter also knelt before his Lord after the miraculous catch of fishes (Luke 5:8–9).

One may ask, "Can't I stand up and pray?" All scripture is profitable to us, so we note that the Pharisee stood when he made his prideful prayer in the holy temple (Luke 18:11). Plus, the Lord pointed out that the hypocrites were fond of standing in the synagogues so they could be seen as they prayed (Matthew 6:5). Since this is specially mentioned in the scriptures, we might take note of our own posture in prayer.

Even our Lord knelt in prayer (Luke 22:41–42). When the ordeal he faced seemed unbearable, he cried, "Remove this cup from me." Then he took his place in submission to the Father's will and prayed, "Nevertheless not my will, but thine, be done." The Son's willing submission, indicated by his words and the bowing of his knees, extends to the end of the ages when he delivers the kingdom to God the Father (1 Corinthians 15:28).

Anyone who has bowed his knees before God knows that this does not indicate forced surrender. In addition to the above examples, we see Paul on his knees in prayer to the Father (Ephesians 3:14). If he was forced to do this, it was by the force of love (2 Corinthians 5:14), since his petition abounds with desire for the blessing of the saints.

And they all brought us on our way, with wives and children. . .and we kneeled down on the shore, and prayed. And when we had taken our leave one of another, we took ship; and they returned home.
ACTS 21:5–6

Take time to be holy, speak oft with thy Lord;
Abide in him always, and feed on his Word.
Make friends of God's children, help those who are weak,
Forgetting in nothing his blessing to seek.

WILLIAM D. LONGSTAFF (1822–1894)
TAKE TIME TO BE HOLY

THE RECIPE FOR HOLINESS

Jesus said, "For their sakes I sanctify myself" (John 17:19). This statement helps explain what it means to be holy. Holiness, or sanctification, isn't cleansing from sin. Jesus Christ had no need for such cleansing. He had no sin, yet he sanctified himself. An example of sanctification is seen in the consecration of Israel's priests. When this occurred, their hands were filled with the sacrifice (Exodus 29:1, 10–14). This shows that real holiness is found in a positive occupation with the things of God rather than a negative absence of sin.

William Longstaff seems to know this. His hymn gives a fourfold recipe for holiness: prayer, the Word, fellowship, and service to the needy. In these, a person is occupied with the things of God. Let's rearrange Longstaff's poetic order to see this clearly. Feeding on God's Word must come first because one can do nothing without nourishment. This is best combined with prayer. The incentive for holiness springs from fellowship and service, the overflow of love to our fellow saints and to all others, as well (1 Thessalonians 3:12).

Our holiness is not displayed in outward appearances that others can see. It is established in front of God our Father, who rewards his believers according to the motives of the heart (v. 13).

And the Lord make you to increase and abound in love one toward another,
and toward all men, even as we do toward you: to the end he may stablish
your hearts unblameable in holiness before God, even our Father, at the
coming of our Lord Jesus Christ with all his saints.
1 THESSALONIANS 3:12–13

Faith of our fathers, living still,
In spite of dungeon, fire, and sword;
O how our hearts beat high with joy
Whenever we hear that glorious word!

FREDERICK W. FABER (1814–1863)
FAITH OF OUR FATHERS

THE FAITH OF OUR FATHERS

The brilliant verse that describes our entrance into the legacy of God's family is Ephesians 2:13: "But now in Christ Jesus ye who sometimes were far off are made nigh by the blood of Christ." Previously, we could not have been further away from God's heritage.

The Ephesian Gentile Trophimus knew this well. He was in Jerusalem with Paul when the rumor that he had approached as near as a Jew to the temple caused the whole city to rise up against the apostle (Acts 21:28–29). They assumed Paul had brought Trophimus into the sanctuary, and they nearly murdered him for this (vv. 30–31). We now know the truth that was understood by Paul and Trophimus but unthinkable to the religious citizens of Jerusalem. That is, every Gentile has far more than physical admission to the Jewish temple. In spirit, we have free access to God the Father (Ephesians 2:18).

Modern believers are related to all God's believers throughout history. The distant patriarchs before Abraham to the youngest in Christ Jesus have three things in common. First, we are fellow citizens. That is, we are under God's government. Second, we are in God's household, in the family of God (v. 19). Third, we are God's dwelling place in spirit (vv. 20–22). Though today we enjoy God's unlimited grace—a favor unknown in Old Testament times—still, in at least these three ways, we share the faith of our fathers.

Now therefore ye are no more strangers and foreigners, but fellowcitizens with the saints, and of the household of God; and are built upon the foundation of the apostles and prophets, Jesus Christ himself being the chief corner stone; in whom all the building fitly framed together groweth unto an holy temple in the Lord: in whom ye also are builded together for an habitation of God through the Spirit.
EPHESIANS 2:19–22

Sweet hour of prayer, sweet hour of prayer,
That calls me from a world of care,
And bids me at my Father's throne
Make all my wants and wishes known.

WILLIAM W. WALFORD (1772–1850)
SWEET HOUR OF PRAYER

PRAYER IN HARMONY WITH GOD

Here is the secret to finding comfort in prayer. Allow the time of prayer to be your rescuer from the world of care. A glance at prayers from the Epistles shows that they are far from the world and intimate with the things of God. For example, the apostle asks for prayer that he will have the utterance to make known the secret of the gospel (Ephesians 6:18–19). He prays for the saints' love for each other and their knowledge and sensibility about the things of importance in the light of Christ's return, and that they will be filled with the fruits of righteousness (Philippians 1:9–11). The truth is, we don't know what we should pray in light of God's purpose (Romans 8:26–28). But the Spirit gives us utterance for such lofty prayer through the Word.

Our concern for others can be expressed to God in the sevenfold prayer of Colossians 1:9–11: the realization of God's will, wisdom and spiritual understanding, a life worthy and pleasing to the Lord, fruit borne of good works, growth in the realization of God, strengthening with power for God's glory, and endurance and patience with joy. In these prayers, we are called away from the world of care.

> *Wherefore also we pray always for you, that our God would*
> *count you worthy of this calling, and fulfil all the good pleasure*
> *of his goodness, and the work of faith with power: that the name*
> *of our Lord Jesus Christ may be glorified in you, and ye in him,*
> *according to the grace of our God and the Lord Jesus Christ.*
> 2 THESSALONIANS 1:11–12

Just as I am, without one plea,
But that thy blood was shed for me,
And that thou bidst me come to thee,
O Lamb of God, I come, I come.

CHARLOTTE ELLIOTT (1789–1871)
JUST AS I AM

THE EXCEEDINGLY ABUNDANT GRACE OF OUR LORD

The phrase signifies that we don't have the power to save ourselves. No person has ever attained to God's salvation by his own strength, determination, or accomplishments. In other words, there is no such thing as "bootstrap" salvation. We cannot pick ourselves up out of sin, clean up our lives, and so please God (Romans 7:21–23). These facts drive the seeker of God to plead, "Wretched man that I am! who shall deliver me from the body of this death?" (v. 24).

Here is the answer to this desperate cry: All that we cannot do, God has done for us in sending his own Son (Romans 8:3–4). This describes God's unlimited grace by which we are freely saved. His exceedingly abundant grace overwhelms unbelief despite the ignorance of the sinner (1 Timothy 1:13–14).

God's grace is so complete that even the faith through which we are saved is not our own. It is God's gift to us and actually belongs to Jesus Christ (Ephesians 1:8; Galatians 2:16). We are not justified and reconciled to God because we traded our belief in the Son of God or our faith in his death for salvation. We have no bargaining chips at this table. God accomplished our salvation entirely independent of us. The following unadorned testimonial of good news is evidence that God took all the initiative to accomplish our salvation: "We were reconciled to God *by the death of his Son*" (Romans 5:10; emphasis added). All we do is stand in this grace and rejoice in the glory of God (vv. 1–2).

Who was before a blasphemer, and a persecutor, and injurious: but I obtained mercy, because I did it ignorantly in unbelief. And the grace of our Lord was exceeding abundant with faith and love which is in Christ Jesus.
1 TIMOTHY 1:13–14

Immortal, invisible, God only wise,
In light inaccessible hid from our eyes,
Most blessed, most glorious, the Ancient of Days,
Almighty, victorious, thy great name we praise.

WALTER C. SMITH (1824–1908)
IMMORTAL, INVISIBLE, GOD ONLY WISE

THIS MORTAL MUST PUT ON IMMORTALITY

The wonderful word *immortal* allows the mind's eye to glimpse the day when the dead will be made alive; when "this corruptible must put on incorruption, and this mortal must put on immortality" (1 Corinthians 15:53).

In the original Greek language of the New Testament, the word translated "immortality" means "undeath," the absence of death. Today Christ Jesus is the only one who has immortality (1 Timothy 6:16). Only he is beyond the reach of death. Immortality is his exclusive possession (1 Corinthians 15:23). The glory of deathlessness shines in him with an intensity that is beyond the possibility of human perception (1 Timothy 6:16). The apostle Paul came as near to seeing this as anyone ever has. The brilliance of it blinded him (Acts 9:3–9).

That our Lord has been made alive is our assurance of immortality (1 Corinthians 15:54). But for now, death is operating in our bodies and will drag us down to the grave if the Lord delays his return. Yet, in that day, the dead in Christ will not simply be restored to life; they will enjoy deathlessness in a body so changed and glorified that it corresponds to the one that is suitable for the head of the universe (Philippians 3:21).

In a moment, in the twinkling of an eye, at the last trump:
for the trumpet shall sound, and the dead shall be raised incorruptible,
and we shall be changed. For this corruptible must put on incorruption,
and this mortal must put on immortality. So when this corruptible
shall have put on incorruption, and this mortal shall have put on
immortality, then shall be brought to pass the saying that is written, Death
is swallowed up in victory.
1 CORINTHIANS 15:52–54

*I will sing the wondrous story
Of the Christ who died for me.
How he left his home in glory
For the cross of Calvary.*

FRANCIS H. ROWLEY (1854–1952)
I WILL SING THE WONDROUS STORY

THE PINNACLE OF GOD'S FOOLISHNESS

Consider the shameful manner of Jesus Christ's death—he was hung on a wooden post that is called "the cross," which the scriptures sometimes call "a tree" (Galatians 3:13). That death brought down the curse of God upon the only man who knew no sin so that he could be our sin offering (2 Corinthians 5:21). Yet the cross has meaning beyond the death of Christ for our sins. It exposes the shame of human religion and the folly of human wisdom.

When Jesus Christ, God's image, lived among the human race (John 1:14), we failed to appreciate him. Our religious intolerance condemned him to a death that is normally reserved for vile criminals. Never before had a man spoken as he did (7:46), yet our wisest men displayed the basic stupidity of human wisdom by crucifying the embodiment of all wisdom (Colossians 2:3). Even so, God has made Golgotha, which is the ultimate scene of weakness and disgrace, the most dazzling exhibition of divine power and glory. There, the Everest of man's wisdom was dwarfed by God's foolishness (1 Corinthians 1:23–25).

To human eyes, death by crucifixion expresses the depths of degradation, powerlessness, and humiliation. To the eyes of faith, Christ's crucifixion eclipses all the power and wisdom of humans. Wise and religious people despise the gospel of God to this day (1 Thessalonians 2:2), but this doesn't diminish the fact that the gospel is powerful enough to save all who believe (Romans 1:16).

*But we preach Christ crucified, unto the Jews a stumblingblock,
and unto the Greeks foolishness; but unto them which are called,
both Jews and Greeks, Christ the power of God, and the wisdom of God.
because the foolishness of God is wiser than men; and the
weakness of God is stronger than men.*
1 CORINTHIANS 1:23–25

Jesus, thy blood and righteousness
My beauty are, my glorious dress;
'Midst flaming worlds, in these arrayed,
With joy shall I lift up my head.

NIKOLAUS VON ZINZENDORF (1700–1760)
JESUS, THY BLOOD AND RIGHTEOUSNESS
TRANSLATED BY JOHN WESLEY (1703–1791)

GOD'S RIGHTEOUSNESS THROUGH CHRIST'S FAITH

Does anyone use the old-fashioned word *righteousness* anymore? We will do well to consider it, because as the hymn says, only in God's righteousness can we lift up our heads with joy before God.

Romans 1:18–3:20 tells all about the conduct of humankind and finds that no one is righteous except God. No one has reached God's standard by doing good or keeping the law. How then can we be justified before God? We must somehow find a way to partake of God's own righteousness. God has provided that way. The channel through which we gain his righteousness is the faith of Jesus Christ (3:26). He is the only one who did good and kept the law. In addition to that, Jesus believed his Father even when God allowed him to die for our sins (Matthew 26:42). Therefore, God's righteousness is revealed in the gospel because it is out of Christ's faith and for our faith (Romans 1:17).

Is this dry, technical theology? No! It is the breathtaking truth about our free justification by God's grace (3:24). It is vital that every believer understand that no one can be judged righteous except by the favor of God. The blood of Christ settles the debt for all sins. Therefore, deliverance from judgment is free to all who believe (v. 25).

But now the righteousness of God without the law is manifested, being witnessed by the law and the prophets; even the righteousness of God which is by faith of Jesus Christ unto all and upon all them that believe: for there is no difference: for all have sinned, and come short of the glory of God; being justified freely by his grace through the redemption that is in Christ Jesus.
ROMANS 3:21–24

Lord, I believe were sinners more
Than sands upon the ocean shore,
Thou hast for all a ransom paid,
For all a full atonement made.

NIKOLAUS VON ZINZENDORF (1700–1760)
JESUS, THY BLOOD AND RIGHTEOUSNESS
TRANSLATED BY JOHN WESLEY (1703–1791)

THE ELIMINATION OF DEATH

Nikolaus von Zinzendorf was the leader of the Moravian Brethren. He opened his estates near Dresden in Saxony to persecuted European believers of all kinds. The Lord used missionaries from the Moravian community to bring John Wesley to faith as he voyaged across the Atlantic to serve in Georgia. Both men were significant in God's work during the eighteenth century. Wesley was especially instrumental in the revival of faith and the social reform movement that some historians believe spared Great Britain from a revolution like that which convulsed France. This hymn shows that both these men realized that, in Christ, God accomplished redemption for all.

John the Baptist's introduction to Jesus Christ demonstrates that same thing: "Behold the Lamb of God, which taketh away the sin of the world" (John 1:29). The amount of sin in the world is incomprehensible, and the idea that the Lamb could take it all away is mind-boggling. At the same time, the prospect that this will occur exhilarates a believer's soul. How will it happen?

At the end of the ages, the last enemy, death, is abolished, put out of business (1 Corinthians 15:26). Since sin reigns only in death, its throne will then no longer exist (Romans 5:20). In other words, when God abolishes death, he leaves no place for sin. John the Baptist's introduction of Jesus Christ to this world is a prophecy of this long-awaited consummation. It tells why the Son lived among us and made his sacrifice on Calvary's cross.

For he must reign, till he hath put all enemies under his feet.
The last enemy that shall be destroyed is death.
1 CORINTHIANS 15:25–26

Lord of all being, throned afar,
Thy glory flames from sun and star;
Center and soul of every sphere,
Yet to each loving heart how near!

OLIVER WENDELL HOLMES (1809–1894)
LORD OF ALL BEING

THE NEARNESS OF GOD

In the first century, Rome was the world's political center. Its power was overcome by the power of God in the gospel (Romans 1:16). In Ephesus, the religious center, the word of the Lord overthrew the world's religion (Acts 19:17–20). Athens was the hub of ancient philosophy. It was the perfect place for the folly of God to defeat the world's wisdom. The account of Paul's visit to Athens gives a pattern for preaching the gospel to the wise of this world (1 Corinthians 1:26). In Athens the apostle found an audience of philosophers (Acts 17:18) atheistic, pleasure-seeking Epicureans, who taught that an accidental gathering of atoms formed the universe. He also encountered austere, polytheistic Stoics, who did not acknowledge sin and for whom reason was the only good.

Paul didn't charge these men with ignorance, but he told about a God who was unknown to them (vv. 22–23). He declared that this God is the Creator who is active in human affairs. Among the Athenians' marvelous temples and elaborate rituals, the apostle declared the uselessness of things made by man's hands. He told the philosophers that God needed nothing from them, yet he gave them everything. He encouraged them to search for God and find him (vv. 24–27).

As Holmes says in his hymn, God is near to loving hearts, yet he is also "not far from every one of us: For in him we live, and move, and have our being" (vv. 27–28).

[God] hath made of one blood all nations of men for to dwell on all the face
of the earth, and hath determined the times before appointed, and the bounds
of their habitation; that they should seek the Lord, if haply they might feel
after him, and find him, though he be not far from every one of us.
ACTS 17:26–27

I know that my redeemer lives, and ever prays for me;
A token of his love he gives, a pledge of liberty.
I find him lifting up my head, he brings salvation near,
His presence makes me free indeed, and he will soon appear.

CHARLES WESLEY (1707–1788)
I KNOW THAT MY REDEEMER LIVES

THE ESSENCE OF OUR FAITH

Christ is living! This exultant thought inspires all the saints. Even Job found in this the essence of his faith and hope. "For I know that my redeemer liveth, and that he shall stand at the latter day upon the earth. . . . Whom I shall see for myself, and mine eyes shall behold" (Job 19:25, 27). Unlike Job, we hold in our hands the scriptures, the entire Word of God. How much more should this accomplished fact control our lives? Christ rose from the dead and ascended to God. He is coming again and will fulfill God's purpose. So what reason can we give not to be disposed to the things above rather than the things of this earth (Colossians 3:2)?

The gospel is good news because it is entirely the work of the wise, loving, and powerful God carried out in and through his beloved Son. Job knew nothing about this grace of God in Christ Jesus that has brought salvation to us. He only knew of God's involvement in all things, and he believed that somehow God would provide a living redeemer (Job 38–41; 19:25). Job endured his trials and through them came to know God had a purpose for them and was operating wisely toward a benevolent end.

People talk about the patience of Job. But we should admire his tenacity to cling to the revelations given him. Through them, he found strength to rely on God in the midst of tremendous suffering. Therefore, we too can hold on to the gospel in every problem of life.

I declare unto you the gospel. . .how that Christ died for our sins according to the scriptures; and that he was buried, and that he rose again the third day according to the scriptures.
1 CORINTHIANS 15:1, 3–4

Grace, 'tis a charming sound,
Harmonious to mine ear;
Heaven with the echo shall resound,
And all the earth shall hear.

PHILIP DODDRIDGE (1702–1751)
GRACE, 'TIS A CHARMING SOUND

THE GRACE OF GOD IN TRUTH

God's future judgment is based on the actions, or works, of individuals (Romans 2:6; Revelation 20:12). The judgment of believers, however, has already occurred in Jesus Christ on the cross. When he died, we died in him. Therefore, "he that is dead is freed from sin" (Romans 6:7). This, and all of God's gracious benefits toward us, are spoiled the moment we connect them with anything that suggests our merit or work. God's grace is freer than the sunlight that brings life to the world. It is "a charming sound, harmonious to mine ear." When God gives, he gives and refuses to allow his gifts to be paid for even if it were possible to pay such a price. Righteousness is given only to a person who believes; that is, who doesn't work for it (4:4–5). Therefore, the grace of God has nothing to do with humanly devised philosophies and religions.

Grace not only saves us; it invigorates us, as well (2 Timothy 2:1). It brings us salvation, justification, reconciliation, and every spiritual blessing in the celestials (Ephesians 1:3). Anyone who appreciates grace, however faintly, is energized by these gifts from God. If we are to covet anything at all, let it be the charming sound of the grace of God in truth (Colossians 1:6).

For the hope which is laid up for you in heaven, whereof ye heard
before in the word of the truth of the gospel; which is come unto you,
as it is in all the world; and bringeth forth fruit, as it doth also in you,
since the day ye heard of it, and knew the grace of God in truth.
COLOSSIANS 1:5–6

Lo! He comes with clouds descending,
Once for favored sinners slain;
Thousand thousand saints attending,
Swell the triumph of his train.

JOHN CENNICK (1718–1755)
LO, HE COMES WITH CLOUDS DESCENDING

THE SECOND COMING OF CHRIST TO ISRAEL

As Jesus sat with his disciples overlooking Jerusalem, they asked, "Tell us, when shall these things be? and what shall be the sign of thy coming, and of the end of the world?" (Matthew 24:3). In his answer, the Lord gave a brief account of the events detailed in the book of Revelation. "Immediately after the tribulation of those days shall. . .appear the sign of the Son of man in heaven," he said. "And then shall all the tribes of the earth mourn, and they shall see the Son of man coming in the clouds of heaven with power and great glory" (vv. 29–30). These words depict Christ coming as the rescuer of Israel (Zechariah 12:9).

Imagine what this will mean for the nation that has rejected Christ for two thousand years. They will see the wounds that were inflicted as he hung on the cross, and the spirit of grace and supplication will overwhelm them (v. 10). They will mourn over the past and bitterly weep because they denied their Messiah. This is a national repentance as all the tribes of the land weep bitterly like a person weeps over the death of a firstborn son (vv. 10–14). Then Israel will be born in a day (Isaiah 66:7–9; Ezekiel 36:26; John 16:20–22; 3:3; Revelation 12:1–2, 5). Like any birth, the blessed rebirth of Israel will not happen without travail (John 16:21). Great tribulation will come (Matthew 24:21). Much of the book of Revelation describes it: "She being with child cried, travailing in birth, and pained to be delivered" (Revelation 12:2). Is this hard to believe? Even Isaiah was amazed at his own prophecy of Israel's rebirth:

Who hath heard such a thing? who hath seen such things? Shall the earth
be made to bring forth in one day? or shall a nation be born at once? for as
soon as Zion travailed, she brought forth her children.
ISAIAH 66:8

Go, labor on: spend, and be spent,
Thy joy to do the Father's will:
It is the way the Master went;
Should not the servant tread it still?

HORATIUS BONAR (1808–1889)
GO, LABOR ON

SUFFERING IN SERVICE

The saints in Philippi not only believed in Christ, but they also suffered for his sake. Both their faith and their suffering were a gift to them from God (Philippians 1:29). Their privilege was to experience the sufferings that come to those who seek to do God's work. Such sufferings are not evidence of God's displeasure, but they are a favor granted to those who are faithful in the operation of God's will.

The Philippians were engaged in the highest service. It involved the comfort of love, the communion of spirit, compassion, and pity; it filled up the apostle Paul's joy (2:1–2) This is our calling, too: "Be likeminded, having the same love, being of one accord, of one mind. Let nothing be done through strife or vainglory; but in lowliness of mind let each esteem other better than themselves. Look not every man on his own things, but every man also on the things of others" (vv. 2–4). This service honors the unity of the Spirit in the uniting bond of peace (Ephesians 4:3) and is sure to bring suffering.

Paul did not expect believers to do these things in their own strength. All we do is *allow* Christ's mind to be in us (Philippians 2:5). All around us we see Adam's offspring exalting themselves through popular entertainment, political ambition, and other worldly pursuits. But Christ, who could assume the place of equality with God, found his delight in submission and humiliation (vv. 6–8). Our service to God is to allow that disposition to be in us just as it was in him.

I seek not yours but you: for the children ought not to lay up for the parents,
but the parents for the children. And I will very gladly spend and be spent
for you; though the more abundantly I love you, the less I be loved.
2 CORINTHIANS 12:14–15

All praise to our redeeming Lord,
Who joins us by his grace;
And bids us, each to each restored,
Together seek his face.

CHARLES WESLEY (1707–1788)
ALL PRAISE TO OUR REDEEMING LORD

ONENESS BRINGS MATURITY

Paul possessed the wisdom of God. That is, by the Spirit he understood the deep things of God (1 Corinthians 2:7, 10). He would have gladly instructed the Corinthians in these things, but he couldn't do so because they were fleshly and immature in Christ (3:1–2). The sign of spiritual immaturity is the same today as it was then—division (v. 3).

The saints in Corinth argued about the servants that God had given to them (v. 4). Some of them were partial to Paul. Some preferred Apollos. This frustrated the outflow of God's favor. It is interesting to note that Apollos certainly taught precisely the same as did Paul, since Paul taught Apollos indirectly through Priscilla and Aquila (Acts 18:24–28). The two men were absolutely one in God's work (1 Corinthians 3:8). The fleshly Corinthians foolishly divided over their preferences between these two men.

In an attempt to remove the spirit of division, Paul compared the Corinthians with a farm and a building. He and Apollos were nothing more than laborers among them (v. 9). Yes, Paul planted the seeds and Apollos watered them, but neither of them could make a single seed grow. Only God gives growth (v. 6).

Who doesn't long for the oneness described in Charles Wesley's hymn? What believer does not desire to know the deep things of God? The eradication of all party spirit allows our hearts to be open to God, who gives growth and maturity.

For while one saith, I am of Paul; and another, I am of Apollos; are ye not carnal? Who then is Paul, and who is Apollos, but ministers by whom ye believed, even as the Lord gave to every man? I have planted, Apollos watered; but God gave the increase. So then neither is he that planteth any thing, neither he that watereth; but God that giveth the increase.
1 CORINTHIANS 3:4–7

We all partake the joy of one; The common peace we feel;
A peace to sensual minds unknown, A joy unspeakable.

CHARLES WESLEY (1707–1788)
ALL PRAISE TO OUR REDEEMING LORD

BE PERFECTLY JOINED TOGETHER

Corinth was the first place where Paul stayed long enough to personally establish the saints in the truth (Acts 18:11). The Corinthians not only believed, many of them also received spiritual gifts and looked forward to the day of Christ's return (1 Corinthians 1:7). They were honored to enter into fellowship with the Son of God (v. 9). Everyone who belongs to Christ has this privilege.

However, divisions among the Corinthians exposed their lack of spirituality. Their factions were removing them from their fellowship in God's Son (v. 12). One camp claimed to follow Paul. These may have been ordinary Corinthian Gentiles. Another preferred Apollos. Perhaps these people liked Apollos's scholarly ways and Alexandrian origin. Those who aligned with Cephas (that is, Peter) may have been Jews who kept the traditions of Israel. Others divided under the banner of Christ.

No work or worker is of any importance in comparison with Christ, who was crucified for us. One can almost hear Paul shout in protest of these divisions: "Is Christ divided? was Paul crucified for you?" (v. 13). Christ is the focus of all God's operations. He is the Crucified One, and he is the head of the body. We identify only with him, not in earthly glory, but in the shameful cross on which he was humiliated and became the lowest of all (1 Corinthians 1:13–31). Even a division under the name "Christ" denies the cross of Christ.

Charles Wesley's hymn calls us away from anything resembling this sectarianism to partake of one joy and feel the common peace that is foreign to fleshly minds. No matter how we describe ourselves or what name we use, in the shadow of the cross, division is indefensible.

I beseech you, brethren, by the name of our Lord Jesus Christ, that ye all
speak the same thing, and that there be no divisions among you.
1 CORINTHIANS 1:10

We give thee but thine own,
Whate'er the gift may be;
All that we have is thine alone,
A trust, O Lord, from thee.

WILLIAM W. HOW (1823–1897)
WE GIVE THEE BUT THINE OWN

THE CASE AGAINST SELF-GLORY

The Corinthians had fallen into fleshly divisions. They preferred one of God's servants above another (1 Corinthians 3:4). In other words, they were puffed up against one another (4:6). So, the apostle asked them, "What do you have that you did not receive? And if you received it, why do you boast as if it were not a gift?" (v. 7 NRSV).

Perhaps the Corinthians had forgotten that everything, spiritual or material, is from God, and that they could not glory in anything as their own. Therefore, they fed their vanity by claiming Apollos or Paul. The truth is, these two men, and everything else the Corinthians had, came from God's bounty through grace.

We have no reason to be proud of our attainments, our joys, or anything else. All we have, all we are, and all we do, we owe to the grace of God. Boasting is forever excluded. Since nothing we have is our own, it is foolish to boast of it. Those who are given everything can boast in none of it. With this understanding, we must pray: "Not unto us, O LORD, not unto us, but unto thy name give glory, for thy mercy, and for thy truth's sake" (Psalm 115:1).

But who am I, and what is my people, that we should be able to make this freewill offering? For all things come from you, and of your own have we given you. For we are aliens and transients before you, as were all our ancestors; our days on the earth are like a shadow, and there is no hope. O LORD our God, all this abundance that we have provided for building you a house for your holy name comes from your hand and is all your own.
1 CHRONICLES 29:14–16 NRSV

Where cross the crowded ways of life,
Where sound the cries of race and clan
Above the noise of selfish strife,
We hear your voice, O Son of Man.

FRANK M. NORTH (1850–1935)
WHERE CROSS THE CROWDED WAYS OF LIFE

THE SON OF MAN

Jesus displayed the kingdom's power by casting out demons and healing all who came to him (Matthew 8:16–18). When multitudes of people, full of demands, surrounded him, he retreated across the Sea of Galilee. There a scribe called him a mere teacher despite the many miracles he had performed (v. 19). This scribe did not comprehend the Lord's power and glory. At this time, Jesus revealed himself as the Son of Man (v. 20).

The title "Son of Man" shows that Jesus Christ is capable of coping with all that Adam's sin has brought into the world. He has regained the sovereignty lost by that first man. His kingdom will extend over humankind, the beasts of the field, and the birds of the air. The ignorant scribe represents Israel, which had no idea Jesus was the promised Messiah. As a result, the jackals reclined in their burrows, the birds had roosts on which to spend the night, yet the weary man whose kingdom includes all creatures found nowhere to rest (v. 20).

Adam was the ruler of all earthly creatures and head of the human race (Genesis 1:28). Jesus Christ, the Son of Man, inherited these glories and will restore them on earth in the coming kingdom age. Long ago, Israel's King David sang of this, looking forward to that glorious day:

> *What is man, that thou art mindful of him? and the son of man,*
> *that thou visitest him? For thou hast made him a little lower*
> *than the angels, and hast crowned him with glory and honour.*
> *Thou madest him to have dominion over the works of thy hands;*
> *thou hast put all things under his feet.*
> PSALM 8:4–6 (SEE ALSO 1 CORINTHIANS 15:25)

I've found a friend, O such a friend!
He loved me ere I knew him;
He drew me with the cord of love,
And thus he bound me to him.

JAMES G. SMALL (1817–1888)
I'VE FOUND A FRIEND

GOD'S CORD OF LOVE

Here is a description of Jesus Christ's friendship: "For scarcely for a righteous man will one die: yet peradventure for a good man some would even dare to die. But God commendeth his love toward us, in that, while we were yet sinners, Christ died for us" (Romans 5:7–8). The thing to remember is this: Since Christ died for us while we were still sinners, we have nothing to fear now that we are justified by faith in him. This is one of the strands that is braided into the cord of love that binds us to Christ. Another one is this: In the death of Jesus Christ, we also died (6:3–4).

It is crucial that all believers understand that they are crucified with Christ, are dead to the world, to the law, and to sin, and are alive to God. So our motto is, "I live; yet not I, but Christ liveth in me" (Galatians 2:20). We are dead by means of the death of Jesus Christ, and we are alive because of his resurrection (Romans 6:4).

What does it mean to say, "Christ lives in me"? This isn't some vague, mystical union with Christ. Our life is the result of the death and resurrection of Jesus Christ's. Outwardly, we live just as other people do; the same things support our natural lives. The difference is that a believer has an inner life that is activated and supported by the faith of Christ and the revelation of his love in giving himself for us. The hymn writer calls this the cord of love.

I am crucified with Christ: nevertheless I live; yet not I, but Christ liveth in me: and the life which I now live in the flesh I live by the faith of the Son of God, who loved me, and gave himself for me.
GALATIANS 2:20

Peace, perfect peace,
in this dark world of sin?
The blood of Jesus whispers peace within.

EDWARD H. BICKERSTETH (1825–1906)
PEACE, PERFECT PEACE

THE PEACE OF GOD

Each of Paul's epistles begins with a salutation of peace to the believers. This was and still is a common greeting in the Middle East. *Salaam* is the Arabic word, and *shalom* is the Hebrew word for peace. This word *peace* takes on an entirely new meaning in light of the death of Jesus Christ. The salutation of peace that begins each of Paul's epistles is conveyed to us from God and is more than a simple greeting or feeling of harmony with others (Romans 1:7; 1 Corinthians 1:3). The gospel is the gospel of peace, and God is the God of peace (Romans 10:15; 15:33). Those who believe the gospel find peace with God. This is thoroughly described in Romans 5:1–8:30.

Most believers know that sin no longer blocks us from the presence of God. This is shown in Romans 3:21–4:25. Yet God isn't satisfied with simply acquitting us from guilt like a judge in a courtroom. Rather, like a father in a family, God craves our love and adoration. His peace is a favor that is infinitely beyond justification. It carries us into full and affectionate fellowship with God. It carries us out of the cold courtroom where Jesus Christ's blood is applied to sinners and into the family circle where the death of God's Son brings reconciliation to us, his enemies, and fills our hearts with peace (Romans 5:8, 10).

Grace to you and peace from God our Father, and the Lord Jesus Christ.
ROMANS 1:7

Peace, perfect peace,
death shadowing us and ours?
Jesus has vanquished death and all its powers.

EDWARD H. BICKERSTETH (1825–1906)
PEACE, PERFECT PEACE

LIFE AND IMMORTALITY THROUGH THE GOSPEL

Certain people, like Lazarus, were raised from the dead before Jesus died and was resurrected, yet Jesus Christ is the first person to be made alive beyond the power of death. All the others who were raised eventually died again. Therefore, Jesus is the firstfruit of those who are made alive (1 Corinthians 15:23).

To better understand this, let's see where death came from: "By one man sin entered into the world, and death by sin; and so death passed upon all men, for that all have sinned" (Romans 5:12). This means that death came through Adam's sin, and because of death, everyone sins. Jesus Christ broke this pattern because he did not sin.

Death entered through a man and departed through a man (v. 17). Through Adam came death. Through Christ, resurrection reaches humankind, disposing of sin and death. However, Christ's act did not simply reverse Adam's original offense. God's goal is greater than this. He does not want to put us back in the garden where Adam was before he sinned. God operates his plan with a forward motion. This is why we are told that Christ's grace is not like Adam's offense (Romans 5:15). The offense simply brought death to humanity. The grace that has come through Christ super-abounds to all humankind. So we read that he not only abolished death, but he also "brought life and immortality to light through the gospel" (2 Timothy 1:10).

But now is Christ risen from the dead, and become the firstfruits of them that slept. For since by man came death, by man came also the resurrection of the dead. For as in Adam all die, even so in Christ shall all be made alive.
1 CORINTHIANS 15:20–22

O for a thousand tongues to sing
My great Redeemer's praise,
The glories of my God and King,
The triumphs of his grace!

CHARLES WESLEY (1707–1788)
O FOR A THOUSAND TONGUES TO SING

THE TRIUMPH OF GOD'S GRACE

Charles Wesley wrote this hymn on the first anniversary of the day the grace of God invaded his life. As he wrote in the ninth of its nineteen verses, "On this glad day the glorious sun of righteousness arose on my benighted soul." Although he was given the grace to write over seven thousand hymns, Wesley knew that a thousand times a thousand tongues, each singing its own unique hymn, cannot fully express the triumph of God's grace.

Some of the earliest recipients of that grace have become our teachers in the school of grace. Concerning the Macedonian believers, Paul wrote that the grace of God super-abounded to the riches of their generosity (2 Corinthians 8:1–2). That is, grace brings us God's love, and that same grace is seen in our love toward others.

The believers in Macedonia were very poor and in the midst of difficult circumstances. Therefore, the apostle didn't expect them to donate to the collection for the poor in Jerusalem. Nevertheless, they begged to take part in it, and they gave beyond their ability (vv. 3–5). These saints had received the ministry of reconciliation, so they had compassion for the poor in Jerusalem and they considered themselves debtors to them (Romans 15:26–27). This was not a work of humanistic charity. The Macedonians knew, "When we were enemies, we were reconciled to God by the death of his Son," and this produced fruit in their lives (5:10). The love of Christ was constraining them, and so they were no longer living "unto themselves, but unto him which died for them, and rose again" (2 Corinthians 5:15).

Grace to you and peace from God our Father and the Lord Jesus Christ.
I give thanks to my God always for you because of the grace of
God that has been given you in Christ Jesus.
1 CORINTHIANS 1:3–4 NRSV

We sing the glorious conquest, before Damascus' gate,
When Saul, the Church's spoiler, came breathing threats and hate;
The rav'ning wolf rushed forward full early to the prey;
But lo! the Shepherd met him, and bound him fast today.

JOHN ELLERTON (1826–1893)
WE SING THE GLORIOUS CONQUEST

OVERWHELMING GRACE

Paul testified three times about his encounter with Jesus Christ on the road to Damascus. These show that he did not feel a need of salvation, was not seeking the Lord's favor, and did not repent of his sins (Acts 9:1–19; 22:1–21; 26:1–18). What happened was this: He was conquered by an exhibition of God's pure grace. That grace overflowed; it was exceeding abundant; it overwhelmed the chief sinner with faith and love; and it made him a pattern for those who would thereafter believe (1 Timothy 1:13–16).

The most wonderful exhibition of God's grace in the sacred scriptures is seen in the call of Saul of Tarsus. Despite what we may think of our own former lives and sinful selves, we should recall that this man was the worst of sinners (v. 15). His heart was so full of threats and murder against the Lord Jesus and the disciples that they were in every breath he breathed (Acts 9:1–2). Saul endorsed the assassination of a man no less saintly that Stephen (7:59–8:1). Could he deserve anything better than swift, severe judgment?

Instead of this, the ascended Lord reproached him with gentle words of grace and love: "Saul, Saul, why persecutest thou me?" (9:4). Saul's heart was calloused, defiant, and rebellious. Yet it was captivated by that display of faith and love in Christ Jesus (1 Timothy 1:14). Ever since then, faith and love have marked the salvation of every believer.

And Saul, yet breathing out threatenings and slaughter against the disciples of the Lord. . . And as he journeyed, he came near Damascus: and suddenly there shined round about him a light from heaven: and he fell to the earth, and heard a voice saying unto him, Saul, Saul, why persecutest thou me?
ACTS 9:1, 3–4

My faith has found a resting place,
Not in device or creed;
I trust the ever living one,
His wounds for me shall plead.

ELIZA E. HEWITT (1851–1920)
MY FAITH HAS FOUND A RESTING PLACE

THE LOVE OF GOD IN CHRIST JESUS

The creeds of human invention may be effective in preserving religious organizations, but they are truly uninviting. They don't touch a person's heart. Faith cannot find a resting place in them. Likewise, various devices or methods of worship and devotion can quickly become mechanical routines and fail to turn a person's affections toward God.

Eliza Hewitt tapped into the single source of flowing, restful faith—the love of Christ as demonstrated in his death. Repeatedly, scripture directs the eyes of our hearts to see that Christ loved us and gave "himself for us an offering and a sacrifice to God for a sweetsmelling savour" (Ephesians 5:2). This love never lets us go, even in our trials and tribulations. God's love hovers over us in the midst of them to temper their distress. In comparison to the love of God, liturgies and creeds are powerless.

The love of God in Christ Jesus will cause death to be swallowed up by immortality (1 Corinthians 15:26; 2 Timothy 1:10). Even if our life in this world seems to lead us far from God, we aren't beyond the reach of God's love (Psalm 139:9–10). The present is perplexing and the future is fearful only to those who don't know this love. Of all the powers in the universe—everything above or beneath—nothing has the power to break the bond that unites the humblest believer to the loving heart of God.

In all these things we are more than conquerors through him that loved us. For I am persuaded, that neither death, nor life, nor angels, nor principalities, nor powers, nor things present, nor things to come, nor height, nor depth, nor any other creature, shall be able to separate us from the love of God, which is in Christ Jesus our Lord.
ROMANS 8:37–39

My heart is leaning on the Word,
The living Word of God,
Salvation by my Savior's name,
Salvation through his blood.

ELIZA E. HEWITT (1851–1920)
MY FAITH HAS FOUND A RESTING PLACE

HOLD THE PATTERN OF SOUND WORDS

It is impossible to overemphasize the importance of the Word of God to a believer's life. We benefit from it in two basic ways. First, the scriptures may be read devotionally. Schedules and plans for daily reading are often used for this purpose, although one might find it difficult to stick with a plan, fall behind, and become disheartened. In addition to this, the goals of the schedule can easily become the purpose of one's Bible reading. The one valid purpose for reading the Word is fellowship with God. How much or how little of the scriptures one reads is not important. A prayerful heart and a thirsty spirit are the only tools one needs.

Second, the scriptures may be carefully studied. Beside an accurate translation, the only tool necessary for this is a concordance. Since "all scripture is given by inspiration of God" (2 Timothy 3:16), attentive students will find that they are handling a living book. If allowed to do so, it will interpret itself in ways that impart Spirit and life to believers (John 6:63). Certainly a person should fellowship with others and consult reliable resources. But never be discouraged from personal Bible study. No one can chew your food for you.

And that from a child thou hast known the holy scriptures, which are able to make thee wise unto salvation through faith which is in Christ Jesus. All scripture is given by inspiration of God, and is profitable for doctrine, for reproof, for correction, for instruction in righteousness: that the man of God may be perfect, thoroughly furnished unto all good works.
2 TIMOTHY 3:15–17

March 15

I need no other argument,
I need no other plea,
It is enough that Jesus died,
And that he died for me.

ELIZA E. HEWITT (1851–1920)
MY FAITH HAS FOUND A RESTING PLACE

THE GREAT CHANGE

Ephesians paints our portrait in dark hues: In past times we were Gentiles in the flesh. Then Israel had all the promises and covenants, and they were not about to share them with us. They derisively called us "the uncircumcision." We were without Christ; we were aliens from the commonwealth of Israel; we were strangers from the covenants of promise. We had no hope. We were without God in the world (Ephesians 2:11–12). We had nothing.

But a great change is gloriously described in Ephesians 2:13–18. Though we were far off, we are now near by the blood of Christ. He became our peace by making Jewish believers and Gentile believers one. He tore down the wall of hatred between the two races. He nullified the precepts and decrees. Jewish and Gentile believers, though vastly different, were made into an entirely new humanity (4:24). Now we both have access to the Father in one spirit. Whereas Israel once had all the divine privileges and we Gentiles were limited to the crumbs that might fall from Israel's table, we now are equal members of Christ's body (3:6; see Matthew 15:26–27).

Eliza Hewitt admires the Lord's death for all its benefits. Truly, "it is enough that Jesus died" since the blood of the cross is the key to this great change. Christ Jesus died for all. And his work is far greater than it first appeared to be. Jesus is no longer only the King of the Jews. He is the Savior of all mankind (1 Timothy 4:10). His blood suffices for all and reconciles all believers in one body to God.

To the praise of the glory of his grace, wherein he hath made us
accepted in the beloved. In whom we have redemption through
his blood, the forgiveness of sins, according to the riches of his grace.
EPHESIANS 1:6–7

Nearer, my God, to thee, nearer to thee!
E'en though it be a cross that raiseth me,
Still all my song shall be, nearer, my God, to thee.
Nearer, my God, to thee, nearer to thee.

SARAH FLOWER ADAMS (1805–1848)
NEARER, MY GOD, TO THEE

THE DAY IS AT HAND

Every lover of God shares Sarah Adams's yearning to be nearer to him. Yet, as members of Christ's body, we presently cannot be nearer to him. On the other hand, each day that passes does bring us nearer to God because we are closer to Christ's second coming. So the apostle says, "It is high time to awake out of sleep: for now is our salvation nearer than when we believed" (Romans 13:11).

Scripture tells of the five great eons or ages that begin and end one by one (1 Corinthians 10:11; 15:23). We now live in "this present evil world" (Galatians 1:4). Within these ages, times and seasons come and go, and the time has come for believers to wake up. This is why Romans 13:11–14 pictures our era as the dawning of day, a period in which darkness gives way to increasing light. The full light of day will bring our complete salvation at Jesus Christ's return.

Just as we wake up in the morning and prepare for the day, we are advised to cast off darkness like pajamas and to put on light (v. 12). Every morning we awake and dress for the day. Similarly, it is time to "put. . .on the Lord Jesus Christ" (v. 14). That is, by grace our conduct points toward the coming of the light and is not tainted with dark endeavors that require shadows of night to hide their shame (v. 13).

And that, knowing the time, that now it is high time to awake out of sleep: for now is our salvation nearer than when we believed. The night is far spent, the day is at hand: Let us therefore cast off the works of darkness, and let us put on the armour of light.
ROMANS 13:11–12 (SEE EPHESIANS 5:10–14)

May the grace of Christ our Savior
And the Father's boundless love
With the Holy Spirit's favor,
Rest upon us from above.

JOHN NEWTON (1725–1807)
MAY THE GRACE OF CHRIST OUR SAVIOR

LOVE, GRACE, AND FELLOWSHIP

We need nothing more to be happy than the love of God, the grace of Christ, and the fellowship of the Holy Spirit (2 Corinthians 13:14).

The grace of Christ is described like this: "For ye know the grace of our Lord Jesus Christ, that, though he was rich, yet for your sakes he became poor, that ye through his poverty might be rich" (8:9; see Philippians 2:6–8). No wonder Paul marveled that the Galatians had transferred from God, who had called them in the grace of Christ, to another gospel (Galatians 1:6; 3:3). How could they abandon grace? They were deceived, so they moved out of grace into the bondage of law. This is the recipe for misery.

The love of God and the fellowship of the Spirit are both described at once in Romans: "The love of God is shed abroad in our hearts by the Holy Ghost which is given unto us" (Romans 5:5). Romans continues to tell of God's love: "For when we were yet without strength, in due time Christ died for the ungodly" (v. 6). This means that God's love, conveyed to us by the Spirit, is expressed in the grace of Christ. These three—love, grace, and fellowship—are inseparable.

The grace of Christ is seen in his deep humiliation at Calvary (2 Corinthians 8:9). It is well known that the love of God is expressed in his making his Son a sin offering for our sakes so that we might become God's righteousness in him (John 3:16; 2 Corinthians 5:21). The communion of the Holy Spirit is the fellowship and unity we share in Christ as recipients of his grace through God's love.

The grace of the Lord Jesus Christ, and the love of God,
and the communion of the Holy Ghost, be with you all. Amen.
2 CORINTHIANS 13:14

How sweet the name of Jesus sounds
In a believer's ear!
It soothes his sorrows, heals his wounds,
And drives away his fear.

JOHN NEWTON (1725–1807)
HOW SWEET THE NAME OF JESUS SOUNDS

THE MEANING OF JESUS' NAME

The name "Jesus" is weighted with meaning for those who see the extent of our Lord's service and suffering. In this name, which is his identity in humiliation, he is elevated from the lowest place to the highest point of creation. From the beginning, Christ was in the form of God, above the heavens (Philippians 2:6). Serving God's will, he took the form of a human slave, was given the name of Jesus, and submitted to the curse of the cross (vv. 7–8). There, Jesus was the lowest of all.

The children of Adam delight to exalt themselves, though the day will come when they will proclaim the lordship of Jesus. In contrast to them, Jesus Christ, who can assume equality with God, delighted in submission to God's will and humiliation in the eyes of man (vv. 6–8). He was the last Adam who died for all, terminating Adam's race. The consequence of his death is that, in God's eyes, all humanity is dead (1 Corinthians 15:45; 2 Corinthians 5:14).

God's Son voluntarily descended from the highest to the lowest place. His exaltation reverses this flow (Philippians 2:9–11). Each time someone believes, the exaltation of the Son advances until the day when all will be subjected to him and the consummation of the ages arrives (1 Corinthians 15:23, 28). Then every tongue will have sounded the sweet name of Jesus, proclaiming, "Jesus Christ is Lord!" to the glory of God the Father (Philippians 2:11).

Who, being in the form of God, thought it not robbery to be equal with God: but made himself of no reputation, and took upon him the form of a servant, and was made in the likeness of men: and being found in fashion as a man, he humbled himself, and became obedient unto death, even the death of the cross.
PHILIPPIANS 2:6–8

Far called, our navies melt away;
On dune and headland sinks the fire:
Lo, all our pomp of yesterday
Is one with Nineveh and Tyre!
Judge of the nations, spare us yet,
Lest we forget, lest we forget!

RUDYARD KIPLING (1865–1936)
GOD OF OUR FATHERS, KNOWN OF OLD

LEST WE FORGET NINEVEH

Nimrod founded Nineveh (Genesis 10:11), and the city occupied a central position on the road between the Mediterranean Sea and the Indian Ocean. Modern-day Mosul, Iraq, is near this site. Wealth flowed into Nineveh from many sources, so it became the greatest and most magnificent of ancient cities. It covered about 2.75 square miles with fifteen great gates opening its walls. At its height as the Assyrian capital, Sennacherib was Nineveh's king (about 700 BC; 2 Kings 19:35–37). But Nineveh was conquered by the Medes and Babylonians and razed to the ground in 612 BC. All memory of it was lost between 400 BC and the mid-nineteenth century when archaeologists discovered its ruins.

Rudyard Kipling wrote his hymn "God of Our Fathers, Known of Old" for the celebration of Queen Victoria's jubilee year, at the height of the power of the British Empire (1887). He compares the significance of Great Britain with that of Nineveh and prays that God will spare his native land the fate of the great ancient city. We may wish to pray in this way for the United States. But let us remember that despite our wishes, God "makes nations great, then destroys them; he enlarges nations, then leads them away" (Job 12:23 NRSV).

He giveth to all life, and breath, and all things; and hath made of one
blood all nations of men for to dwell on all the face of the earth, and hath
determined the times before appointed, and the bounds of their habitation.
ACTS 17:25–26

> *A guilty, weak, and helpless worm,*
> *Into thy hands I fall;*
> *Be thou my strength and righteousness,*
> *My Savior, and my all.*

ISAAC WATTS (1674–1748)
HOW SAD OUR STATE BY NATURE IS

OF WORMS AND WISDOM

A weak and helpless worm? Yes, Isaac Watts considered himself the equivalent of a damp, dirt-eating invertebrate in comparison with God's Son. This extreme statement shows that Watts understood how exalted the Son truly is. Perhaps he thought, "I am as far below Christ in the order of things as a worm is below me."

Let's read the scriptures and draw our own conclusions about this. Colossians says that all the treasures of wisdom and knowledge are found in Christ (2:3). This points to Proverbs 8:12–31, which is the testimony of wisdom. Such wisdom portrays the Son of God: "The LORD possessed me in the beginning of his way. . . . I was set up from everlasting, from the beginning, or ever the earth was. When there were no depths, I was brought forth; when there were no fountains abounding with water. Before the mountains were settled, before the hills was I brought forth. . . . When he prepared the heavens, I was there: when he set a compass upon the face of the depth: When he established the clouds above: when he strengthened the fountains of the deep. . .when he appointed the foundations of the earth: Then I was by him, as one brought up with him: and I was daily his delight, rejoicing always before him" (vv. 22–30).

These words describe only a portion of the Son's history. If more proof is needed to convince us of the height of Christ's status above us, we can also consider his present and future glories, compare ourselves to these, and decide if we wish to join Isaac Watts in his humility.

In whom are hid all the treasures of wisdom and knowledge.
COLOSSIANS 2:3

Under his wings I am safely abiding,
Though the night deepens and tempests are wild,
Still I can trust him; I know he will keep me,
He has redeemed me, and I am his child.
Under his wings, under his wings,
Who from his love can sever?

WILLIAM O. CUSHING (1823–1902)
UNDER HIS WINGS

WE ARE SAVED IN HIS LIFE

Tiny chicks can be no safer than when they are beneath the warm wings of their mother. Outside this shelter, though the chicks don't know it, birds of prey circle overhead awaiting an opportunity to swoop down and claim one for a meal. Jesus used the figure of a hen and her chicks to depict the relationship he desired to have with Israel (Matthew 23:37). His beloved nation rejected his love, so he was left exposed to the powers of darkness. Now, in this era of Israel's apostasy, the gospel has come to the Gentiles (Acts 28:28).

We are hidden from the destroying powers of darkness, not under Christ's wings, but in Christ himself. So we read, "Your life is hid with Christ in God" (Colossians 3:3). This is greater by far than the protection of figurative wings. Christ is our life, and we are saved in that life (Romans 5:10; Colossians 3:4).

Let us review Christ's life: He was in the form of God, but he left that behind and humbled himself to the death of the cross (Philippians 2:6–8). Then he was given his tomb with the wicked (Isaiah 53:9). God raised him from that tomb and has highly exalted him. We are saved in his life. When we believed, we were baptized into Christ's death and entombed together with him. Now, just as the Father raised Christ Jesus from the dead, we are walking in newness of life (Romans 6:3–4). With this understanding, believers think of their life like this:

For in that he died, he died unto sin once: but in that he liveth,
he liveth unto God. Likewise reckon ye also yourselves to be dead
indeed unto sin, but alive unto God through Jesus Christ our Lord.
ROMANS 6:10–11

Open my eyes, that I may see
Glimpses of truth thou hast for me;
Place in my hands the wonderful key
That shall unclasp and set me free.

CLARA H. SCOTT (1841–1897)
OPEN MY EYES, THAT I MAY SEE

THE MINISTRY OF THE SPIRIT

As Jesus neared the end of his life, he made this surprising statement: "I still have many things to say to you, but you cannot bear them now" (John 16:12 NRSV). This means that the Lord's teachings in the Gospels don't tell us everything he'd like us to know. A universe of truth was awaiting revelation in Christ's death, resurrection, and exaltation. So after those astonishing events, God's truth came through the Spirit of truth (v. 13). As time passed, Israel rejected the gospel offered by the Lord's twelve apostles, and the apostle Paul was called to minister to the other nations (Galatians 2:7–8). His ministry involved truths that had never before been revealed (Acts 26:16; Ephesians 3:3, 5). These were among the many things the Lord could not speak about while he ministered in Israel.

The King James Version says that Paul ministered to fulfill the Word of God (Colossians 1:25). The word *fulfill* should be more precisely translated "complete." The apostle completed God's Word. Unlike the other scriptures, Paul's revelation extends outside the ages (1 Corinthians 2:7, 11; 15:23–24) and beyond the earth (Ephesians 2:6; Philippians 3:20; Colossians 3:3). He tells of Israel's glorious Messiah, and also of Christ the hope of glory among the nations (Colossians 1:27). In his epistles, justification by faith is made clear (Romans 3:24–30; Galatians 3:8), the dispensation of reconciliation is inaugurated (Romans 5:10–11; 2 Corinthians 5:18–19), and the secret hidden from the ages in God is revealed (Ephesians 3:3–6, 9; Colossians 1:25–27).

Thus, the apostle Paul's writings complete the Word of God. His ministry of the Spirit was even more glorious than any that had gone before (2 Corinthians 3:8). Through it, the Spirit guides us into all truth.

Howbeit when he, the Spirit of truth, is come, he will guide you into all truth.
JOHN 16:13

Thy works, not mine, O Christ,
Speak gladness to this heart;
They tell me all is done;
They bid my fear depart.

HORATIUS BONAR (1808–1889)
THY WORKS, NOT MINE, O CHRIST

THE LAW VS. GRACE

The conflict between our works and Christ's work is seen in the book of Galatians. There believers are challenged: "This only would I learn of you, Received ye the Spirit by the works of the law, or by the hearing of faith?" (3:2). Of course, the Galatians began in faith just as we all did. But they had to answer this question: "Are ye so foolish? having begun in the Spirit, are ye now made perfect by the flesh?" (v. 3). We should consider how we might answer that question. Can we, like Horatius Bonar, abandon our efforts of self-perfection and live today just as we began—by grace through faith (Ephesians 2:8)?

Acts tells of the opposition of the church in Jerusalem to Paul and his gospel to the nations. Multitudes of Jews believed during the Pentecostal era (Acts 2:41; 4:4), but they could not shake off their fondness for Jewish law and accept that Paul preached a gospel that was tailored by God for the nations (21:20–21). Their questionings, strife, and debates dragged Gentile believers from grace and faith down to law and works. In Galatia, Judaizers preached a different gospel, one of law blended with grace (Galatians 1:6–7; 3:2–3).

God intended that Israel minister to the nations, helping them on the way of salvation (Acts 3:25; Galatians 3:8). Instead of this, the book of Acts tells all about their opposition to the gospel. In the face of this, Paul was all things to all people in order to gain them for God: To the Jews, he became a Jew. To those under the law, he was under law (1 Corinthians 9:19–22). But, at last, he had to put a stop to all discussion of these subjects, saying:

> *Avoid foolish questions, and genealogies, and contentions,*
> *and strivings about the law; for they are unprofitable and vain.*
> TITUS 3:9

*God of the earth, the sky, the sea!
Maker of all above, below!
Creation lives and moves in thee,
Thy present life in all doth flow.*

SAMUEL LONGFELLOW (1819–1892)
GOD OF THE EARTH, THE SKY, THE SEA

THE SPHERE OF HUMAN EXISTENCE

Paul told the unbelieving Athenians the essential truth about the sphere of human existence. "In him we live, and move, and have our being," he said (Acts 17:28). We all exist in God, both believers and those who do not yet believe. This remarkable statement notified those idolatrous Greek philosophers of the unique components that make up human beings.

These are seen in the model prayer that we will do well to pray for our loved ones: "The very God of peace sanctify you wholly; and I pray God your whole spirit and soul and body be preserved blameless unto the coming of our Lord Jesus Christ" (1 Thessalonians 5:23). This prayer corresponds to Acts 17:28. Our soul lives, our body moves, and our spirit has its being in God.

As Paul stood on the Areopagus (or Mars Hill, Acts 17:19, 22), a prominence that represented the pinnacle of human wisdom, the apostle said, "In him we live" (v. 28). This tells of the human soul that was first made living when God breathed into Adam (Genesis 2:7). With our souls we analyze all that we see, hear, touch, taste, and smell in our body. This body is evident in the phrase "in him we. . .move," because we are immobile without it. Finally, scripture reveals that our being is centered in our spirit because this single component returns to God at death (Ecclesiastes 12:7).

The philosophers called the apostle Paul "this babbler," as if he raucously cawed like a crow (Acts 17:18). Did they realize that, in one sentence, he condensed more knowledge about God and humankind than could be found in all the philosophies of Greece? We prize this masterly analysis of humans and their relation to the Creator:

For in him we live, and move, and have our being.
ACTS 17:28

In Christ there is no east or west,
In him no south or north;
But one great fellowship of love
Throughout the whole wide earth.

WILLIAM DUNKERLEY (1852–1941)
IN CHRIST THERE IS NO EAST OR WEST

THE ONE GREAT FELLOWSHIP OF LOVE

When writing to the Corinthians, Paul first mentions the one great fellowship of love that William Dunkerley so admires in his hymn. "God is faithful," says the apostle, "by whom ye were called unto the fellowship of his Son Jesus Christ our Lord" (1 Corinthians 1:9). He placed the Corinthians in that great fellowship, even though there were divisions among them (vv. 10–11). But their schisms can't match those we see today. The Corinthian factions still met together in one place (11:17, 20). The idea that believers from the same locality might divide into independent churches was unknown to them. But now sectarianism is an incurable affliction that defies all efforts to restore the Church's unity.

Knowing this, what are we to do? The apostle advises two things: One, keep the Spirit's unity in the bond of peace (Ephesians 4:3). Two, seek fellowship with all who call on the name of the Lord out of a pure heart (2 Timothy 2:22). The visible unity of believers no longer exists. Nevertheless, let's nurture fellowship with all believers, despite man-made divisions. Soon we will all be caught up into the presence of Christ and every barrier will be gone (1 Thessalonians 4:16–17). Until then, let us do our part to realize this oneness with every believer we meet.

I therefore, the prisoner of the Lord, beseech you that ye walk
worthy of the vocation wherewith ye are called, with all lowliness
and meekness, with longsuffering, forbearing one another in love;
Endeavouring to keep the unity of the Spirit in the bond of peace.
EPHESIANS 4:1–3

God, in the gospel of his Son,
Makes his eternal counsels known;
Where love in all its glory shines,
And truth is drawn in fairest lines.

BENJAMIN BEDDOME (1717–1795).
GOD, IN THE GOSPEL OF HIS SON

THE THREEFOLD GOSPEL

Here is the gospel in its simplest form: "I declare unto you the gospel
. . .how that Christ died for our sins according to the scriptures; and
that he was buried, and that he rose again the third day according to
the scriptures" (1 Corinthians 15:1, 3–4).

The gospel is not one fact but three: Christ died for our sins,
he was entombed, and he has been raised. These add up to what
Benjamin Beddome calls God's eternal counsels. Men did not crucify
the Savior, though their hands planted that cross on Golgotha. Jesus
was "delivered by the determinate counsel and foreknowledge of God"
(Acts 2:23). This terminated Adam's race and solved the problem of
sin (Romans 6:7; 2 Corinthians 5:14).

In his burial, every believer was buried, "that like as Christ was raised
up from the dead. . .so we also should walk in newness of life" (Romans
6:4). In addition, Christ emerged from the grave as God's firstfruits in
resurrection; the first to triumph over death. All who belong to Christ
when he returns will follow him out of death's grasp (1 Corinthians
15:23). Then, as the eons run their course, all is subjected to the Son
until death itself is abolished and its prisoners are released (v. 26). Then
the end has come and God's counsels are complete (v. 28).

For as in Adam all die, even so in Christ shall all be made alive. But every
man in his own order: Christ the firstfruits; afterward they that are Christ's
at his coming. Then cometh the end. . . . For he must reign, till he hath put
all enemies under his feet. The last enemy that shall be destroyed is death.
1 CORINTHIANS 15:22–26

O Lord, how shall I meet you,
How welcome you aright?
Your people long to greet you,
My hope, my heart's delight!

PAUL GERHARDT (1607–1676)
O LORD, HOW SHALL I MEET YOU?

THE DEAD IN CHRIST SHALL RISE FIRST

The saints in Thessalonica were concerned about how the dead believers would meet the Lord at his return. They were comforted to learn that the resurrection of Christ guarantees that all who belong to him will be raised (1 Thessalonians 4:14). Jesus revealed that Israel will enjoy the resurrection of life, which will occur after the period of God's wrath when Christ again sets foot on earth (John 5:29; Revelation 20:5). However, we who are justified in Christ's blood will be saved from that wrath (Romans 5:9). Christ Jesus has delivered us from the wrath of that great tribulation (1 Thessalonians 1:10; 5:9; Revelation 11:18). The hymn writer Paul Gerhardt and all who believe during this era of grace will meet the Lord in the air, before Christ's return to the earth (1 Thessalonians 4:17).

This same resurrection was also unfolded to the Corinthians (1 Corinthians 15:51–53). They learned that living as well as dead believers will be given incorruptible, spiritual, celestial bodies. Without these, we cannot meet the Lord in the air. The crowning glory of our blessed expectation was made known to the Philippians. They were blessed to learn that our bodies of humiliation will be transfigured to conform to that glorious body that blinded Paul when he saw the Lord (Philippians 3:21; Acts 9:3, 8, 18). We who believe in Jesus Christ have the honor of holding in our hearts this hope of our calling (Ephesians 4:4).

> *Behold, I shew you a mystery; We shall not all sleep, but we shall all be changed, In a moment, in the twinkling of an eye, at the last trump: for the trumpet shall sound, and the dead shall be raised incorruptible, and we shall be changed. For this corruptible must put on incorruption, and this mortal must put on immortality.*
> 1 CORINTHIANS 15:51–53

O dearest Jesus, what law hast thou broken
That such sharp sentence should on thee be spoken?
Of what great crime hast thou to make confession
What dark transgression?

JEAN DE FÉCAMP (ABOUT 1000–1079)
O DEAREST JESUS

CURSED IS EVERYONE WHO HANGS ON A TREE

Jesus Christ, the image of the invisible God, is in the garden of Gethsemane anticipating death by crucifixion (Matthew 26:36–45; Colossians 1:15). He retreats to pray. The firstborn of every creature asks his friends to watch with him. The one in whom all things were created is sorrowful and depressed (Matthew 26:38). He is before all things, yet he falls on his face to pray (v. 39). All things cohere in him; still he asks his Father if he might avoid the coming suffering. He once said, "I came down from heaven, not to do mine own will, but the will of him that sent me" (John 6:38), and he always delighted in God's will even though it brought him opposition and hatred. Despite this, his will balks at the terrors of the curse and the abandonment by God that it will cause. The prospect of the cross is so horrific that he prays three times, "Not as I will, but as thou wilt!" a declaration that seems far more appropriate for us than for him.

Jean de Fécamp asks in his hymn, "O dearest Jesus, what law hast thou broken that such sharp sentence should on thee be spoken?" Only this: Against his will, Jesus was hung on a cross (Deuteronomy 21:22–23). Because of this, he was cursed and forsaken by God. "For it is written, Cursed is every one that hangeth on a tree" (Galatians 3:13).

And when the sixth hour was come, there was darkness over the whole land until the ninth hour. And at the ninth hour Jesus cried with a loud voice, saying, Eloi, Eloi, lama sabachthani? which is, being interpreted, My God, my God, why hast thou forsaken me?
MARK 15:33–34

Lo, how a rose e'er blooming
From tender stem hath sprung!
Of Jesse's lineage coming,
As men of old have sung.

GERMAN CAROL (FIFTEENTH CENTURY)
LO, HOW A ROSE E'ER BLOOMING
TRANSLATED BY THEODORE BAKER (1851–1934)

THE STUMP AND THE SPRIG

This lovely song compares Jesus Christ to two delicate plants: One is the rose of Sharon (Song of Solomon 2:1), and the other is the tender shoot emerging out of the stem or stump of Jesse (Isaiah 11:1). Let's contemplate the tender shoot, a reference to the lineage of our Lord.

Jesus Christ is often called the Son of David in the four Gospels and Acts because he was descended from Israel's king (Romans 1:3). David himself was Jesse's son. Why then does Isaiah call the Messiah a shoot from the stump of Jesse? This is because Jesse lived and died in humble obscurity and his family was originally of no repute (1 Samuel 18:18). To emphasize his lowly origins, sometimes David was called the son of Jesse. This was a contemptuous title for the formidable king (22:7). The royal family that sprang from Jesse's seed and grew tall like a cedar was eventually cut down. By the time Jesus was born in the city of David, Israel's kingly tree was a dry stump.

But "there is hope of a tree, if it be cut down, that it will sprout again, and that the tender branch thereof will not cease" (Job 14:7). So figuratively speaking, from the stump of the tree that grew out of lowly Jesse, emerged Jesus Christ—a frail sprig whose kingdom will flourish with trees for a thousand years (Isaiah 41:18–20).

> *A shoot shall come out from the stump of Jesse, and a branch shall*
> *grow out of his roots. The spirit of the LORD shall rest on him,*
> *the spirit of wisdom and understanding, the spirit of counsel and might,*
> *the spirit of knowledge and the fear of the LORD.*
> ISAIAH 11:1–2 NRSV

The people that in darkness sat
A glorious light have seen;
The light has shined on them who long
In shades of death have been.

JOHN MORRISON (1750–1798)
THE PEOPLE THAT IN DARKNESS SAT

LIGHT HAS SPRUNG UP

Jesus was raised near Galilee, a remote part of Israel far from Jerusalem, whose inhabitants were considered uncouth by other Israelites. There, he ministered the gospel of the kingdom (Matthew 4:17).

A sketchy map of Jesus' work is found in Matthew 4:15. He began in the region around Nazareth and Cana. These were in the land allotted to the tribe of Zebulon. It did not touch the Sea of Galilee but bordered Naphtali to the northeast. In Naphtali lay the towns of Capernaum, called "his own city" (9:1), Chorazin, and Bethsaida—towns that saw so many of his miraculous works (11:21). This was Galilee of the Gentiles, a borderline region where pagan nations mingled with the Jews.

Scripture pictures the people who lived there as sitting down immoblized in the region of the shadow of death. They preferred that shadow over the light that was in Christ (Matthew 4:16; John 1:4; 3:19). Even so, he was the great light that arose there to enlighten those who for generation upon generation had labored in the shadowy light of the law.

Although that great light has been temporarily extinguished for Israel, he will shine again for his people one day. Then they will live and reign with their Messiah for a thousand years (Revelation 20:3–4). Finally, that light will shine for God's people in unimaginable fullness in New Jerusalem. This city, which their father Abraham longed to see (Hebrews 11:8–10), has no night. Lamplight and sunlight are not needed there because the Lord God is its illumination (Revelation 22:5).

The land of Zabulon, and the land of Nephthalim, by the way of the sea, beyond Jordan, Galilee of the Gentiles; the people which sat in darkness saw great light; and to them which sat in the region and shadow of death light is sprung up.
MATTHEW 4:15–16

O come, O come, Emmanuel,
And ransom captive Israel,
That mourns in lonely exile here
Until the Son of God appear.

LATIN HYMN (TWELFTH CENTURY)
O COME, O COME, EMMANUEL

THE MEANING OF *EMMANUEL*

God is an invisible Spirit whom no one has ever seen (John 1:18; 4:24). However, Christ is "the image of the invisible God" (Colossians 1:15). In other words, as Isaiah predicted, his name is Emmanuel, meaning "God with us" (Isaiah 7:14; Matthew 1:23).

How did Jesus Christ bring God to Israel and the nations? The book of Hebrews uses the figure of sunshine to explain this. There we read that the Son is the "brightness of [God's] glory" (1:1–3). A better translation for "brightness" is "effulgence," which means "shining" or "radiance." Some people enjoy sitting in the sun for its warmth or tanning effects. Of course, they aren't actually in the sun, they are in the sunshine—the sun's effulgence. The sun is hidden behind the radiant beams that bring its energy to us in beneficial ways that we can cope with. Similarly, the Son is the effulgence of the invisible God.

Even as the loving Father, God cannot be known except through the Son (John 14:9–10). It is only through his "express image" that God reveals himself. Though he is now seated at the right hand of the Majesty on high (Hebrews 1:3), the Son is still the unique way we comprehend and approach the Almighty God.

Who being the brightness of his glory, and the express image of his person,
and upholding all things by the word of his power, when he had by himself
purged our sins, sat down on the right hand of the Majesty on high.
HEBREWS 1:3

O come, desire of nations, bind
All peoples in one heart and mind;
Bid envy, strife, and quarrels cease;
Fill the whole world with heaven's peace.

LATIN HYMN (TWELFTH CENTURY)
O COME, O COME, EMMANUEL

THE DESIRE OF NATIONS

Not only does believing Israel long for her Messiah, the coming Christ is the desire of the nations, as well. He will come and fulfill God's long-ago promise to Abraham: "In thee shall all families of the earth be blessed" (Genesis 12:3).

This desire is first seen only in individual Gentiles: Balaam spoke of the star that will come out of Jacob and the scepter that will rise out of Israel (Numbers 24:17). Job knew of a living redeemer (Job 19:25). Magi journeyed from far away to worship the baby Jesus (Matthew 2:1–2). A Canaanite woman accepted meager crumbs from Israel's table (15:22–27). Eventually, multitudes of people from every nation heard the disciples announce the Messiah's kingdom in Jerusalem (Acts 2:1–5).

Step by step the nations enter God's blessing in Christ until the fullness of the nations comes in at the close of this age (Romans 11:25). At first, the Messiah was sent only to the lost sheep of the house of Israel (Matthew 15:24). He told the twelve apostles to "go nowhere among the Gentiles" (10:5–6 NRSV). Later, the apostles learned that Gentile converts to Judaism could share Israel's blessings in the gospel (Acts 10:39–48.) A huge step was taken when God opened a door of faith to Gentiles who were not Jewish converts (13:46–47). Finally, the salvation of God was sent directly to the nations without the mediation of Israel (28:28). And now we are among untold numbers of Gentiles desiring to see the return of Christ.

Yet once, it is a little while, and I will shake the heavens, and the earth, and the sea, and the dry land; and I will shake all nations, and the desire of all nations shall come: and I will fill this house with glory, saith the LORD of hosts.
HAGGAI 2:6–7

In the bleak midwinter, frosty wind made moan,
Earth stood hard as iron, water like a stone;
Snow had fallen, snow on snow, snow on snow,
In the bleak midwinter, long ago.

CHRISTINA G. ROSSETTI (1830–1894)
IN THE BLEAK MIDWINTER

GRACE AND THE HARDENED HEART

Scholars agree that Jesus Christ was not born in the wintertime. Never-theless, the Savior's birth is observed during what is in many regions the darkest and coldest time of the year—the bleak midwinter. In her hymn, Christina Rossetti poetically depicts the world before the arrival of Jesus Christ: Snow had fallen snow on snow, snow on snow, snow on snow. Anyone who has lived in the northern tier of the United States knows what this is like. Job's description of humanity without God is also chilling, and much more graphic: "They lie all night naked, without clothing, and have no covering in the cold" (24:7 NRSV).

Another illustration of man without God is found in John's Gospel. On the night of Christ's betrayal, "It was cold: and they warmed themselves: and Peter stood with them, and warmed himself" (18:18). People are still trying to warm themselves around fires they themselves have kindled. Though we should know better, even we believers may seek strength and comfort in material possessions, personal accomplishments, or social position.

At that fire, Peter had a practical experience of what every self-righteous person eventually learns—"What I hate, that I do" (see Romans 7:15). Peter lied when questioned about his Master (John 18:25). Worldly self-righteousness had made his heart cold toward the Lord. At that very moment, in the bleak midwinter of his hardened heart, a glance from Jesus Christ brought a flood of grace to the lapsed apostle, and this overwhelmed his unbelief (Luke 22:61–62; see 1 Timothy 1:13–14).

Who was before a blasphemer, and a persecutor, and injurious: but I
obtained mercy, because I did it ignorantly in unbelief. And the grace of our
Lord was exceeding abundant with faith and love which is in Christ Jesus.
1 TIMOTHY 1:13–14

Earth has many a noble city; Bethlehem, thou dost all excel;
Out of thee the Lord from heaven
Came to rule his Israel.

AURELIUS CLEMENS PRUDENTIUS (348–ABOUT 413)
EARTH HAS MANY A NOBLE CITY

THE EXALTATION OF BETHLEHEM

The family of Jesus Christ was associated with Bethlehem from the time of Boaz and Ruth (Matthew 1:5; Ruth 1:1–2; 4:13–17). Here was the childhood home of David the king who longed for water from its wells (2 Samuel 23:15–16). Before David, Bethlehem was so insignificant that it is missing from the gazetteers of the cities of Judah in Joshua 15 and Nehemiah 11. Micah uses this insignificance as the background to display Bethlehem's future greatness: "But thou, Bethlehem Ephratah, though thou be little among the thousands of Judah, yet out of thee shall he come forth unto me that is to be ruler in Israel; whose goings forth have been from of old, from everlasting" (5:2). Jesus Christ gave honor to little Bethlehem but, in keeping with his humility, gained no honor from it, since he was raised in despised Nazareth (John 1:46).

Out of Bethlehem came a ruler "whose goings forth have been from of old, from everlasting." These rich words echo Philippians 2:6, which reveals that Christ, before he humbled himself and came to be in the likeness of humanity, was inherently in the form of God, just as the Word was with God in the beginning (John 1:1). The ruler mentioned by Micah can only be Christ. None other fits the bill.

God's grace is seen even in the location of the birth of his Son. Bethlehem had nothing to recommend it. Human wisdom would have chosen Jerusalem for the birthplace and home of Israel's king. Bethlehem would never be considered worthy to be honored by the Messiah's birth. In this little town, we again see God exalting people of low degree (Luke 1:52).

And Joseph also went up from Galilee, out of the city of Nazareth, into Judaea, unto the city of David, which is called Bethlehem. . .with Mary his espoused wife, being great with child.
LUKE 2:4–5

Angels from the realms of glory,
Wing your flight o'er all the earth;
Ye who sang creation's story
Now proclaim Messiah's birth.

JAMES MONTGOMERY (1771–1854)
ANGELS FROM THE REALMS OF GLORY

THE EXULTANT ANGELS, PART 1

From long before the days of David, shepherds have guarded their flocks in the countryside around Bethlehem. They use a sheepfold with a stone wall to protect their flock at night. The shepherd sleeps in its entrance, thus becoming the door of the sheepfold (John 10:7).

Shepherds were doing this when Israel's great shepherd was born (Luke 2:8–16). That night, the darkness around their sheepfold was illumined by God's glory, and an angel stood nearby. Though the shepherds were afraid, the messenger reassured them, announcing the birth of the Messiah. The citizens of Israel slept through this earth-shattering event, but the multitude of heavenly hosts hailed the Son of God's coming in human form with unrestrained joy.

As James Montgomery points out in his hymn, such an angelic celebration had happened once before: When God laid the foundations of the earth, "the morning stars sang together, and all the sons of God shouted for joy" (Job 38: 7). They were elated to see preparations being made for the coming of the one who would reconcile all things to God (Colossians 1:20).

These celebrations show that Christ's coming affects more than humanity. They reach from the highest of heaven's hosts to the lowest of humankind. All God's great purposes of blessing will flow through Christ to the utmost bounds of creation. What more can man wish for or God desire?

And, lo, the angel of the Lord came upon them, and the glory of the Lord shone round about them: and they were sore afraid. And the angel said unto them, Fear not: for, behold, I bring you good tidings of great joy, which shall be to all people. For unto you is born this day in the city of David a Saviour, which is Christ the Lord.
LUKE 2:9–11

Hark! The herald angels sing, "Glory to the newborn King;
Peace on earth, and mercy mild, God and sinners reconciled!"
Joyful, all ye nations rise, join the triumph of the skies;
With th' angelic host proclaim, "Christ is born in Bethlehem!"

CHARLES WESLEY (1707–1788)
HARK! THE HERALD ANGELS SING

THE EXULTANT ANGELS, PART 2

The visit of the herald angels to the shepherds of Bethlehem is evidence that the effects of the birth of Jesus Christ stretched from the highest of heaven's angelic hosts to the lowest of humankind as represented by the shepherds (Luke 2:13–15). However, it was God's pleasure that Israel's Messiah was rejected and crucified, so the peaceable kingdom has not yet been established (Isaiah 32:16–19). Actual peace has not appeared on earth, nor has goodwill suddenly sprung up among men. Even the heavenly hosts have seen only the beginning of the coming glory (1 Peter 3:22).

The heavenly messengers may not have known of God's plan to use the blood of the cross to accomplish reconciliation (Colossians 1:20). The timing of the Son's arrival on earth to die also may not have been understandable to them. But they apparently had gained a glimpse of the goal—glory to God throughout heaven and earth (Luke 2:14). They knew that the birth of the baby they celebrated would cause God's great purpose to be fulfilled to the utmost bounds of creation (1 Corinthians 15:28).

In contrast to the sight of the heavenly messengers, when the shepherds hurried to confirm the angel's message, they came upon a humble scene: a lowly family in a dim stable with the baby Messiah cradled in a feed trough. The only glory there was spiritual, and only heaven celebrated the Savior's birth.

And suddenly there was with the angel a multitude of the heavenly host praising God, and saying, Glory to God in the highest, and on earth peace, good will toward men.
LUKE 2:13–14

Sing praise to God who reigns above,
The God of all creation,
The God of power, the God of love,
The God of our salvation.

JOHANN J. SCHÜTZ (1640–1690)
SING PRAISE TO GOD WHO REIGNS ABOVE

THE TRAINING OF GOD'S GRACE

Johann Schütz's phrases stretch from the highest point to rock bottom; from the power and love of the reigning God of creation down to the salvation of sinners. This unimaginable gap was bridged because "the grace of God that bringeth salvation hath appeared to all men" (Titus 2:11). These words describe the coming of the one who dwelt among us, full of grace and truth (John 1:14). No wonder the scriptures repeatedly greet us with the beautiful words, "Grace to you."

What does the saving grace of God described in Titus actually do for us? It trains us "that, denying ungodliness and worldly lusts, we should live soberly, righteously, and godly in this present world" (2:12). Titus 2:11–12 is a miniature outline of Paul's approach to the gospel, which begins with grace—revelatory details of God's purpose—and concludes with explanations of saintly behavior (Ephesians 1:1–3; 4:1–5). This order is quite important. First comes grace, then conduct. We are not expected to live up to a certain standard so that we might then deserve grace. The God of our salvation first gives rich grace freely to all. His grace is without equal in its ability to train us to live in godly fashion, even in this evil age.

> *For the grace of God that bringeth salvation hath appeared*
> *to all men, teaching us that, denying ungodliness and worldly lusts,*
> *we should live soberly, righteously, and godly, in this present world;*
> *looking for that blessed hope, and the glorious appearing*
> *of the great God and our Saviour Jesus Christ.*
> TITUS 2:11–13

*My hope is built on nothing less
Than Jesus' blood and righteousness.
I dare not trust the sweetest frame,
But wholly trust in Jesus' name.*

EDWARD MOTE (1797–1874)
MY HOPE IS BUILT

THE SALVATION OF ISRAEL

The right of sanctuary is an ancient custom in Middle Eastern lands. A person who is in danger of death by an avenger can invoke the name of a powerful person and find salvation through that name. If the avenger refuses to listen to this appeal and takes the man's life, the person on whose name the dead man has called must swiftly retaliate, defending the honor of his name.

This idea found its way into the gospel. The Corinthian believers called on the name of the Lord (1 Corinthians 1:2), and the book of Romans mentions the invocation of the Lord's name (10:5–13). First Corinthians shows that Gentiles benefit from the Lord's sacred name. Romans 10, on the other hand, is concerned with the salvation of Israel (v. 1). The safe haven of the name Jesus will become the nation's only resort when the world's persecution finally threatens its existence and God's vengeance visits the earth at the end of this age. In the extreme dangers of those years, the Jews may wish they could ascend to heaven to bring the Messiah down, or even descend into the deep to bring him back from the dead (vv. 6–7). This being impossible, the chosen nation, which has held itself aloof from the other nations for thousands of years will learn that there is no difference, "For the same Lord over all is rich unto all that call upon him" (v. 12). Then, believing hearts and confessing mouths will summon the Deliverer (vv. 9–10). Israel will be saved together with all others who in that day seek refuge in his name (10:13; 11:26).

For there is no difference between the Jew and the Greek: for the same Lord over all is rich unto all that call upon him. For whosoever shall call upon the name of the Lord shall be saved.
ROMANS 10:12–13

When I survey the wondrous cross
On which the Prince of Glory died,
My richest gain I count but loss,
And pour contempt on all my pride.

ISAAC WATTS (1674–1748)
WHEN I SURVEY THE WONDROUS CROSS

WE ARE JUSTIFIED FREELY BY HIS GRACE

Let us view the cross of Christ in the same way as Isaac Watts. He understood that, of all who have ever lived on this earth, only Jesus Christ fully pleased God and kept the law (Romans 8:3–4). Plus, Jesus believed in the goodness of his Father even when it pleased God to make his soul an offering for our sins (Isaiah 53:10). The words of Isaac Watts's hymn should find a place in the heart of everyone who is justified by God's grace through the deliverance in Christ (Romans 3:24). That deliverance, which takes place exclusively on the ground of grace, silences all boasting except for our boast in Christ and in God our justifier (vv. 26–27).

A person who is justified before God is legally not guilty of sin. This is not the same as forgiveness, which means that, though one is guilty of sin, he or she is pardoned for it. Such forgiveness is based on a person's repentance (Acts 2:38). In contrast, justification is based on God's voluntary favor, because no one deserves it (Romans 3:23). Christ Jesus has brought about a deliverance from judgment that is free to all who believe, and even that belief is through the faith of Jesus Christ. All this marvelous truth is elsewhere condensed into one sentence: "For by grace are ye saved through faith; and that not of yourselves: it is the gift of God" (Ephesians 2:8).

Being justified freely by his grace through the redemption that
is in Christ Jesus: Whom God hath set forth to be a propitiation
through faith in his blood, to declare his righteousness for the
remission of sins that are past, through the forbearance of God;
To declare, I say, at this time his righteousness: that he might be just,
and the justifier of him which believeth in Jesus.
ROMANS 3:24–26

His dying crimson, like a robe,
Spreads o'er his body on the tree;
Then I am dead to all the globe,
And all the globe is dead to me.

Isaac Watts (1674–1748)
When I Survey the Wondrous Cross

THE WORD OF THE CROSS

God told Noah, "The end of all flesh is come before me," speaking of a physical end to human flesh (Genesis 6:13). Today, though humankind is again physically flourishing, because of Christ's death, God sees all people as being dead (2 Corinthians 5:14). This is the word, or preaching, of the cross (1 Corinthians 1:18).

Not long after Gentiles first believed in Jesus Christ, religious people began pressuring them to add the Jewish law to their faith, hoping to "make a fair shew in the flesh" (Galatians 6:12). This is typical of religion, which for the most part is an attempt to make something for God out of one's natural ability and effort—that is, the flesh. However, the apostle says, "God forbid that I should glory, save in the cross of our Lord Jesus Christ, by whom the world is crucified unto me, and I unto the world" (v. 14). Isaac Watts echoes this attitude in his hymn.

The death of Christ is entirely effective for our salvation from sin, and our fleshly efforts are useless to improve on it. That death occurred upon a shameful and degrading cross. How can we boast in our flesh and glory in the world in the light of the humiliation of the Lord of all? Nothing we are and nothing we do can benefit us before God, because we are crucified with Christ on that same cross, and our life is hidden in him (Galatians 2:20; Colossians 3:3).

The word of the cross applies not only to believers but also to the whole world. It is impossible to improve the world enough to please God (Romans 3:20). So let us join the apostle in beseeching the world to be reconciled to him (2 Corinthians 5:19–20).

No flesh [will] be justified in his sight.
Romans 3:20

Forbid it, Lord, that I should boast,
Save in the death of Christ my God!
All the vain things that charm me most,
I sacrifice them to his blood.

ISAAC WATTS (1674–1748)
WHEN I SURVEY THE WONDROUS CROSS

TO BOAST IN THE CROSS

The apostle Paul only boasted in the cross (Galatians 6:14). It put an end to the flesh, whether his or ours or the world's. This is why Isaac Watts sang, "My richest gain I count but loss and pour contempt on all my pride." Because of the cross of Christ, a new creation exists in which the flesh—our gain and pride—has no place (2 Corinthians 5:14–17; Galatians 6:15).

Believers are willing to part with sin and evil and to take Jesus Christ as their Savior. Thank the Lord for this. But, unlike Watts, or, even more, the apostle Paul, we usually do not wish to part with the goodness, personal advantages, and capabilities of our flesh, and only be found in Christ. May God cause us to realize that Christ's death put an end to all that we are in ourselves. Our desire to be valued before God or among the saints makes us antagonistic toward the cross. Pride in our national origin or family status, our superior character, and personal attainments is fleshly, and this clashes with the meaning of the cross of Christ. What is that meaning? Simply this: "[You] are dead, and your life is hid with Christ in God" (Colossians 3:3).

Here is the paradox: A person either boasts in the cross, as Isaac Watts's hymn exemplifies, or finds himself or herself unwittingly its enemy (Philippians 3:18).

For I determined not to know any thing among you,
save Jesus Christ, and him crucified.
1 CORINTHIANS 2:2

O boundless salvation! deep ocean of love,
O fullness of mercy, Christ brought from above,
The whole world redeeming, so rich and so free, ...
Now flowing for all men, come, roll over me!

WILLIAM BOOTH (1829–1912)
BOUNDLESS SALVATION

JESUS CHRIST, GOD'S PROPITIATION

Imagine a man, down on his luck, singing this hymn at one of William Booth's Salvation Army missions in a London slum. He knows his need. He knows his weakness. He asks the ocean of God's redeeming mercy in Christ to flow over him like the tide.

Jesus told a story about such a man—a tax collector, despised by his countrymen for taking their money and delivering it to the Roman oppressors at a profit. He and another man happened to be praying in the temple at the same time (Luke 18:9–14). The other man, a Pharisee, prayed a boasting, self-righteous prayer. Blind to his sins, he imagined that God was pleased with his sham religion.

The traitorous tax collector, however, showed spiritual intelligence. "Be merciful to me a sinner," he prayed. This is better translated, "Propitiate for me, a sinner." From where he stood, the man could see the smoke of the sacrifice ascending to God out of the temple, and he grasped the great truth of propitiation: Though he was a sinner, he could approach God and obtain favor because of the sacrifice that God provided. In telling this man's story, Jesus called attention to himself as the one great propitiatory offering, well pleasing to God.

Whom God hath set forth to be a propitiation through faith in his blood, to declare his righteousness for the remission of sins that are past, through the forbearance of God; to declare, I say, at this time his righteousness: that he might be just, and the justifier of him which believeth in Jesus.
ROMANS 3:25–26

April 12

Come, thou long-expected Jesus
Born to set Thy people free;
From our fears and sins release us,
Let us find our rest in thee.

<small>CHARLES WESLEY (1707–1788)</small>
<small>COME, THOU LONG-EXPECTED JESUS</small>

THE GOOD SAMARITAN'S LOVE

The half-dead man in the parable of the good Samaritan is typical of a person exhausted by his effort to qualify for salvation (Luke 10:25–37). When people arrive at this point, they will finally find rest in Christ.

This man, descending from blessed Jerusalem to cursed Jericho, is attacked and left for dead (Joshua 6:26). His is the lot of all who break the law, for "cursed be anyone who does not uphold the words of this law by observing them" (Deuteronomy 27:26 NRSV; see Galatians 3:10). He represents every human being, "for all have sinned, and come short of the glory of God" (Romans 3:23).

Religion and its ceremonies are useless to help him. This is evident in the priest who keeps as far from the wounded man as possible. He does this because the law of his religion does not allow him to be defiled with death. A Levite, who represents dedicated service to religion, also must avoid the dying man. These two show that behavior upheld by law does not cure sin but actually perpetuates it (Romans 5:20; 7:8–10). They may not have begun their religious careers with hardened hearts, but over time, legalism kills compassion.

Then the Samaritan arrives. Because he is not under religious law, he can compassionately display the love that the law demands. What's more, since the wounded Jew is his enemy, his behavior surpasses that demand (Matthew 5:44; Luke 10:27). His actions prove that where sin increases, grace abounds all the more (Romans 5:20).

For what the law could not do, in that it was weak through the flesh, God
sending his own Son in the likeness of sinful flesh, and for sin, condemned
sin in the flesh: that the righteousness of the law might be fulfilled in us,
who walk not after the flesh, but after the Spirit.
<small>ROMANS 8:3–4</small>

Israel's strength and consolation,
Hope of all the earth thou are;
Dear desire of every nation,
Joy of every longing heart.

CHARLES WESLEY (1707–1788)
COME, THOU LONG-EXPECTED JESUS

THE PROPHECY OF SIMEON

"There was a man in Jerusalem whose name was Simeon; this man was righteous and devout, looking forward to the consolation of Israel" (Luke 2:25 NRSV).

The name Simeon means "hearing" in Hebrew. He signifies those in ancient Israel who could hear the underlying message in the law of the Lord and who looked for the fulfillment of the prophetic promises. How did he know to look for the newborn Messiah? Perhaps he was so familiar with scripture that he knew the years spoken of by Daniel had elapsed (Daniel 9:25–26). An aged saint like Simeon could hope for no greater gain than to set his eyes on the Lord's servant before he died. In the dark days in which we live, there are saints like Simeon and Anna who see the signs of Christ's coming and pray for the privilege of surviving until that glorious day.

Simeon's faith was similar to Abraham's. He saw Israel not merely as the blessed nation but as a blessing to the other nations of the world (Genesis 18:18; Luke 2:32). He was not so narrow as Israel's leaders, and he was aware of their apostasy (Luke 2:34–35). So, while speaking to Mary, Simeon hinted at the sufferings of Christ and his rejection by Israel. The old man held the wonderful infant in his arms, and as he spoke, the shadow of the accursed tree loomed in the distance (Galatians 3:13–14).

And there was one Anna, a prophetess. . . . And she was a widow of about fourscore and four years, which departed not from the temple, but served God with fasting and prayers night and day. And she coming in that instant gave thanks likewise unto the Lord, and spake of him to all them that looked for redemption in Jerusalem.
LUKE 2:36–38

April 14

How silently, how silently, the wondrous gift is given;
So God imparts to human hearts the blessings of his heav'n,
No ear may hear his coming, but in this world of sin,
Where meek souls will receive him still, the dear Christ enters in.

PHILLIPS BROOKS (1835–1893)
O LITTLE TOWN OF BETHLEHEM

THE SILENT WORK OF THE SPIRIT

From birth and life, to death and resurrection, Jesus Christ did all his work as a misunderstood, even hated, man in a remote province of the Roman Empire. He hardly caused a ripple in the official histories. "How silently, how silently, the wondrous gift is given."

Critics of the faith think that the maneuvering of man caused its spread until it became the great tree we call Christianity (Luke 13:19). The truth is far from this. The faith of Jesus Christ has grown in the same silent way it began. The outward edifice of religion has nothing to do with it. His death on the cursed cross that was planted by rude soldiers on Golgotha has an effect that is far too potent to require the help of human hands (Acts 17:24–25). Whatever is positive and lasting is the Spirit's work alone, and with few exceptions the Spirit works silently.

Southern Galatia, in what is now south-central Turkey, was an out-of-the-way place like Galilee. Yet that land was the seedbed from which grew the work of the apostle to the nations. His ministry went from glory to glory (2 Corinthians 3:18) until it became wholly a ministry of the Spirit that silently breathes life into every believer's faith to this day.

When they had gone throughout Phrygia and the region of Galatia, and were forbidden of the Holy Ghost to preach the word in Asia, after they were come to Mysia, they assayed to go into Bithynia: but the Spirit suffered them not. And they passing by Mysia came down to Troas.
ACTS 16:6–8

My heart inquired with anxious care, Will God forever spurn?
Shall we no more his favor see? Will mercy ne'er return?
Forever shall his promise fail? Has God forgotten grace?
Has he withdrawn his tender love, in anger hid his face?

AUTHOR UNKNOWN
I THOUGHT UPON THE DAYS OF OLD
PARAPHRASE OF PSALM 77

GOD IS AT PEACE WITH SINNERS, PART 1

Thoughts like those expressed in this hymn still trouble people, even though they are entirely out of date. Today all humankind has crossed the great divide of Calvary. There is no need for people to plead with God or fret that he has turned away from them. Here's why: "God was in Christ, reconciling the world unto himself, not imputing their trespasses unto them. . . . Now then we are ambassadors for Christ, as though God did beseech you by us: we pray you in Christ's stead, be ye reconciled to God" (2 Corinthians 5:19–20). Sinners needn't plead with God. He is at peace with the world because of Christ's death. His ambassadors are the ones pleading, "Be reconciled with God!"

All one need do is believe God. Abraham proves this: "To him that worketh not, but believeth on him that justifieth the ungodly, his faith is counted for righteousness" (Romans 4:5). Such faith doesn't come because of something we do. It is all because of what the Lord Jesus has done. His grace overwhelms our unbelief with faith and love (1 Timothy 1:14).

"The doctrine of reconciliation" is the dry term theologians use to describe this glorious truth of scripture. Despite theology, consider the deep feeling and undreamt of meaning in the following sentence that describes God's conciliatory heart: "God commendeth his love toward us, in that, while we were yet sinners, Christ died for us" (Romans 5:8).

For if while we were enemies, we were reconciled to God through the death of his Son, much more surely, having been reconciled, will we be saved by his life. But more than that, we even boast in God through our Lord Jesus Christ, through whom we have now received reconciliation.
ROMANS 5:10–11 NRSV

I asked in fear and bitterness: Will God forsake me in distress?
Shall I his promise faithless find? Has God forgotten to be kind?
Has he in anger hopelessly removed his love and grace from me?

AUTHOR UNKNOWN
TO GOD WILL I DIRECT MY PRAYER
PARAPHRASE OF PSALM 77

GOD IS AT PEACE WITH SINNERS, PART 2

A nation's ambassador speaks with the authority of that nation so long as he or she delivers officially approved messages. Ambassadors who stray from their nation's doctrines or policies are liable to lose their position. We are God's ambassadors to this world so long as we deliver his message of conciliation. This is seen in 2 Corinthians 5:18–21.

What is the meaning of the word *conciliation*? If two people are in conflict and one of them decides to be at peace with the other, that person is one who has a conciliatory attitude toward the other person. However, the two can only be reconciled when the second person also decides to be at peace. We were once God's enemies, but Christ made peace on God's side through the blood of his cross (Romans 5:10; Colossians 1:20). The word "reconciled" is used in 2 Corinthians 5:18–20 because the peace described there is one-sided. However, when people believe in Christ, they find God's peace and are not only conciliated but also forever reconciled to God.

Here is the message that God expects his ambassadors to deliver to this world: "God gave his beloved Son to be a sin offering for your sake. Therefore, he is not counting your offenses against you. In fact, he gives you his own righteousness in Christ and is at peace with you. Why has God done this? It is because, in his love, he knows that you cannot do it yourself. God is actually pleading with you to be conciliated, to be at peace with him. He has done everything necessary to make this possible. All you need do is respond to his plea. Be reconciled to God."

Therefore being justified by faith, we have
peace with God through our Lord Jesus Christ.
ROMANS 5:1

As with gladness, men of old
Did the guiding star behold
As with joy they hailed its light
Leading onward, beaming bright
So, most glorious Lord, may we
Evermore be led to thee.

WILLIAM C. DIX (1837–1898)
AS WITH GLADNESS, MEN OF OLD

THE LANGUAGE OF GOD'S SEEKERS

Three wise men appear yearly in manger scenes and Christmas pageants. However, scripture doesn't say there were only three seekers from the East, but that they brought three types of gifts (Matthew 2:11). The magi represent those people who observe nature—people like outdoorsmen, scientists, and gardeners. Nature leads its pupils to the worship of its Creator.

Many attempts have been made to explain the star of Bethlehem as a purely natural occurrence. Could it be that the wise men followed a meteor, a comet, or the conjunction of a number of planets? Astronomers can find no such celestial light during the time of the birth of Christ. The magi probably saw the star at the time of Christ's birth. After some time for preparation, they made their slow journey to Bethlehem, arriving when the child was a toddler. No simple star could guide the magi for such a long period and then take its place directly above Bethlehem.

This was an extraordinary heavenly light, the likes of which these stargazers from the East had never seen. It heralded the birth of a most extraordinary baby. The star teaches us that God speaks to seekers in the language they understand. For the wise men, this was the language of astronomy. Our Father is fluent in the secret language of every person who has ever been born.

For the invisible things of him from the creation of the world are clearly seen, being understood by the things that are made, even his eternal power and Godhead; so that they are without excuse.
ROMANS 1:20

Yet with the woes of sin and strife the world has suffered long;
Beneath the angel strain have rolled two thousand years of wrong;
And man, at war with man, hears not the love-song which they bring;
O hush the noise, ye men of strife and hear the angels sing.

EDMUND H. SEARS (1810–1876)
IT CAME UPON THE MIDNIGHT CLEAR

THE CONCILIATED GOD

Instead of expecting the unbelieving world to hear the angels' song of peace on earth, perhaps we believers could more fully understand that God's peace has actually come in us. Then, wearing the preparation of the gospel of peace on our feet, we can bring that peace into the world (Ephesians 6:15).

To this end, let's review a vital fact: "In Christ God was reconciling the world to himself, not counting their trespasses against them, and entrusting the message of reconciliation to us" (2 Corinthians 5:19 NRSV). This verse describes the work of the God of peace (Romans 15:33). God is not presently at war with humankind; rather, he is conciliated with the world. His attitude is so conciliatory that he is not taking into account the world's offenses. This is why he is called the God of peace and gave Paul the ministry of reconciliation (2 Corinthians 5:18). Like the apostle, as God's ambassadors, let's beseech the world to be reconciled to God and enjoy his peace (v. 20).

God is beseeching people to be at peace with him. Many gospel preachers reverse this, telling people to beg God for his peace. Instead of this, let us tell the citizens of this tumultuous world that God made Christ to be sin for them so they can be made God's righteousness in him and live in peace (v. 21).

And all things are of God, who hath reconciled us to himself by Jesus Christ,
and hath given to us the ministry of reconciliation; to wit, that God was
in Christ, reconciling the world unto himself, not imputing their trespasses
unto them; and hath committed unto us the word of reconciliation.
2 CORINTHIANS 5:18–19

Now to the Lord sing praises all you within this place,
And with true love and brotherhood each other now embrace;
This holy tide of Christmas all others doth deface. . . .
O tidings of comfort and joy.

EIGHTEENTH-CENTURY CAROL, LONDON, ENGLAND
GOD REST YE MERRY, GENTLEMEN

WHY THE ANGELS CELEBRATED

This song's peculiar phrase "This holy tide of Christmas all others doth deface" simply means, "The Christmas season is the greatest of all." Many people say something like this every year. However, they probably mean that they love the shopping, lights, parties, gifts, food, and family gatherings. But this saying has a much deeper meaning.

What is greater than the birth of Jesus? Nothing can have more meaning than this. Even angels celebrated the birth of the Savior of the world (Luke 2:13). The only other time such a celestial celebration occurred was when God laid the earth's foundation (Job 38:4–7). Apparently, nothing had happened since then that was of such interest to the celestial multitudes until Jesus was born. This hints at the purpose for the creation of the earth and the birth of Jesus.

God created humankind in his image and likeness so that the Son, who is his express image, could come to this earth in the likeness of a man (Philippians 2:7; Hebrews 1:3). Indeed, the Son had to be in the form of man so he could die (Hebrews 10:4–5). His death enabled God to reconcile all things to himself—things in earth, and things in heaven, including the angelic hosts who celebrated his birth that long-ago night in Bethlehem (Colossians 1:20).

That at the name of Jesus every knee should bow, of things in heaven, and things in earth, and things under the earth; and that every tongue should confess that Jesus Christ is Lord, to the glory of God the Father.
PHILIPPIANS 2:10–11

The people who in darkness walked
Have seen a glorious light;
On them broke forth the heavenly dawn
Who dwelt in death and night.

JOHN MORRISON (1746–1798)
THE PEOPLE WHO IN DARKNESS WALKED

THE LIGHT OF THE GENTILES

This hymn refers to Matthew 4:16, a quotation of Isaiah 9:2, which describes the people of Israel at the time Jesus lived among them, especially those in the regions near the Sea of Galilee. At the Messiah's arrival, divine light dawned for God's beloved nation. If the Jews had accepted him, they would have become a light for the Gentiles and carried God's salvation to the end of the earth (Isaiah 49:6).

However, the Gospels tell of Israel's rejection of Jesus Christ. The book of Acts follows with the story of the nation's rejection of his apostles and the gospel of the kingdom. How then could the Gentiles find salvation since Israel abdicated its responsibility to bring its light to them? Enter the apostle Paul. God gave him the grace to be "the minister of Jesus Christ to the Gentiles, ministering the gospel of God" (Romans 15:16). Peter and the others confirmed this assignment when Paul visited them in Jerusalem (Galatians 2:7). If Paul hadn't been separated from the rest to bring the truth of the gospel to the non-Jewish world, we wouldn't know the Lord as we do today (Acts 13:2).

When Paul encountered Israel's negative response to the gospel, he personally claimed the responsibility that should have been assumed by the entire nation. He declared the prophet Isaiah's words, "I have set thee to be a light of the Gentiles, that thou shouldest be for salvation unto the ends of the earth," and the Gentiles who heard him rejoiced (vv. 47–48). We can thank God that Paul was not disobedient to that heavenly vision (26:19).

> *Be it known therefore unto you, that the salvation of*
> *God is sent unto the Gentiles, and that they will hear it.*
> ACTS 28:28

Thou knowest, Lord, thou know'st my life's deep story,
And all the mingled good and ill I do;
Thou seest my shame, my few stray gleams of glory,
Where I am false and where my soul rings true.

HENRY W. HAWKES (1843–1917)
THOU KNOWEST, LORD

THE FUNCTION OF EVIL IN GOD'S PURPOSE

The parable of the prodigal son gives a near perfect illustration of how God uses evil as an instrument of good (Luke 15:11–32). The young man wandered in evil ways and experienced sorrow and suffering as a result. Through this, he gained insight into life and its fortunes. We don't take pleasure in his consorting with harlots, the famine that came upon him, his hunger, the husks he had to eat, the swine with which he lived. These things are evil in themselves. But can we deny that, under the guiding and controlling hand of God, they finally resulted in good?

The father knew how his son's escapade would turn out and was watching for the boy's return. Then he embraced and kissed him, no questions asked. In spite of this, the prodigal rattled off his speech: "Father, I have sinned against heaven, and in thy sight." The father cut him short with a flood of gifts, as if saying, "Forget about sin! It was designed to reveal the depth of my love and has done its work. It is past and forgotten. Now is the time to feast. Let us rejoice and be happy in each other's love."

Meanwhile, the prodigal's brother exploded with pent-up anger that his sibling had received such honors. For years, he had cheated himself of joy and happiness by harboring the false notion that his father's love could be purchased with good behavior (v. 29). The father's response: "All that is mine is yours and always has been" (v. 31, paraphrase). The younger son came to know the father by departing from him, and this experience of evil became the means of showing the father's love to the elder son.

I form the light, and create darkness: I make peace, and create evil.
ISAIAH 45:7

Were you there when they crucified my Lord?
Were you there when they crucified my Lord?
Oh! Sometimes it causes me to tremble, tremble, tremble.
Were you there when they crucified my Lord?

AFRICAN-AMERICAN SPIRITUAL
WERE YOU THERE?

WERE YOU THERE WHEN THEY CRUCIFIED MY LORD? PART 1

Whether they know it or not, everyone has the same answer to the question posed in this hymn. The answer is, "Yes, I was there." All humanity was at the Crucifixion, not as an observer, but as a participant. This is seen in this description of Christ's love: "For the love of Christ constraineth us; because we thus judge, that if one died for all, then were all dead" (2 Corinthians 5:14). In other words, at the cross everyone died. There, Christ was our sin offering, the reality of the sacrifice described in Leviticus (v. 21; Leviticus 4:29, 33).

The following is a common, though erroneous, idea about Christ's death: We deserve to die for our sins, but Jesus Christ died instead of us. That, however, is not how it worked. If that idea were accurate, we would still be alive and 2 Corinthians 5:14 would be untrue.

In Leviticus, the person who brings the sin offering identifies with it by laying his hands on the animal's head. This identification is most significant. It means that the sacrificial animal doesn't die *instead* of the one who offers it; rather, the one who offers dies *in* the animal he sacrifices. In God's eyes, when the sacrifice dies, the one who offers it is dead, and so his sins are gone. This explains our death in Christ and why the scripture says, "He that is dead is freed from sin" (Romans 6:7). This, and our resurrection in Christ, is the basis of all true spirituality.

> *Count yourselves dead to sin but alive to God in Christ Jesus.*
> ROMANS 6:11 NIV

Were you there when they nailed him to the tree?
Were you there when they nailed him to the tree?
Oh! Sometimes it causes me to tremble, tremble, tremble.
Were you there when they nailed him to the tree?

AFRICAN-AMERICAN SPIRITUAL
WERE YOU THERE?

WERE YOU THERE WHEN THEY CRUCIFIED MY LORD? PART 2

Romans 6 says that we died with Christ. Indeed, we were there when they nailed him to the tree. This leads us to the core meaning of the cross and the secret of spirituality: "We died to sin; how can we live in it any longer? Or don't you know that all of us who were baptized into Christ Jesus were baptized into his death?" (vv. 2–3 NIV). This understanding revolutionizes a believer's life—*we died*—with Christ. So the following words describe the way we live to God: "If we be dead with Christ, we believe that we shall also live with him. . . . For in that he died, he died unto sin once: but in that he liveth, he liveth unto God. Likewise reckon ye also yourselves to be dead indeed unto sin, but alive unto God through Jesus Christ our Lord" (vv. 8, 10–11).

Since we did not physically die, but Christ was crucified for us, we can reckon that his death is ours, fully terminating our connection with sin. His resurrection is ours also, and so in him we live in the presence of God. This realization of our death to sin and life in Christ gives us power to cope with sin, because we know that, through God's abundant grace, sin cannot bring us into condemnation (8:1).

I am crucified with Christ: nevertheless I live; yet not I, but Christ liveth in me: and the life which I now live in the flesh I live by the faith of the Son of God, who loved me, and gave himself for me.
GALATIANS 2:20

Unresting, unhasting, and silent as light,
Nor wanting, nor wasting, thou rulest in might;
Thy justice, like mountains, high soaring above
Thy clouds, which are fountains of goodness and love.

WALTER C. SMITH (1824–1908)
IMMORTAL, INVISIBLE, GOD ONLY WISE

GOD'S MOUNTAINOUS JUSTICE

Humankind's attitude is that God is unjust. This is why scripture asks, "Is there unrighteousness with God?" (Romans 9:14). The troublesome case of Jacob and Esau forces us to consider our view of God's justice (vv. 10–13). Humanly speaking, Jacob should have served his older brother, because the birthright always went to the eldest. Instead, the elder served the younger (Genesis 25:23). Our sense of fair play says this is wrong. "Rebecca deceived Isaac," we say, "and Esau was cheated" (see 27:18–29).

But we must ask, "Why did God love Jacob and hate Esau?" (see Malachi 1:2–3). Did Esau say or do something wrong? Was Jacob so excellent that he deserved the Lord's blessings? We are quick to blame Jacob, and even Rebecca, for this apparent injustice. Did Jacob's cunning gain him the blessing? Did Rebecca's scheming rob Esau? The right question to ask is: Who ordered all this to take place?

God formed his plan and chose the actors in it, including Jacob, Rebecca, you, and me. These choices do not materialize out of man's will but are entirely of God (Romans 9:16). Let's be glad for this and recognize God as God (1:21). Only he can make judgments that ensure the success of his purpose. There is no injustice in this. Our wisdom is so far short of God's that we would degrade the Creator and promote the creature (vv. 22–23). We fancy that our wills compete with the will of God the Father, out of whom all is (11:36).

True wisdom acknowledges the stupidity of this, admitting God's magnificence and our insignificance. God's love for Jacob and hatred of Esau are not reactions to their behavior but are determined by his steadfast purpose.

For as the heavens are higher than the earth, so are my ways higher than
your ways, and my thoughts than your thoughts.
ISAIAH 55:9

To all, life thou givest, to both great and small;
In all life thou livest, the true life of all;
We blossom and flourish as leaves on the tree,
And wither and perish but naught changeth thee.

WALTER C. SMITH (1824–1908)
IMMORTAL, INVISIBLE, GOD ONLY WISE

THE WORDS OF LIFE

One day the Lord Jesus encountered a crowd of people who were clamoring for physical food. He told them, "The flesh profiteth nothing: the words that I speak unto you, they are spirit, and they are life" (John 6:63). The day before this happened, he had fed them abundantly through a miracle that overflowed with twelve baskets full of leftovers (vv. 12–13). That is why they came to him again, begging, "Lord, evermore give us this bread" (v. 34). That physical bread would keep their flesh alive, but it would not give them life. By it they could live for a while and then die. Their true need was to believe the words spoken by the Son because faith would bring them life in the coming kingdom.

Those people heard the words of the living Word of God. How life-giving these must have been! But most of them did not believe him. That day even many of the Lord's disciples walked out on him (v. 66). In spite of this, a few knew that they had nowhere else to go. They understood that he had the words of life (v. 68).

We must care for our physical body. At the same time, we are wise to remember that our flesh and blood cannot inherit the kingdom of God (1 Corinthians 15:50). To be vitalized spiritually, we have nowhere to go but to the sacred scriptures, the words of life that reveal God in his Son, Jesus Christ.

And that from a child thou hast known the holy scriptures, which are able to make thee wise unto salvation through faith which is in Christ Jesus.
2 TIMOTHY 3:15

We sing the glorious conquest, before Damascus' gate,
When Saul, the Church's spoiler, came breathing threats and hate;
Christ's light shone down from heaven and broke across the path.
His presence pierced and blinded the zealot in his wrath.

JOHN ELLERTON (1826–1893)
WE SING THE GLORIOUS CONQUEST

THE PATTERN OF GRACE

"What is grace?" The answer to this question is given in the person of Saul, the Church's leading persecutor, and the chief sinner (1 Timothy 1:13, 15). "I am the least of the apostles," he confessed, "because I persecuted the church of God" (1 Corinthians 15:9). Yet this man, who was "less than the least of all saints" was given this grace to "preach among the nations the unsearchable riches of Christ" (Ephesians 3:8). This transformation happened because the grace of the Lord overwhelmed him with faith and love in Christ Jesus (1 Timothy 1:12–16).

Saul of Tarsus first appears in scripture while approving Stephen's execution (Acts 7:59–8:1). He devastated the Church and breathed out threats and murder against the believers. Surely, none of these saints thought that one day Saul would be given a crown of righteousness (2 Timothy 4:8). While they were suffering at his hand, did they imagine that Christ was displaying his patience in order that Saul could become the pattern of grace for all who would thereafter believe (1 Timothy 1:16)? It seems unlikely, yet that is what happened.

Before he encountered Christ, Saul did not repent, reform, or seek God's favor. He imagined that he was serving God as he destroyed the Church. Yet, suddenly, overwhelmed by grace, Saul was called and changed into the brilliant advocate of that transcendent grace—Paul, the apostle to the nations. Later Paul described that moment: "Where sin abounded, grace did much more abound" (Romans 5:20).

> *By the grace of God I am what I am: and his*
> *grace which was bestowed upon me was not in vain.*
> 1 CORINTHIANS 15:10

Come, let us join our cheerful songs with angels round the throne.
Ten thousand thousand are their tongues, but all their joys are one.
"Worthy the Lamb that died," they cry, "to be exalted thus!"
"Worthy the Lamb," our lips reply, "for he was slain for us!"

ISAAC WATTS (1674–1748)
COME, LET US JOIN OUR CHEERFUL SONGS

THE VICTORIOUS LAMB

Long before the twenty-four celestial elders declare that the Lamb is worthy, Jesus Christ was identified as God's Lamb. This title recalls the lamb that was slain for the Passover (Exodus 12:21; John 1:29). Israel's priests freely used this animal in their rituals. It was used as a sin offering, a guilt offering, and for the cleansing of a leper (Leviticus 4:32; 5:6; 14:12). But never before Jesus Christ appeared did a lamb take away the sin of the world (John 1:29).

The ancient priests did not use the lamb only for sin offerings, however. It was used for worship and communion, as well. Every morning and every evening the encamped Israelites saw the smoke of a sacrificed lamb rise from the tabernacle (Exodus 29:38–42). A lamb was also used as a peace offering, and, together with the wave offering, is a symbol of the resurrection (Leviticus 23:11). Thus, the scripture uses seven sacrifices to depict the sacrificial work of God's Son.

A young lamb is nearly helpless. This image of Christ is the exact opposite of his disposition as the lion of the tribe of Judah (Revelation 5:5). All his achievements are the result of his submitting in weakness to the suffering, humiliation, and death of the cross. This includes his worthiness as the lion to open the sealed scroll (vv. 2–8). Eventually, the little, sacrificial Lamb of God will lead in victory over a monstrous dragon and all the assembled powers of darkness.

And they sung a new song, saying, Thou art worthy to take the book, and to open the seals thereof: for thou wast slain, and hast redeemed us to God by thy blood out of every kindred, and tongue, and people, and nation.
REVELATION 5:9

I sing the mighty power of God, that made the mountains rise,
That spread the flowing seas abroad, and built the lofty skies.
I sing the wisdom that ordained the sun to rule the day;
The moon shines full at God's command, and all the stars obey.

ISAAC WATTS (1674–1748)
I SING THE MIGHTY POWER OF GOD

GOD'S INSCRUTABLE WAYS

Lately we have witnessed a great debate about how the creation came into being. Did it evolve slowly out of primitive elements, or did God create it in seven days? This controversy, however, is simply a distraction from this vital truth: "From him and through him and to him are all things" (Romans 11:36 NRSV).

Can there be a more comprehensive statement about creation than this? God is the source of all, the channel of all, and the object of all. The universe sprang out of him, not out of nothing; it has its course in him, and he is its conclusion. Scriptural truth puts to rest all disputes about the origin of the universe and explains universal history. However, no one can comprehend this unless they have been given the gift of faith.

Creation is *out of* God. Creation is *to* him. God is responsible for all the activities of creation, including those of humankind. This means that creation is through him. What is the goal of all things? God is carefully guiding his creatures and creation until he becomes all in all (1 Corinthians 15:28).

God's judgments and ways are far too deep for human perception (Romans 11:33). We can taste the sweetness of a fresh peach, but we don't know how the tree made that peach. Similarly, we can enjoy the knowledge of God's goal for creation, but the process by which he attains it is far too complex for us to comprehend.

O the depth of the riches both of the wisdom and knowledge of God! how
unsearchable are his judgments, and his ways past finding out! For who
hath known the mind of the Lord? or who hath been his counsellor?
ROMANS 11:33–34

Immortal, invisible, God only wise,
In light inaccessible hid from our eyes,
Most blessed, most glorious, the Ancient of Days,
Almighty, victorious, thy great name we praise.

WALTER C. SMITH (1824–1908)
IMMORTAL, INVISIBLE, GOD ONLY WISE

THE IMAGE OF THE INVISIBLE GOD

John's Gospel tells us, "No man hath seen God at any time, the only begotten Son, which is in the bosom of the Father, he hath declared him" (John 1:18). But readers of the Hebrew scriptures will ask, "Didn't Israel's prophets actually see God from time to time?" For example, Isaiah said, "I saw. . .the Lord sitting upon a throne, high and lifted up" (Isaiah 6:1). This and similar experiences were not actual sightings of the Almighty but glimpses of messengers, or angels, through whom God communicated with Israel (Hebrews 2:2). Theologians call Isaiah's experience, and others like it, a *theophany*.

Only the Son is "the brightness of [God's] glory, and the express image of his person" (1:3). Therefore, when Philip asked Jesus, "Show us the Father" (John 14:8), the Lord replied, "He that hath seen me hath seen the Father" (v. 9). The disciples saw the Father manifested in Jesus Christ, who loved and led them, taught and fed them like a father does his children. The Son is uniquely the Word, the expression of God (1:1). The Father is evident in all his words and works (1:14; 14:10), and is seen nowhere else in the universe but in him.

In whom we have redemption through his blood, even the forgiveness of sins: who is the image of the invisible God, the firstborn of every creature: for by him were all things created, that are in heaven, and that are in earth, visible and invisible, whether they be thrones, or dominions, or principalities, or powers: all things were created by him, and for him.
COLOSSIANS 1:14–16

What wondrous love is this, O my soul, O my soul!
What wondrous love is this, O my soul!
What wondrous love is this that caused the Lord of bliss
To lay aside his crown for my soul.

AMERICAN FOLK HYMN (C. 1835)
WHAT WONDROUS LOVE IS THIS

GOD'S GREAT LOVE

Those who examine the original Greek language of the New Testament find that John 3:16 is most accurately translated like this: "For thus God loves the world, so that he gives his only begotten Son." This shows the quality of God's love—"*thus* God loves"—not its quantity. Nor is this love a thing of the past. God *loves* the world. His gift of the Son expresses timeless love.

Jesus spoke these words to Nicodemus (v. 1), who only knew God as Israel's demanding lawgiver. The only way he could expect a gift from God was through his obedience to God's law. Jesus told him that God is not confined to Israel but is a bountiful benefactor who gives life to all who believe (v. 16).

God's great love causes him to plead that his enemies be reconciled to him (2 Corinthians 5:18–20). He is at peace with us and wants us to be at peace with him. The gospel is not primarily concerned with the sinner. Rather, it tells of God's love for humankind and of the sufferings and triumphs of Christ that display that love (Romans 5:8). Therefore, God has not given us a message of judgment, but the word of reconciliation (2 Corinthians 5:18). One day the nations of the earth will see God's wrath (1 Thessalonians 1:10; Revelation 6:16–17). For the present, God insists on being at peace with the people of this world no matter how they treated his Son (2 Corinthians 5:19).

> *But God, who is rich in mercy, for his great love wherewith*
> *he loved us, even when we were dead in sins, hath quickened*
> *us together with Christ, (by grace ye are saved).*
> EPHESIANS 2:4–5

Thou didst thyself in God delight
Thy heart's desires are thine by right;
To see thy travail gratified—
So shall thy soul be satisfied.

ANONYMOUS,
OH WONDROUS GOD OF WONDROUS GRACE

THE FRUIT OF THE TOIL OF GOD'S SOUL

God's words in Genesis 1 declare the coming of light, order, and life (vv. 2–31). This is still being told in all the earth: "The heavens are telling the glory of God; and the firmament proclaims his handiwork" (Psalm 19:1 NRSV). God's words also restored and gladdened the hearts of the people of Israel (vv. 7–14). We modern believers have heard words of truth and love that echo the words of Genesis 1:3: "God, who commanded the light to shine out of darkness, hath shined in our hearts, to give the light of the knowledge of the glory of God in the face of Jesus Christ" (2 Corinthians 4:6).

The darkness of human unbelief, stubbornness, and enmity are like the primeval chaos. They cannot withstand the power of life-giving light. God's words deal with disorder and darkness and always end with good (Genesis 1:31). In his wisdom, God has allowed the rulers of the darkness of this world to subject his creation to the vanity of suffering, corruption, and travail (Romans 8:20; Ephesians 6:12). But he has done this knowing that it will end in good: "The creature itself also shall be delivered from the bondage of corruption into the glorious liberty of the children of God" (Romans 8:21).

What will God see when his creation's groaning in chaos and darkness ends? To his glory, every knee will bow and every tongue will declare that Jesus Christ is Lord, and then he will be all in all (1 Corinthians 15:28; Philippians 2:10–11). God's satisfaction in this consummation is the fruit of the toil of his soul that is centered in the travail of his Son.

He shall see of the travail of his soul, and shall be satisfied: by his knowledge shall my righteous servant justify many; for he shall bear their iniquities.
ISAIAH 53:11

Glory be to Jesus, who, in bitter pains,
Poured for me the lifeblood from his sacred veins!
Grace and life eternal in that blood I find;
Blest be his compassion, infinitely kind.

ITALIAN HYMN (EIGHTEENTH CENTURY)
GLORY BE TO JESUS
TRANSLATED BY EDWARD CASWALL (1814–1878)

THE PRIESTS OF ISRAEL AND THE LAMB OF GOD

When the high priest of Israel was judging Jesus, he asked him, "Are you answering nothing?" (see Matthew 26:62). He didn't understand that Jesus' silence was a sign that he was like the animal that priests routinely led to the altar of sacrifice: "He was oppressed, and he was afflicted, yet he opened not his mouth: he is brought as a lamb to the slaughter" (Isaiah 53:7).

The interrogating priest then invoked the name of God: "I put you under oath before the living God, tell us if you are the Messiah, the Son of God" (Matthew 26:63 NRSV). This triggered Jesus' testimony to the truth: "You have said so," he answered (v. 64 NRSV).

All this served God's purpose, since the only reason Israel's priesthood existed was to slaughter the sacrifice, although the innumerable lambs they had offered for centuries all amounted to vain repetition. These only covered sin; they could not take it away (Hebrews 9:13–14). The priests who had offered those countless lambs were about to slay the Lamb of God whose lifeblood would change sin into righteousness and enmity into reconciliation. Their hatred and malice was the blade that shed the blood of the true and final sacrifice, and so accomplished the will of God (Acts 2:23).

> *And when he was accused of the chief priests and elders,*
> *he answered nothing. Then said Pilate unto him, Hearest thou*
> *not how many things they witness against thee? And he answered*
> *him to never a word; insomuch that the governor marvelled greatly.*
> MATTHEW 27:12–14

> *The great Creator of the worlds,*
> *The sovereign God of heaven,*
> *His holy and immortal truth*
> *To all on earth hath given.*

EPISTLE TO DIOGNETUS (ABOUT 150)
THE GREAT CREATOR OF THE WORLDS
TRANSLATED BY F. BLAND TUCKER (1895–1984)

THE WORD OF TRUTH

Untold millions have found God's steadfast truth in the writings of Paul, who was stubbornly determined that the believers would possess the truth of the gospel (Galatians 2:5) and that everyone should be presented mature before God (Colossians 1:28).

When Paul wrote his first letter to Timothy, the Church was the pillar and base of the truth (1 Timothy 3:15; AD 57). But by the time he wrote 2 Timothy, the pillar and base were no more. All the churches in Asia had abandoned the apostle and his gospel (2 Timothy 1:15; about AD 65). Still, Paul wrote with confidence, "The foundation of God standeth sure." This is surely true today (2:19).

Those who seek God should value the second letter to Timothy the apostle's last word. Here we find the answer to this question: How shall we serve the Lord in the midst of the unbelief and apostasy of this present day?

Second Timothy begins with the exhortation to have the pattern of sound words (1:13)—those of the apostle himself. It closes with the charge to proclaim the Word (4:2). Its center is anchored in the instruction to correctly divide the Word of truth, assigning each truth its proper place. If this is not done, they can become dangerous error (2:15–18). A mature knowledge of scripture is the one great need in these degenerate days (3:16–17).

For this is good and acceptable in the sight of God our Saviour; who will have all men to be saved, and to come unto the knowledge of the truth. For there is one God, and one mediator between God and men, the man Christ Jesus; who gave himself a ransom for all, to be testified in due time.
1 TIMOTHY 2:3–6

He sent no angel of his host
To bear his mighty word,
But him through whom the worlds were made,
The everlasting Lord.

EPISTLE TO DIOGNETUS (ABOUT 150)
THE GREAT CREATOR OF THE WORLDS
TRANSLATED BY F. BLAND TUCKER (1895–1984)

THE COMING AND GOING OF THE WORD OF GOD

The opening sentence of the Gospel of John tells of the Son of God as the Word. This is because John was writing to Hebrew believers who had always possessed the oracles of God (Romans 3:2). He informs them that this divine expression had, from the beginning, been the Son of God. He then summarizes the revelation given to Israel, which concludes in John the Baptist's testimony that the true light had come (John 1:2–9). When the Word became flesh, the divine expression converged in Jesus Christ, and grace and truth came into the world (v. 14).

John's Gospel records seven miraculous signs that were performed by Jesus before his death. Each of these signs shows that he is the incarnate Word of God: Notice that when he speaks, the miracle is done. Water becomes wine (2:7–9), a dead boy lives (4:50), and a sick man is healed (5:8). At his word, five thousand people are fed (6:10–11), his disciples are rescued at sea (6:16–21), a blind man is given sight (9:7), and Lazarus is raised from the dead (11:43–44).

John's account describes the two phases of Jesus Christ's earthly life: He came out from God and was going away to God (13:3). In the beginning, he was with God. Next, he came in the flesh as the divine expression—the Word—to minister to Israel. But his people rejected him (1:11; 12:37–38). Then Jesus knew that the hour had come for him to leave the world and return to the Father (13:1). The remainder of the book of John tells of his journey back to God.

And the Word was made flesh, and dwelt among us.
JOHN 1:14

Jesus shall reign where'er the sun
Doth his successive journeys run;
His kingdom stretch from shore to shore,
Till moons shall wax and wane no more.

ISAAC WATTS (1674–1748)
JESUS SHALL REIGN

THE COMING KINGDOM

The book of Daniel provides the first clear view of the coming kingdom (2:45). It tells of King Nebuchadnezzar's dream of an image in the form of a man made of a variety of metals—a gold head, silver breast and arms, brass belly and thighs, iron legs, and feet of both iron and clay. In simple terms, these represent the historical succession of the world's kingdoms. In his dream, Nebuchadnezzar saw a stone that fell and collided with the image's feet. This pulverized the various metals like chaff, and they were blown away with the wind (vv. 31–35). This stone then turned into a mountain—the promised kingdom—that filled the entire earth.

Nebuchadnezzar's dream is remarkable in its description of the swift fall of the world's kingdoms. It doesn't show the pleasant influences of righteousness causing a gradual improvement in this world until it is perfected. Instead, we can anticipate the quick, violent demise of the world's kingdoms and the immediate appearance of the thousand-year kingdom with all its righteous authority (v. 44).

The mountain is a geological sign that includes all the metals seen in the image and many more minerals in correct proportions and harmony. It represents the messianic kingdom. With divine wisdom, Christ's earthly rule will foster and protect every element necessary to create a perfectly complete social and political structure that will stand until the coming of the new heaven and the new earth (Revelation 20:6; 21:1).

And the seventh angel sounded; and there were great voices in heaven, saying, The kingdoms of this world are become the kingdoms of our Lord, and of his Christ; and he shall reign for ever and ever. And the four and twenty elders, which sat before God on their seats, fell upon their faces, and worshipped God.
REVELATION 11:15–16

Soldiers of Christ, arise,
And put your armor on,
Strong in the strength which God supplies
Through his eternal Son.

CHARLES WESLEY (1707–1788)
SOLDIERS OF CHRIST, ARISE

THE CONCILIATED SOLDIER

Beginning in Exodus, throughout the Hebrew scriptures, and in recent history, Israel has struggled with flesh and blood—that is, human beings on the earth. But the Church is not the same as Israel. We do not wrestle with flesh and blood, but with wicked spirits in the celestial realms (Ephesians 6:12). If people oppose us for our faith in God and his Word, it is because adversarial spiritual forces are using them against us. It is not our place to strive against flesh and blood. Rather, our attitude toward such people is conciliatory, displaying the gospel of peace (v. 15).

The apostle Paul is our example in this. Even before his final visit to Jerusalem, he knew that thousands of believers there were zealous for the law (Acts 21:20). Lies were spread among them concerning his ministry (v. 21). They sent agents to the Gentile churches to undo the apostle's work of grace by introducing the law (Galatians 1:6–9). He was in danger among them, having already suffered because of their plots. Many times he was warned that affliction awaited him in Jerusalem (Acts 20:19, 22–23; 21:10–11). Even the leaders of the church there cautioned him (21:22).

Did he struggle with flesh and blood? No. He was conciliatory toward the legalistic Jewish believers in Jerusalem, and he agreed to participate in harmless ceremonies in hopes of winning them over to God's grace (Acts 21:23–24; Romans 5:2; 1 Corinthians 9:20). In this way, Paul was made all things to all people, so that he could save some (1 Corinthians 9:22).

Bless those who persecute you; bless and do not curse them. . . . Do not repay
anyone evil for evil, but take thought for what is noble in the sight of all. If
it is possible, so far as it depends on you, live peaceably with all.
ROMANS 12:14, 17–18 NRSV

Stand then in his great might,
With all his strength endued,
But take, to arm you for the fight,
The panoply of God.

CHARLES WESLEY (1707–1788)
SOLDIERS OF CHRIST, ARISE

THE WHOLE ARMOR OF GOD

We live in an evil day, but God's armor enables us to stand in it (Galatians 1:4; Ephesians 6:11, 13–14). We find our spiritual security and confidence in the knowledge and experience of scriptural truth. The armor of God depicts the most vital of these truths (vv. 14–17).

First is the truth itself, which braces us like a broad belt around our waist. A person who acknowledges the truth is rescued from the snare of Satan (2 Timothy 2:25–26). Second is righteousness, a breastplate covering the heart. Nobody is righteous (Romans 3:10). But because Christ was made sin for us, we are God's righteousness in him (2 Corinthians 5:21). Knowing this protects our heart from condemnation (Romans 8:33–34).

Third, the gospel of peace is like shoes—the only part of the armor that contacts earth; the rest is for celestial warfare. We imitate the God of peace in our peaceful interactions with others (Romans 12:18). Fourth, faith shields us from the flaming darts of Satan. This shield doesn't burn up, because it does not represent our faith, but the faith of Jesus Christ, which is the gift to us from God (Romans 3:22; Ephesians 2:8).

Fifth, the expectation of salvation is like a helmet over the mind repelling all doubt that God will save believers from the wrath to come (1 Thessalonians 5:8–9; Revelation 6:17). And, as always, the Word of God is the Spirit's sword that will surely defeat Satan as it did when our Lord was tempted in the wilderness (Matthew 4:1–11).

The night is far spent, the day is at hand: let us therefore cast off the works of darkness, and let us put on the armour of light.
ROMANS 13:12

We limit not the truth of God to our poor reach of mind,
By notions of our day and sect, crude, partial, and confined.
No, let a new and better hope within our hearts be stirred:
The Lord has yet more light and truth to break forth from his Word.

GEORGE RAWSON (1807–1889)
WE LIMIT NOT THE TRUTH OF GOD

GOD'S COUNSEL WILL STAND

The magi from the East spent great energy and resources to search out the newborn King of the Jews (Matthew 2:1–2). Contrast these men with the priests, scribes, and populace of Israel who should have rejoiced at the news brought by the Eastern travelers. Instead, all of Jerusalem was disturbed when they heard about the Christ child's birth (v. 3). Bethlehem was barely two hours' journey from Jerusalem, but no one went with the magi to worship the Messiah (John 1:11).

This didn't matter. The nation's ignorance didn't hinder Jesus Christ from completing his commission. What's more, God used Israel's stubbornness for good, since we Gentiles obtained mercy because of their unbelief (Romans 11:15, 30). Their poor reach of mind did not limit the truth of God.

Many years later, Jesus Christ presented Nicodemus with the idea of being born anew. This was beyond the reach of Nicodemus's mind, even though he was leader of the Jews (John 3:3–4). He could not grasp that in the future all Israel will be born in a day, and the desired kingdom will come (Isaiah 66:7–10; John 16:20–23). Although Israel is presently in unbelief, one day the fullness of the Gentiles will come in, and all Israel will be saved when their deliverer appears (Romans 11:25–26).

Let us not despair at the notions of our day and place—crude, partial, and confined as they are. "My counsel shall stand," says the Lord, "and I will do all my pleasure" (Isaiah 46:10).

> *According to the purpose of him who worketh*
> *all things after the counsel of his own will. . .*
> EPHESIANS 1:11

> *Who dares to bind to one's own sense the oracles of heaven,*
> *For all the nations, tongues, and climes and all the ages given?*
> *That universe, how much unknown! The ocean unexplored!*
> *The Lord has yet more light and truth to break forth form his Word.*

GEORGE RAWSON (1807–1889)
WE LIMIT NOT THE TRUTH OF GOD

THE SOURCE OF SPIRITUAL DIGNITY

As Paul traveled from place to place, he visited local synagogues (Acts 17:1–2). The message he brought to the Jews at the synagogue in Antioch of Pisidia is characteristic of what he spoke in all these Jewish gatherings (13:14–41). He told them that Jesus is the offspring of David come to be their Savior and to bring in the promised kingdom (vv. 22–23, 34). This is an extension of the kingdom gospel declared by Jesus and John the Baptist (Matthew 3:2; 4:17). Paul spoke to the synagogues in Antioch of Pisidia, Iconium, Thessalonica, Berea, Athens, Corinth, and Ephesus. The Jews opposed him in all of these cities except Athens.

Berea was also an exception because there people from Thessalonica agitated the throngs (Acts 17:13). For their part, the Bereans "were more noble than those in Thessalonica, in that they "received the word with all readiness of mind, and searched the scriptures daily, whether those things were so" (v. 11). The apostle's success among the Bereans was the result of their willingness to examine the scriptures. Somehow, these people overcame the trend in Judaism that replaced the scriptures with tradition and the teachings of the elders. Still today, spiritual dignity is found in disregarding fashionable dogma and accepting only what is in accord with scripture.

Thy words were found, and I did eat them; and thy word was unto me the joy and rejoicing of mine heart.
JEREMIAH 15:16

Darkling our great forefathers went the first steps of the way;
'Twas but the dawning yet to grow into the perfect day.
And grow it shall, our glorious sun more fervid rays afford:
The Lord hath yet more light and truth to break forth from his Word.

GEORGE RAWSON (1807–1889)
WE LIMIT NOT THE TRUTH OF GOD

THE BELT OF TRUTH

Our spiritual armor begins with the belt of truth: "Stand therefore, having your loins girt about with truth" (Ephesians 6:14). Like an ancient soldier's broad girdle, truth gives a believer strength and stability.

Three fundamental truths are of great value to us, strengthening our lives. They are justification (Romans 3:21–4:25), reconciliation (5:1–6:23), and God's supremacy (chaps. 8–11). These truths are the essential form of doctrine that was delivered to the church in Rome (16:17). The saints in Rome are exemplary because they did more than just read Paul's letter. They took its teaching to heart and remained in it. In other words, their loins were girded with its truth.

When Paul urged the saints to pray for all humankind, he was confident they could do this because they were strengthened with the following truths: God wills all humankind to be saved, come to a realization of the truth, and worship the one God according to the apostle's teaching (1 Timothy 2:1–7). Our Lord spoke of this strengthening when he said, "If ye continue in my word, then are ye my disciples indeed; and ye shall know the truth, and the truth shall make you free" (John 8:31–32). The delusions of philosophy, self-help, and tradition do not liberate. The net of bondage these use to constrict and entangle the mind are in stark contrast to the broad, strengthening belt that is the truth of the Word of God.

> *When ye received the word of God which ye heard of us,*
> *ye received it not as the word of men, but as it is in truth,*
> *the word of God, which effectually worketh also in you that believe.*
> 1 THESSALONIANS 2:13

How firm a foundation, ye saints of the Lord,
Is laid for your faith in his excellent word!
What more can he say than to you he hath said,
You, who unto Jesus for refuge have fled?

ATTRIBUTED TO JOHN KEENE KIRKHAM AND JOHN KEITH
HOW FIRM A FOUNDATION
PUBLISHED IN JOHN RIPPON'S *A SELECTION OF HYMNS*, 1787

MATERIALS FOR GOD'S BUILDING

When scripture pledges that the foundation of God stands sure (2 Timothy 2:19), it is no doubt referring to the foundation laid by Paul (1 Corinthians 3:10–11). God is the architect of his building (Hebrews 11:10), and the apostle was God's master builder. Apollos and other teachers were used by God to build on the foundation laid down by Paul. The character of the doctrines with which these teachers edified the Church is figured in various materials: gold, silver, precious stones, wood, hay, and stubble (1 Corinthians 3:12).

The baser materials are human philosophies and traditions that replace and obscure scriptural truth. In contrast to these, the precious building materials are found in the master builder's own epistles. These are characterized in a few key verses:

God's supremacy: "For from him and through him and to him are all things" (Romans 11:36 NRSV). *Man's justification:* "By the righteousness of one the free gift came upon all men unto justification of life" (5:18). *God's conciliation:* "God was in Christ, reconciling the world unto himself, not imputing their trespasses unto them" (2 Corinthians 5:19). *Creation's destiny:* "And, having made peace through the blood of his cross, by him to reconcile all things unto himself." (Colossians 1:20). *The ultimate goal:* "That God may be all in all." (1 Corinthians 15:28). The believer who builds with these truths will have a strong structure in which to dwell in faith.

According to the grace of God which is given unto me, as a wise
masterbuilder, I have laid the foundation, and another buildeth thereon.
But let every man take heed how he buildeth thereupon.
1 CORINTHIANS 3:10

*Jesus, the very thought of thee
With sweetness fills the breast;
But sweeter far thy face to see,
And in thy presence rest.*

BERNARD OF CLAIRVAUX (1091–1153)
JESUS, THE VERY THOUGHT OF THEE
TRANSLATED BY EDWARD CASWALL (1814–1878)

WE SHALL BE SAVED FROM WRATH

Bernard of Clairvaux sang of the day when we see the Lord face-to-face. This is called the day of the Lord, which begins with the resurrection (1 Thessalonians 4:16; 5:2). At that moment, whether dead or living, all believers will see the Lord (4:15–17). Although this is true, people are often made to fear the wrath of God at the time of the Lord's coming. But the apostle's words describe our hope, our expectation— not our fear. This is why we are told to comfort one another with these words about the future (v. 18).

True, the day of the Lord will be full of terror and destruction. But this is not for us, because "God hath not appointed us to wrath, but to obtain salvation by our Lord Jesus Christ" (5:9). We who believe in Jesus Christ are delivered from the day of wrath described in the book of Revelation (6:16–17; see also Romans 5:9; 1 Thessalonians 1:10).

Will some believers suffer in the coming tribulation and miss the inexpressible comfort of the day described in this hymn? To find out, let's consider the believers in Thessalonica. They, like us, must have been harassed by their failings. Yet scripture describes them, without exception, as "children of the light" and "children of the day" (1 Thessalonians 5:5). This is because each one of them received the gospel by faith independent from works. Their salvation, like ours, was based on pure grace (Ephesians 2:8–9). The death of Christ, not our conduct, is the foundation on which our salvation rests.

But God commendeth his love toward us, in that, while we were yet sinners, Christ died for us. Much more then, being now justified by his blood, we shall be saved from wrath through him.
ROMANS 5:8–9

How sweet the name of Jesus sounds
In a believer's ear!
It soothes his sorrows, heals his wounds,
And drives away his fear.

JOHN NEWTON (1725–1807)
HOW SWEET THE NAME OF JESUS SOUNDS

THE LORD'S NAME AND THE BELIEVER'S HEART

The first epistle to the Corinthians is addressed to the church at Corinth and to "all that in every place call upon the name of Jesus Christ our Lord" (1 Corinthians 1:2). This shows that the first-century believers, just like John Newton in later years, experienced the sweetness and solace of the Lord's name.

On the day of Pentecost, Peter spoke of those who call on the Lord's name when he quoted the apocalyptic prophet, Joel. He declared that, in the midst of the terrors of the end of this age, "Whosoever shall call on the name of the Lord shall be saved" (Acts 2:21; see Joel 2:32). For all Peter knew, the end of the age had nearly come on that day in Jerusalem. If Israel had believed the gospel, the thousand-year reign of Christ would have begun. In God's wisdom, this was not to be. Still, people continued to call on the name of the Lord.

Over thirty years later, Paul wrote to the Romans, "The same Lord over all is rich unto all that call upon him. For whosoever shall call upon the name of the Lord shall be saved" (Romans 10:12–13). And, in his final epistle, the apostle describes the basis of our fellowship during the disbelief of these last days. Doctrinal conformity is not necessary, nor should we center our fellowship on church government or the knowledge of the truth. Rather, our fellowship is based on the heart's motive: "Follow righteousness, faith, charity, peace, with them that call on the Lord out of a pure heart" (2 Timothy 2:22). Contrary to the way of the world, God does not consider a person's outward appearance; he looks at the heart, and so should we (1 Samuel 16:7).

Now the end of the commandment is charity out of a pure heart, and of a good conscience, and of faith unfeigned.
1 TIMOTHY 1:5

Weak is the effort of my heart,
And cold my warmest thought;
But when I see thee as thou art,
I'll praise thee as I ought.

JOHN NEWTON (1725–1807)
HOW SWEET THE NAME OF JESUS SOUNDS

THE RAISING OF EUTYCHUS

Two resurrections are recorded in the book of Acts—those of Dorcas and Eutychus. Dorcas was full of good works and acts of charity. When she died, Peter was called to Joppa and shown all the clothing Dorcas had sewn, presumably for the poor. People thought this woman's works qualified her to be raised from the dead. And so she was (Acts 9:36–40). She represents Israel, to which Peter ministered (Galatians 2:7). James, who ministered to the Jews, as well (James 1:1), explains in his epistle the melding of grace and works by which Israel is saved. By these standards, Dorcas qualified.

Eutychus was among the Gentiles present in Troas when Paul addressed the believers there. It was midnight, and Eutychus, sitting on a window ledge, fell asleep, tumbled three stories to the ground, and was picked up dead. This young man was apparently nothing like the virtuous Dorcas. He was not even able to remain watchful while Christ's apostle spoke. Nevertheless, Paul brought him back to life (Acts 20:7–10). Eutychus represents believers like you and me who are saved by grace though faith, not by our works (Ephesians 2:8).

In anticipation of the Lord's soon return, it is desirable that we not sleep, but watch and be sober (1 Thessalonians 5:6). However, as surprising as it may be, and in keeping with the gospel of God's grace, because Jesus Christ died for us, whether we wake or sleep, we will live together with him (vv. 9–10). This is the lesson of Eutychus.

> *It is high time to awake out of sleep: for now*
> *is our salvation nearer than when we believed.*
> ROMANS 13:11

Oh, wondrous grace for all mankind, That spreads from sea to sea!
It heals the sick and leads the blind, And sets the prisoner free;
The soul that seeks it cannot fail
To see the Savior's face,
And Satan's power cannot prevail
If we are saved by grace.

FANNY J. CROSBY (1820–1915)
A MESSAGE SWEET IS BORNE TO ME

THE TYRANNY OF GRACE

All of Paul's epistles begin with a similar salutation: "Grace to you." This phrase sounds the glorious theme of the gospel of God. That is, grace and grace alone is the means of our salvation. In fact, anything that pleases God springs from his own gracious provision and direction. This understanding enables a believer to walk humbly with God (Micah 6:8), while people who imagine that they can do something that pleases God have not yet comprehended God's grace. The awareness that grace is tyrannical—that it allows nothing that we are, or anything we can do, to coexist with it—cuts deeply into our pride.

We are told to work out our own salvation (Philippians 2:12). Yet, before we can even pause to think how we might conjure a way to do this in the strength of our flesh, we learn that God is the force that accomplishes it (v. 13). For instance, Paul labored more abundantly than all the other apostles. Yet he testified that it was "not I, but the grace of God which was with me" (1 Corinthians 15:10). He attributed all that he had become since he first encountered grace on the Damascus road to that same grace of God. This means that, whatever about us is true, honest, just, pure, lovely, of good report; any virtue, any praise does not give us reason to boast but only opportunity to thank God for his saving grace (Philippians 4:8).

Who hath saved us, and called us with an holy calling, not according to our works, but according to his own purpose and grace, which was given us in Christ Jesus before the world began.
2 TIMOTHY 1:9

May the mind of Christ, my Savior,
Live in me from day to day,
By his love and power controlling
All I do and say.

KATE B. WILKINSON (1859–1928)
MAY THE MIND OF CHRIST, MY SAVIOR

THE RENEWAL OF THE MIND

First Corinthians 2:16 says, "We have the mind of Christ"—an astonishing concept. How can this be possible? The answer is found in Romans 12:2, which tells us we can be transformed by the renewing of the mind. But this prompts another question: How does a person's mind become renewed? It is through the gospel of Christ—"the power of God unto salvation to every one that believeth" (1:16). A person's mind is changed when he or she understands the gospel. God's gracious purpose and Christ's faithful service become comprehensible; the world, its inhabitants, and their hope for the future are cast in a completely new light.

Notice that Romans 12 begins with a reminder of the mercies of God (v. 1). These are the themes of the gospel illuminated in Romans 1–11. They include God's righteous justification of all sinners (5:18–19), his peaceful attitude toward his enemies (v. 10), the dominance of grace over sin (v. 20), the effectiveness of Christ's death (6:3), God's gracious gift of life in Christ (v. 23), the believer's freedom from condemnation (8:1), the creation's freedom from corruption (vv. 19–21), Israel's destiny (chapts. 9–11), and on and on, culminating in one of the clearest revelations of God in all the scriptures (11:32–36). An immersion in these truths makes one's mind so new that it resembles the mind of Christ (Philippians 2:5).

> *And be not conformed to this world: but be ye transformed*
> *by the renewing of your mind, that ye may prove what*
> *is that good, and acceptable, and perfect, will of God.*
> ROMANS 12:2

Break thou the bread of life, dear Lord, to me,
As thou didst break the loaves beside the sea;
Beyond the sacred page I seek thee, Lord;
My spirit pants for thee, O living Word!

MARY A. LATHBURY (1841–1913)
BREAK THOU THE BREAD OF LIFE

THE KINGDOM'S ABUNDANCE

Many people, even those who are not yet believers, know this saying: "Man shall not live by bread alone" (Luke 4:4). The completion of this thought may be less known: "but by every word of God." This brings to mind the story of a miraculous event that shows Christ as the life of the world and the true bread of God (John 6:1–13; 33). In this story, the lack of food is a thousandfold: five thousand people have only enough food to feed five—a picture of humankind today, spiritually hungry and far from true food.

When Jesus Christ lived in Israel, the powers of the kingdom were present with him (Hebrews 6:5). Therefore, when the multitudes were fed, they were experiencing the coming kingdom. In that future age, physical food will be bountiful. In addition to that, the head and heart will be fed, as well, because the earth will be full of the knowledge of the Lord (Isaiah 11:9–11).

Today, when people believe in Christ Jesus, the bread of life is broken for them and suddenly available in abundance. Their panting spirit is satisfied. The same will be true throughout the earth when the kingdom comes. Its spiritual plenty will not arrive gradually by natural development, character building, and education. Instead, just as Christ fed the multitudes, out of famine will come a miraculous multiplication and distribution of the knowledge of God.

And they shall teach no more every man his neighbour, and every man his brother, saying, Know the LORD: for they shall all know me, from the least of them unto the greatest of them.
JEREMIAH 31:34

O send thy Spirit, Lord, now unto me,
That he may touch my eyes, and make me see:
Show me the truth concealed within thy Word,
And in thy book revealed I see the Lord.

MARY A. LATHBURY (1841–1913)
BREAK THOU THE BREAD OF LIFE

THE SPIRIT OF WISDOM AND REVELATION

People usually pray for material blessings like food, shelter, health, and wealth. Mary Lathbury's prayer is different. It tells of her longing to see the truth that is concealed in God's Word—a spiritual blessing.

The epistle to the Ephesians, the peak of divine revelation, does not mention physical blessings on this earth. Instead, we find that the Father has "blessed us with all spiritual blessings in heavenly places in Christ" (Ephesians 1:3). We certainly must have our physical needs met, but such blessings are not as scarce or valuable as these celestial, spiritual endowments. So the apostle prays that the Father will give us "the spirit of wisdom and revelation in the knowledge of him" (v. 17). The best blessing is to know God and his plans and purposes for us. Therefore, let us join the apostle in praying for this spirit.

Every believer has God's Spirit (1 Corinthians 2:12). Not one is left out. But if we are to know "what is the hope of his calling, and what [are] the riches of the glory of his inheritance in the saints, and what is the exceeding greatness of his power to us-ward who believe," the eyes of our understanding must be enlightened (Ephesians 1:18–19). For this, God has made available the spirit of wisdom and revelation, which agrees with the written Word of God. The believer who prays for this spirit will go from strength to strength (Psalm 84:7).

That the God of our Lord Jesus Christ, the Father of glory, may give unto
you the spirit of wisdom and revelation in the knowledge of him. . .
EPHESIANS 1:17

Bless thou the truth, dear Lord, to me, to me,
As thou didst bless the bread by Galilee;
Then shall all bondage cease, all fetters fall;
And I shall find my peace, my all in all.

MARY A. LATHBURY (1841–1913)
BREAK THOU THE BREAD OF LIFE

GOD—THE ALL IN ALL

It is rare to hear the expression "all in all" applied to the Father, but when God blesses the truth to us, multiplying and distributing it abundantly as Jesus did the bread at Galilee, we will ultimately see the Creator's goal to be all in all to his creatures (1 Corinthians 15:28).

Some of the Corinthian believers misunderstood the truth, saying there was no resurrection of the dead (v. 12). This provided opportunity for God to be seen as all in all. The resurrection is the bedrock of the gospel's truth, and it includes our Lord's death, because only one who is dead can be raised from the dead. Also, without his resurrection, we are still in our sins, because a dead Christ cannot save (v. 17). However, there is no doubt that we are saved in his life (Romans 5:10).

On the way to God becoming all in all, death entered through Adam and departed through Christ: "For as in Adam all die, even so in Christ shall all be made alive" (1 Corinthians 15:22). The first to be made alive was Christ—the firstfruits. Therefore, God is all in Christ Jesus at this time. He is our prototype. The next step will come when all who belong to Christ when he returns are made alive (v. 23). Then God will be all in all to his believers. The final step will come at the consummation when death is abolished and God gloriously becomes all in all (vv. 26, 28).

And when all things shall be subdued unto him, then shall
the Son also himself be subject unto him that put all things
under him, that God may be all in all.
1 CORINTHIANS 15:28

Loved with everlasting love,
Led by grace that love to know;
Gracious Spirit, from above,
Thou hast taught me it is so!

GEORGE WADE ROBINSON (1838–1877)
I AM HIS, AND HE IS MINE

HOW TO LOVE GOD

Believers desire to love God with all their heart (Matthew 22:37). How can this be possible? The apostle John gives us this hint: "Not that we loved God, but that he loved us, and sent his Son" (1 John 4:10). Paul agrees and goes further to describe how love for God fills our hearts: "The love of God is shed abroad in our hearts by the Holy Ghost which is given unto us" (Romans 5:5).

John wrote this most famous description of God's love: "God so loved the world, that he gave his only begotten Son" (John 3:16). This theme sounds again in Paul's letter to the Romans: "For when we were yet without strength, in due time Christ died for the ungodly" (Romans 5:6). We were irreverent and infirm, helpless and godless, yet Christ died for us. That act of pure grace describes God's love for us. The Holy Spirit poured that love into our hearts. Or, as George Robinson's hymn says, "Gracious Spirit, from above, Thou hast taught me it is so!"

God goes even further to win us over by recommending his love to us "in that, while we were yet sinners, Christ died for us" (v. 8). God's way of winning a person's whole heart is to first pour his own love into it—a love that is demonstrated in Christ's death for us though we were entirely undeserving of that favor.

> *But God, who is rich in mercy, for his great love wherewith*
> *he loved us, even when we were dead in sins, hath quickened*
> *us together with Christ, (by grace ye are saved).*
> EPHESIANS 2:4–5

Behold the Savior of mankind
Nailed to the shameful tree!
How vast the love that him inclined
To bleed and die for thee!

SAMUEL WESLEY (1662–1735)
BEHOLD THE SAVIOR OF MANKIND

SCENES AT THE CRUCIFIXION

Golgotha was alive with the presence of God. This is seen not only in Christ, the victim, and in the faithful who followed him there. Even the people who hated Christ displayed God's presence.

Pontius Pilate, the Roman governor, was the only actor in the Crucifixion tragedy that pled the case of Jesus Christ (Matthew 27:15–19). His wife, troubled by a dream, tried to discourage her husband from convicting Jesus (v. 19). Barabbas, the rebel and murderer whose name means "son of the father," was the first person delivered from death by the crucifixion of Christ (v. 21).

Soldiers dressed Jesus in a scarlet robe, crowned him with thorns, and thrust a reed into his hand for a scepter. Then they praised, "Hail! King of the Jews" (vv. 27–31 NRSV), foreshadowing the coming of his kingdom. People gambled for his clothes, fulfilling the scriptures: "They parted my garments among them, and upon my vesture did they cast lots" (v. 35; see Psalm 22:18). Israel's chief priests gave a sermon at the foot of the cross (vv. 41–43). "He [is] the King of Israel," they mocked, "let him now come down from the cross, and we will believe him" (see v. 42). They could not even accept the Lord's resurrection of Lazarus; how could they believe in anything concerning Jesus Christ (Luke 16:30–31; John 11:43–44)?

Yet, as they mocked, he died for each of them. Finally, at the very moment of Jesus' death, a Gentile prophesied, "This was the Son of God" (Matthew 27:54), unknowingly anticipating the day of his return as Israel's King and Lord over the nations of the earth.

And Pilate wrote a title, and put it on the cross. And the writing was
JESUS OF NAZARETH THE KING OF THE JEWS. . .and it was
written in Hebrew, and Greek, and Latin.
JOHN 19:19–20

Jesus lives, and so shall I:
Death, thy sting is gone forever!
He for me hath deigned to die,
Lives the bands of death to sever.

CHRISTIAN FÜRCHTEGOTT GELLERT (1715–1769)
JESUS LIVES, AND SO SHALL I
TRANSLATED BY PHILLIP SCHAFF (1819–1893)

THE FAITH OF ABRAHAM

This hymn declares as a fact something that has not yet happened—the resurrection of believers. Abraham also believed in something that was yet to occur. He believed in God "who gives life to the dead and calls into existence the things that do not exist" (Romans 4:17 NRSV).

Abraham believed when all the evidence was against God. He knew he was as good as dead, and his wife was unable to conceive, yet he did not doubt that God could and would fulfill the promise that he would be the father of many nations (vv. 17–19). For this to come about, Sarah had to give birth, and indeed she did so. Abraham believed in God, who is above death. The father of faith did not cease believing when asked to sacrifice Isaac, whose very birth was life from the dead. A dead Isaac would nullify the promise, because Abraham's descendants had to spring from Isaac. So Abraham assumed that God was able to raise Isaac from the dead (Hebrews 11:17–19). By this faith, God justified Abraham (Romans 4:22, 24–25).

The simple act of believing in God's operation in Christ justifies us, just as Abraham was justified. We are as dead as Abraham and as barren as Sarah. However, the sin Jesus Christ bore for us is all gone (v. 25). So God gave life to Jesus Christ when he raised him from the dead, and he will do the same for us (Romans 8:11).

> *[Righteousness] will be reckoned to us who believe in him who*
> *raised Jesus our Lord from the dead, who was handed over to*
> *death for our trespasses and was raised for our justification.*
> ROMANS 4:24–25 NRSV

Great is Thy faithfulness, O God my Father;
There is no shadow of turning with thee;
Thou changest not, thy compassions, they fail not;
As thou hast been, thou forever will be.

THOMAS O. CHISHOLM (1866–1960)
GREAT IS THY FAITHFULNESS

THE UNCHANGING SAVIOR

Thomas Chisholm's words bring to mind Hebrews 13:8: "Jesus Christ the same yesterday, and to day, and for ever." Certainly, this is so. But consider this: John the Baptist said Christ was a young lamb—the Lamb of God—and Daniel called him the Ancient of days (John 1:36; Daniel 7:9). The one who now pours love into our hearts will pour indignation on the nations at the end of the age (Romans 5:5; Revelation 19:15). The same one who wearily sat on Sychar's well is now seated at God's right hand (John 4:6; Mark 16:19). He who was once lowly is now exalted (Acts 7:55). He who healed many people when he lived among humankind refused to remove Paul's thorn in the flesh (2 Corinthians 12:7–9). The one who hung on Calvary's cross and lay in the tomb is now alive, ascended to God's right hand.

The key to understanding Hebrews 13:8 is this: In Greek, the phrase "the same" is a pronoun. That is, it refers to Jesus Christ's personality, not to his administration of God's plan. His service must change to harmonize with God's purpose, but he himself remains the same. We are entirely different than he is. Even so, as our flesh fails and our days decline, we are privileged to believe in an unchanging Savior whose compassions do not fail.

Jesus said unto them, Verily, verily, I say unto you,
Before Abraham was, I am.
JOHN 8:58

May 24

God, our Father, we adore thee!
We, thy children, bless thy name!
Chosen in the Christ before thee,
We are "holy without blame."
We adore thee! We adore thee!
Abba's praises we proclaim!

GEORGE W. FRAZER (1830–1896)
GOD OUR FATHER, WE ADORE THEE

OUR GOD; OUR DADDY

It is not often noted that Jesus struggled to do God's will when he prayed in the Garden of Gethsemane. He had never done his own will, always preferring the Father's, but at Gethsemane he asked if it was possible for the bitter cup of crucifixion to be taken away (Mark 14:36; John 5:30). It was at that time he called his Father by the sweet and tender name of *Abba*.

In Jesus' day, the people of Israel were bilingual. They used an Aramaic dialect in day-to-day affairs, and understood Greek, a universal language in that place and time. The word *Abba* is Aramaic; it corresponds to our endearing title Daddy. That Jesus called his Father "Daddy" shows how intimate they were and reveals Jesus' sincere trust in his God (1 Peter 1:3).

We have a similar intimacy with God because we are the children of God. He "sent forth the Spirit of his Son into [our] hearts, crying, Abba, Father" (Galatians 4:6). That Spirit assures us that we are justified from sin and at perfect peace with God. This is entirely unlike those who, by fleshly effort, are trying to please God. They have the spirit of bondage and fear, whereas we have the spirit of sonship (Romans 8:15).

In ancient days, Hebrew children lovingly called out to their fathers, "Abba!" and they do so to this day. Our own children trustingly say, "Daddy." Likewise, we are entirely free in the majestic company of the Almighty, the Father of our Lord Jesus Christ who is our Father, as well (Ephesians 3:14). Jesus called him Abba, and so can we.

And he said, Abba, Father, all things are possible unto thee; take away this cup from me: nevertheless not what I will, but what thou wilt.
MARK 14:36

> *There are depths of love that I cannot know*
> *Till I cross the narrow sea;*
> *There are heights of joy that I may not reach*
> *Till I rest in peace with thee.*

FANNY J. CROSBY (1820–1915)
I AM THINE, O LORD

LOVE NEVER ENDS

Faith, hope, and love are the three enduring gifts that believers share in this era of God's grace (1 Corinthians 13:13). Faith and hope, however, do not continue in the future glory. Only love will carry on beyond the coming of Christ Jesus. So Fanny Crosby did well to sing of love's depths that are yet to be known.

Through prayer and the Word, let us continue to strengthen our faith in God and rejoice in hope of his glory (Romans 5:2). At the same time, we know that these will not exist in the coming ages. Hope will be past because all our expectations will be gloriously realized. Faith will be unnecessary because the things that are not seen now will become evident to all (Hebrews 11:1). Clearly, the greatest of the three remaining gifts is love. It never ends.

Love is first on the list of the Spirit's pleasant fruits (Galatians 5:22). It joins us to the Lord and unites us with our fellow saints in the new creation where no fleshly distinctions exist between us because faith operates through love (v. 6). Since these differences are abolished, we bear one another in love in a spirit of unity (Ephesians 4:2–6). God's own love is poured out in our hearts through the Spirit (Romans 5:5). We therefore possess more than enough passion to love God, his believers, and even those who do not yet believe. All of this illustrates that we have been transferred from the jurisdiction of darkness into the kingdom of love presided over by the Son of God (Colossians 1:13).

Love never ends.
1 CORINTHIANS 13:8 NRSV

Almighty Father of mankind,
On thee our hopes remain;
And when the day of trouble comes
I shall not trust in vain.

MICHAEL BRUCE (1746–1767)
ALMIGHTY FATHER OF MANKIND

THE CONSTANT GOD

In AD 66, Israel rebelled against the Roman Empire, and tens of thousands of Jews fled for safety to other countries. James addressed his epistle to these refugees—"the twelve tribes which are scattered abroad" (1:1). He was the leader of the church in Jerusalem, which was composed entirely of Jews. How disappointed those believers must have been to see their fellowship crushed and scattered. Had their faith come to nothing? Had God rescinded his promises? Would they never see their Messiah and his kingdom? Were they no longer the firstfruits of his creatures (v. 18)?

James corrected them: "Do not err, my beloved brethren. Every good gift and every perfect gift is from above, and cometh down from the Father of lights, with whom is no variableness, neither shadow of turning" (vv. 16–17). In other words, God is faithful to his promises.

Our physical blessings find their ultimate source in the sun. All life on earth is directly or indirectly dependent upon it. Just as natural good descends from the sun, all spiritual good comes from God. So James compares God in his constancy to the sun.

The people of Jerusalem passed through a trauma of great proportions. In AD 70, their ancient, holy city was torn to the ground and many thousands were killed. This was a shocking reminder to them that on the earth there are shadows and turning. Circumstances here are continuously changing, but God is constant. He operates all things in accord with the counsel of his will (Ephesians 1:11).

The gifts and the calling of God are irrevocable.
ROMANS 11:29 NRSV

Sweet will of God, still fold me closer;
Till I am wholly lost in thee;
Sweet will of God, still fold me closer,
Till I am wholly lost in thee.

LEILA N. MORRIS (1862–1929)
SWEET WILL OF GOD

SERVICE IN GOD'S WILL

The desire to serve God is common in believers. However, we sometimes belittle our service in comparison with others who are more gifted or those who have been given greater opportunity.

Who could be greater among God's servants than our Lord? He "was a minister of the circumcision for the truth of God, to confirm the promises made unto [Israel's] fathers" sent to the lost sheep of the house of Israel (Romans 15:8; see Matthew 15:24). Dare we ask how well he did in ministry to his nation? The prophet Isaiah answers for him: "I have labored in vain, I have spent my strength for naught, and in vain. . . . Though Israel be not gathered, yet shall I be glorious in the eyes of the LORD, and my God shall be my strength" (Isaiah 49:4–5).

Another servant, Noah, was a preacher of righteousness in his generation (2 Peter 2:5). How much fruit did his testimony bear? Humanly speaking, not much was harvested. Only he and his family were saved in accord with the will of God. Satisfactory service has nothing to do with apparent success. Our service is offered only for the gratification of the one to whom it is given.

We have been chosen to serve in this day of darkness and apostasy with our own distinctive gifts and prospects. This we do, and in harmony with the spirit of the perfect servant, we leave the results to God.

I thank thee, O Father. . .that thou hast hid these things from the wise and prudent, and hast revealed them unto babes: even so, Father; for so it seemed good in thy sight.
LUKE 10:21

I am the Lord's! O joy beyond expression,
O sweet response to voice of love divine;
Faith joyous "Yes" to the assuring whisper,
"Fear not! I have redeemed thee; thou art mine."

<small>Lucy A. Bennett (1850–1927)</small>
<small>I Am the Lord's</small>

THE FEARLESS TESTIMONY

Second Kings 6:15–23 tells the marvelous story of Elisha's bloodless victory over Syria, Israel's powerful adversary. Several times, God gave the prophet visions that betrayed the secret plans of the Syrian king. Elisha passed this information on to Israel's king, thus rescuing him. The frustrated king of Syria learned through spies that Elisha was living in Dothan, and he decided to take him prisoner by surrounding him there. Early one morning, Elisha's servant discovered that a "host . . .with horses and chariots" (v. 15) encircled them. He cried out to Elisha, "Alas, my master! [What] shall we do?" (v. 15).

Elisha was calm, saying, "Fear not: for they that [are] with us are more than they that [are] with them" (v. 16). Then Elisha prayed that the young man's eyes would be opened to see. The servant then saw that "the mountain was full of horses and chariots of fire round about Elisha" (v. 17), a vivid example of this saying: "[He] maketh his angels spirits, and his ministers a flame of fire" (Hebrews 1:7).

Elisha was God's testimony in the kingdom of Israel thousands of years ago. It was in God's interest to defend him. Today God has included us in the purpose for the ages, which he has made in Christ Jesus. We have nothing to fear in this world. By the gift of his grace and the working of his power, God preserves the Church as the testimony to the heavenlies of his manifold wisdom (Ephesians 3:10–11).

> *There shall be no loss of any man's life among you, but of the ship.*
> *For there stood by me this night the angel of God, whose I am,*
> *and whom I serve, Saying, Fear not, Paul; thou must be brought before*
> *Caesar: and, lo, God hath given thee all them that sail with thee.*
> <small>Acts 27:22–24</small>

If thou hadst bid thy thunders roll,
And light'nings flash, to blast my soul,
I still had stubborn been;
But mercy has my heart subdued,
A bleeding Savior I have viewed,
And now I hate my sin.

JOHN NEWTON (1725–1807)
LORD, THOU HAST WON, AT LENGTH I YIELD

THE HISTORY OF MERCY

Stubbornness is the history of mercy: "For God has imprisoned all in disobedience so that he may be merciful to all" (Romans 11:32 NRSV). Furthermore, humankind's stubbornness is as much God's work as is his merciful response to that stubbornness. This is so clear yet so surprising, it is worth repeating: God locks up all together in stubbornness so that he can be merciful to all.

Everyone is born with a disposition that is opposed to God (Romans 8:7). We live in the current of this world and are in accord with the evil prince of the power of the air (Ephesians 2:2). We are "by nature the children of wrath" (v. 3), hoarding a treasure of "wrath against the day of wrath and revelation of the righteous judgment of God" (Romans 2:5).

Then, suddenly, a stupendous change occurs. This is expressed in two words: "But God" (Ephesians 2:4). In the past, we could not claim God's blessing. We were "without Christ, being aliens from the commonwealth of Israel, and strangers from the covenants of promise, having no hope, and without God in the world" (v. 12). Does scripture then say, "But men and women, despite their former sinfulness, summoned strength from within themselves, made the right decision, and by great effort qualified themselves for divine deliverance"? No! It says,

But God, who is rich in mercy, for his great love wherewith he loved us,
even when we were dead in sins, hath quickened us together with Christ,
(by grace ye are saved).
EPHESIANS 2:4–5

May 30

O God how rich, how vast thy love,
Whoe'er can thee repay?
Thy love is past man's finding out,
Thy grace no man can say.

HORATIUS BONAR (1808–1889)
O GOD HOW RICH, HOW VAST THY LOVE

OUR SALVATION: THE DELIGHT OF HIS WILL

We believers in Christ were once like all other people. None are righteous. None understand. None seek after God. All are unprofitable. None do good. No, not one (Romans 3:10–12). Though we may wish to think otherwise, all this is true. We were not seeking God; rather, he attracted us by his grace as we behaved ourselves "in the lusts of our flesh, fulfilling the desires of the flesh and of the mind; and were by nature the children of wrath, even as others" (Ephesians 2:3).

"But God, who is rich in mercy. . ." (2:4). These words are so beautiful in contrast with the description of our former selves. The great love with which God loved us fills our hearts with the enormity of his mercy. We were dead in sins, yet God made us alive together with Christ and swept us up in the vastness of his love.

Once we realize that we are saved purely by grace, we will have it no other way. This ends our selfishness, and it centers our thoughts on God, who purposed and provided to us the full measure of his great salvation. God loves to give to humankind. Nothing is asked in return but our glad acceptance and appreciation. This is in accord with the delight of his will and in keeping with "the glorious gospel of the blessed God" (1 Timothy 1:11).

For by grace are ye saved through faith;
and that not of yourselves: it is the gift of God.
EPHESIANS 2:8

*But if man's heart should e'er suppose
He could repay thy love,
It only means he nothing knows
Of love, all loves above.*

HORATIUS BONAR (1808–1889)
O GOD HOW RICH, HOW VAST THY LOVE

CHRIST'S CONSTRAINING LOVE

We naturally want to please God, yet this does not come naturally to us. Scripture solves this dilemma with these six words: "The love of Christ constraineth us" (2 Corinthians 5:14).

Envy, covetousness, anger, impatience—and who knows what other sins—can crop up in our hearts like weeds at any time. We may be startled by an incident or offended by someone and, out of the blue, react in a shameful way. When selfish desires are not fulfilled, we may become irritable. Flattery can draw us into arrogance.

The love of Christ runs contrary to all this. The apostle Paul said that it constrained him to be well pleasing to God and to devote himself to the one who died and was raised for his sake (vv. 9, 15). Christ's love will likewise constrain our motives and behavior.

Christ's love is not a sentimental, impotent thing. It is virile, competent, and effective. Its energy is found in the message of the cross, which is the power of God to us for salvation from the tyranny of sin and our old humanity (Romans 1:16; 1 Corinthians 1:18). That message informs us that we were crucified with Christ, and now we live by the faith of the one who loved us so much as to give himself up (Galatians 2:20). Let us pray to know the love that was displayed at Golgotha and be glad it collides with our self-centered world, constraining us to live according to the word of the cross.

For the love of Christ constraineth us; because we thus judge, that if one died for all, then were all dead: and that he died for all, that they which live should not henceforth live unto themselves, but unto him which died for them, and rose again.
2 CORINTHIANS 5:14–15

THE JACOBEAN BARGAIN

God's graciousness in Jacob's dream is remarkable. Jacob was really a criminal—a fugitive who had stolen his brother's birthright. Instead of disciplining him, God confirmed the promise of the land, assured Jacob of numberless descendants, and made him the channel of blessing to the whole earth (Genesis 28:13–15). Notice that Jacob's response betrays how little he understood God's grace toward him (vv. 18–22).

God had poured riches into Jacob's life, but he immediately tried to get the better of God by driving a sharp bargain: If God would be with him, keep him, feed him, clothe him, and restore him to his father in peace, he—Jacob—would pay for this by giving back a tenth of it. What a bargain! To all intents and purposes, Jacob proposed to pay for merchandise by returning a portion of it to the merchant. Such a deal would bankrupt anyone but God. Bethel is a cinematic display of God's gracious goodness in contrast to the selfishness of humankind.

There are probably Jacobs today who think that by tithing they have repaid the Lord for his benefits. If the return of a tenth of our income robs us of the awareness that we owe all to God, it is better to give nothing. God doesn't need it. Rather, he wants thankful hearts and adoring spirits. Our heritage is far richer than Jacob's, so let us pay ten times a tenth in our thanksgiving and worship to God.

Thanks be to God for his indescribable gift!
2 CORINTHIANS 9:15 NRSV

Nothing between, Lord, nothing between;
Nothing of earthly care,
Nothing of tear or prayer,
No robe that self may wear,
Nothing between.

ELIZA H. HAMILTON (C. 1878)
NOTHING BETWEEN

WHAT SHALL WE SAY TO THESE THINGS?

The truth is, there is nothing between God's love and us. Yes, we are sometimes disappointed in ourselves for surrendering to earthly cares and stumbling on selfish failures. But our feelings are not the same as God's. He is always for us (Romans 8:31). Nothing can compare with the awareness of our place in the heart of God, who "spared not his own Son, but delivered him up for us all, [therefore] how shall he not with him also freely give us all things?" (v. 32). God gave his best gift when he sacrificed his Son. He will not withhold anything from those who have received his beloved.

What in the universe is against us? In Christ, God has justified us. In addition, all judgment has been given to the Son, who died for us and lives to plead for us at God's right hand. God is the judge of all, and he has vindicated us. Only Christ has the right to condemn, and he is our Savior! "What shall we then say to these things? If God be for us, who can be against us?" (v. 31). What we cannot say is that these things are not true.

Wrapping up his argument for God's absolute love, Paul asks, "Who shall separate us from the love of Christ?" He lists seventeen items and concludes that nothing can ever separate us from "the love of God. . .in Christ Jesus, our Lord" (vv. 35, 39).

Who shall lay any thing to the charge of God's elect? It is God
that justifieth. Who is he that condemneth? It is Christ that died,
yea rather, that is risen again, who is even at the right hand of God,
who also maketh intercession for us.
ROMANS 8:33–34

Father, 'twas thy love that knew us
Earth's foundation long before:
That same love to Jesus drew us
By its sweet constraining pow'r,
And will keep us, and will keep us,
Safely, now and ever more.

JAMES G. DECK (1807–1884)
FATHER, 'TWAS THY LOVE THAT KNEW US

THE LOVE OF GOD IN CHRIST

"I proceeded forth and came from God," said Jesus to the Pharisees, "neither came I of myself, but he sent me" (John 8:42). This brings to mind the Father's great love for us. In order to know God, let us appreciate his love displayed in Christ, his beloved, the Son of his love (Colossians 1:13).

Some people set up God in contrast to the Son as if one is unrelated to the other. To them, God is stern and relentless. The Son, on the other hand, is tender, merciful, and loving. The way they see it, only Jesus Christ prevents the angry God from striking the guilty sinner. He holds back God's wrath with one hand and extends the other in compassion and mercy toward the sinner. This awful caricature disagrees with two fundamental principles: First, love is the motive behind all that God does (1 John 4:16). Second, God is the prime mover in redemption. Therefore we read, "God was in Christ, reconciling the world unto himself" (2 Corinthians 5:19).

God is the origin of redemption; Christ reveals God's will and achieves his purpose. Christ's redemptive work was not the cause of the Father's love to love us. Rather, Christ's redemption flows out of that love.

> *The love of God is shed abroad in our hearts by the Holy Ghost*
> *which is given unto us. For when we were yet without strength,*
> *in due time Christ died for the ungodly. . . . But God commendeth*
> *his love toward us, in that, while we were yet sinners, Christ died for us.*
> ROMANS 5:5–6, 8

We think of the man in thy presence,
Set down there, exalted as head;
Once raised by the might of thy power,
When numbered along with the dead.

AUTHOR UNKNOWN
WE THINK OF THE MAN IN THY PRESENCE

THE EXALTATION OF JESUS CHRIST

The name Jesus is full of significance. It is the Greek word for the Hebrew *Joshua*, which is a shortened form of *Jehovah-Hoshea*, "Jehovah-Savior." Jehovah is the title of the almighty God in association with the ages in which he is revealing himself. The cross of Christ the Savior stands at the center point of those ages. Therefore, Jesus is the fitting name of the Savior whom God sent into this age to rescue creation from the oppression of sin, devastation, and death.

As this hymn says, Jesus was numbered along with the dead. From that lowest place, Jesus is exalted as head of all. His reward for subjecting himself to utter humiliation is the worship and acclamation of the universe (Philippians 2:6–11). So we read, "At the name of Jesus every knee should bow. . .and. . .every tongue should confess that Jesus Christ is Lord" (vv. 10–11).

This praise will not wait until the end when the last enemy is subdued (1 Corinthians 15:26, 28). Presently, Christ is "at the right hand of God, with angels, authorities, and powers made subject to him" (1 Peter 3:22 NRSV). When he returns, the earth will know him as King. Eventually, even beings under the earth, whatever they may be, will worship and obey him. Celestial, terrestrial, and subterranean—all will bow the knee in worship and acclaim that Jesus, the Crucified One, is Lord. And this is for one grand purpose the glory of God, the Father (Philippians 2:11).

For to this end Christ both died, and rose, and revived, that he might be Lord both of the dead and living. . . . For it is written, As I live, saith the Lord, every knee shall bow to me, and every tongue shall confess to God.
ROMANS 14:9, 11

Thou great and good, thou just and wise,
Thou art my Father and my God;
And I am thine by sacred ties;
Thy son, thy servant, bought with blood.

ISAAC WATTS (1674–1748)
GREAT GOD, INDULGE MY HUMBLE CLAIM

THE UNITY OF THE FATHER AND THE SON

Love is the essence of God's being (1 John 4:16). This fact lies at the foundation of our faith and of all things. In harmony with this vast love, scripture calls God "Father." The writings of John focus attention on the love of God and often refer to the Father. They record that Jesus, time and again, referred to God as "My Father."

The relationship between the Son and the Father is seen in one simple statement: "[He] is the image of the invisible God" (Colossians 1:15). An image is in every possible way an exact representation of its original. This is especially true of the living image of God. Only in him can we see the Father. Many of us, however, are like Philip. When the Lord said, "If ye had known me, ye should have known my Father also," Philip replied, "Lord, show us the Father, and it sufficeth us." Jesus then explained, "Have I been so long time with you, and yet hast thou not known me, Philip? he that hath seen me hath seen the Father" (John 14:7–9).

The unity of the Father and the Son is so close that, by observation, there is no difference. The love, care, and provision of the Father were entirely manifested in Jesus Christ. It was impossible to know him without, at the same time, becoming acquainted with the Father. God is invisible, but this is not a problem for those of us who believe, since his Son is "the brightness of his glory, and the express image of his person" (Hebrews 1:3).

Then said they unto him, Where is thy Father? Jesus answered,
Ye neither know me, nor my Father: if ye had known me,
ye should have known my Father also.
JOHN 8:19

Of all the gifts thy love bestows,
Thou giver of all good!
E'en heav'n itself no richer knows
Than Jesus and his blood.

WILLIAM COWPER (1731–1800)
OF ALL THE GIFTS THY LOVE BESTOWS

THE LOVE THAT TRANSCENDS KNOWLEDGE

The apostle John was an eyewitness of Jesus Christ's love, and his Gospel describes the sacrificial quality of that love. Paul, on the other hand, was an apostle of the ascended Christ. He did not know the Lord in the flesh. So he tells how God's love in Christ reaches the whole creation. The combined testimony of these two men expresses the tender intimacy and vast reach of the sacrifice at Calvary.

John recorded these words of the Good Shepherd: "Therefore doth my Father love me, because I lay down my life, that I might take it again. No man taketh it from me, but I lay it down of myself. I have power to lay it down, and I have power to take it again" (John 10:17–18). Christ was competent in every way to die the death that would forever heal the breach between God and his creation.

Although Jesus Christ had authority to command legions of angels (Matthew 26:53), he made the journey from Gethsemane to Golgotha all alone. There he used his power to lay down his life. As he did so, he prayed a prayer of sweetest fragrance: "Father, forgive them; for they know not what they do" (Luke 23:34). What words more deeply express the potency of his love? He asked his Father to trade mercy for ignorance and grace for guilt. That exchange was made that day when the sky darkened over Jerusalem.

With this in view, we pray to "know the love of Christ, which passeth knowledge, [and to] be filled with all the fulness of God" (Ephesians 3:19).

Who will have all men to be saved, and to come unto the knowledge of the truth. For there is one God, and one mediator between God and men, the man Christ Jesus; who gave himself a ransom for all, to be testified in due time.
1 TIMOTHY 2:4–6

To God be the glory, great things he has done;
So loved he the world that he gave us his Son,
Who yielded his life an atonement for sin,
And opened the life gate that all may go in.

FANNY J. CROSBY (1820–1915)
TO GOD BE THE GLORY

GLORIFY GOD AS GOD

The glory of God is the goal toward which all creation travels, and the achievement of the cross will cause this to be realized. Though God's glory is the goal, this does not mean that he has not always been glorious. Rather, he has not yet been recognized and glorified by his creation. God has always been righteous, wise, and filled with love, but this is difficult for us to appreciate because of the presence of sin and corruption. This is why humanity does not glorify God as God (Romans 1:21). Instead, we project upon him our own ignorance and limitations, going about our business as if God did not create all things, is not in total control of that creation, and cannot successfully operate his purposes for it from beginning to end (11:36).

How will God ever be fully glorified as God? As time passes, God's glory will be realized and enjoyed by each of his creatures until they are genuinely righteous and incorruptible. Then, from their very core, they will bring him glory. We who now believe began to appreciate God's glory when we first believed in Christ. We mature in the faith as we grasp who and what God is and what he has accomplished in the Son. This is the way God is glorified. The end of this path will come "in a moment, in the twinkling of an eye, at the last trump: for the trumpet shall sound, and the dead shall be raised incorruptible, and we shall be changed" (1 Corinthians 15:52). Then we will glorify God to such an extent that even our bodies will be glorious (Philippians 3:21).

Moreover whom he did predestinate, them he also called: and whom he called, them he also justified: and whom he justified, them he also glorified.
ROMANS 8:30

No wrath God's heart retaineth
To usward who believe
No dread in ours remaineth
As we his love receive.

MARY B. PETERS (1813–1856)
BY THEE, O GOD, INVITED

A STUDY OF THE WORD *WRATH*

Two things are necessary for personal study of the scriptures: a copy of the Bible, unadorned by notes or commentary, and a concordance. This does not mean we shouldn't look to others to help us know the truth. For example, a believer does not have to personally discover the truth of justification by faith. Martin Luther did this for us. But, until we go to the scriptures and make that truth our own revelation, it will not become an influence in our life and faith. No teaching or ministry qualifies as the bread of life. Only God's Word is our spiritual food (Luke 4:4).

Mary Peters uses the word *wrath* in her hymn. What is wrath, scripturally speaking? A concordance shows that the King James Version uses this word forty-seven times. The first is John the Baptist's warning against the wrath to come (Matthew 3:7). An examination of each occurrence of the word brings the student to Romans 5:9, which says that we will be saved from wrath because we are justified by the blood of Christ. Scripture teaches that God's wrath comes on the children of disobedience (Colossians 3:6) and that God has not appointed us to wrath (1 Thessalonians 5:9).

Eventually our concordant study leads to the book of Revelation and the answer to our question. Almost a third of the occurrences of "wrath" are here. This book records the pouring out of God's wrath on the earth (Revelation 16:1). Most of the events in Revelation occur during the last three and one-half years of this age. They give meaning to the word *wrath*. Now we see, with the help of a concordance, the full expression of wrath, and that the phrase "saved from wrath" means that believers will not experience the terrifying events at the close of this age.

Much more then, being now justified by his blood, we shall be saved from wrath through him.
ROMANS 5:9

Abba, Father! We adore thee, Humbly now our homage pay;
'Tis thy children's bliss to know thee, None but children "Abba" say.
This high honor we inherit, Thy free gift through Jesus' blood;
Thine own Spirit with our spirit, Witnesseth we're sons of God.

ROBERT S. HAWKER (1804–1873)
ABBA, FATHER! WE APPROACH THEE

THE INDWELLING HOLY SPIRIT

Paul's epistles begin by describing the human heart as foolish, darkened, lustful, hard, and unrepentant (Romans 1:21, 24; 2:5). But they end with a heart that is clean and pure (1 Timothy 1:5; 2 Timothy 2:22). This agrees with Peter's statement to the conference in Jerusalem that God, who knows human hearts, purified the hearts of the Gentiles by faith (Acts 15:9).

How is it possible for God to do this? Nowhere does Paul say that our nature has changed. However, we do find that God has given us the earnest of the Spirit in our hearts (2 Corinthians 1:22). His sending the Spirit into our hearts has made us sons of God who call out to him, "Abba, Father" (Galatians 4:6). In other words, our hearts have been cleansed by the indwelling of the Holy Spirit (Romans 8:11). The place where God dwells is always made holy by his presence.

The temple at Jerusalem, for example, had beautiful buildings, the sacred ritual, and the proper sacrifices, but these great things did not make it holy. Without the presence of the glory of God, it was nothing more than an orderly pile of stone (2 Chronicles 7:1). Likewise, dry, desert ground was made holy when the Lord met Moses there (Exodus 3:5). A believer's body is God's temple because the divine Spirit indwells the human heart. The purity this Spirit imparts to our hearts enables us to glorify God in our bodies.

> *Know ye not that your body is the temple of the Holy Ghost which is in you...and ye are not your own? For ye are bought with a price: therefore glorify God in your body, and in your spirit, which are God's.*
> 1 CORINTHIANS 6:19–20

Of the Father's love begotten, Ere the worlds began to be,
He is Alpha and Omega, He the source, the ending he,
Of the things that are, that have been, And that future years shall see.

AURELIUS CLEMENS PRUDENTIUS (348–ABOUT 413)
OF THE FATHER'S LOVE BEGOTTEN
TRANSLATED BY JOHN M. NEALE (1818–1866)

THE THREE TITLES OF CHRIST

The last book of scripture concludes God's revelation to mankind. It also describes the end of the divine purpose within the ages. Plus, it depicts the final scene of the ages (Revelation 21:1). Each of these three aspects of Christ's work furnishes him with an appropriate title (22:13). He is the first and the last letter of the alphabet used in God's revelation. He is also the beginning and the end, because all began in him and will be headed up in him. And he is the first and the last in time during which God's plan is carried out.

Our Lord is the Alpha and the Omega—the first and last letters in the Greek alphabet. Like the English *A* and *Z*, the first letter often symbolizes a beginning and the last an ending. In revealing himself, God has used innumerable characters, but the first one was Christ and the last one will be Christ. God commences and concludes his revelation in him.

Christ inaugurates and completes God's purpose; therefore he is the beginning and the end. "He himself is before all things" (Colossians 1:17 NRSV). That is, he is the inauguration of God's purpose. At its completion, all is headed up in Christ (Ephesians 1:10).

The designation "the first and the last" points to the time aspect. The scriptures deal with a number of eons or ages. Christ was active at their beginning in the work of creation (Revelation 3:14). At their ultimate consummation, he will have subdued all things, including the last enemy, death. Then he will deliver the kingdom to the Father, and God will at last be all in all (1 Corinthians 15:24–26, 28).

I am Alpha and Omega, the beginning and the end, the first and the last.
REVELATION 22:13

*Jesus! That name we love, Jesus, our Lord! Jesus, all names above,
Jesus, the Lord! Thou, Lord, our all must be; Nothing that's good have we;
Nothing apart from thee. Jesus, our Lord!*

JAMES G. DECK (1807–1884)
JESUS! THAT NAME WE LOVE

JESUS CHRIST IS LORD

Paul rarely used the name Jesus unaccompanied by a title, because this is the name of God's Son as he lived on this earth. Paul never knew Jesus Christ in the flesh, but he first encountered him in his ascension. So Paul usually accompanies the name Jesus with the titles Lord or Christ or both. This acknowledges the Son's inherent, official preeminence.

A person who meets the president of the United States calls him "Mr. President" or "President Bush" or at least "Sir." To call him "George" may be taken as an insult or a denial of his position and power. His family may address him by a private name without giving offense, but it is unwise for others to omit his title. Let us not fail to give God's Son his proper place in our hearts and prayers by calling our Master "Lord" and our Savior "Christ."

We do love the name Jesus, however. It is "all names above" because it refers to the depth of his humiliation. On the day he was obedient to the death of the cross, the skies darkened, and his Father's face turned away. When he was the suffering sacrifice, he brought a glory to that name that exalts it above every name. From the moment of his resurrection, knees began to bow to him and tongues began to confess, "Jesus Christ is Lord." You have done this, and so have I. His exaltation continues today and will continue until the end. Then, every knee will bow and every tongue will acclaim Jesus Christ as Lord (1 Corinthians 15:23–28; Philippians 2:10–11).

And being found in fashion as a man, he humbled himself, and became obedient unto death, even the death of the cross. Wherefore God also hath highly exalted him, and given him a name which is above every name.
PHILIPPIANS 2:8–9

THE VOICE OF THE BLOOD OF CHRIST

The blood of Christ speaks better things than that of Abel (Hebrews 12:24). Abel's blood cried, "Vengeance!" so Cain spent his life accursed from the earth. Jesus Christ's death also brought down a curse, but not on his murderers. He bore the curse himself (Galatians 3:13). The voice of the blood of Christ sings, "Grace and peace!"

Nothing has had such profound effect upon the world as the Crucifixion of Jesus Christ. It is transforming alienated humankind into adoring worshippers. It conciliates God to the world. All those who receive that conciliation are reconciled to him (2 Corinthians 5:18–21). But this does not exhaust the power of the blood. It is the basis of all future blessings even beyond the consummation of the ages (1 Corinthians 15:23–24).

The phrase "the blood of Christ" expresses the permanent power of our Lord's death (Ephesians 2:13). In the Jewish ritual, blood was sprinkled once a year in the Holy of Holies on the day of propitiation. This sacrifice was effective for twelve months. Likewise, the suffering of Christ is past, but its effectiveness is unending. Figuratively speaking, his blood remains always within the holiest in heaven as a witness to his offering (Hebrews 9:20–25).

The phrase "the blood of his cross" takes us deeper. This is only found in Colossians 1:20, and it combines Christ's death—the blood—with the means of that death—the cross. The blood speaks of pain and agony. The cross speaks of humiliation and shame. These combine to bring peace to the universe and to reconcile all things to God.

And, having made peace through the blood of his cross, by him to reconcile all things unto himself; by him, I say, whether they be things in earth, or things in heaven. . .
COLOSSIANS 1:20

Come, Lord, and tarry not;
Bring the long looked for day;
O why these years of waiting here,
These ages of decay?

HORATIUS BONAR (1808–1889)
COME, LORD, AND TARRY NOT

THE LOVE OF HIS APPEARING

It is sometime in the middle of the decade of AD 60. The believers in the province of Asia have turned away from the apostle Paul (2 Timothy 1:15). The churches are slipping into apostasy, having a form of godliness but denying its power (3:1–5). The time of Paul's departure from this life is near.

What has become of Paul's plans—a trip to Spain (Romans 15:24), wintering in Nicopolis (Titus 3:12), a visit to the Colossians (Philemon 22)? There is no record that any of these were accomplished. No one stands with him in the Roman court. All forsake him (2 Timothy 4:16). In the midst of apparent failure, Paul faces death in triumph (vv. 6–8). He has kept the faith, and a reward awaits him. He has always longed for the coming of Christ, and he assures Timothy and all who believe that the victor's wreath of righteousness will crown those who love the appearing of Jesus Christ (v. 8). This fact alone is sufficient incentive for us not only to love but also to proclaim our expectation of Christ's glorious return.

Jesus Christ's testimony in the book of Revelation ends with these words: "Surely I come quickly." The loving response is, "Even so, come, Lord Jesus" (22:20). We have no other help, no other hope; yet we long for him not merely for our own happiness, but that his glory will be seen and all creation will be be blessed (Romans 8:21). Let us continually pray, "Come, Lord Jesus!"

For I am now ready to be offered, and the time of my departure is at hand. I have fought a good fight, I have finished my course, I have kept the faith: Henceforth there is laid up for me a crown of righteousness, which the Lord, the righteous judge, shall give me at that day: and not to me only, but unto all them also that love his appearing.
2 TIMOTHY 4:6–8

Himself he could not save,
Our sins' full weight must fall
Upon the sinless one;
For nothing less can God accept
In payment of that fearful debt.

ALBERT MIDLANE (1825–1909)
HIMSELF HE COULD NOT SAVE

THE SWEET-SMELLING SAVOR

We were all once like ancient Israel, wearying God with our sins and iniquities (Isaiah 43:24). In response, God sent his Son and made him a sin offering to take our sins in his body onto the accursed tree (2 Corinthians 5:21; 1 Peter 2:24). As a result, we have the following astonishing fact: "God was in Christ, reconciling the world unto himself, not imputing their trespasses unto them" (2 Corinthians 5:19).

God has entrusted this glorious good news to us. Consider this: "We are ambassadors for Christ, as though God did beseech you by us: we pray you in Christ's stead, be ye reconciled to God" (v. 20). We are honored to make known to this world God's immeasurable love, which is poured out so all may become God's righteousness in Christ (v. 21). This is almost too great for our limited comprehension. It is as if we have encountered God in a burning bush. We are suddenly on holy ground (Exodus 3:5). In Christ, all barriers are down. Our sins are no longer a hindrance, because God made his Son, who did not know sin, to be a sin offering for us.

As the hymn says, "Nothing less can God accept in payment of that fearful debt." Nor can we contribute anything of value to this divine achievement of peace and righteousness. Yet God has enriched us with two jewels of divine truth set in our hearts: In Christ, God was with us (Matthew 1:23). In Christ, we are with God (Colossians 3:3).

Thanks be to God for his indescribable gift!
2 CORINTHIANS 9:15 NRSV

Not all the blood of beasts
On Jewish altars slain
Could give the guilty conscience peace
Or wash away the stain.

ISAAC WATTS (1674–1748)
NOT ALL THE BLOOD OF BEASTS

THE FINALITY OF THE WORK OF CHRIST

This hymn refers to Hebrews 9, which contrasts the Jewish rituals in the tabernacle with the Lord's sacrifice (vv. 1–14). This chapter shows that Israel never learned the lesson of God's design for the tabernacle. He divided its holy places into two compartments, and he hid himself behind thick curtains in the inner one. There he was out of reach to all but the high priest, who only entered this sacred area once a year (v. 7). Today we can see that the way to God was not open to Israel, and the rituals of the tabernacle were powerless to open it. The tabernacle and its offerings were temporary measures, lasting only until Christ would clear away all barriers by his better sacrifice. The book of Hebrews reveals that the rituals and sacrifices connected with Israel's tabernacle and temple were patterns of something far more profound. They portrayed the sacrifice of Christ himself and the final putting away of sin.

Hebrews tells of the finality of the work of Christ. Israel's priests had to offer sacrifices continually (10:1). These were presented year after year and could never finally perfect the people who offered them. Yet Christ remains a priest continually. He offered one sacrifice and is now seated at the right hand of God, his work complete. His one offering is permanent; he is forever able to perfect those who are sanctified by it (7:3; 10:12, 14).

And every priest standeth daily ministering and offering oftentimes the same sacrifices, which can never take away sins: but this man, after he had offered one sacrifice for sins for ever, sat down on the right hand of God; from henceforth expecting till his enemies be made his footstool. For by one offering he hath perfected for ever them that are sanctified.
HEBREWS 10:11–14

Glory be to Jesus, who, in bitter pains,
Poured for me the life blood from his sacred veins!
Grace and life eternal in that blood I find;
Blest be his compassion, infinitely kind.

EDWARD CASWALL (1814–1878)
GLORY BE TO JESUS

GOD'S INFINITE COMPASSION

The scriptures describe a number of people as being just or righteous. Abel, Lot, Zechariah and his wife Elizabeth, Mary's husband Joseph, John the Baptist, and Joseph of Arimathea are a few of these. The word *righteous* is actually used three times in connection with Abel (Matthew 23:35; Hebrews 11:4) and three times in connection with Lot (2 Peter 2:7–8). All these people were certainly just in comparison with those around them. Compare Abel with Cain, for example. Lot was righteous in contrast with his neighbors in Sodom, and Zechariah was exceptional in comparison to the corrupt priesthood of his day.

But in Romans, we confront the absolute righteousness of God, and we learn that no flesh will be justified in his sight (3:20). In this light, even these saints are like all other people: They fall short. That shortfall is called sin.

All failure is sin. For example, the book of Judges mentions men who were so expert with the sling that when they shot they never "sinned" (20:16). That is, they never missed the mark. This is the real meaning of sin. Not only is sin the disobedience of laws and commands, but it is also our failure to attain absolute perfection. To sin is to fall short, to miss the mark.

A single sin brought about the moral chaos that we see all around us (Genesis 3:6): "Wherefore, as by one man sin entered into the world, and death by sin; and so death passed upon all men, for that all have sinned" (Romans 5:12). This brings us to the infinite compassion mentioned in today's hymn.

But the free gift is not like the trespass. For if the many died through the one man's trespass, much more surely have the grace of God and the free gift in the grace of the one man, Jesus Christ, abounded for the many.
ROMANS 5:15 NRSV

It passeth knowledge, that dear love of thine!
My Jesus! Savior! yet this soul of mine
Would of that love, in all its depth and length,
Its height and breadth, and everlasting strength
Know more and more.

MARY SHEKLETON (1827–1883)
IT PASSETH KNOWLEDGE

BE IMITATORS OF GOD

"To know the love of Christ, which passeth knowledge" (Ephesians 3:19). What believer would not join Mary Shekleton in this prayer? Let's consider what life is like where this prayer is offered and answered.

Ephesians 5 begins with a seemingly impossible appeal: "Be imitators of God" (v. 1 NRSV). But scripture immediately tells us how to do this: "And live in love, as Christ loved us and gave himself up for us" (v. 2 NRSV). Colossians provides the details of such a life: "As God's chosen ones, holy and beloved, clothe yourselves with compassion, kindness, humility, meekness, and patience. Bear with one another and, if anyone has a complaint against another, forgive each other; just as the Lord has forgiven you, so you also must forgive. Above all, clothe yourselves with love, which binds everything together in perfect harmony" (Colossians 3:12–14 NRSV).

In the ages to come, we will be used by God to display his transcendent grace among the celestials (Ephesians 2:6–7). Shouldn't we now prepare for that service by being gracious to the people around us? In this way, because of our present portion of grace, we are imitators of God. Believers who make the prayers of Ephesians their plea to him take great strides to this end (1:17–19; 3:14–19).

If there be therefore any consolation in Christ, if any comfort of love, if any
fellowship of the Spirit, if any bowels and mercies, fulfil ye my joy, that ye
be likeminded, having the same love, being of one accord, of one mind. Let
nothing be done through strife or vainglory; but in lowliness of mind let
each esteem other better than themselves. Look not every man on his own
things, but every man also on the things of others.
PHILIPPIANS 2:1–4

> *But though I cannot tell, or sing, or know,*
> *The fullness of thy love while here below,*
> *My empty vessel I may freely bring:*
> *O thou, who art of love the living spring,*
> *My vessel fill.*

MARY SHEKLETON (1827–1883)
IT PASSETH KNOWLEDGE

THE GOSPEL'S SKELETON

Christ is the sole subject of the gospel. Three events in his life form its core, each of which occurred within a period of three days: Jesus Christ died, was entombed, and rose again (1 Corinthians 15:3–4). He died for our sins, and his resurrection is proof of their elimination. This is so simple yet so magnificent. It is the message that saves humankind. Mary Shekleton knew she could not fully understand the fullness of God's love. Though it is completely revealed in the gospel, its depths cannot be found, and its heights of glory cannot be crested. Still, we thank God that the Spirit has poured it into our hearts (Romans 5:5).

God's love is expressed in the gospel, which is concerned with the Son and the part of his career that causes our salvation. Without three facts—Christ's death, burial, and resurrection—there is no gospel (1 Corinthians 15:1–4). Yet this is only a skeleton outline of the complete story. There is much more to be said about the effects of Jesus Christ's sacrifice upon God and man. So 1 Corinthians 15:3–4, the verses that provide this outline, twice use the following phrase: "according to the scriptures." These two verses are a thumbnail sketch of vast fields of truth mapped out in detail elsewhere in the sacred scriptures. Only these "are able to instruct you for salvation through faith in Christ Jesus" (2 Timothy 3:15 NRSV).

For I delivered unto you first of all that which I also received, how that Christ died for our sins according to the scriptures; and that he was buried, and that he rose again the third day according to the scriptures.
1 CORINTHIANS 15:3–4

He is speaking to his Father,
Tasting deep that bitter cup,
Yet he takes it, willing rather
For our sakes to drink it up.

JOSIAH HOPKINS (1786–1862)
LORD, THY LOVE HAS SOUGHT AND FOUND US

THE SON'S OBEDIENCE TO HIS FATHER'S WILL

The book of Hebrews gives a glimpse of Jesus Christ as he prayed in Gethsemane: "Who in the days of his flesh, when he had offered up prayers and supplications with strong crying and tears unto him that was able to save him from death. . .yet learned he obedience by the things which he suffered" (5:7–8). Elsewhere we read of him "being found in appearance as a man, he humbled himself and became obedient to death—even death on a cross!" (Philippians 2:8 NIV).

God's will was foremost in the life of Jesus Christ, and it was his nature to be obedient to that will. "My meat is to do the will of him that sent me," he explained to his disciples, "and to finish his work" (John 4:34). But that obedience was put to the test time after time. At the beginning of Jesus' public ministry, Satan tempted him to avoid the cross (Matthew 4:8–9). Later Peter repeated Satan's appeal (16:21–23). The week of his death, Greeks sought out the Lord Jesus as if he were a celebrity to be exalted (John 12:20). In response, he simply said that his glory was to die like a seed in the ground (vv. 23–24). Later, when he was troubled in soul, he would not say, "Father save me from this hour." Instead, he prayed, "Father, glorify thy name" (vv. 27–28). Finally, in Gethsemane, as this same battle raged within his soul, Jesus Christ, struggling in tearful prayers, became obedient to the death of the cross (Philippians 2:8).

And he was withdrawn from them about a stone's cast, and kneeled down, and prayed, saying, Father, if thou be willing, remove this cup from me: nevertheless not my will, but thine, be done. . . . And his sweat was as it were great drops of blood falling down to the ground.
LUKE 22:41–42, 44

And to an ocean fullness, His mercy doth expand;
His grace is all-sufficient And by his wisdom planned.

ANNE R. COUSIN (1824–1906)
THE SANDS OF TIME ARE SINKING

THE END OF THE LORD

God used a physical illness and a request for healing to further Paul's maturity. Second Corinthians 12:7–10 tells the story of the thorn in the apostle's flesh. This festering foreign object symbolizes a physical ailment that caused suffering for Paul. He called it "the messenger of Satan to buffet me" (v. 7).

God once delivered another man to Satan: Job was flawless, faithful, upright, fearing God, and withdrawing from all evil (Job 1:1). Why would God allow such an exemplary person to be plagued by Satan? Job's story teaches this: A person with a faith that glorifies God in severe suffering knows God's all-sufficient grace more than a person who basks in blessing. James condenses this lesson to one sentence: "Ye have heard of the patience of Job, and have seen the end of the Lord" (James 5:11). Job describes the Lord's end, or purpose, for his suffering like this: "I had heard of you by the hearing of the ear, but now my eye sees you" (Job 42:5 NRSV).

Satan assumes God's saints cannot bear misfortune without turning their back on him (Job 1:11). However, Satan does not include God's grace in the equation. God's strength is perfected not in our blessings or accomplishments but in our weakness; his grace is sufficient in any case (2 Corinthians 12:9).

Paul was given many trials—beatings, shipwreck, hunger, thirst, robbers, cold, nakedness, and manifold dangers—yet these were minor in comparison to the revelations given to him (2 Corinthians 11:23–12:1). A person could glory in such phenomenal revelations forever. But through suffering Paul learned grace and said:

Most gladly therefore will I rather glory in my infirmities, that the power of Christ may rest upon me. Therefore I take pleasure in infirmities, in reproaches, in necessities, in persecutions, in distresses for Christ's sake: for when I am weak, then am I strong.
2 CORINTHIANS 12:9–10

June 21

*God moves in a mysterious way
His wonders to perform;
He plants his footsteps in the sea,
And rides upon the storm.*

William Cowper (1731–1800)
God Moves in a Mysterious Way

The Image of the Invisible God

William Cowper's couplet is well loved among believers and is familiar even to people who may never have sung a hymn. We do not wish to diminish the pleasure in its wisdom. However, the fact is, we do know how God performs his wonders.

God is an invisible Spirit, so he was formerly a mystery (John 4:24; 1 Timothy 6:16). The Son of God is the visible, tangible embodiment of the invisible God (Colossians 1:15). Only in Christ can we see God (John 14:9–10). All other images that pretend to portray him are condemned because they are false, dishonoring, and misrepresentative of God (Deuteronomy 5:8). Although no one can see God, the disciples saw all his attributes in the Son.

Long before Jesus walked in Galilee, all creation was in the Son just as the tree and its fruit are found in the seed (Colossians 1:16). God created everything in him. The celestial and terrestrial spheres and every form of power and authority exist through him and for him. In addition to this, all things are held together in him for the accomplishment of God's purpose (v. 17). All this was formerly a mystery, but since Jesus Christ came and the apostle completed the Word of God (v. 25), that mystery is revealed and we know that God exclusively operates through Christ.

*Who is the image of the invisible God, the firstborn of every creature:
For by him were all things created, that are in heaven, and that are in earth, visible and invisible, whether they be thrones, or dominions, or principalities, or powers: all things were created by him, and for him: and he is before all things, and by him all things consist.*
Colossians 1:15–17

O Christ, he is the fountain.
The deep, sweet well of love!
The streams of earth I've tasted
More deep I'll drink above.

ANNE R. COUSIN (1824–1906)
THE SANDS OF TIME ARE SINKING

FROM THE FATHER THROUGH THE SON

In former days, people drew water in buckets from wells or collected it at springs. Their water had its source deep in the earth where they could not go. The scriptures similarly describe the Father and the Son: "There is one God, the Father, from whom are all things and for whom we exist, and one Lord, Jesus Christ, through whom are all things and through whom we exist" (1 Corinthians 8:6 NRSV). In other words, the Father is the source and the Son is the course of all things. As the hymn writer sang, "O Christ, he is the fountain."

All is out of God (Romans 11:36). This is the most basic principal of truth. But God does not deliver all things to us directly. All that is out of God comes to us through the Son, the deep, sweet well of life. This is important because it describes the relationship of the Father and Son and our relationship to both of them.

The word *diameter* means the distance through a circle. *Dia* is a Greek word meaning "through." So "all things came into being through—dia—him" (John 1:3 NRSV). The King James Version says "by him" in this verse. However, the Greek word for "by" is not found here. Elsewhere, we read, "The world was came into being through—dia—him" (John 1:10 NRSV), and "God, through—dia—Jesus Christ, will judge the secret thoughts of all" (Romans 2:16).

Closer to home, the order is the same: We all love to taste the living streams that save from grief and strife. These come to us from God himself as our Savior who brings us redemption through his beloved Son (1 Timothy 1:1; 4:10; Ephesians 1:6–7).

I proceeded forth and came from God.
JOHN 8:42

Jesus, thou art my righteousness,
For all my sins were thine;
Thy death hath bought of God my peace,
Thy life hath made him mine.

CHARLES WESLEY (1707–1788)
FOREVER HERE MY REST SHALL BE

CHRIST, OUR RIGHTEOUSNESS

The best expression of God's love for humankind is found in 2 Corinthians 5:21—God makes Christ to be sin for us. This means that our sin was made Christ's and was destroyed in his death on the cross. Let's review this magnificent truth.

God was in Christ reconciling the world to himself (v. 19). When people receive that reconciliation, they become God's righteousness in Christ, and they are at peace with God (v. 21). What good news! God's condemnation of sin was exhausted by Christ's death. As a result, we become his righteousness in Christ. This is the basis of peace.

On the cross, Christ was made sin and absorbed the force of God's condemnation. Now, we have true righteousness—the righteousness of God in Christ. While we were still God's enemies, God dealt with sin in Christ by making him sin for our sakes (Romans 5:10). Now people can receive God's conciliation by faith and lift up their heads in peace.

In introducing this love of God, scripture declares, "All things are of God" (2 Corinthians 5:18). This means that God did all this in Christ without human assistance. The death of the Son is the only reason we are reconciled with God. The evidence that God is satisfied with Christ's work is that he does not charge men and women with their trespasses (v. 19). We who understand these things are God's ambassadors, bearing this message to the world: "Be ye reconciled to God" (v. 20).

And all things are of God, who hath reconciled us to himself by Jesus Christ. . . . God was in Christ, reconciling the world unto himself, not imputing their trespasses unto them. . . . For he hath made him to be sin for us, who knew no sin; that we might be made the righteousness of God in him.
2 CORINTHIANS 5:18–19, 21

A mind at perfect peace with God;
What a word is this!
A sinner reconciled through blood;
This, this indeed is peace.

CATESBY PAGET (NINETEENTH CENTURY)
A MIND AT PERFECT PEACE WITH GOD

THE SOLUTION TO SIN AND ENMITY

Believers mature when they see God's reasons for sending the Son into the world. Such understanding enables us to appreciate the love God has lavished upon us and to joyfully return that love to him.

Catesby Paget considered herself "a sinner reconciled through blood." This statement touches two vital matters in Christ's work that solve humankind's fundamental problems in relation to God—sin and enmity. The first is solved because we are justified freely in God's grace through the redemption that is in Christ Jesus (Romans 3:25). That is, our justification by faith solves the problem of our sin.

Our enmity, or hostility, toward God is best illustrated in the life of Saul of Tarsus. He first appears in the divine record when Stephen is stoned to death (Acts 7:58; 8:1). This deed is second only to the Crucifixion in expressing Israel's opposition to the Messiah. Saul was zealously committed to that opposition. He endorsed Stephen's murder and then devastated the church (v. 3). He later described himself as "a blasphemer, and a persecutor, and injurious" (1 Timothy 1:13). No one in Israel deserved a worse fate than he. So what did God do about this virulent enemy? He didn't send Peter and the apostles to reason with Saul. Rather, the ascended Christ himself appeared to the madman, not to reckon his offenses against him, not to strike him dead, but to grant him mercy and overwhelm him with grace (v. 14). In an instant, Saul was transformed from Christ's worst human enemy to his most faithful friend. This exemplifies God's reconciliation of all mankind.

Therefore being justified by faith, we have peace with God through our Lord Jesus Christ: by whom also we have access by faith into this grace wherein we stand, and rejoice in hope of the glory of God.
ROMANS 5:1–2

So nigh, so very nigh to God,
I cannot nearer be;
For in the person of his Son
I am as near as he.

CATESBY PAGET (NINETEENTH CENTURY)
A MIND AT PERFECT PEACE WITH GOD

IN CHRIST AND IN THE LORD

When the hymn writer says she is "in the person of his Son," does this mean "in Christ," or "in the Lord"? These two have distinct scriptural meanings. In fact, they may be misunderstood and considered contradictory. For example, there is no difference between male and female in Christ (Galatians 3:28), but the wife is to be subject to her husband in the Lord (Colossians 3:18). If we focus on what we are in Christ and neglect our life in the Lord, we will be unbalanced. The opposite of this is also true. A student of scripture will be profited while considering these topics using a concordance.

In brief, the sphere of a believer's blessing is in Christ. The book of Ephesians is rich in this truth. There we learn that God has blessed us with every spiritual blessing in the celestials in Christ (1:3). We are chosen, recipients of an allotment, sealed with the Holy Spirit of promise, and made alive in Christ (vv. 4, 11, 13; 2:5–6). In him we find strength for every situation, we are complete, and we are transferred beyond the grasp of our sins and offenses (Philippians 4:13; Colossians 2:10–15).

At the same time, we were bought with a price, so we are slaves of Christ (1 Corinthians 7:22–23). That price freed us from sin and enslaved us to righteousness (Romans 6:18; 1 Corinthians 6:20). The phrase "in the Lord" reflects this aspect of our lives. The three words, "in the Lord," speak of our service (Ephesians 6:21), our labor (Romans 16:12), our place as slaves (Colossians 4:7), and our deportment (Ephesians 5:8). Anticipating our need for instruction in this truth, Ephesians 5 and 6 include a short course on what it means to be in the Lord.

Salute Tryphena and Tryphosa, who labour in the Lord. Salute the beloved
Persis, which laboured much in the Lord.
ROMANS 16:12

We may not touch his hands and side,
Nor follow where he trod;
But in his promise we rejoice,
And cry, "My Lord and God!"

HENRY ALFORD (1810–1871)
WE WALK BY FAITH

THE WAY OF GOD'S SALVATION

Those few people who believed in Jesus while he lived in Israel believed by sight because he was physically among them. At the time of Christ's resurrection, Mary Magdalene reported to the disciples, "I have seen the Lord" (see John 20:18). The disciples said the same thing to Thomas, who is the best example of those people who believe by sight (v. 25). Not until he touched the wounds on the body of the resurrected Christ did Thomas cry, "My Lord and my God" (v. 28). In fact, he may be the only person who ever believed by touch.

After the ascension (Acts 1:8–9), those in Jerusalem who believed through the work of the Twelve did so because they saw miracles. When Christ returns, the people of Israel will believe because they physically see the Christ whom they pierced on the cross (Zechariah 12:10; Revelation 1:7).

Today, however, we are saved through faith (Ephesians 2:8). We cannot see Jesus Christ, but God has given us the gift of faith to believe in him. So our salvation comes entirely from God—it has nothing to do with who we are, where we have been, or what we may or may not have seen and done. Our righteousness is of faith that it may accord with grace (Romans 4:16).

For by grace are ye saved through faith; and that not of yourselves: it is the
gift of God: not of works, lest any man should boast.
EPHESIANS 2:8–9

Teach me, Lord, some rapturous measure,
Meet for me thy grace to prove,
While I sing the countless treasure
Of my God's unchanging love.

ROBERT ROBINSON (1735–1790)
COME, THOU FOUNT OF EVERY BLESSING

GOD IS LOVE

Three little words reveal God's character—God is love (1 John 4:16). Behind all things beats his heart of infinite, unchanging love. From our point of view, life on earth may seem a never-ending, aimless tangle. Yet when the purposes of divine love have run their course, the history of the ages will be written with the one small word that declares what God is.

When light passes through a prism, it is disassembled and appears as the seven colors of the rainbow. Each color is a manifestation of light, although none shows the full spectrum. When the colors are perfectly combined, however, pure light results. This is true of love, as well. As it passes through the prism of the divinely arranged conditions of this world, it appears to us as mercy, righteousness, goodness, power, faithfulness all of the many divine attributes. None of these qualities stand alone as love, yet without each one, love would not be what it is.

Just as blue differs from red in the rainbow, so God's righteousness is to his mercy in the spectrum of love. Each proceeds from God's heart to accomplish the purpose of love, which is to create and call forth love in his creation. Love's victory comes when humanity, transformed by its elements, utterly loves God. For ages, we have borne the image of the earthy; then we will bear the image of the heavenly, and the universe will be flooded with divine affection.

Love never fails.
1 CORINTHIANS 13:8 NIV

O to grace how great a debtor
Daily I'm constrained to be!
Let thy goodness, like a fetter,
Bind my wandering heart to thee.

ROBERT ROBINSON (1735–1790)
COME, THOU FOUNT OF EVERY BLESSING

GRACE TO YOU

"Do men gather grapes of thorns," asked the Lord Jesus, "or figs of thistles?" (Matthew 7:16). The answer to this question is no. Likewise, the question, "Can the Ethiopian change his skin, or the leopard his spots?" compels us to admit that self-improvement is out of the question (Jeremiah 13:23). Therefore, we must look to God, and pray that he will make us "perfect in every good work to do his will, working in [us] that which is wellpleasing in his sight" (Hebrews 13:21).

God will answer our prayer, because he "is able to do exceeding abundantly above all that we ask or think, according to the power that worketh in us" (Ephesians 3:20). Then, when we see that prayer being answered, our attitude will surely be in harmony with the truth: "Let the one who boasts, boast in the Lord" (1 Corinthians 1:31 NRSV). In other words, we will sing with Robert Robinson, "O to grace how great a debtor daily I'm constrained to be!"

Deep in the epistles of Paul is found this description of the way God changes our lives: "For the grace of God that bringeth salvation hath appeared to all men, Teaching us that, denying ungodliness and worldly lusts, we should live soberly, righteously, and godly, in this present world" (Titus 2:11–12). Grace reigns through righteousness, and it powerfully affects us day by day (Romans 5:21). Grace teaches us to present ourselves to God as those who are alive from among the dead, and to offer our members as instruments of righteousness (6:13). This is how we live soberly, righteously, and godly in this world.

Grace to you.
ROMANS 1:7; PHILEMON 1:3

Grace, 'tis a charming sound,
Harmonious to mine ear;
Heaven with the echo shall resound,
And all the earth shall hear.

PHILIP DODDRIDGE (1702–1751)
GRACE, 'TIS A CHARMING SOUND

WE SHOULD NOT TRUST IN OURSELVES

Grace is often defined as "unmerited favor." This is true in a limited sense, especially as it relates to sinners. Actually, God's entire operation is accomplished by grace. Therefore, God calls very few wise, powerful, or noble people. Instead, he has "chosen the foolish things of the world to confound the wise; and. . .the weak things of the world to confound the things which are mighty" (1 Corinthians 1:27). The reason for this points us to grace: It rules out all boasting of human flesh (v. 29). In other words, all is of God (2 Corinthians 5:18).

The scriptures abound with examples of how "the foolishness of God is wiser than men; and the weakness of God is stronger than men" (1 Corinthians 1:25). Sisera, captain of the Canaanite army, was slain by a woman with a glass of milk and a tent peg (Judges 5:24–26). Gideon and three hundred men defeated multitudes of Midianites with pitchers, torches, and a shout (Judges 7:16–22). A shepherd boy defeated Goliath with a sling (1 Samuel 17:49). The tiny, despised nation of Israel rules the earth (Daniel 7:27). The Church is blessed in Christ with every spiritual blessing among the celestials (Ephesians 1:3). All these announce God's grace.

The service of the apostle Paul, the man who brought to us the gospel of the grace of God (Acts 20:24), began with three days of helplessness (9:8–9). He was energetic and intelligent but also self-reliant and capable. So God enrolled him in the school of grace:

In Asia. . .we were pressed out of measure, above strength, insomuch that
we despaired even of life: But we had the sentence of death in ourselves, that
we should not trust in ourselves, but in God which raiseth the dead.
2 CORINTHIANS 1:8–9

*I know not why God's wondrous grace
To me he hath made known,
Nor why, unworthy, Christ in love
Redeemed me for his own.*

DANIEL W. WHITTLE (1840–1901)
I KNOW WHOM I HAVE BELIEVED

I KNOW WHOM I HAVE BELIEVED

Paul the aged wrote his last letter to Timothy, encouraging him not to be ashamed of the Lord's testimony or of him, the imprisoned apostle to the nations (2 Timothy 1:7–8). Why would Timothy be ashamed? Perhaps it was because the situation in the churches was bleak. If perilous times had not yet come, they were certainly near (3:1). So Timothy was advised to draw upon his spirit of power, love, and sanity to suffer evil with the gospel.

It is doubtful that Timothy asked, "Why me? Why should I suffer?" By the time he received his second letter from Paul, Timothy had known and worked with the apostle for about fifteen years. He knew of his mentor's holy calling in God's purpose and grace and that this grace was given to us in Christ Jesus before the ages began (1:9). Every believer has the same holy calling and the same salvation as Timothy. And, though few modern believers must suffer evil for the gospel like Timothy and Paul did, we can be encouraged by Paul's words just as Daniel Whittle was. He made them the chorus of his beautiful hymn (v. 12):

> *But I know whom I have believed,*
> *And am persuaded that he is able*
> *To keep that which I've committed*
> *Unto him against that day.*

But be thou partaker of the afflictions of the gospel according to the power of God; who hath saved us, and called us with an holy calling, not according to our works, but according to his own purpose and grace, which was given us in Christ Jesus before the world began, but is now made manifest by the appearing of our Savior Jesus Christ, who hath abolished death, and hath brought life and immortality to light through the gospel.
2 TIMOTHY 1:8–10

I know not when my Lord may come,
At night or noonday fair,
Nor if I'll walk the vale with him,
Or meet him in the air.

DANIEL W. WHITTLE (1840–1901)
I KNOW WHOM I HAVE BELIEVED

THE LOVE OF HIS APPEARING

When Paul realizes his death is near, he briefly reviews his life: "I have fought a good fight, I have finished my course, I have kept the faith" (2 Timothy 4:7). Then he looks to the future and adds, "Henceforth there is laid up for me a crown of righteousness, which the Lord, the righteous judge, shall give me at that day" (v. 8). Not surprisingly, however, Paul doesn't think only of himself but also of those who are running the race with him: "And not to me only, but unto all them also that love his appearing" (2 Timothy 4:8).

Is there a living believer who doesn't long for the victor's wreath and, even more, to be with the Lord on that day? Such a love for the Christ and his appearing is born in his love for us. The heart of the apostle's ministry is his desire that we would know that knowledge transcending love (Ephesians 3:19). He often urges us to consider it: "Christ also hath loved us, and hath given himself for us an offering and a sacrifice to God" (5:2); "Christ also loved the church, and gave himself for it" (v. 25); "I live by the faith of the Son of God, who loved me, and gave himself for me" (Galatians 2:20).

Notice that Christ's love for us is firmly linked to his sacrifice. His love is proven by his death. Let us kindle our love of him and his appearing by prayerfully weighing these things in our hearts. And, if one hears the question that once grieved Peter, "Do you love me?" (John 21:15 NRSV) remember that whether one loves him a little or a lot, it is always possible to deepen that love by the sight of the sacrifice revealed in scripture.

Grace be with all them that love our
Lord Jesus Christ in sincerity. Amen.
EPHESIANS 6:24

> But I know whom I have believed,
> And am persuaded that he is able
> To keep that which I've committed
> Unto him against that day.
>
> DANIEL W. WHITTLE (1840–1901)
> I KNOW WHOM I HAVE BELIEVED

PAUL THE OFFSCOURING OF ALL THINGS

In the final stage of the apostle's life, people were ashamed of him. Perhaps this was because of the slander he suffered when he was arrested in Jerusalem or the years he spent imprisoned as his work lay fallow (Acts 23:12–14). Certainly, those who were Judaizing Paul's work of grace among the nations had turned many people against him (Galatians 1:6–7).

In fact, all in Asia turned from him, and some desired to add affliction to his bonds (2 Timothy 1:15; Philippians 1:16). The effects of this slander had even reached his fellow worker, Timothy. So the apostle urged the young man not to be ashamed of him (2 Timothy 1:8). Even at his trial, everyone forsook Paul, although, to its credit, the household of Onesiphorus was not ashamed of him (1:16; 4:16).

This man was partaking of the afflictions of the gospel in accord with the power of God (1:8). Is it strange that someone would suffer evil because of his stand for the glorious good news of God's grace? No, not when we bear in mind that this gospel calls for the crucifixion of the flesh (Galatians 2:20; 5:24). It not only excludes human boasting but also aims for nothing less than the reconciliation of all God's estranged creatures (Colossians 1:20). Since human beings are inherently proud, they covet their fleshly glory, loving the darkness rather than the light (John 3:19). This is why Paul was defamed and "made as the filth of the world, and. . . the offscouring of all things" (1 Corinthians 4:13).

For the which cause I also suffer these things: nevertheless I am not ashamed: for I know whom I have believed, and am persuaded that he is able to keep that which I have committed unto him against that day.
2 TIMOTHY 1:12

When clothed in his brightness, transported I rise
To meet him in clouds of the sky,
His perfect salvation, his wonderful love,
I'll shout with the millions on high.

FANNY J. CROSBY (1820–1915)
HE HIDETH MY SOUL

"BEHOLD, I SHOW YOU A MYSTERY"

Here is an extraordinary statement: "He will transform the body of our humiliation so that it may be conformed to the body of his glory" (Philippians 3:21 NRSV). Scripture schedules this great occasion at the time of our Savior's advent (v. 20). First Corinthians hints at the celestial bodies that are in our future (15:40), but Philippians tells us why we will need them: We are citizens of heaven (3:20 NRSV).

If we are still living when the resurrection day arrives, our bodies will be transfigured to be like Jesus' body. Now, our bodies are unsuitable for our heavenly destiny; they are weak, mortal, corruptible, earthbound, and humiliating. As such, we cannot take them to our celestial home. So Christ will transfigure them for us. This will happen "in a moment, in the twinkling of an eye" (1 Corinthians 15:52).

The Greek word translated "moment," is *atomoo*. This is the source of the word *atom*. It literally means "uncut." The ancients knew nothing of subatomic particles like protons and neutrons. They thought the atom was the smallest unit in existence. It could not be cut into a smaller piece.

The glorious change in the bodies of the living believers will take place in an atom—not an atom of matter, but of time—the shortest time imaginable at the junction between the past and the future.

> *Behold, I shew you a mystery; We shall not all sleep, but we shall all be changed, in a moment, in the twinkling of an eye, at the last trump: for the trumpet shall sound, and the dead shall be raised incorruptible, and we shall be changed.*
> 1 CORINTHIANS 15:51–52

Consecrate me now to thy service, Lord,
By the power of grace divine;
Let my soul look up with a steadfast hope,
And my will be lost in thine.

FANNY J. CROSBY (1820–1915)
I AM THINE, O LORD

WE ARE HIS WORKMANSHIP

American believers are prosperous in a material sense, yet scripture tells us "if in this life only we have hope in Christ, we are of all men most miserable" (1 Corinthians 15:19). In contrast to us, the apostle Paul lived a life of hardship and persecution. As his life ended, he was shackled, fed prison fare, and left with little to call his own (2 Timothy 4:13). Even worse, the people to whom he had brought the light of the gospel of the glory of Christ—the ones who should have rewarded him with undying loyalty and friendship—turned against him (1:15).

He was "troubled on every side, yet not distressed. . .perplexed, but not in despair; Persecuted, but not forsaken; cast down, but not destroyed" (2 Corinthians 4:8–9). His vast spiritual wealth and rich reward for his labor and suffering were imperceptible. He is the pattern for believers (1 Timothy 1:16).

Scripture places no limit on the riches and glories that await us (2 Corinthians 4:17). These aren't promised because we deserve them. Indeed, the opposite is true. However, since God intends to display his grace and love to the heavenly hosts, we who were "without Christ, being aliens from the commonwealth of Israel, strangers from the covenants of promise, having no hope, and without God in the world" (Ephesians 2:12) are fit to be his representatives because of the grace he has lavished upon us. So, like Fanny Crosby, let us look up with steadfast hope and believe we will receive the magnificent promises of honor and glory that are ours in Christ Jesus (Romans 8:18).

Henceforth there is laid up for me a crown of righteousness, which the Lord, the righteous judge, shall give me at that day: and not to me only, but unto all them also that love his appearing.
2 TIMOTHY 4:8

Let nothing now my heart divide,
Since with thee I am crucified, and live to God in thee.
Dead to the world and all its toys,
Its idle pomp and fading joys, Jesus, my glory be.

CHARLES WESLEY (1707–1788)
COME, JESUS LORD, WITH HOLY FIRE

THE CRUCIFIXION OF THE CRIMINALS

Charles Wesley's hymn recalls a basic gospel truth: "I am crucified with Christ" (Galatians 2:20). The thieves and criminals who were physically crucified with Christ help us understand this (Matthew 27:38; Mark 15:27; Luke 23:32).

Our Lord not only died, but he underwent the humiliating ordeal of crucifixion. The world (Galatians 6:14), the flesh (5:24), the old humanity (Romans 6:6), you and me (6:8–11; Colossians 2:20), and the apostle himself (Galatians 2:20) are like the criminals, deserving of the same sentence. When we agree with the justice of our crucifixion, we will better grasp its meaning (Luke 23:41).

The unbelieving malefactor represents the world. He blasphemed and challenged Jesus Christ to immediately save him (Luke 23:39). In the same way, the world wants to be saved from its impossible predicament, but without crucifixion.

One of the criminals who was crucified with Christ had faith. He didn't ask for instant relief like the unbeliever did. Instead, he rebuked his companion for his lack of godly fear; he acknowledged the justice of his own judgment; he recognized the Savior's sinlessness (vv. 40–41). Apparently he'd heard of the promised kingdom and believed. So he looked forward in faith to his salvation in that future day (v. 42). We see ourselves in him. We who are crucified with Christ will find no glory and little relief in the present life. However, as the faithful saying declares: "If we have died with him, we will also live with him" (2 Timothy 2:11 NRSV).

That I may know him, and the power of his resurrection, and the fellowship
of his sufferings, being made conformable unto his death; if by any means I
might attain unto the resurrection of the dead.
PHILIPPIANS 3:10–11

Come, let us tune our loftiest song
And raise to Christ our joyful strain;
Worship and thanks to him belong,
Who reigns and shall forever reign.

ROBERT A. WEST (1809–1865)
COME, LET US TUNE OUR LOFTIEST SONG

THE REIGN OF CHRIST AND THE PURPOSE OF GOD

Nothing is done in heaven or earth that does not serve to advance the purpose of the ages, because God operates all in accord with the counsel of his will (Ephesians 1:11).

Robert West's hymn mentions Christ's reign, and 1 Corinthians 15:25 describes the extent and reason for it: "He must reign, till he hath put all enemies under his feet." How long will Christ rule? Until all things are subjected to him (v. 28). Why does Christ reign? To subdue all things, and his government operates to do this in the whole universe the one exception to it is God himself (v. 27).

Christ will bring creation to such a state of perfection that all need of government vanishes. Even the effects of evil, which for mankind are concentrated in death, will be gone. When the universe has been purged of all other evil, death becomes inoperative and yields up its victims (v. 26).

Presently, God is all in Christ. God will be all in the believers when we are made alive on the day of resurrection. When death is abolished at the consummation, the marvelous outcome of God's purpose and the result of Christ's reign will arrive: God will be all in all (vv. 23–28).

For he must reign, till he hath put all enemies under his feet. The last enemy that shall be destroyed is death. For he hath put all things under his feet. . . . And when all things shall be subdued unto him, then shall the Son also himself be subject unto him that put all things under him, that God may be all in all.
1 CORINTHIANS 15:25–28

July 7

*I am not skilled to understand
What God hath willed,
What God hath planned;
I only know that at his right hand
Is one who is my Savior!*

DORA GREENWELL (1821–1882)
I AM NOT SKILLED TO UNDERSTAND

GOD HAS CHOSEN THE
WEAK THINGS OF THE WORLD

God called only a few noble or wise people in Israel through the work of Jesus Christ. The most prominent of these are Nicodemus and Joseph of Arimathea, who are associated with the leadership of Israel (John 7:50; Mark 15:43). They were evidently called to perform one great service for God: to bury Jesus Christ. The Romans would have left his body hanging on the cross until it rotted away or was devoured by birds. This would not do, because Christ's burial is one of the three essentials of the gospel (1 Corinthians 15:3–4). Apparently, only these men among the disciples had the authority and the wealth to bury the Lord.

To this day the great, the noble, and the wise are a small minority among the saints of God (1:26). If high birth or exceptional wisdom or any other attainment were required for God's calling, few would measure up, and God would get little glory.

In her hymn, Dora Greenwell admits her shortcomings. Her example encourages us to stop looking for anything of value in ourselves. Let us not boast in our wisdom, holiness, or righteousness but find these only in Christ. Then let us boast to our heart's content in that which we have in him (vv. 1:30–31).

But of him are ye in Christ Jesus, who of God is made unto us wisdom, and righteousness, and sanctification, and redemption: that, according as it is written, He that glorieth, let him glory in the Lord.
1 CORINTHIANS 1:30–31

Returning sons he kisses,
And with his robe invests;
His perfect love dismisses
All terror from our breasts.

MARY B. PETERS (1813–1856)
BY THEE, O GOD, INVITED

THE GREAT GIFT AND BASIC FORCE OF THE GOSPEL

The prodigal son illustrates a wonderful truth: "Where sin abounded, grace did much more abound" (Romans 5:20). The prodigal imagined he would return to his father and, at best, become a hired hand (Luke 15:19). But his father's abounding grace—the robe, the ring, the sandals, and the fatted calf—put an end to that notion (vv. 22–23). It is the same with us. We do nothing; we are worthy of nothing, yet we are given all spiritual blessings (Ephesians 1:3).

Grace is the great gift and basic force of the gospel described in Romans. It begins with Paul, who received grace as the power of his apostleship (Romans 1:5). Its greeting is inscribed in the heart of everyone who has realized this gift: "Grace to you and peace from God our Father, and the Lord Jesus Christ" (v. 7). We know that all have sinned and come short of God's glory. Even so, we are freely justified by his grace (3:23–24).

Such justification is by faith because this is in harmony with grace (4:16). The gospel goes further to describe our peace with God as the grace in which we stand (5:1–2). The answer to Adam's offense is grace, because the grace of God and the gift in grace super-abound (5:14–15). Those who obtain this abundance of grace reign in life (5:17). All this is seen in a brief statement from the man who, while devastating the church, encountered grace on the Damascus road (Acts 9:3–6). This is his testimony: "Where sin abounded, grace did much more abound" (Romans 5:20).

[God]. . .even when we were dead in sins, hath quickened us together with Christ, (by grace ye are saved;) and hath raised us up together, and made us sit together in heavenly places in Christ Jesus.
EPHESIANS 2:4–6

Be thou supreme, O Jesus Christ, Nor creed, nor form, nor word,
Nor holy church, nor human love, Compare with thee, my Lord.

J. TEMPERLEY GREY
BE THOU SUPREME

THE SUPREMACY OF CHRIST

Since we are bought with a price, Christ owns the rights to our entire being (1 Corinthians 7:23). Therefore, to a believer, he is supreme; he is all. However, in this world, he is *also* rather than *all*. The world's catalog of religious leaders includes Buddha, Krishna, Confucius, Mohammed, and Moses. Somewhere on the list is also found the name Jesus Christ—one of many. But a believer cannot view him that way. He is not merely good; he is the best. His servants cannot simply say he is great; he is the greatest to them. Lovely is not sufficient. If he is not the loveliest, something is lacking in a person's faith.

The scriptures tell of King Herod's plot to kill the king of Israel in his infancy (Matthew 2:16). But Christ is supreme over him and every other enemy, both fleshly and spiritual. Satan personally attempted to bribe God's Son away from obedience to his Father (4:10). Through Peter, Satan the adversary argued that the Savior should avoid the cross. "Get thee behind me Satan!" declared the one who later, on that cross, triumphed over all sovereignties and authorities (Matthew 16:22–23; see Colossians 2:14–15).

The same story runs through this age as Christ overwhelms all who encounter him until the day he rides out of heaven as the King of kings and Lord of lords (Revelation 19:16). Eventually, all will be like the three disciples on the Mount of Transfiguration who saw *Jesus only* (Matthew 17:8; see Philippians 2:10–11). The present world reverses this and sees a man who is *only Jesus*. Despite this, the consummation will come when he is supreme over all, and God becomes all in all (1 Corinthians 15:25–28).

> *And when all things shall be subdued unto him,*
> *then shall the Son also himself be subject unto him that*
> *put all things under him, that God may be all in all.*
> 1 CORINTHIANS 15:28

> *O Father God, we owe thee all!*
> *All that we are and have!*
> *With grateful thanks before thee fall,*
> *'Tis all that we can give.*

HORATIUS BONAR (1808–1889)
O FATHER GOD, WE OWE THEE ALL

THANKSGIVING IN SUFFERING

First Thessalonians tells us, "In every thing give thanks: for this is the will of God in Christ Jesus concerning you" (5:18). It does not say to give thanks *for* everything; rather, it tells us to be giving thanks *in* everything. The context informs us that *everything* includes our sorrows and sufferings (2:14; 4:13).

We give thanks *for* all our spiritual blessings (Ephesians 1:3; 5:20). Thessalonians, however, speaks of the opposition to the gospel, of separation and death among the saints, and invites us to give thanks in the midst of such suffering. God's grace has brought us such a rich supply of blessings so that in every trial, in every loss, and in every attack upon our service in the Lord, we can be thankful.

The overall theme of 1 Thessalonians is our hope, our expectation. This expectation builds up a reservoir of thankfulness in a believer. Though life will bring us dark hours, in these we can give thanks. Our thanksgiving is not for the darkness, but that God is our deliverer out of the coming wrath—a truly dark hour (1:10). In sufferings, we give thanks not for the present pain, but for the glory and joy in the presence of our Lord Jesus Christ at his coming (2:14, 19). We can give thanks, not for our affliction and distress, but that our hearts are being established "unblameable in holiness before God. . .at the coming of our Lord Jesus Christ with all his saints" (3:13).

While others are downcast by the tiresome events of this evil age, believers have the grace to be comforted, not by tears of sorrow, but by the assurance that Christ will descend from heaven for us (4:13, 16).

Wherefore comfort one another with these words.
1 THESSALONIANS 4:18

July 11

Let sorrow do its work, send grief or pain;
Sweet are thy messengers, sweet their refrain,
When they can sing with me: More love, O Christ, to thee.

ELIZABETH PRENTISS (1818–1878)
MORE LOVE TO THEE, O CHRIST

SWEETNESS THROUGH SUFFERING

Elizabeth Prentiss gloried in her afflictions. She must have found that they guided her to God's poured-out love—the source of her love for him (Romans 5:3–5).

As we endure suffering in this life and so know God's love, we are being prepared to govern with Christ in the future (2 Timothy 2:12). Someone once observed that every physician should be thrown out of the window—that is, should experience suffering firsthand before practicing on a patient. Then they can manage suffering in others sympathetically and successfully. It is the same with governing. As we feel the pain and consequences of mortality, and endure its suffering and humiliation, we are prepared to rule in the ages to come. Our reigning with Christ will be so successful that government will eventually be ruled out (1 Corinthians 15:28).

The prophet Ezekiel was once given a book in which was written lamentations, mourning, and woe. He was told to eat this book—to take in all of its meaning. He did so, and it tasted as sweet as honey (Ezekiel 2:9–3:3). This is meaningful because Ezekiel, with Israel, was in the midst of captivity and persecution in Babylon—the bitter background for the sweet blessings prepared for them (Ezekiel 11:16–20).

Each of our lives is a book written within and without in travail. But as we take in God's Word and learn of his purposes, we will find sweetness in every experience God gives us. All this is in preparation for the ages to come when he will show "the exceeding riches of his grace in his kindness toward us through Christ Jesus" (Ephesians 2:7).

And not only so, but we glory in tribulations also: knowing that tribulation worketh patience; and patience, experience; and experience, hope: And hope maketh not ashamed; because the love of God is shed abroad in our hearts by the Holy Ghost which is given unto us.
ROMANS 5:3–5

More about Jesus; in his Word, Holding communion with my Lord;
Hearing his voice in every line, Making each faithful saying mine.

ELIZA E. HEWITT (1851–1920)
MORE ABOUT JESUS

THE WORD OF HIS GRACE

Eliza Hewitt is in the blessed lineage of those who treasure the written Word of God. She was like Daniel, who, during the Babylonian captivity, turned to the writings of Jeremiah to learn of God's deliverance of Israel (Daniel 9:2); and Paul, who, when imprisoned in Rome, wanted only three things: his cloak, his scrolls, and his parchments (2 Timothy 4:13). The scrolls were surely copies of the scriptures. Likewise, William Tyndale, who, when imprisoned near Brussels, condemned to die for translating the Bible, asked for his Hebrew Bible, grammar, and study tools; and Martin Luther, when on trial for heresy, appealed only to the testimony of scripture.

From the beginning, God's adversary, Satan, has attacked God's Word by asking, "Has God said. . . ?" (Genesis 3:1). So let us be sure that as we honor the Word with our mouths, we also keep our minds occupied with its contents. Our love for scripture must be accompanied by similar love with our mind in which we are assured that our faith is founded on fact.

Jesus Christ shows us that salvation from satanic seduction is found in the love of the truth (2 Thessalonians 2:9–12). When tempted by Satan, he referred to the Word of God: "Man shall not live by bread alone, but by every word that proceedeth out of the mouth of God" (Matthew 4:4). We are rescued out of this present evil age as we turn to God and the word of his grace (Acts 20:32; Galatians 1:4). Conscience, intuition, philosophy, tradition, reason, books and magazines, a person or church, a favorite theology, creed, or denomination—these fall far short of the Word of God.

And now, brethren, I commend you to God, and to the word of his grace,
which is able to build you up, and to give you an inheritance among all
them which are sanctified.
ACTS 20:32

Once as prodigals we wandered,
In our folly far from thee,
But thy grace, o'er sin abounding
Rescued us from misery.

JAMES G. DECK (1807–1884)
ABBA, FATHER! WE APPROACH THEE

THE SUPER-EXCESSIVE GRACE OF GOD, PART 1

Though the prodigal son was far from his father's house, his elder brother was far from his father's heart (Luke 15:11–32). Like the elder brother, the Pharisees were always in the temple, yet their affection was far from God. The tax collectors and sinners were outcasts from the Jewish nation and its religion. Yet, like the prodigal, they knew their predicament and craved God's mercy.

The elder son illustrates religion based on self-righteous conduct and law-keeping. Even if such behavior is sincere, it does not allow the Father a chance to express his love. The debauchery and decadence of the prodigal, however, drew forth his father's love in abundance. While writing his hymn, James Deck had the insight to say that the prodigal and his father illustrate a beautiful gospel adage: "Where sin abounded, grace did much more abound" (Romans 5:20).

The prodigal's best hope was to be a servant, not a son. But his delighted father gave him the place of honor in his house. The best robe covered his filthiness; sandals protected his feet; a ring beautified the hand that fed the swine. Feasting and merriment began and did not end (Luke 15:24). It was the same with the outcasts of Israel: They were not put on probation; they did not have to make amends through good conduct. They simply sat down and feasted with Jesus Christ. And to this day, by the effectiveness of God's work in Christ, sin does not prevent any person from freely enjoying the super-excessive grace of God (Romans 5:20).

As Jesus sat at meat in his house, many publicans and sinners sat also together with Jesus and his disciples: for there were many, and they followed him. And when the scribes and Pharisees saw him eat with publicans and sinners, they said... How is it that he eateth and drinketh with publicans and sinners?
MARK 2:15–16

All that we were our sin, our guilt,
Our death was all our own:
All that we are we owe to thee,
Thou God of grace alone.

HORATIUS BONAR (1808–1889)
ALL THAT WE WERE

THE SUPER-EXCESSIVE GRACE OF GOD, PART 2

Paul coined new words to tell of great truths. For instance, he took the Greek word for excess and strengthened it with the word that is translated "over" or "super." This created a word meaning "superexceed" found in Romans 5:20, which is best translated like this: "Where sin increases, grace superexceeds." Grace is not only adequate or more than enough, it is super-excessively above the great multiplication of sin. This was seen when Jesus Christ fed the multitudes. All were satisfied, and there was a huge surplus (Matthew 14:20). This illustrates that God's wealth of grace far exceeds our need.

Can sin increase to the point that it blocks the flow of grace? No. Grace overflows, overwhelms, and obliterates every obstacle and superexceeds the utmost increase of sin. Though sin increases, God's grace does not; it is simply and always super-excessive.

We witness this on the Damascus road when grace righteously takes the foremost sinner and makes him God's apostle. In his extreme sin, Paul found grace in such rich excess that it enabled him to bring us the gospel of God's grace the only way of salvation (Acts 20:24). The word *grace* is found in every section of Paul's epistles because that one word best describes his gospel. Grace is the characteristic truth of the gospel. Without it, we sinners have no good news.

To the praise of his glorious grace that he freely bestowed on us in the Beloved. In him we have redemption through his blood, the forgiveness of our trespasses, according to the riches of his grace that he lavished on us.
EPHESIANS 1:6–8 NRSV

Thy mercy found us in our sins,
And gave us to believe;
Then, in believing, peace we found,
And in thy Christ we live.

HORATIUS BONAR (1808–1889)
ALL THAT WE WERE

THE POTTER'S POWER OVER THE CLAY

The scriptures show that God is like a potter with power over his clay (Romans 9:21). Because he has designed, planned, and purposed everything, only God knows who is best suited to advance his purpose. Abraham, for example, did not choose God. God chose him (Genesis 12:1). Likewise, Isaac did not choose to be Abraham's promised son. God said, "In Isaac shall thy seed be called," even though Ishmael had priority as the firstborn (21:12). Jacob is the prime example of God's freedom to choose among his creatures. Isaac's favorite was Esau, his firstborn, but this didn't matter. God's choice was Jacob (Genesis 25:23; 27:27–30; Romans 9:11–13). When men try to override God's choice, like Joseph's brothers did, they only further God's plan and acknowledge God's choice (45:8; 43:26).

The divine potter shapes a variety of vessels. Each one is designed to fill a particular need. God even makes his power known by molding vessels of wrath fitted for destruction. In this way he makes the riches of his glory known in the vessels of mercy (Romans 9:22–23). But this is not the end of the story. There are presently vessels of wrath and vessels of mercy. None of these has chosen his or her part in God's plan.

Formerly, God had mercy on Israel while all the other nations were in unbelief. Now, Israel is stubborn, and God is being merciful to the nations. Since the gifts and the calling of God are irrevocable, Israel will one day obtain mercy again, and in the end God will have mercy on all (11:29–32).

Then I went down to the potter's house, and, behold, he wrought a work on the wheels. And the vessel that he made of clay was marred in the hand of the potter: so he made it again another vessel, as seemed good to the potter to make it.

JEREMIAH 18:3–4

All that we are, as saints on earth,
All that we hope to be,
When Jesus comes and glory dawns,
We owe it all to thee.

HORATIUS BONAR (1808–1889)
ALL THAT WE WERE

THE BELIEVERS' SPIRITUAL HISTORY WITH CHRIST

Colossians uses the little phrase "with Christ" three times to trace our spiritual history. First, we died with Christ (Colossians 2:20). This is the hallmark of Paul's ministry and is found in each of his epistles. It is always linked with the second piece of our history: We are raised with Christ (3:1). This resurrection goes hand in hand with his ascension. That is why we are to "seek those things which are above, where Christ sitteth on the right hand of God" (v. 1). This is echoed elsewhere in the message that God "hath raised us up together, and made us sit together in heavenly places in Christ Jesus" (Ephesians 2:6).

Someone may say, "Right now, I'm living a physical life on earth. How does all this spiritual talk help me?" The gospel is about Christ's death, burial, and resurrection. This includes our death and resurrection with him (Romans 6:3–4; 1 Corinthians 15:1–5). When believers come to understand this, they finally know why it is good news.

We pray to be enlightened to know the hope of our calling (Ephesians 1:18) "That blessed hope, and the glorious appearing of the great God and our Savior Jesus Christ" (Titus 2:13). So scripture plainly says, "If in this life only we have hope in Christ, we are of all men most miserable" (1 Corinthians 15:19).

This leads to the last phase of our spiritual history: "Your life is hid with Christ in God" (Colossians 3:3). At this moment, our true life is in Christ. One day, a new chapter of our history will open when our expectation is made real: "When Christ, who is our life, shall appear, then shall ye also appear with him in glory" (v. 4).

But our citizenship is in heaven, and it is from there
that we are expecting a Savior, the Lord Jesus Christ.
PHILIPPIANS 3:20 NRSV

Hast thou heard him, seen him, known him?
Is not thine a captured heart?
Chief among ten thousand own him;
Joyful choose the better part.

AUTHOR UNKNOWN
HAST THOU HEARD HIM?

THE COMPLETED WORD OF GOD

Peter once stood with John in the temple and told the authorities, "We cannot but speak the things which we have seen and heard" (Acts 4:20). These men were privileged to walk with Jesus Christ two thousand years ago. But a modern believer who longs to be there, too, robs himself of something far richer.

Unlike the other apostles, Paul never personally knew Christ in the flesh. But, unlike them, he did see the Lord in his ascension. He was told, "Thou shalt be his witness unto all men of what thou hast seen and heard" (22:15). If believers wish to be like Paul and see great visions, they will do well to turn their attention to the sacred scriptures. The written Word of God is a complete, comprehensive revelation. Only this Word makes it possible for us to become acquainted with our God.

Twenty years after he first encountered the Lord, Paul admitted that he had seen only part of God's revelation, and he looked forward to its perfection (1 Corinthians 13:9–10). The common thought is that this perfect revelation will come in the future. This is not so. The truths brought to light in Ephesians, Philippians, and Colossians complete the Word of God (Colossians 1:25). This is why it then became possible for a believer to "stand perfect and complete in all the will of God" (4:12), and the apostle had confidence that he could "present every man perfect in Christ Jesus" (1:28), an impossibility if the divine revelation were not perfect.

God has withheld nothing from us. Although we eagerly await Christ's coming, there is no need to await a perfect knowledge of him. Rather, what is needed is a vigorous faith in the Word and persistent examination of all that is revealed there.

> *I suffer trouble, as an evil doer, even unto bonds;*
> *but the word of God is not bound.*
> 2 TIMOTHY 2:9

*What has stripped the seeming beauty
From the idols of the earth?
Not a sense of right or duty,
But the sight of peerless worth.*

AUTHOR UNKNOWN
HAST THOU HEARD HIM?

THE IMAGE OF GOD VS. IDOLS

The peoples of the earth prefer three notions that replace faith in God, who created all things. Those who say there is no God are atheistic (Psalm 14:1). Others won't seek God and don't desire any knowledge of him. They are agnostic (10:4; Job 21:14). Idolatrous people try to make their god visible by forming an idol and then worshipping it (Isaiah 44:9–10). They exchange "the glory of the immortal God for images resembling a mortal human being or birds or four-footed animals or reptiles" (Romans 1:23 NRSV). In other words, they render divine service to the creature rather than the Creator.

Why is God so opposed to these idols? It is because they are caricatures that misrepresent and dishonor him. In some cases, idols may suggest a few of God's attributes. Yet these are partial and distorted. He is jealous of them because they divert our love away from him. Also, idols lack essential life, love, and light. Only the living, loving, enlightening image of the invisible God revealed in scripture can bring the divine essence and attributes to us (Colossians 1:15–16).

Jesus Christ lived and died among the Jewish believers to whom the book of Hebrews was written. They were very interested in understanding who he was and is. So this epistle begins by explaining the Son's relationship with the God revealed in their scriptures: He is the effulgence of God's glory and the express image of all God's roles and qualities (Hebrews 1:1–3). The sun is invisible to human sight, but the photosphere that surrounds it—its effulgent radiation—is evident to our eyes. Likewise, the Son brings God within reach of human awareness.

Professing themselves to be wise, they became fools, and changed the glory of the uncorruptible God into an image made like to corruptible man, and to birds, and fourfooted beasts, and creeping things.
ROMANS 1:22–23

'Tis that look that melted Peter,
'Tis that face that Stephen saw,
'Tis that heart that wept with Mary,
Can alone from idols draw.

AUTHOR UNKNOWN
HAST THOU HEARD HIM?

FAITH AND THE WORD OF GOD

Peter, Stephen, and Mary Magdalene were faithful believers. But the examples used in this hymn illustrate not faith, but belief by sight.

Who has never wanted to compel others to believe in Christ? We imagine, *If only some great miracle would show them the hand of God. Perhaps God will send them a dream or a vision.* In other words, we have more confidence in sight than in faith to bring a person to God. This is why we try to produce reasonable, logical evidence to convince our unbelieving friends. In the future, visible proof will be produced at the great white throne judgment (Revelation 20:11–12). Then everyone will be convinced by irresistible evidence. But this is not God's way today. Now faith must rest upon his unadorned Word, without evidence. So we read, "Faith cometh by hearing, and hearing by the word of God" (Romans 10:17).

We may prefer the old saying, "Seeing is believing." Scripture says the opposite in the example of believing Abraham, who "against hope believed in hope, that he might become the father of many nations, according to that which was spoken" (4:18). The patriarch didn't believe because of what his eyes saw, but according to what his ears heard.

Faith in God is a gift, no matter what it is based upon (Ephesians 2:8). However, faith like Abraham's, based solely on hearing the Word, is God's special gift for today. We live in a time of grace, when faith is entirely associated with the declaration concerning Christ. Although this has no attraction for the flesh, our greatest privilege is to believe solely on the basis of that Word.

> *Thomas, because thou hast seen me, thou hast believed:*
> *blessed are they that have not seen, and yet have believed.*
> JOHN 20:29

Thy faithfulness, Lord, each moment we find,
So true to thy Word, so loving and kind!
Thy mercy so tender to all the lost race,
The vilest offender may turn and find grace.

CHARLES WESLEY (1707–1788)
THY FAITHFULNESS LORD, EACH MOMENT WE FIND

GOD'S FAITHFULNESS TO ISRAEL

The New Testament is full of revealed secrets, or mysteries. Among the many are the mystery of the marriage of Christ and the Church in Ephesians (5:32) and the mystery of godliness in 1 Timothy (3:16). All such secrets are important to our understanding of God's will, including the one that transparently shows God's great faithfulness—the secret that Israel's present condition of unbelief is not permanent (Romans 11:25–26). Blindness has happened to Israel only "until the full number of the Gentiles has come in" (v. 25 NRSV). Then, Israel's deliverer will come and the beloved nation will see him, the one they pierced (Zechariah 12:10; John 19:37). All Israel will be saved, and it will regain its proper place on this earth, becoming the light of the world, just as God intended (Isaiah 49:6).

Israel is still the beloved of God, no matter what its present attitude toward him. God does not regret any favor he has shown to Israel (Romans 11:29). In fact, no individual or nation that God calls will ever ultimately disappoint him. He knows what they are and what they will do. The people of Israel will eventually fulfill their part in the divine plan, and then they too will sing, "Great is thy faithfulness, mercy, and love."

And he said, It is a light thing that thou shouldest be my servant to raise up the tribes of Jacob, and to restore the preserved of Israel: I will also give thee for a light to the Gentiles, that thou mayest be my salvation unto the end of the earth.
ISAIAH 49:6

July 21

What was it, blessed God,
Led thee to give thy Son,
To yield thy well-beloved
For us by sin undone?
'Twas love unbounded led thee thus,
To give thy well-beloved for us.

ANN T. GILBERT (1782–1852)
WHAT WAS IT, BLESSED GOD?

CHRIST'S DEATH FOREKNOWN

Let us reverently listen to a bit of the Son's affectionate prayer to the Father: "Thou lovedst me before the foundation of the world" (John 17:24). This one, loved by God, is "the Lamb slain from the foundation of the world" (Revelation 13:8).

God loves the Son *and* the world. So his beloved Son came to us exhibiting that love through death (Romans 5:8). These things illuminate God's unsearchable judgments and ways past finding out (11:33). That Christ's sacrifice was foreknown helps us understand such judgments (1 Peter 1:19–20). The Son's death was not inserted to repair an unexpected disaster—the advent of sin. That redemption precedes sin is a part of God's plan. There never would have been sin unless God had previously prepared a sacrifice for it. Christ's death was foreknown by God. In this we see that God operates all things according to the counsel of his own will (Ephesians 1:11).

Adam's transgression and Christ's sacrifice were necessary to advance God's great purpose to reveal the depth of his love and the expanse of his affection to his creatures. Knowing this, we must join the apostle to exclaim, "O the depth of the riches both of the wisdom and knowledge of God!" (Romans 11:33).

Ye were not redeemed with corruptible things, as silver and gold. . .but with the precious blood of Christ, as of a lamb without blemish and without spot: who verily was foreordained before the foundation of the world, but was manifest in these last times for you.
1 PETER 1:18–20

Have thine own way, Lord! Have thine own way!
Thou art the potter, I am the clay.
Mold me and make me after thy will,
While I am waiting, yielded and still.

ADELAIDE A. POLLARD (1862–1934)
HAVE THINE OWN WAY, LORD

THERE IS NO DIFFERENCE

God "made of one blood all nations of men for to dwell on all the face of the earth" (Acts 17:26). This is another way of saying that all humanity has been formed out of one lump of clay (Romans 9:21). This figure of the clay from which a potter molds his vessels brings to mind our earthy origin: "And the Lord God formed man of the dust of the ground" (Genesis 2:7). Myriads of saints and sinners—vessels for honor and vessels for dishonor—lay dormant in the lump of dirt that long ago became the first man.

Moses, Samuel, and David the king are there, as are Isaiah, Daniel, and Jeremiah. There are the twelve apostles and the heroes and martyrs of the early Church. The fools and the philosophers of all time are in that clay; the heroes and cowards, the noble and the base, all pirates and priests—everyone is there waiting to be molded into the part he or she is are destined to play in the drama of the ages.

This is why "there is no difference between the Jew and the Greek" (Romans 10:12). The Lord's rich grace is for all people, because we are all out of the same lump. And, as it is for grace, so it is for sin: "There is no difference: For all have sinned, and come short of the glory of God" (3:22–23). The field is level concerning both guilt and grace. Social class, intellectual attainment, national divisions—all flesh is removed because there is no difference. Therefore, "The same Lord over all is rich unto all that call upon him" (10:12).

But now, O LORD, thou art our father; we are the clay,
and thou our potter; and we all are the work of thy hand.
ISAIAH 64:8

Oh wondrous God of wondrous grace,
Thou hast redeemed our fallen race;
Upon the tree of Calvary
Didst die for all humanity.

AUTHOR UNKNOWN
OH WONDROUS GOD OF WONDROUS GRACE

THE EXPLANATION OF THE UNIVERSE

The cross of Christ is the explanation of the universe. There, God obtained the goal of creation: humanity perfected in love and obedience. Jesus Christ is not simply a superior individual unrelated to humankind and untouched by its afflictions. If this were so, his presence on earth and death on the cross would be beyond our understanding. Instead, Christ is the last Adam (1 Corinthians 15:45). This places upon him the entire burden of human sin and misery. It means that his cross is the defining moment of human history.

The last Adam was greater than the first Adam because he embodied ideal humanity. Therefore, Adam's race reached its perfection in him, and his victory will become the victory of all humanity. His cross is not simply a preface to salvation, it is salvation itself. Jesus Christ, the only man who needed no salvation, achieved salvation for all. He is now raised from the dead and exalted. In him, God's goal is achieved.

The crisis of the cross dominates the history of the world for this reason: By it, humanity is remade in the image of the Lord from heaven.

> *And so it is written, The first man Adam was made a living soul; the last Adam was made a quickening spirit. . . . The first man is of the earth, earthy: the second man is the Lord from heaven. As is the earthy, such are they also that are earthy: and as is the heavenly, such are they also that are heavenly. And as we have borne the image of the earthy, we shall also bear the image of the heavenly.*
> 1 CORINTHIANS 15:45, 47–49

I am crucified with Christ,
And the cross hath set me free;
I have ris'n again with Christ,
And he lives and reigns in me.

A. B. SIMPSON (1843–1919)
I AM CRUCIFIED WITH CHRIST

LOVE, LIFE, AND CRUCIFIXION

In God's sight, sin had to be wiped out. Jesus Christ, the one who knew no sin, was the only one who could accomplish this. When he hung on the cross, God made him a sin offering for our sakes so that we can become God's righteousness in him (2 Corinthians 5:21). When his blood was shed, it was sufficient for all humankind and for all creation. We were there when the offering was made, and the resurrection is evidence of its acceptance (Galatians 2:20). God now views us through the cross. Therefore, we are holy and flawless in his sight (Colossians 1:22).

Realistically, however, we are still fleshly and have the problems of this life. Our values are of this world. But A. B. Simpson's hymn reminds us of a greater reality: "I am crucified with Christ: nevertheless I live; yet not I, but Christ liveth in me: and the life which I now live in the flesh I live by the faith of the Son of God, who loved me, and gave himself for me" (Galatians 2:20). As believers realize their true position—crucified and risen with Christ—their values and attitudes change; they are led to the final phrases of this verse, "who loved me, and gave himself for me," and they grow in the realization of God's love.

We know that God's love for us is vast (Ephesians 2:4). Too often our response to it is feeble. However, the more we grow in the knowledge of him through the scriptures, the stronger our love will become. How would our daily contacts with others change if they were based on our knowledge of God's love for them? How different this world would be if this love were the primary motive in all believers' lives.

Husbands, love your wives, even as Christ
also loved the church, and gave himself for it.
EPHESIANS 5:25

Buried with Christ and raised with him, too,
What is there left for me to do?
Simply to cease from struggling and strife,
Simply to walk in newness of life.

T. RYDER
BURIED WITH CHRIST

CONSIDER YOURSELF DEAD TO SIN

We Christians may find it difficult to believe that we have died to sin (Romans 6:2). We will admit that we *ought* to die to sin, but our experience at times contradicts the scripture. Which should we believe?

The apostle insists that not only himself, nor a special class of people, but all who are in Christ died to sin. He doesn't appeal to anyone's experience, even his own. He simply declares the truth and instructs us to "consider yourselves dead to sin and alive to God in Christ Jesus" (v. 11 NRSV). He directs our attention to Christ's death, burial, resurrection, and present life in God, and declares that those in Christ Jesus participate in all these achievements. There is no consideration of our personal condition or experience.

Christ died to sin, and all who belong to him are baptized into that death. Thus, we, too, died to sin. Our relationship to sin is the same as Christ's present involvement with it. And just as he lives to God, so in him a believer walks in newness of life. This is not an experience to be enjoyed, but a revelation of what has happened to all who are baptized into Christ. Our task is not to experience it, but to reckon it true.

Union with Christ, death with him, burial together with him, resurrection, and being alive to God in him are all spiritual facts that are true for everyone who believes (vv. 3–4). Faith placed us into the one who accomplished it all. As the hymn writer says, we should stop struggling and striving to make it true. Christ died, was buried, and rose from the dead (1 Corinthians 15:3–4). Because of this, we are now walking in newness of life.

For ye are dead, and your life is hid with Christ in God.
COLOSSIANS 3:3

Once it was the blessing, now it is the Lord;
Once it was the feeling, now it is his word;
Once his gift I wanted, now, the giver own;
Once I sought for healing, now himself alone.

A. B. Simpson (1843–1919)
Once It Was the Blessing

The Transition to Maturity

With these few lines, A. B. Simpson sketches a contrast between the immature and the mature believer. He does this in an affirmative way, not weighing anyone who may be in the beginning stages of spiritual understanding. Indeed, any amount of faith and knowledge of truth is advanced far beyond the prevailing attitudes in this present evil age (Galatians 1:4).

Still, scripture describes a path from childishness to maturity (1 Corinthians 3:1; Philippians 3:15). Before they received the rich revelation of truth presented in the prison epistles (Ephesians, Philippians, and Colossians), the saints were in a period of adolescence. This is described in the letters to the Corinthians. The believers were not lacking in spiritual gifts, because these had a purpose at that time: They were to lead them to maturity and then be set aside (1 Corinthians 1:7; 13:10; 14:20). Paul's prison epistles introduce that maturity (Philippians 3:15; Colossians 1:28, 4:12). He toiled and struggled, admonished and taught in order to present everyone mature in Christ (Colossians 1:28–29).

The era between Paul's call and his imprisonment was a historic transition. At its beginning, the non-Jewish saints were like proselytes to Judaism (Acts 15:1). At its end, they were entirely independent of Israel (28:28). The teachings and experiences of that time laid the foundation for the final revelation of the Church as the perfect complement of Christ (Ephesians 1:22–23).

For the perfecting of the saints, for the work of the ministry, for the edifying of the body of Christ: Till we all come in the unity of the faith, and of the knowledge of the Son of God, unto a perfect man, unto the measure of the stature of the fulness of Christ.
Ephesians 4:12–13

Once I hoped in Jesus, now I know he's mine;
Once my lamps were dying, now they brightly shine;
Once for death I waited, now his coming hail;
And my hopes are anchored safe within the veil.

A. B. SIMPSON (1843–1919)
ONCE IT WAS THE BLESSING

MATURITY AND THE SECRET OF CHRIST

Even while a prisoner, Paul was "admonishing and teaching everyone with all wisdom, so that we may present everyone perfect in Christ" (Colossians 1:28 NIV). So he wrote the book of Colossians, in which he made the extraordinary claim that he had completed, or filled up, the Word of God (v. 25).

Colossians was not the last of the scriptures to be written. The apostle completed the Word of God in another sense. The other New Testament writings present the nations as secondary to Israel (Romans 1:16). However, Colossians and its companion, the letter to the Ephesians, present the secret, or mystery, of Christ, which shatters the barriers of Judaism (Ephesians 3:4; 4:3). In them, all restrictions upon the Gentiles vanish.

In his time on earth, Jesus Christ never left the land of Israel. But now he is among the nations (Colossians 1:27). Paul met Christ outside the land as the glorified Son of God. Gradually, through Paul's ministry, the Lord unfolded the following secret: All that he had been to Israel in flesh and more is multiplied in spirit to the nations (Ephesians 2:11–18). Whereas Israel is promised the earthly kingdom of Christ, we have a preeminent place in his celestial realms (Matthew 19:28; Ephesians 2:6–7).

The secret of Christ is of tremendous importance. It brings us to maturity; it fills the heart with love and satisfies the mind's need to understand the truth; it discloses the treasures of wisdom and knowledge; it explains the universe from its creation to its reconciliation (Colossians 1:15–20).

Continue in prayer, and watch in the same with thanksgiving; withal praying also for us, that God would open unto us a door of utterance, to speak the mystery of Christ, for which I am also in bonds.
COLOSSIANS 4:2–3

There is one amid all changes Who standeth ever fast,
One who covers all the future, The present and the past;
It is Christ the Rock of Ages, The first and the last.

A. B. SIMPSON (1843–1919)
THERE IS ONE AMID ALL CHANGES

LET ME HIDE MYSELF IN THEE

The book of Romans, the document that defines the gospel of Christ, ends with the Rock of Ages. There we read that the gospel's mystery had been kept in silence through the ages. Paul divulged this secret because the eternal God commanded it (Romans 16:25–26). The word that is translated "eternal" in this verse is the Greek word for eons or ages. So, more correctly, here he is the God of the ages. This title shows God in relation to the eons of time, unfailingly working in grace to correct and remove the effects of Adam's disobedience.

The Hebrew scriptures give a similar title to God: *El Aulam.* There the prophet Isaiah informs us, "In the Lord God you have an everlasting rock" (Isaiah 26:4 NRSV), or rock of the eons El Aulam. In other words, from the beginning to the end of the ages, Jehovah is faithful to his covenant with Israel and will deliver the beloved nation. To Israel and to the church, he is the Rock of Ages. So long as any refuge or support is needed, it will be found in him.

Our God, the Rock of Ages, is revealed in his Son (Colossians 1:15). We have been given faith to believe in Christ (Ephesians 2:8). So we are assured, "Whosoever believeth on him shall not be ashamed" (Romans 10:11). We cannot be disgraced, because Christ is our righteousness (1 Corinthians 1:30). The gospel has paved for us a path of joy and peace in spirit on which we sing words like these, written by Augustus Toplady:

Not the labor of my hands can fulfill thy law's demands;
Could my zeal no respite know, could my tears forever flow,
All for sin could not atone, thou must save, and thou alone.
Rock of Ages, cleft for me, let me hide myself in thee.

Lord of all being, throned afar, Thy glory flames from sun and star;
Center and soul of every sphere, Yet to each loving heart how near!

OLIVER WENDELL HOLMES (1809–1894)
LORD OF ALL BEING

THE GLORY OF OUR INHERITANCE

The glory of God expressed in the flames of the sun and stars is evident to every believer's eyes. However, the eyes of our hearts need enlightenment to see another kind of glory—"the riches of his glorious inheritance among the saints" (Ephesians 1:18 NRSV).

Christ is presently seated at the right hand of God, the highest position in the universe. He outranks every sovereign and authority, every power, every lordship (Ephesians 1:20–21). His name is superior over every name in heaven and on earth (Philippians 2:10). All must be subject to him.

With this in mind, here is the glory we must see: Christ, the head of his body, the Church, possesses the supremacy—the headship over all. We as members of his body participate in Christ's governmental power. We are his complement, the counterpart through which, in the coming eons he will administer the universal government (1 Corinthians 6:3). The chosen nation of Israel will be allied with Christ, their king, to rule the earth while the Church will be one with him as the head of the body in his reign over the rest of the universe (Luke 22:30; Ephesians 1:20–23).

For this reason, we cannot help but join the apostle in his prayer for us:

That the God of our Lord Jesus Christ, the Father of glory, may give unto you the spirit of wisdom and revelation in the knowledge of him: the eyes of your understanding being enlightened; that ye may know what is the hope of his calling, and what the riches of the glory of his inheritance in the saints, and what is the exceeding greatness of his power to us-ward who believe, according to the working of his mighty power, which he wrought in Christ, when he raised him from the dead, and set him at his own right hand in the heavenly places.
EPHESIANS 1:17–20

How tedious and tasteless the hours
When Jesus I no longer see;
Sweet prospects, sweet birds and sweet flowers,
Have all lost their sweetness to me;
The midsummer sun shines but dim,
The fields strive in vain to look gay.
But when I am happy in him,
December's as pleasant as May.

JOHN NEWTON (1725–1807)
HOW TEDIOUS AND TASTELESS

THE JOY OF BELIEVING

In Colossians, we are urged to sing psalms, hymns, and spiritual songs to God with grace in our hearts (3:16). A heart charged with an appreciation of God's grace cannot help but overflow, and singing is the ideal way to do this. John Newton knew such joy, and he overflowed with many hymns, including "Amazing Grace."

The word for grace in the ancient Greek language is charis, and it is related to the word we translate as "joy." Anyone who knows the joy of believing can understand grace. The Greeks used the word *grace* to describe art, music, beautiful things—anything that gives joy. The desire to impart joy to others was also called grace. The joy passed along by something beautiful was grace. Any activity that gave joy was grace. This was the meaning of the word long before it found its way into scripture. There we see God communicating his joy to the hearts of his creatures. This is grace. The gladness of God's heart as he blesses us in Christ is grace. This word describes the love of God that seizes every opportunity to gladden sinful, needy, and graceless men and women.

Grace is God's love flowing to creatures that do not deserve his love. This is why, in Paul's epistles, God's love to sinners is called grace. All God does for us in Christ and all that the gospel displays of God's good will is grace. Thus, grace explains the cross of Christ because there grace took hold of sin, conquered it, and canceled it.

Now the God of hope fill you with all joy and peace in believing, that ye may abound in hope, through the power of the Holy Ghost.
ROMANS 15:13

I love my Lord, but with no love of mine,
For I have none to give;
I love thee, Lord, but all the love is thine,
For by thy love I live.
I am as nothing, and rejoice to be
Emptied, and lost, and swallowed up in thee.

JEANNE GUYON (1648–1717)
I LOVE MY LORD

GOD'S LOVE AND OUR LOVE

The people who love God are those into whom God has poured his love. In other words, we love God because he first loved us (Romans 5:5; 1 John 4:19). Just as the sun can only be seen in its own light, so God is loved with the love he has given us. Despite the differences that divide believers, our love for God reveals that we all belong to him.

The book of Romans mentions a believer's love one time: "All things work together for good to them that love God, to them who are the called according to his purpose" (Romans 8:28). But Romans has much to say about faith, whose constant companions are hope and love (1 Corinthians 13:13). Love goes along with faith, and the greater our faith the more passionate our love. Nevertheless, all believers are lovers of God because the divine lover has captured their hearts through faith.

One may anxiously ask, "How can I know that I'm called according to God's purpose?" The answer is found in another question: "Do I love God?" Our love for God witnesses to the fact that God has called us (1 Corinthians 8:3). It is true that in these last days people love their own gratification more than they love their God (2 Timothy 3:4). Nevertheless, we are reassured of our love as we occupy ourselves with God in his Word. As we discover and deepen our love for him, the certainty that we are participating in his purpose grows, and this will consummate in our glorification (Romans 8:29–30).

But if any man love God, the same is known of him.
1 CORINTHIANS 8:3

> I have seen the face of Jesus.
> Tell me not of aught beside;
> I have heard the voice of Jesus
> All my soul is satisfied.
> In the radiance of the glory
> First I saw his blessed face,
> And forever shall that glory
> Be my home, my dwelling place.

EMMA F. BEVAN (1827–1909)
I HAVE HEARD THE VOICE OF JESUS

GLORY IN THE FACE OF JESUS CHRIST

As the children of Israel trekked through the wilderness, God's tabernacle went with them. When they camped, the tabernacle was set up in the midst of the camp. When God wanted the people to relocate, the visible sign of his presence—the cloud—was lifted from the tabernacle and they moved on (Exodus 40:36). The people followed the cloud until it stopped in a new place where they again pitched their tents. In the cloud by day and the fire by night, Israel saw its divine leader. These assured them of God's presence (v. 38).

God is with us even more today. However, we do not need visible signs of his presence because we are not in flesh, but in spirit (Romans 8:9). Therefore, the transcendent greatness of his power is seen through the eyes of our hearts (Ephesians 1:18–19). Though God's presence was seen in the cloud upon the ancient tabernacle, the light of God's glory was within it, invisible to those outside (Exodus 40:34). That glory now shines in our hearts "to give the light of the knowledge of the glory of God in the face of Jesus Christ" (2 Corinthians 4:6). This light is hidden in the core of a believer's being, unseen by the world. Our physical bodies have darkness inside and light outside. Spiritually, this is reversed: God's revelation and glory are within while darkness grips the outer world.

But we all, with open face beholding as in a glass the glory of the Lord, are changed into the same image from glory to glory, even as by the Spirit of the Lord.
2 CORINTHIANS 3:18

Jesus himself drew near,
And joined them as they walked,
And soon their hearts began to burn,
As of himself he talked.

A. R. HAVERSHON
DRAW NEAR, O LORD

ALL SCRIPTURE IS PROFITABLE

The Bible is a closed book to the people of this world because the natural man cannot receive the things of the Spirit of God (1 Corinthians 2:14). They need someone to open the book for them. To a lesser degree, this is also true of God's saints. We are like the disciples on the way to Emmaus who where sad because they could not understand the events they had recently witnessed in Jerusalem.

The resurrected Christ came to help these men. But before he made known the meaning of the things they had seen, in a rebuke he told them the reason for their lack of understanding. "O fools, and slow of heart to believe all that the prophets have spoken," he said. "Ought not Christ to have suffered these things, and to enter into his glory?" (Luke 24:25–26). Christ didn't rebuke them for not believing the scriptures. Nor did he congratulate them for believing some scriptural truth. They were faulted for being slow to believe "all that the prophets have spoken."

Through the prophets, the Spirit of Christ testified about his sufferings and the resulting glories (1 Peter 1:11). The disciples were quick to believe in Christ's glories but were tardy in accepting his suffering. They contended with one another over their positions in the kingdom but rebuked the Lord when told of his betrayal and death (Matthew 16:21–22; Mark 10:37, 41). In them, we see our own tendency to cling to what we prefer to believe instead of embracing all that the scriptures reveal. Our hearts will burn like those of the two disciples in Emmaus when we allow the Spirit to open to us all the scriptures.

All scripture is given by inspiration of God, and is profitable for doctrine,
for reproof, for correction, for instruction in righteousness.
2 TIMOTHY 3:16

O safe to the rock that is higher than I,
My soul in its conflicts and sorrows would fly;
So sinful, so weary, thine, thine, would I be;
Thou blest "Rock of Ages," I'm hiding in thee.

WILLIAM O. CUSHING (1823–1902)
HIDING IN THEE

THE BELIEVER'S HIDDEN LIFE

The four Gospels tell of our Lord's public ministry. But he had a hidden life, as well as the years he lived in anonymity in Nazareth. When Nathanael learned of Jesus' humble origins, he exposed a popular attitude: "Can there any good thing come out of Nazareth?" (John 1:46). Israel expected a spectacular Messiah. God sent an unobtrusive man who was prepared in obscurity.

We believers have our own despised Nazareth. It is our hidden life with Christ in God (Colossians 3:3). The world in its wisdom rewards the showy and extravagant. God ordains the unseen and unassuming. Our hidden life is that which makes us complete in Christ (2:10). The world has no interest in these marvels. Mention them, and you will be met with disinterest if not derision (1 Corinthians 1:23).

Our completed, hidden life is summarized in three words: death, burial, and resurrection (15:3–4). These were Christ's experience literally, and they are ours in him. Colossians refers to circumcision, the cutting off of the flesh. This signifies death. Baptism pictures both burial and resurrection (Colossians 2:11–12). Our hidden life is complete because, in Christ, we descended into death; his burial was our baptism; in his resurrection, we were raised from the dead. Faith in God's operation in Christ is all that is needed to place us beyond the tomb in full possession of the privileges of the new creation.

In addition to that, we are ascended with him since God has seated us together among the celestials in Christ Jesus (Ephesians 2:6). There, our life is "hid with Christ in God." Therefore, "when Christ, who is our life, shall appear, then shall ye also appear with him in glory" (Colossians 3:3–4).

Set your affection on things above, not on things on the earth.
COLOSSIANS 3:2

When Christ their life shall be made manifest,
When he shall come with all his pow'r to rule,
Their glory, hidden long, shall be confessed;
Arise and shine! O bright and beautiful.

E. F. RICHTER
CHRIST THEIR LIFE

THE HIDDEN LIFE AND THE PRESENT LIFE

Our citizenship is in heaven, and this earth is not our realm (Philippians 3:20). No doubt, Christ our life will appear and earthly politics and society will be remade. For the present, we rest in him and wait until that time comes when we will appear with Christ Jesus in glory (Colossians 3:4). The Holy Spirit of promise is our assurance that this will occur (Ephesians 1:13–14).

That all these marvels are hidden is seen in Abraham's burial of Sarah in private, in expectation of resurrection (Genesis 23:4; Hebrews 11:19). Our burial was also hidden. It occurred in the baptism of death that Jesus Christ suffered for us (Mark 10:38). When he arose, we rose in him. When he ascended, we left the earth behind for a seat at God's right hand (Ephesians 2:5–6; Colossians 3:1).

A person might inquire, "Since all this is realized only by faith, please describe our present, practical life." As always, scripture answers, "Ye have put off the old man with his deeds; and have put on the new man, which is renewed in knowledge after the image of him that created him" (vv. 9–10).

In other words, our present life looks like this: "As God's chosen ones, holy and beloved, clothe yourselves with compassion, kindness, humility, meekness, and patience. Bear with one another and, if anyone has a complaint against another, forgive each other; just as the Lord has forgiven you, so you also must forgive. Above all, clothe yourselves with love, which binds everything together in perfect harmony. And let the peace of Christ rule in your hearts, to which indeed you were called in the one body. And be thankful" (vv. 12–15 NRSV).

> *Do all in the name of the Lord Jesus,*
> *giving thanks to God and the Father by him.*
> COLOSSIANS 3:17

Salvation's found in thee alone;
Thy blood speaks peace upon God's throne.
A ransom offer at his call—
A price o'erpaid by far, for all.

AUTHOR UNKNOWN
OH WONDROUS GOD OF WONDROUS GRACE

THE VALUE OF THE RANSOM PAYMENT

God alone has set the price of mankind's ransom, and he has accepted our Lord's payment. Jesus Christ's resurrection from the dead is proof of God's satisfaction. Exactly what was the ransom payment? Scripture names two prices: The Son of Man gave his soul a ransom for many, and the Mediator gave himself a ransom for all (Matthew 20:28; 1 Timothy 2:6).

A person's soul is the history and expression of his experience. So, the ransom of the Son of Man's soul recalls that Jesus Christ, born of a woman, came to serve, not to be served. Though he was rich, for our sake he became poor. He was in the form of God, yet emptied himself, assumed a human form, and descended to the death of the cross. He knew no sin yet was made sin for us. In other words, he was humiliated to the uttermost. These bitter experiences are the price he paid for the ransom of many. They compose the soul that he poured out unto death (Mark 14:34).

In Matthew, Jesus says the ransom is for many (20:28), but our God is more than the God of many believers; he is the God of all creation. The exalted Christ is the Mediator with God who gives not just his soul, but himself as the ransom for all. The immeasurable value of Christ's suffering and shame is amplified by the glory and power of his resurrection and ascension. Even when lowered to the poverty of the cross, he ransomed the many. Now he is no longer poor, but himself is the embodiment of infinite wealth at the right hand of God. There the Mediator pays the ransom for all.

For there is one God, and one mediator between God and men, the man Christ Jesus; who gave himself a ransom for all, to be testified in due time.
1 TIMOTHY 2:5–6

Not what I am, O Lord, but what thou art;
That, thee alone, can be my soul's true rest;
Thy love, not mine, bids fear and doubt depart,
And stills the tempest of my tossing breast.

HORATIUS BONAR (1808–1889)
NOT WHAT I AM, O LORD

THE TREASURE IN EARTHEN VESSELS

The book of Acts describes some of the circumstances behind Paul's afflictions. He spent a year and a half in Ephesus where exorcists, the powers of darkness, the avaricious guild of silversmiths, and fanatical idolaters opposed the proclamation of the gospel (19:13–41). The apostle wrote to the church in Corinth and described the harshness of his circumstances—it was beyond endurance. Yet he knew that God had rescued him and would be rescuing him in the future. Otherwise, he did not expect to survive (2 Corinthians 1:8–10).

The Lord did not take away Paul's afflictions. Instead, he was immune to breakdown and ruin. "We are troubled on every side," he wrote, "yet not distressed; we are perplexed, but not in despair; Persecuted, but not forsaken; cast down, but not destroyed" (4:8–9).

Where did this protection from defeat come from? Was it only for Paul, or can we expect it, as well? In Paul's day, precious treasures were often concealed in fragile earthenware containers. Scripture makes this a figure of believers: "We have this treasure in earthen vessels, that the excellency of the power may be of God, and not of us" (v. 7). God's power does not simply offset the fragility and weakness of our earthen vessel; it far exceeds it.

The great truth of 2 Corinthians 4:7–10 applies to all who believe. The power for our living and service to the Lord is of God and not of us. When we give up our fleshly struggles, our experiences in stressful situations are similar to Paul's. That is, the transcendence of the power is of God and not of us.

For we which live are always delivered unto death for Jesus' sake, that the
life also of Jesus might be made manifest in our mortal flesh.
2 CORINTHIANS 4:11

> *My times are in thy hand;*
> *O God, I wish them there;*
> *My life, my friends, my soul I leave*
> *Entirely to thy care.*

WILLIAM F. LLOYD (1791–1853)
MY TIMES ARE IN THY HAND

THE RAINBOW AND THE THRONE

Ezekiel's prophecy begins with a whirlwind out of the north and a great cloud flashing fire round about. Out of this emerge four living creatures rushing along on wondrous wings and wheels with the appearance of lightning. This vision inaugurates the prophet, empowering him for a faithful, fearless ministry.

Above the wheels, the animals, and the cloudy, flashing atmosphere is the likeness of a throne. On it is a human form (Ezekiel 1:26–27). "Like the bow in a cloud on a rainy day, such was the appearance of the splendor all around" (v. 28 NRSV). This higher scene is not frantic or baffling. There are no tumbling clouds, wild winds, or flashing fires. Ezekiel rises above the crosscurrents of this world with a sight he can bear: a man under a rainbow administrating the universe.

A person can discover God's powerful attributes by observing creation (Romans 1:19–20). But the knowledge of the gracious, universal headship of the Son of God comes by revelation. Even so, this world will one day be glad to submit to the authority of its redeemer. The vast creation will acknowledge his will, acclaim his power, and above all, praise and worship his for it (Philippians 2:10).

Now, the pathway seems to be a cloudy, storm-ridden labyrinth. But above this, the eyes of faith see the throne and the rainbow of God's promise. With such a vision, we breathe this prayer: "My times are in thy hand" (Psalm 31:15).

That in the dispensation of the fulness of times he might gather together in one all things in Christ, both which are in heaven, and which are on earth; even in him: in whom also we have obtained an inheritance, being predestinated according to the purpose of him who worketh all things after the counsel of his own will.
EPHESIANS 1:10–11

Hark! the voice of love and mercy Sounds aloud from Calvary;
See, it rends the rocks asunder, Shakes the earth, and veils the sky:
"It is finished!" "It is finished!" . . . Hear the dying Savior cry.

JONATHAN EVANS (1749–1809)
HARK! THE VOICE OF LOVE AND MERCY

THE FINAL FINISH

On the hill of Golgotha, a few disciples strain to hear the words of their dying Master. Imagine their anxiety when he cries, "My God, my God, why didst thou forsake me?" (Matthew 27:46). Hadn't he once said, "He that sent me is with me: the Father hath not left me alone" (John 8:29)? But now he wails that the Father has forsaken him.

And what do they think of the next cry from his lips: "It is finished"?

We now view the cross through the empty tomb and so recognize this as a shout of triumph. But to the grieving disciples, it seems to be a desolate cry. Things have not turned out as expected. The Father has forsaken the one they suppose is the Messiah. Before their eyes, he gives up in despair. They cannot tell that, rather than desperation, this is Christ's declaration that the work he was sent to do is finished.

His cross is at the heart of everything to come, and much will happen before the purpose of the ages is complete. The declaration that "the kingdoms of this world are become the kingdoms of our Lord, and of his Christ" is a major milestone along that way (Revelation 11:15). Even then, however, the end has not come. One day the heavens will pass away with a great noise, the elements will melt with fervent heat, and the earth will burn up (2 Peter 3:10). This cataclysm, like the deluge in Noah's day, clears the way for a fresh start. It is not the end; it is the beginning of the new creation (Revelation 20:11; 21:1) in which the Lamb will reign until the last enemy—death—is abolished (1 Corinthians 15:26). Then God becomes all in all, and the consummation of the ages arrives at last (vv. 23, 28).

Then cometh the end.
1 CORINTHIANS 15:24

There's a little word that the Lord has giv'n
For our help in the hour of need:
Let us reckon ourselves to be dead to sin,
To be dead and dead indeed.

A. B. SIMPSON (1843–1919)
THERE'S A LITTLE WORD

RECKON YOURSELF DEAD

The gospel is not a self-improvement program. We have already been presented holy, blameless, and unreprovable in God's sight (Colossians 1:22). This astonishing statement is not wishful thinking; it is how we look from God's vantage point. We know it is true because we accept God's declaration of the good news. The inspired record tells of our part in this marvelous arrangement: "Reckon ye also yourselves to be dead indeed unto sin, but alive unto God through Jesus Christ our Lord" (Romans 6:11).

To reckon is to acknowledge by faith that this is so. However, faith does not rely on feeling. After all, we feel like we are alive. Let us rest our faith on God's dependable declaration. The secret to spirituality is not in trying to overcome sin or in daily dying to sin. Anything that depends on our own efforts is doomed to failure (7:24). The Lord's words are pure, tried in a furnace, purified seven times (Psalm 12:6). So we should discern them accurately. It is not our part to die. All we need do is accept that we are already dead and alive again in Christ Jesus.

Christ died to sin once and for all time (Romans 6:10). This has a dual meaning. He paid the penalty that we should have paid for our *sins*. But he also died to *sin*, which is the force within humanity's flesh that makes it unable to please God (7:24; 8:8). Christ died *for our sins*, he died *to sin*, and we died in him. This is why sin has no more dominion over us (6:3, 14). Our part is simply to take the word the Lord has given for our help and reckon ourselves dead to sin and alive to God in Christ.

He that is dead is freed from sin.
ROMANS 6:7

There's another word that the Lord has giv'n,
In the very same verse we read
Let us reckon ourselves as alive in him,
As alive and alive indeed.

A. B. SIMPSON (1843–1919)
THERE'S A LITTLE WORD

RECKON YOURSELF ALIVE

To say we believe in Christ means that we believe in his death in all of its significance. Our belief is an acknowledgment that we were included in his death and resurrection. By believing in Christ, we are reckoning ourselves dead to sin and accepting that our death in Christ has freed us from slavery to sin (Romans 6:11, 14). In addition to that, by faith in Christ we reckon that we are walking in newness of life (v. 4). Scripture tells us this is true, and the Spirit within us agrees. Therefore, only lack of knowledge, or unbelief, can keep us from enjoying it, not as a feeling but as a fact.

Because the understanding of this is so momentous, you may wish to pray that the God of our Lord Jesus Christ, the Father of glory, will give you the spirit of wisdom and revelation in the knowledge of him (Ephesians 1:17). That spirit enables a believer to grasp and appropriate these precious truths. As our faith is harmonized with their reality, it compels us to present ourselves to God as those who are alive from among the dead and to give our members as implements of righteousness for his use (Romans 6:19).

> *Now if we be dead with Christ, we believe that we shall also live with him. . . . For in that he died, he died unto sin once: but in that he liveth, he liveth unto God. Likewise reckon ye also yourselves to be dead indeed unto sin, but alive unto God through Jesus Christ our Lord.*
> ROMANS 6:8, 10–11

> While we trust in feeling or inward frames
> We shall always be tossed about,
> Let us anchor fast to the Word of God.
> And reckon away our doubt.

A. B. SIMPSON (1843–1919)
THERE'S A LITTLE WORD

HOW TO DISCERN THE TRUTH

When A. B. Simpson mentions our being "tossed about," he is referring to Ephesians 4:14, which says we should no longer be children, "tossed to and fro, and carried about with every wind of doctrine, by the sleight of men, and cunning craftiness, whereby they lie in wait to deceive." Simpson is saying that our feelings do not prove our death with Christ. The Word of God is our proof. The deception mentioned in Ephesians 4:14 can only be countered by scriptural truth.

"How," one may ask, "can I discern the truth?" Scripture instructs us on this topic: First, "hold fast the form of sound words, which thou hast heard of me, in faith and love which is in Christ Jesus" (2 Timothy 1:13). That is, only use scriptural terms, especially the apostle Paul's language, when considering and fellowshipping about the scriptures. This seems obvious, but it is rarely done. Note that without a spirit of faith and love, even this will fall short.

Also, correctly divide the Word of truth (2:15). The context of this statement explains its meaning: Hymenaeus and Philetus did not deny the resurrection; they misplaced it. They made it past when, in fact, it is future (vv. 17–18). All truth has its appropriate place. If it is transferred to another era, it becomes error. For example, Gentile believers were told that they had to keep Jewish laws if they were to be saved (Acts 15:1). This misplaced the truth. Moses gave the law, but everything changed when Jesus Christ brought grace and truth (John 1:17).

It will greatly help you to understand scripture if you mark not only what is spoken or written, but of whom and to whom, with what words at what time, where, to what intent, with what circumstances, considering what goes before and what follows.
JOHN WYCLIFFE, EARLY BIBLE TRANSLATOR (1324–1384)

May the word of God dwell richly
In my heart from hour to hour,
So that all may see I triumph
Only through his power.

KATE B. WILKINSON (1859–1928)
MAY THE MIND OF CHRIST, MY SAVIOR

THE WORD OF CHRIST

This hymn rephrases Colossians 3:16, which says, "Let the word of Christ dwell in you richly in all wisdom; teaching and admonishing one another in psalms and hymns and spiritual songs, singing with grace in your hearts to the Lord." In all scripture, only this verse mentions the word of Christ. This is because Colossians, of all the sacred writings, expressly presents the secret of Christ (4:3; 2:2). Here we see the past primacy of the Son (1:15–17), his present headship of the body as the firstborn from the dead (vv. 18–19), and his future reconciliation of the universe (v. 20).

This history of God's work in Christ—the word of Christ—should be woven into the psalms, hymns, and spiritual songs that believers, with grace in their hearts, sing to one another. An inspired worship team might compose a song about Christ the image of the invisible God and the firstborn of every creature (v. 15). A new hymn is needed that exalts the one in whom all is created—all in the heavens and on the earth, the visible and the invisible (v. 16). A psalm that expresses the profound fact that all is created through him and for him would surely build up believers. What better way to be filled than to sing out the rich word of Christ? (v. 17; see Ephesians 5:18–19).

> *Speaking to yourselves in psalms and hymns and spiritual songs,*
> *singing and making melody in your heart to the Lord.*
> EPHESIANS 5:19

May the peace of God my Father
Rule my life in everything,
That I may be calm to comfort
Sick and sorrowing.

KATE B. WILKINSON (1859–1928)
MAY THE MIND OF CHRIST, MY SAVIOR

THE PATTERN OF SOUND WORDS

Colossians is again rephrased in this verse. Bible verses are frequently rephrased in our hymns for various reasons. Poetic form—the requirements of a hymn's meter and rhyming scheme—is a common explanation. Or perhaps the hymn writer is unfamiliar with scriptural language. Kate Wilkinson's hymn quotes the King James Version of the Bible, which is incorrect in this case. In the original Greek, Colossians 3:15 recommends not the peace of God, but the peace of Christ.

Scripture advises us to "hold fast the form of sound words, which thou hast heard of me" (2 Timothy 1:13). Therefore, whether writing hymns or simply fellowshipping with others, it is always best to avoid popular, traditional, and/or purely theological terms and adhere to scriptural language.

The scriptures are the sole source of God's revelation. Nowhere else can we see God, his purpose, his Christ, and his work. God did not choose mere human words to express these things, but he purified our language into a divine vocabulary to transfer his thoughts to us (Psalm 12:6). Therefore, the ways in which words are used in scripture gives them meaning that is found nowhere else. Surely, it takes some discipline and a little time to learn and use this vocabulary. But a person does not need to become a scholar to do so. When we simply draw on our innate love of God and his Word, we will gladly hold fast the form of sound, scriptural words.

I have not departed from the commandment of his lips;
I have treasured in my bosom the words of his mouth.
JOB 23:12 NRSV

Cast all thy care, and not a part,
The great things and the small;
The Lord's all-loving, mighty heart
Has room and thought for all.

M. M. MOULE
CAST THOU THY CARE UPON THE LORD

THE SCRIPTURAL RELIEF FOR WORRY

Using plants and animals as examples, our Lord exhorted us not to worry about practical needs such as food and drink and clothing (Matthew 6:25–34). How can we do this?

The scriptures show a progression in the experience of believers in relation to worry. This develops as God's grace becomes more fully known. Psalm 55:22 offers this solution to worry: "Cast thy burden upon the LORD, and he shall sustain thee." This is good, although it requires that we have enough strength to lift the ceaseless burdens of this life and cast them upon God. Likewise, Matthew 6:25–34 is encouraging, even though its relief is conditional. That is, if we are able to first seek the kingdom and its righteousness, then "all these things shall be added" (v. 33). First Peter 5:7 is a beloved verse, although, like Psalm 55:22, it involves our work—"casting all your care upon him; for he careth for you."

Philippians 4:6–7 tells how to get beyond the reach of anxiety: "Do not worry about anything, but in everything by prayer and supplication with thanksgiving let your requests be made known to God. And the peace of God, which surpasses all understanding, will guard your hearts and your minds in Christ Jesus" (NRSV).

These verses do not promise that our prayers will be answered. Nor do they say that our cares will be taken away. They go far deeper than this. God is guiding all things to the divine goal, and he is not hindered by the worries that distress us (Romans 8:28). When we present our requests to God through prayer and petition with thanksgiving, we agree with God's will, no matter if our prayers are answered or not. Then we enter into an inexplicable peace that guards our hearts and minds from further worries. Though this is difficult to explain, it can be experienced through prayer.

Do not worry about anything.
PHILIPPIANS 4:6 NRSV

Help me then in every tribulation
So to trust thy promises, O Lord,
That I lose not faith's sweet consolation
Offered me within thy holy Word.
Help me, Lord, when toil and trouble meeting,
Ever to take, as from a father's hand,
One by one, the days, the moments fleeting,
Till I reach the promised land.

LINA SANDELL (1832–1903)
DAY BY DAY
TRANSLATED BY A. L. SKOOG (1856–1934)

THE COMFORT OF OUR EXPECTATION

Lina Sandell, the beloved Swedish hymn writer, treasured the sweet consolation of God's Word. Perhaps she was thinking of this verse as she wrote her hymn: "Wherefore comfort one another with these words" (1 Thessalonians 4:18). The words of comfort offered in scripture are often words of expectation—hope that is found only in the word of the truth of the gospel (Colossians 1:5).

For example, believers in Thessalonica were losing heart because some of their friends and family, brothers and sisters in the Lord, had died. These people needed comfort (1 Thessalonians 5:14). They didn't know about the coming resurrection of the dead, so they had no idea what would become of their loved ones. So Paul told them what to expect: "Since we believe that Jesus died and rose again, even so, through Jesus, God will bring with him those who have died" (4:14 NRSV).

First Corinthians 15 is the detailed explanation of the resurrection, where we find these words: "If in this life only we have hope in Christ, we are of all men most miserable" (v. 19). Certainly, our faith is all about what Christ has done in the past, but it also includes our expectation of what is to come. In the midst of the tumult and uncertainty of this world, believers are comforted in this hope.

For the grace of God has appeared, bringing salvation to all, training us to renounce impiety and worldly passions, and in the present age to live lives that are self-controlled, upright, and godly, while we wait for the blessed hope and the manifestation of the glory of our great God and Savior, Jesus Christ.
TITUS 2:11–13 NRSV

Peace, perfect peace, in this dark world of sin?
The blood of Jesus whispers peace within.

EDWARD H. BICKERSTETH (1825–1906)
PEACE, PERFECT PEACE

PEACE, PERFECT PEACE

When Adam disobeyed, he was ousted from the Garden of Eden. As generations passed, the enmity between God and man grew greater as we strengthened the barriers between our Creator and us. To this day, like Adam, we hide from the only one who can give us what we desperately need.

Although Paul's letters to the Corinthians addressed many problems, in fact the people had only one: their distance from God caused them to have no peace. They were the first people to learn that "God was in Christ, reconciling the world unto himself, not imputing their trespasses unto them" (2 Corinthians 5:19). That is to say, God has removed all barriers of enmity and has cut the way of peace. This is the very same good news of peace that was heralded when Christ was born (Luke 2:14).

God's adversary, Satan, is aware that this ministry of reconciliation tears down the walls of separation between man and God. He knows it brings people into God's love. No wonder he has "blinded the minds of them which believe not, lest the light of the glorious gospel of Christ, who is the image of God, should shine unto them" (2 Corinthians 4:4).

Satan's deception has made us not just sinners but also enemies of God. Humanity is utterly estranged from the Creator. But the work of Christ brought salvation and justification. Even more, it removed everything that might impede the boundless stream of God's love. The Lord sent his ambassador to beseech the world to be reconciled to God (5:20). Those who respond find God whispering within them, "Peace, perfect peace."

Therefore being justified by faith, we have
peace with God through our Lord Jesus Christ.
ROMANS 5:1

O let us rejoice in the Lord evermore,
Though all things around us be trying,
Though floods of affliction like sea billows roar,
It's better to sing than be sighing.

A. B. SIMPSON (1843–1919)
IT'S BETTER TO SING

REJOICE IN THE LORD ALWAYS

Jesus Christ began his public ministry with the word, "Repent!" (Matthew 4:17). But Israel has not yet repented and appreciated her need of salvation (John 1:11). His disciples were slow to believe, too. Peter rebuked and opposed the Lord (Matthew 16:22). They contended with one another for prominent positions (20:21–24) and failed to understand the significance of Christ's words (Luke 24:25–26). Even so, the first word of Christ's ministry in resurrection is "Rejoice!" (Matthew 28:9 NRSV).

Jesus Christ had completed the most heroic journey of all time. Being in the form of God, he was above the heavens. But he voluntarily sank from the highest to the lowest place in the universe. He took the form of a slave and came to this world in the likeness of humanity. Then, obedient to God's will, he humbled himself to die a most degrading death by crucifixion (Philippians 2:6–8). As the gospel says, "Christ died for our sins" (1 Corinthians 15:3). His journey continued as he was buried. And finally, "He rose again the third day" (v. 4). No wonder he declared, "Rejoice!"

This joy did not come from his circumstances. On the day of Jesus' resurrection, God's people still rejected their Messiah, as they do to this day. His disciples had not yet understood the things they had seen and heard. Yet he said, "Rejoice!"

And now the faith that was Christ's on that epic journey is ours to live by (Galatians 2:20). In our hands, we hold the scriptures that describe God's will from beginning to end. Even though we are in the midst of a crooked and perverse generation, we are luminaries here, holding forth this word of life (Philippians 2:15–16). This is why the apostle encourages us:

Rejoice in the Lord always; again I will say, Rejoice.
PHILIPPIANS 4:4 NRSV

I'll sing of the wonderful promise
That Jesus has given to me;
"My strength is made perfect in weakness,
My grace is sufficient for thee."
And lest my poor heart should forget it,
Or ever forgetful should be,
He still keeps repeating the promise,
My grace is sufficient for thee.

A. B. SIMPSON (1843–1919)
MY GRACE IS SUFFICIENT

THE MIGHT OF HIS STRENGTH, PART 1

The strength that is perfected in our weakness is also called "the exceeding greatness of his power" (Ephesians 1:19). This was operating in Christ when God raised him from the dead and seated him at his right hand among the celestials (v. 20). But as A. B. Simpson points out and as scripture repeatedly declares, this strength is not only associated with God and Christ but with all the believers, as well. Anyone who will join the apostle in prayer to receive the spirit of wisdom and revelation will come to know "the exceeding greatness of his power to us-ward who believe, according to the working of his mighty power" (v. 19).

God's Spirit operated in Christ when he raised him from among the dead and lifted him to the pinnacle in the universe. This displays God's mighty power at work. Doesn't this power operate in us? Can't it do exceeding abundantly above all that we ask or think (3:20)? Doesn't scripture assure us, "He that raised up Christ from the dead shall also quicken your mortal bodies by his Spirit that dwelleth in you" (Romans 8:11)? Surely, this is all true. This is why we will find answers when we pray for a life that is "worthy of the Lord unto all pleasing, being fruitful in every good work, and increasing in the knowledge of God; strengthened with all might, according to his glorious power" (Colossians 1:10–11).

Now to him who by the power at work within us is able to accomplish abundantly far more than all we can ask or imagine, to him be glory in the church and in Christ Jesus to all generations, forever and ever. Amen.
EPHESIANS 3:20–21 NRSV

It is not our grace that's sufficient, But his grace, it ever must be:
Our graces are transient and changing; His grace is unfailing as he.
And so I am ever repeating His wonderful promise to me,
My strength is made perfect in weakness,
My grace is sufficient for thee.

A. B. Simpson (1843–1919)
My Grace Is Sufficient

THE MIGHT OF HIS STRENGTH, PART 2

Let us consider strength and weakness. Abraham, for example, believed the promise that he would have descendants (Genesis 12:7). Many years later, Sarah still had not given birth. Yet Abraham, the spiritual father of us all, believed in God who gives life to the dead and calls into existence the things that do not exist (Romans 4:16–17). He believed that he would become the father of many nations, because God said his descendants would be as numerous as the stars in the sky (Genesis 15:5). His faith didn't weaken when he considered that his body was as good as dead. Rather, his faith grew stronger as he gave glory to God, convinced that God was able to do what he had promised (Romans 4:18–21).

Moses was eighty years old when, out of the burning bush, God called him (Acts 7:23, 29–30). Moses wrote, "The days of our life are seventy years, or perhaps eighty, if we are strong; even then their span is only toil and trouble; they are soon gone, and we fly away" (Psalm 90:10 NRSV). Yet, when he was seventy, he was strengthened for another fifty years in which he led God's people out of Egypt and through the wilderness. At the end of his labors, the 120-year-old Moses had strength to climb a mountain to survey the length and breadth of the Promised Land. "Moses was an hundred and twenty years old when he died: his eye was not dim, nor his natural force abated" (Deuteronomy 34:7). We too can be invigorated like these men. Here's how:

I have learned, in whatsoever state I am, therewith to be content. . . . I can do all things through Christ which strengtheneth me.
Philippians 4:11, 13

Did we in our own strength confide, our striving would be losing;
Were not the right man on our side, the man of God's own choosing:
Dost ask who that may be? Christ Jesus, it is he;
Lord Sabaoth, his name, from age to age the same,
And he must win the battle.

MARTIN LUTHER (1483–1546)
A MIGHTY FORTRESS IS OUR GOD

THE MIGHT OF HIS STRENGTH, PART 3

Martin Luther refers to Lord Sabaoth in this well-known hymn about God's warfare. This term is usually translated "Lord of hosts." It is used in Isaiah 1:9, which is quoted in Romans 9:29 to show that God still protects Israel. Scripturally speaking, the Lord of hosts is related to the chosen nation—Israel. Luther transferred this to the church during the Reformation's intense years of spiritual warfare. However, the church's spiritual power is different than Israel's. Ours is the exceedingly great power of God that operated in Christ when he raised him from the dead (Ephesians 1:19–20). Consider this for a moment: Ours is the power that raised Christ from the dead!

It is well known that Christ did not remain in the tomb. He was raised from among the dead. His friend Lazarus was also raised, but there is much more to Christ's resurrection than we see in the awakening of Lazarus: Lazarus died again, but Christ dies no longer. He died to sin once for all time (Romans 6:9–10). What's more, Christ's resurrection means that everyone who has ever passed into death will likewise be made alive (1 Corinthians 15:26).

Therefore, Colossians assigns two wonderful titles to our Lord: He is the firstborn of every creature (1:15). This means he preceded all that has ever come into being. And he is the firstborn from among the dead. Of all who have died, he is the first to be made alive (v. 18). The power that brought forth the universe was placed in Christ at the beginning (v. 15), and power to bring forth the dead was placed in him when he became the firstborn from among the dead.

I am the resurrection.
JOHN 11:25

Strong are the walls around me,
That hold me all the day;
But they who thus have bound me,
Cannot keep God away:
My very dungeon walls are dear,
Because the God I love is here.

JEANNE GUYON (1648–1717)

THE WORD OF GOD IS NOT BOUND

Madame Guyon came by her imprisonment honestly. She was perse-cuted, arrested, and jailed in the Bastille in Paris simply because her piety and love of God attracted many admirers.

The prototype of all imprisoned saints is the apostle Paul who, in about AD 58, was imprisoned for at least five years. His attitude provides us with the proper perspective in our own limitations. "I suffer trouble, as an evil doer, even unto bonds," he wrote, "but the word of God is not bound" (2 Timothy 2:9). Not even Paul could know how true this statement was. He completed the Word of God, but did he know that the glorious truths he wrote in that prison would enflame the hearts and enrich the faith of believers more than twenty centuries later?

None of us can know the glorious purposes that are at work within us. Despite appearances, these are for our good and, even more, benefit those whom we will contact in the future. If we could appreciate the depth, the measure, and the meaning of God's far-reaching purposes, we would never again complain of hardships or restrictions.

The Word of God is not bound, whether it concerns his counsel and will in the purpose of the ages or the counsel of his will in our daily affairs. He declares "the end from the beginning, and from ancient times the things that are not yet done, saying, My counsel shall stand, and I will do all my pleasure" (Isaiah 46:10).

For this cause also thank we God without ceasing, because,
when ye received the word of God which ye heard of us,
ye received it not as the word of men, but as it is in truth,
the word of God, which effectually worketh also in you that believe.
1 THESSALONIANS 2:13

Pressed out of measure, pressed beyond all length,
Pressed so intensely, seeming beyond strength;
Pressed in the body, pressed within the soul,
Pressed in the mind till darksome surges roll.

AUTHOR UNKNOWN
PRESSED OUT OF MEASURE

THE GOD OF ALL COMFORT

Paul's sufferings did not happen as a result of offenses or errors on his part. They were the consequence of his announcing the gospel of Christ. Therefore, he called these the sufferings of Christ (2 Corinthians 1:5). Not long before he wrote to the Corinthians, he had been in grave danger at the hands of a mob in Ephesus. Plus, he was suffering from some physical ailment (12:7). Meanwhile, he had learned that the Corinthians were also suffering, though this was the result of their own misconduct. Still, he comforted them. God prepared him for this ministry of consolation through his many afflictions (1:4). In this way, Paul reveals God to us in a new light as the Father of mercies and the God of all comfort (v. 3).

This illustrates how God uses sin and suffering to draw our hearts closer to him and to one another. What's more, afflictions liberate us from confidence in ourselves so we can rely on God (vv. 9–10). Therefore, though the apostle does not give thanks for his sufferings, he does ask believers to join him in thanksgiving for the gift of comfort in suffering (v. 11). Later he will tell them he glories and delights in his infirmities because in his weakness he finds the power of Christ (12:9–10). May each believer find in affliction God's all-sufficient grace that turns weakness into strength.

> *Blessed be God, even the Father of our Lord Jesus Christ,*
> *the Father of mercies, and the God of all comfort; who comforteth*
> *us in all our tribulation, that we may be able to comfort them which*
> *are in any trouble, by the comfort wherewith we ourselves are*
> *comforted of God. For as the sufferings of Christ abound in us,*
> *so our consolation also aboundeth by Christ.*
> 2 CORINTHIANS 1:3–5

What a friend we have in Jesus,
All our sins and griefs to bear!
What a privilege to carry
Everything to God in prayer!
O what peace we often forfeit,
O what needless pain we bear,
All because we do not carry
Everything to God in prayer!

JOSEPH SCRIVEN (1819–1886)
WHAT A FRIEND WE HAVE IN JESUS

THE POSSIBILITY OF UNCEASING PRAYER

First Thessalonians begins and ends with unceasing prayer (1:2; 5:17).
Let's consider whether such prayer is possible.

This epistle does not start with a call to prayer but with an example
of a man who prays. There, the apostle Paul offers his prayer of ceaseless
remembrance of the Thessalonians' faith, love, and hope (1:2–5). He
then tells of the power of faith and love as they are seen in his life and
those of the believers (1:6–4:12). Finally, he comforts them in hope
with a view of the resurrection and the Lord's return (4:13–5:11). Only
then does he appeal for unceasing prayer.

This outline of 1 Thessalonians illustrates that prayer is the outcome
of our realization of God's grace. The apostle's request for unceasing
prayer is a plea to always consider God and all he has done. This produces
prayer that never ceases. We do not initiate such prayer; it is the fruit of
God's grace. It is our heart's reply to our Lord Jesus Christ's death for
our sakes (5:10); to the expectation that he will descend and snatch us
away to be together with him (4:16–17); to the fact that, through him,
we obtain salvation (5:9). Since there is no end to grace, there is likewise
no end of prayer.

Because we embrace God's transcendent grace, the twenty-one
exhortations that close 1 Thessalonians are not burdensome to us. They
simply describe our lives as the children of light (5:12–26). We find
these three words nested in their midst:

Pray without ceasing.
1 THESSALONIANS 5:17

Faithful are all who love the truth,
And dare the truth to tell;
Who steadfast stand at God's right hand,
And strive to serve him well.

WILLIAM G. TARRANT (1853–1928)
COME, LET US JOIN WITH FAITHFUL SOULS

HOW TO BREAK THE BREAD OF LIFE

A mysterious person appears in scripture to teach us about truth. Elihu seems to have been a passerby who stopped to listen to Job and his friends in hope of learning more of God's ways (Job 32–37). He probably did not intend to participate in the debate. But Job's self-justification and the friends' lack of answers forced him to speak (32:19–20).

Job's friends defend an established doctrinal system while Elihu speaks on God's behalf (36:2). They rely on human wisdom; he depends on the divine Spirit (32:8). They lean on each other; he counts on the divine presence (36:4). Read these chapters and notice how Elihu clears the field and prepares it for God's operation within Job.

He distances himself from the three and points out the superficiality of experience, the error of tradition, and the futility of personal achievement. He outlines God's dealings with humans and proves that we are utterly ruined and cannot recover what we have lost. He points out that God deals with us through a mediator who interprets the invisible God and pays the price for man's redemption (33:19–28).

This obscure young man confounds the greatness of the older men. Their pomp is vanquished by his modesty. The book of Job is ponderous to read until Elihu breaks the bread of life for us. Then, when the Lord speaks from the whirlwind, he takes Elihu's words for his theme: "God is greater than man" (see Job 38:1-12).

Elihu teaches us a deep, essential lesson: Let the theme of our study and speaking be nothing other than Christ Jesus, the bread of life himself. Then, like Job, we will eventually say, "I had heard of you by the hearing of the ear, but now my eye sees you" (Job 42:5 NRSV).

I am that bread of life.
JOHN 6:48

*Lord, speak to me that I may speak
In living echoes of thy tone;
As thou has sought, so let me seek
Thine erring children lost and lone.*

FRANCES R. HAVERGAL (1836–1879)
LORD, SPEAK TO ME

WHAT DOES THE LORD SPEAK ABOUT?

Second Corinthians 13:3–6 tells about the Lord's speaking to us. There the believers were seeking proof of Christ speaking in Paul. So he immediately pointed them to the gospel.

This is how Christ speaks in a believer: First comes the message of humility, apparent weakness, and stupidity seen in the cross: "He was crucified through weakness" (v. 4). This is followed by the message of life and power in resurrection: "He liveth by the power of God" (v. 4). Christ's speaking in Paul is seen in his union with Christ in death and resurrection.

The Corinthians looked for assurance that Paul was really an apostle of Christ. But Paul knew that they needed to become more aware of what Christ had done for them. So he described our faith and instructed them to test themselves to see if they were in that faith just as he was (vv. 4–5). He wasn't questioning their salvation. He wanted them to put more thought into the fact that Christ Jesus was in them, crucified out of weakness and living by the power of God.

The Corinthians needed the Lord's speaking about his grace displayed in death and resurrection. This grace kept them from being disqualified, that is, reprobate (v. 5). This grace qualified Paul as an apostle. It was not that he had great leadership abilities or eloquence. The evidence of Christ speaking in Paul was the apostle's display of Christ's disposition. It was not seen in the number of his miracles or how many followers he had. The question is, Was he gracious and conciliatory? The Corinthians could find out that Paul was qualified by listening to Christ speak about their position in grace (v. 6).

*For we also are weak in him, but we shall live
with him by the power of God toward you.*
2 CORINTHIANS 13:4

I am thine, O Lord, I have heard thy voice,
And it told thy love to me;
But I long to rise in the arms of faith
And be closer drawn to thee.

FANNY J. CROSBY (1820–1915)
I AM THINE, O LORD

THE JOY OF OUR EXPECTATION

In this couplet, Fanny Crosby displays the joy of hope (1 Thessalonians 2:19). First Thessalonians tells of this joy because it was written "that ye sorrow not, even as others which have no hope" (4:13). It accomplishes this so well that we are enabled to do the seemingly impossible—always rejoice (5:16).

The Thessalonian believers actively displayed faith and brotherly love (1:7–9; 4:9–10). But they lacked calmness and interfered in others' affairs (4:11). They were sorrowful, fearful, and disorderly (4:13; 2 Thessalonians 2:2; 3:6–15). In their defense, we may ask how they could rejoice and be at peace when they were so afflicted and the world around was so opposed to their God (1 Thessalonians 2:14–16). Above all, they had a false notion of the future (4:13). None of us could rejoice, even occasionally, with such a dark view of things.

Paul knew that once the Thessalonians saw their hope—the expectation for their future—their dismal outlook would be replaced by joy. So he revealed to them the details of the Lord's coming for us. That is, the dead believers will be made alive, and those who are alive will be snatched away with them to meet the Lord in the air (4:13–18). He told them we will not experience God's wrath at the end of this age but will obtain his salvation (5:9). These truths make it possible for us to always rejoice.

Just because we don't always rejoice doesn't mean we can't or that we have no reason to do so. Our expectation for the future gives us reason to rejoice even in the midst of our most trying circumstances.

Now the God of hope fill you with all joy and peace in believing, that ye
may abound in hope, through the power of the Holy Ghost.
ROMANS 15:13

Sweet hour of prayer, sweet hour of prayer,
May I thy consolation share,
Till, from Mount Pisgah's lofty height,
I view my home and take my flight.

WILLIAM WALFORD (1772–1850)
SWEET HOUR OF PRAYER

A VIEW OF OUR CELESTIAL HERITAGE

From Mount Pisgah's lofty height, the Lord showed Moses the entire Promised Land (Deuteronomy 34:1–3). Just as the man of God saw Israel's future from that pinnacle, we see all that awaits us from the vantage point of scripture. This view can occupy every hour of prayer from now until it comes to pass.

Israel is forever tied to its earthly heritage. But ours is a celestial heritage. Our blessings are among the heavenlies. We are seated there in Christ, where, in the coming ages, God will display in us the exceeding riches of his grace (Ephesians 1:3; 2:6–7). Since our realm is in the heavens, even now we are oriented to that which is above (Philippians 3:20; Colossians 3:2). This is why "when Christ, who is our life, shall appear, then shall ye also appear with him in glory" (v. 4).

God's purpose includes not only the earth but the entire universe. So when the trumpet of God sounds and the dead in Christ rise, those of us who are living will be snatched away to meet the Lord in the air. As he brings Israel's promised kingdom to earth, we will take the testimony of grace to the celestials (Ephesians 2:6–7). For this task, we will need the transfigured bodies mentioned in Philippians 3:21 and detailed in 1 Corinthians 15. If the Lord delays, we will die like seeds. As for our body, "it is sown in dishonour; it is raised in glory: it is sown in weakness; it is raised in power: it is sown a natural body; it is raised a spiritual body" (vv. 43–44). Clothed in such bodies, we will enjoy our celestial heritage.

For this corruptible must put on incorruption,
and this mortal must put on immortality.
1 CORINTHIANS 15:53

August 28

This robe of flesh I'll drop and rise
To seize the everlasting prize;
And shout, while passing through the air,
"Farewell, farewell, sweet hour of prayer!"

WILLIAM WALFORD (1772–1850)
SWEET HOUR OF PRAYER

THE EVENTS OF THE FINAL DAY

The return of Christ is the beginning of the end of the present age. Then, as William Walford says in his hymn, we'll drop our robes of flesh and rise to meet the Lord in the air (1 Thessalonians 4:17). This closes the long era of God's grace and sets in motion the contrasting period of God's swift wrath. The inspired terms that describe Christ at this time portray his character differently from those with which we are familiar today. The gentle directions of the Good Shepherd will be replaced by the commander's shout. Rather than the teacher's patient words, we will hear the chief messenger's voice. The ministrations of the Great Physician will be no longer needed. Then we will hear the trumpet of God (v. 16).

The Lord's commanding shout comes first. This is a military order that demands instant obedience (v. 16). In this present wicked day, we are able to stand because we are equipped with the armor of God (Ephesians 6:12–13). But then the commander will call us to do direct battle in the heavens against the prince of the power of the air (2:2).

The archangel mentioned here must not be Gabriel, and here's why: Malachi 1:1–2 shows that the Son is the chief messenger seen in 1 Thessalonians 4:16. No angel, no matter how superior, would be sent to call Christ's members to be with him always. The Lord's body responds only to its head.

There are three distinct actions in this grand event. The commander's shout will raise the dead believers. The messenger's voice instructs those who are still alive. Trumpets have historically been used to direct troop movements. So might it be that the figurative trumpet of God will call us all to our place with the Lord in the air? However this occurs, we pray:

Amen. . . . Come, Lord Jesus.
REVELATION 22:20

Soon shall the trump of God
Give out the welcome sound,
That shakes death's silent chamber walls,
And breaks the turf-sealed ground.

HORATIUS BONAR (1808–1889)
SOON SHALL THE TRUMP OF GOD

OUR RESURRECTED BODIES

Some believers in Corinth struggled with the idea of resurrection. "How are the dead raised up?" they asked. "With what body do they come?" The answer is found in the sowing of seed (1 Corinthians 15:35–38).

When a grain of wheat is planted in the ground, it dies and is given life. But does an identical seed come forth? No. It shoots up into a stalk, sends down roots, and bears many kernels that are like the original seed. A seed's dying and rising creates forms and functions entirely unlike the original seed. It is the same when believers are made alive at the last trumpet. The secret of the resurrection is that our bodies undergo extreme change in the resurrection (vv. 50–54).

After his resurrection, the Lord appeared among his disciples in an extraordinary body. It became invisible, it entered locked rooms; yet it was a real body with flesh and bones. Christ was not a spirit. He could be touched, and he ate food. The saints who rule with Christ on the earth in his kingdom will have such bodies (1 John 3:2). But we have a celestial destiny. So our bodies of humiliation will be transfigured to conform to Christ's glorious body (Philippians 3:20–21).

Christ Jesus was in that glorious body when he called Paul. It was so much more glorious than the body he displayed before his ascension that its brightness wounded the future apostle's eyes (Acts 9:8). Peter and the others sometimes did not recognize their resurrected master, but they were not blinded by light. Paul saw him in a body that was brighter than the noonday sun (26:12–13). Our glory will be like this when our humble bodies are exchanged for ones that are like that of the ascended Lord.

We shall all be changed, in a moment, in the twinkling of an eye, at the last trump.
1 CORINTHIANS 15:51–52

Blest are the sons of peace
Whose hearts and hopes are one,
Whose kind designs to serve and please
Through all their actions run.

JOHN FAWCETT (1740–1817)
BLEST BE THE TIE THAT BINDS

THE PURSUIT OF PEACE

The portions of Paul's epistles that deal with the believers' conduct are saturated with a peaceful spirit. Romans 12:9–21; Ephesians 4:1–5; and Colossians 3:12–20 are only three examples of this. A direct exhortation to peace is found in Romans 14:19: "Let us therefore follow after the things which make for peace."

The word "therefore" in this verse indicates that our pursuit of peace is based on something that has already been mentioned. This peace is not based on humanitarianism or some other philosophy. It is the operation of the peace placed within us by God. This began when we were justified by faith and found "peace with God through our Lord Jesus Christ" (5:1). As we grow in this peace, God places in us the message of his reconciliation with the world (2 Corinthians 5:19). And since God is making his appeal for peace with the world through us, how can we not imitate God and pursue peace, as well (v. 20; Ephesians 5:1)?

Scripture does not say that we *must* pursue peace or even that we *should* do so. This is not a commandment or an obligation. We do it because we ourselves are at peace. This may not spring up in our lives overnight, but it is certainly the result of our growth toward maturity. Whether or not we see any positive effect in others is beside the point and is entirely in God's hands. As we pursue peace, imitating the God of peace, we are the ones who benefit; our spirits are blessed and our faith is strengthened.

> *Be ye therefore followers of God, as dear children;*
> *and walk in love, as Christ also hath loved us, and hath given himself*
> *for us an offering and a sacrifice to God for a sweetsmelling savour.*
> EPHESIANS 5:1–2

High on the cross the Savior hung,
High in the heav'ns he reigns:
Here sinners by th' old serpent stung
Look, and forget their pains.

ISAAC WATTS (1674–1748)
AS WHEN THE HEBREW PROPHET RAISED

THE UPLIFTING OF CHRIST, PART 1

Jesus Christ foretold his being lifted up on the cross in judgment for our sin (John 12:32). Such deliverance through an uplifting is seen elsewhere in scripture, as well.

"And the waters increased, and bare up the ark, and it was lift up above the earth" (Genesis 7:17). The waters of judgment lifted up the ark in the days of the deluge. Within it, Noah, his family, and the animals found salvation. That all creatures were represented there means that all was included in Christ on the cross. So we read that "if one died for all, then were all dead" (2 Corinthians 5:14). Christ bore the flood of judgment upon sin. We are safe because our salvation is in him.

Twice Moses lifted up his rod. When God instructed him to lift it up and strike the waters of Egypt, he did so and they were turned to blood (Exodus 7:20). In Egypt, the Nile River and its tributaries are the only fresh water. They are the life of the world. But the judgment of the cross has crucified the world to us (Galatians 6:14). This is why we can smell the stench of death in the world system (Exodus 7:21). At the same time, we are crucified to the world. So let us not be surprised that the world considers us dead by its standards.

Moses lifted his rod the second time when the waters of the sea were parted (14:13–18). In this one action, Israel escaped from Egypt and God destroyed Pharaoh and his army so the people could not be recaptured. These events picture our salvation in Christ, who saves us from death and abolishes death so we will never again be subject to it (1 Corinthians 10:1–4; 2 Timothy 1:10).

And as Moses lifted up the serpent in the wilderness, even so must the Son of man be lifted up.
JOHN 3:14

When God's own Son is lifted up,
A dying world revives;
The Jew beholds the glorious hope,
Th' expiring Gentile lives.

Isaac Watts (1674–1748)
As When the Hebrew Prophet Raised

The Uplifting of Christ, Part 2

Events in Samson's life (Judges 15:9–20) display God's salvation through the uplifting of Christ. Like our Lord, Samson was taken without a struggle and handed over to a ruling nation for execution. Then the Spirit of God came upon him, and he killed a thousand Philistines with the jawbone of a donkey. When Samson cried out in thirst, God opened a spring on a hill and water came out to quench his thirst. The hill where this occurred was called Ramath-lehi, which means "the uplifting (or hill) of the jawbone." The spring of water was named En-hakkore, meaning "the well of him that cried." Christ fought a great battle when he was lifted up on the hill Golgotha, "the place of the skull." He also cried out in thirst. Then God opened the well of the water of life for all.

Jesus said, "As Moses lifted up the serpent in the wilderness, even so must the Son of man be lifted up" (John 3:14). Here he referred to the events recorded in Numbers 21:5–9. Then fiery serpents bit and killed many Israelites. God easily could have caused those serpents to go away. Instead, he let them remain and provided a means of healing. This was a serpent made of bronze lifted up on a pole. By looking at it, those who were bitten by the serpents lived.

Long ago, the serpent bit Adam, figuratively speaking, and since then death has passed along to the entire human race (Romans 5:12). The cure is Jesus Christ, lifted up on the cross like the bronze serpent. He was made sin for us so we can be the righteousness of God in him (2 Corinthians 5:21). So we are assured that "as in Adam all die, even so in Christ shall all be made alive" (1 Corinthians 15:22).

And I, if I be lifted up from the earth, will draw all men unto me.
John 12:32

Lifted up was he to die;
"It is finished!" was his cry;
Now in heav'n exalted high.
Hallelujah! What a Savior!

PHILIP BLISS (1838–1876)
HALLELUJAH! WHAT A SAVIOR

THE UPLIFTING OF CHRIST, PART 3

God's purpose for the entire universe focused on a lone, cursed, executed man. This display of divine love did not occur in the heavens as a grand exhibit to the whole world. God didn't need all the promised land to enact this greatest of events. Nor was it a well-ordered ritual in the temple of Jerusalem, the Holy City. His purpose was reduced to about a square foot of earth; enough to mount a pole in the ground upon which to hang the one through whom and for whom all was created (Colossians 1:17).

Jesus Christ knew he would be lifted up from the earth in this way. Though it was not evident at the time, his cruel death held the promise of unlimited expansion. It was the beginning of his drawing all to himself (John 12:32).

Angels heralded his birth from the womb of a woman. They announced his emergence from the tomb, as well. "Why seek ye the living among the dead?" asked two brilliant angels. "He is not here, but is risen" (Luke 24:5–6). That day, Jesus became the firstborn from the dead and the firstfruits of them that slept (1 Corinthians 15:20; Colossians 1:18). While hanging on the cross, Christ was the last Adam (v. 45); now he is the firstborn and the firstfruit. These two titles indicate that many more will follow the Savior out of death.

For therefore we both labour and suffer reproach, because we trust in the living God, who is the Saviour of all men, specially of those that believe.
1 TIMOTHY 4:10

O holy city, seen of John, Where Christ the Lamb doth reign,
Within whose foursquare walls shall come
No night, nor need, nor pain,
And where the tears are wiped from eyes
That shall not weep again.

WALTER R. BOWIE (1882–1969)
O HOLY CITY, SEEN OF JOHN

SCENES IN THE FINAL AGE

We discover inspiring scenes in the last two chapters of the Bible. Let us allow our vision to be expanded by faith in what is written there. Our preconceived ideas on these subjects fall away as we let the scriptures speak about this surprisingly simple topic. Here are a few of the many amazing details:

New Jerusalem covers a perfect square that is nearly 1,380 miles on each side (Revelation 21:16). It is equally as high. It must be pyramidal, because this form permits buildings of any height. A pyramid the size of New Jerusalem has more surface area than the continental United States. Though this magnificent city is heavenly, it is located on the earth (v. 2; Hebrews 11:10; 12:22). Outside its walls are nations ruled by kings just as some are today (Revelation 21:24).

Surprisingly, perfection has not been reached in New Jerusalem because "the leaves of the tree [are] for the healing of the nations" (22:2). Healing is needed only where there is sickness. But these healing leaves are so powerful that none die (21:4). Plus, it is not that there are no more tears; rather, God shall wipe away all tears. So any tears that still exist there must be tears of joy, because sorrow and pain are no more. Furthermore, the city will enjoy peace and quiet because there will be no crying out, shouting, or clamor within her walls (v. 4).

What is pictured in Revelation 21 and 22 is elsewhere called the administration of the fullness of times. During this age, the universe will become entirely headed up in Christ (Ephesians 1:10). Its end is described in 1 Corinthians 15:24–28 when death is abolished, all is subjected to the Son, and God becomes all in all.

I John saw the holy city, new Jerusalem.
REVELATION 21:2

Of mercy and of justice my thankful song shall be;
O Lord, in joyful praises my song shall rise to thee.
Within my house I purpose to walk in wisdom's way;
O Lord, I need thy presence; how long wilt thou delay?

AUTHOR UNKNOWN
OF MERCY AND OF JUSTICE
PARAPHRASE OF PSALM 101

HOW TO WALK IN WISDOM

When telling of the mystery of Christ, the apostle advises that we "walk in wisdom toward them that are without" (Colossians 4:5). Since the Son is the image of the invisible God, all the treasures of wisdom and knowledge are concealed in him (1:15, 2:3). Our knowledge of him is the foundation of our lives, and all we need for a walk in wisdom is found in the secret of Christ (Colossians 1:15–20).

We believers hold in our hearts this truth, which is the revelation of the secret of Christ: "In him all things in heaven and on earth were created. . .all things have been created through him and for him" (v. 16 NRSV). Our friends, neighbors, fellow workers, their families, and even their dogs and cats were created through Christ just as we were. They were created for him, as well. We share this in common with them, even though they may not yet believe. This fact alone should entirely change our attitude toward others.

Our walk among those in this world can be saturated with wisdom when we realize that, through Christ, all things are reconciled to God (v. 20). This is a big part of the secret of Christ. We are blessed to know that "God was in Christ, reconciling the world unto himself, not imputing their trespasses unto them" (2 Corinthians 5:19). Wisdom for our walk can be found in the knowledge that God has committed the message of reconciliation to us (vv. 19–20). This message revolutionizes the feelings of our hearts toward others.

How that by revelation he made known unto me the mystery; (as I
wrote afore in few words, whereby, when ye read, ye may understand my
knowledge in the mystery of Christ). . .
EPHESIANS 3:3–4

Beloved, let us love: love is of God;
In God alone hath love its true abode.
Beloved, let us love: for they who love,
They only, are his sons, born from above.

HORATIUS BONAR (1808–1889)
BELOVED, LET US LOVE

GOD'S INDESCRIBABLE GIFT

God's absolute power and righteousness are especially seen in the obedience of his Son to the death of the cross. The fact that Jesus Christ died for our sins, was entombed, and has been raised is the key to realizing the character of our God and Father.

God's power for salvation and the righteousness in his operations are seen in the gospel as the expression of his love. The apostles John and Paul both describe the work and faith of Christ as the demonstration of this love. John wrote, "For God so loved the world, that he gave his only begotten Son, that whosoever believeth in him should not perish, but have everlasting life" (John 3:16). And Paul said, "God commendeth his love toward us, in that, while we were yet sinners, Christ died for us" (Romans 5:8).

God's gift of his Son conveys his selfless, unyielding, and effective compassion. That love is selfless in that he gave his Son for our benefit (1 Corinthians 13:5). It is unyielding because nothing, not even our fears and failures, can separate us from it (Romans 8:35–39; 1 Corinthians 13:8). It is effective in that it brings nothing but blessings (Ephesians 1:4–6; 2:4–7).

Love is patient; love is kind; love is not envious or boastful or arrogant or
rude. It does not insist on its own way; it is not irritable or resentful; it
does not rejoice in wrongdoing, but rejoices in the truth. It bears all things,
believes all things, hopes all things, endures all things. Love never ends.
1 CORINTHIANS 13:4–8 NRSV

Love divine, all loves excelling,
Joy of heaven to earth come down;
Fix in us thy humble dwelling;
All thy faithful mercies crown!

CHARLES WESLEY (1707–1788)
LOVE DIVINE, ALL LOVES EXCELLING

WE ARE OBJECTS OF THE FATHER'S LOVE

Abraham loved Isaac with a deep, warm, and robust love. But when his son was still a lad, God instructed Abraham to sacrifice him (Genesis 22). The word *son* appears ten times in Genesis 22. As you read this chapter, pause each time it appears and feel the love there. Could Abraham have endured a severer test than this? Surely this father loved nothing on earth more than his son.

Likewise, David loved Absalom. Despite his rebellion, Absalom was the object of David's strong love. When he heard that the young man's rebellion had led to his death, the king wept with sorrow and cried, "O my son Absalom, my son, my son Absalom! would God I had died for thee, O Absalom, my son, my son!" (2 Samuel 18:33). The love of a father for his son is most intense and deep.

But the love of God the Father toward his Son, Jesus Christ, excels all loves. Note their loving relationship: "I will be to him a Father, and he shall be to me a Son" (Hebrews 1:5). Note the trust in their love: "The Father loveth the Son, and hath given all things into his hand" (John 3:35). Note the pleasure in the Father's love: "This is my beloved Son, in whom I am well pleased" (Matthew 3:17). As we read in the Greek New Testament, our Lord is simply "the Son of His [God's] love" (Colossians 1:13 NKJV).

And as for us, according to the delight of his will, God has designated us as his children (Ephesians 1:5). Let us go to him as his children, fearless, with our hearts soaring in love, crying "Abba Father!" and, as his heirs, rejoicing in joyous thanksgiving (Romans 8:15; Galatians 4:6).

Wherefore thou art no more a servant, but a son;
and if a son, then an heir of God through Christ.
GALATIANS 4:7

September 7

Jesus, thou art all compassion, Pure unbounded love thou art;
Visit us with thy salvation; Enter every trembling heart.

CHARLES WESLEY (1707–1788)
LOVE DIVINE, ALL LOVES EXCELLING

THE FIRST ACT OF LOVE IN HUMAN HISTORY

Adam was made in the image and likeness of God and given authority over the lower creation (Genesis 1:26). He was also charged not to eat of the tree of the knowledge of good and evil (2:17). Therefore, it is not likely that the serpent could have influenced him. The serpent was so crafty that he did not approach Adam directly. Instead, he dealt with the man through Eve, who was one flesh with her husband (v. 24).

Adam ate of the forbidden tree only after Eve had done so and had involved all their descendants in the transgression. In this way, Adam resembles Jesus Christ who didn't sin but voluntarily involved himself in our offense and bore our sin on the cross (Romans 5:15). Adam didn't personally take of the tree; he only ate what his wife gave him after she had tasted it (1 Timothy 2:13–14). If he hadn't done this, Eve, his helper and complement (Genesis 2:20–23), would have suffered the penalty alone.

Imagine what Adam said to Eve after she had eaten of the fruit of the tree of the knowledge of good and evil. Surely he explained the awful consequence her transgression had brought into God's creation. Since the serpent didn't deceive Adam, why did he taste that fruit? It was because he loved Eve just as he did his own flesh (Ephesians 5:28–30). How could he bear to think that his wife might suffer the penalty of her offense alone? Her deed was the firstfruit of evil among humankind, and it motivated the first act of love. Adam's love for his wife beautifully suggests Christ's love for his body, the Church. With such compassion, Christ suffered complete separation from God and the most degrading of deaths, hallowing and cleansing us to make a glorious Church (vv. 25–27).

And Adam was not deceived, but the woman
being deceived was in the transgression.
1 TIMOTHY 2:14

Alone thou goest forth,
O Lord, in sacrifice to die;
Is this thy sorrow naught to us
Who pass unheeding by?

PETER ABELARD (1079–1142)
ALONE THOU GOEST FORTH
TRANSLATED BY F. BLAND TUCKER (1895–1984)

THE CURSE OF THE CROSS

Moses prescribed stoning as the method for capital punishment in Israel (Leviticus 24:14). This was a comparatively swift and painless death. A single blow on the head could stun the victim into unconsciousness. The Romans' way of crucifixion was far more painful and shameful. They usually attached their victim's arms above his head to a single upright stake and left him there to die. In this position, the weight of the body restricts its ability to breathe. Death comes by suffocation—a lingering and humiliating spectacle. In that position, Jesus Christ was made a curse for us (Galatians 3:13).

There is no glamour in the cross of Christ; no light, only dense darkness; no power, only weakness; no glory, only shame. Jesus was hung just high enough that his feet did not touch the ground. The disgraceful Crucifixion is the end of the Son's descent from the highest glory to the lowest humiliation (Philippians 2:6–8). Scripture leaves nothing to the imagination when describing this: "For our sake [God] made him to be sin who knew no sin" (2 Corinthians 5:21 NRSV)

Here is how Jesus felt as he hung there: "I am poured out like water, and all my bones are out of joint. My heart has turned to wax; it has melted away within me. My strength is dried up like a potsherd, and my tongue sticks to the roof of my mouth; you lay me in the dust of death" (Psalm 22:14–15 NIV).

Christ hath redeemed us from the curse of the law, being made a curse for us: for it is written, Cursed is every one that hangeth on a tree.
GALATIANS 3:13

Lord, I am glad thou know'st my inmost being,
Glad thou dost search the secrets of my heart;
I would not hide one folly from thy seeing,
Nor shun thy healing touch to save the smart.

HENRY W. HAWKES (1843–1917)
THOU KNOWEST, LORD

THE EFFECT OF THE SCRIPTURES

If believers wish to allow God's light to reach their inmost being, to experience God's searching of the heart's secrets, and to know his healing touch, they must be intimately involved with God's Word. Our direct engagement with the sacred scriptures connects us with God and his power for salvation and frees us from occupation with sin.

A person cannot look in opposite directions at the same time. Therefore, scripture encourages us to actively reckon ourselves alive to God. This renders us dead to sin because we cannot regard our sin and God's righteousness simultaneously (Romans 6:11). As we understand Christ's saving activity at the cross, his entombment, and resurrection, a bright light is cast on the shadow of sin and reveals its awfulness. The truth of the gospel leads to happiness for our deliverance from sin's dominion, and it cancels our tendency to amuse ourselves with sin. Even better, it prevents our fruitless, fleshly efforts to abolish sin from our lives, and it enables us to boast in the cross of our Lord Jesus Christ (Galatians 6:14).

We are often encouraged to imitate the apostle Paul (1 Corinthians 4:16; Philippians 3:17). If we focus on scripture, we will notice that he was determined to know nothing except Jesus Christ and him crucified (1 Corinthians 2:2). This word of the cross, which is found throughout Paul's epistles, will dim the things of this world that distract us from God and his salvation.

The word of God is living and active, sharper than any two-edged sword,
piercing until it divides soul from spirit, joints from marrow;
it is able to judge the thoughts and intentions of the heart.
HEBREWS 4:12 NRSV

Our earth we now lament to see
With floods of wickedness overflowed,
With violence, wrong, and cruelty,
The killing fields our constant abode,
Where men like fiends each other tear,
In all the hellish rage of war.

CHARLES WESLEY (1707–1788)
OUR EARTH WE NOW LAMENT TO SEE

GOD'S LOVE AND THE WORLD'S DEPRAVITY

People see the world's suffering, injustice, and disarray and ask, "Why doesn't God do something about this?" Some use this as an excuse to question the existence of God, who created the world for his pleasure and glory. To him, the creation was very good. But the work of an enemy whom humankind prefers over its Creator has changed this. So no one should expect the present world, which has fallen under the organized power of Satan, to bring pleasure to the holy God (Ephesians 2:1–2).

Yes, God seems to be indifferent toward the world. But this is actually evidence of his deep interest in it. People who challenge God to do something about the world's condition do not see that this delay confirms his love. As long as he postpones the day of his wrath, the world's inhabitants have opportunity to receive his salvation. The fact that God's ambassadors are still here beseeching the world, "Be ye reconciled to God!" is proof of the Creator's love (2 Corinthians 5:19–20).

God has not abandoned this world. In the fullness of time, he sent his beloved Son into it to reveal his love and redemptive purpose. What more could be expected? Yet this revelation of God, rich in grace, revealed something else: The world has no appreciation of infinite love and goodness. So why doesn't God simply bring in the judgment? It is because he formed a purpose before the world ever existed (Ephesians 3:11). This will be carried out in righteousness to its consummation.

He has fixed a day on which he will have the world judged in righteousness
by a man whom he has appointed, and of this he has given assurance to all
by raising him from the dead.
ACTS 17:31 NRSV

Thy cross I'll place before me, Its saving power be o'er me,
Wherever I may be; Thine innocence revealing,
Thy love and mercy sealing, The pledge of truth and constancy.

PAUL GERHARDT (1607–1676)
UPON THE CROSS EXTENDED

GOD'S WISDOM IN CHRIST

According to human wisdom, the word of the cross is stupidity. But as Paul Gerhardt's hymn points out, for believers it is the power of God (1 Corinthians 1:18). This is seen in the experience of Naaman the Syrian (2 Kings 5). In God's wisdom, the clean water of the rivers near Damascus would not cure Naaman's leprosy, no matter what he expected (v. 12). Only the muddy waters of the Jordan River could heal him. Likewise, God made Christ, who didn't know sin, to be sin for us. Only in that way could we be God's righteousness in him (2 Corinthians 5:21). Man's arguments and creeds—all the Syrian waters—cannot heal our sin.

The brass serpent also illustrates this principle (Numbers 21:6–9). Those who were bitten by serpents saw the brass serpent that Moses hung on a pole and were healed (John 3:14). This brings to mind the act of the ancient serpent, Satan, who brought sin into the world (Genesis 3:1). Yet God promised that the seed of the first sinful woman would bruise that serpent's head. Human wisdom could not imagine that this seed would appear to be a serpent. Yet the Son of Man, like the brass serpent in the wilderness, was suspended on a pole in order to destroy the one who had the power of death (Hebrews 2:14).

People cannot deliver themselves from sin in waters of their own choosing, nor can they glamorize the Savior. Wise philosophies, theologies, self-help programs, and the like—however clean and attractive—are of no use. The world must find deliverance in Christ where God in his wisdom provides it.

We preach Christ crucified, unto the Jews a stumblingblock, and unto the
Greeks foolishness; but unto them which are called, both Jews and Greeks,
Christ the power of God, and the wisdom of God.
1 CORINTHIANS 1:23–24

Lord, circumcise our hearts, we pray,
Our fleshly natures purge away;
Thy name, thy likeness may they bear:
Yea, stamp thy holy image there!

SEBASTIEN BESNAULT (D. 1724)
O HAPPY DAY, WHEN FIRST WAS POURED

THE SYMBOLISM OF CIRCUMCISION

The Jews take pride in their distinction from the other nations. The scriptural sign of this contrast is circumcision. This physical ritual is mentioned in the Greek scriptures because Jewish believers mistakenly thought that Gentile believers had to be circumcised and keep the Jewish law in order to be saved (Acts 15:1). However, no physical act can shield a person from God's judgment; not baptism, the Lord's Supper, or church attendance. Only faith in Christ can save us, because by this we participate in his death (Romans 6:5–7).

In the rite of circumcision a bit of flesh is cut off. This is simply a sign indicating the failure of all human flesh in God's eyes. Spiritually speaking, we have put off all our flesh in the circumcision of Christ (Colossians 2:11). This is the reality of Christ's death—the end of the flesh. In other words, our faith in Christ acknowledges the fact that we can trade nothing we are or do for favorable treatment by God. Therefore, "we are the circumcision, which worship God in the spirit, and rejoice in Christ Jesus, and have no confidence in the flesh" (Philippians 3:3).

Anything we possess of value is not in ourselves but is in Christ who, like all Jewish boys, was circumcised on the eighth day (Luke 2:21). But his real circumcision came at the cross when he was cut off from the land of the living (Jeremiah 11:19); his flesh was stripped off and laid in the tomb. We have also stripped off the body of flesh in the circumcision of Christ and so possess the spiritual reality of which the physical rite is only the symbol.

And the LORD thy God will circumcise thine heart, and the heart of thy seed,
to love the LORD thy God with all thine heart, and with all thy soul, that
thou mayest live.
DEUTERONOMY 30:6

Fight the good fight with all thy might!
Christ is thy strength, and Christ thy right;
Lay hold on life, and it shall be
Thy joy and crown eternally.

JOHN S. B. MONSELL (1811–1875)
FIGHT THE GOOD FIGHT WITH ALL THY MIGHT

HOW TO FIGHT THE GOOD FIGHT

We need no personal strength to fight faith's good fight (1 Timothy 6:12). Like us, Timothy was called to this life of faith, and God gave him all he needed to live it. The spiritual assets that Paul encourages Timothy to pursue are similar to the figurative armor of God that we all receive (v. 11; Ephesians 6:13–17).

This armor of God covers our whole body, and except for the sword of the Spirit is only for defense. Within it, we are at rest. It is entirely sufficient to defeat the spiritual forces of wickedness (v. 12). God's truth gives us strength to withstand the attacks of error. Christ's righteousness protects our hearts from the wounds of iniquity. The gospel of peace with which we contact the world reconciles us with all people, especially those who are used by the spirit-powers to attack us. Faith, the gift of God, keeps us cool in the midst of the fiery fight (1 Thessalonians 5:8). The expectation of salvation assures us that judgment will never fall upon us.

We also receive the Word of God—the Spirit's sword. Yet this too has nothing to do with human strength. Our offensive power is every word that proceeds out of God's mouth (Luke 4:4).

But thou, O man of God, flee these things; and follow after righteousness, godliness, faith, love, patience, meekness. Fight the good fight of faith, lay hold on eternal life, whereunto thou art also called, and hast professed a good profession before many witnesses.
1 TIMOTHY 6:11–12

They come, God's messengers of love,
They come from realms of peace above,
From homes of never fading light,
From blissful mansions ever bright.

ROBERT CAMPBELL (1814–1868)
THEY COME, GOD'S MESSENGERS OF LOVE

OUR PRESENT RELATIONSHIP WITH ANGELS

The chief feature of our time is that God works with us through faith, which is a conviction about matters that are not seen. Therefore, we walk by faith, not by sight (2 Corinthians 5:7; 1 Timothy 1:4; Hebrews 11:1). Faith and sight are contrasted in scripture to teach us to base our life on that which is not yet seen (Romans 8:24–25).

Many people are interested in God's messengers, which are usually called angels. Let's consider them in light of our life of faith. A concordance reveals that their ministry is mostly related to Israel. They appear frequently in the Hebrew scriptures as God deals with the chosen nation. They are seen in the Gospels mostly in relation to the birth, death, and resurrection of Israel's Messiah. Angels are occasionally involved in the events described in Acts and are often seen in the final scenes of this age depicted in Revelation. In all of these cases, God's messengers are physically seen, so they are not related to our present life of faith.

Between the era of Acts, when Israel relinquished the blessings of the gospel (Acts 28:28), and that of Revelation when Israel again appears on the stage of the divine drama, angels are not active among us. Rather, by faith we see that we are presently a display for their instruction and will one day judge them (1 Corinthians 4:9; 6:3).

God's messengers hold lofty positions in the universe. But in Christ, we are in a much closer relationship to God than they are (Colossians 3:3). We have something far better than angels to help us in our faith. We are led by God's Spirit (Romans 8:14). Moreover, we have God's Word. Therefore, the illumination of our lives is not the light cast by angels, but that of scriptural revelation.

Know ye not that we shall judge angels?
1 CORINTHIANS 6:3

With Christ we share a mystic grave, with Christ we buried lie;
But 'tis not in the darksome cave by mournful Calvary.
The pure and bright baptismal flood entombs our nature's stain;
New creatures from the cleansing wave with Christ we rise again.

JOHN M. NEALE (1818–1866)
WITH CHRIST WE SHARE A MYSTIC GRAVE

THE BAPTISM OF JESUS CHRIST

Though our Lord was baptized in the Jordan River, he spoke of another baptism that would release him from the restrictions he experienced in his earthly ministry (Luke 12:50). Until that baptism, all baptisms were shadows. The washings of the law and the waters of Jordan did not remove the filth of the flesh, much less the moral defilement that came between our Creator and us. Still, these shadows point to the real thing.

What can wash away our defilement? Nothing but the death of Christ.

Jesus Christ's crucifixion is true and real and a parable of something deeply spiritual. When people die, their friends can no longer fellowship with them. Similarly, the cross severed Christ from the fellowship he had enjoyed with his Father from before the creation of the world. Even more, just as God consumed the ancient offering with fire from heaven, when Christ was made the sin offering for us on the cross, God sent fire into his bones (Leviticus 9:24; Lamentations 1:13).

God required our cleansing, and Jesus Christ's baptism accomplished it. Water could not do this, not even literal fire. Only the fierce fury of God's wrath could consume our sin. We may never know all that Jesus Christ's baptism involved. But we do know that only he could bear it; that it laid him in the grave; that he triumphantly rose from it and ascended to God's right hand. Because we see him there, we are assured that our sins, which he bore on the cross, are gone, because they can never share God's presence.

> *But I have a baptism to be baptized with;*
> *and how am I straitened till it be accomplished!*
> LUKE 12:50

In Christ there is no east or west,
In him no south or north;
But one great fellowship of love
Throughout the whole wide earth.

WILLIAM A. DUNKERLEY (1852–1941)
IN CHRIST THERE IS NO EAST OR WEST

OUR PLACE IN CHRIST

Ephesians 1:10 says that the heavens and the earth will be headed up in Christ. This is the first notice of our Lord's universal headship. It is our privilege to be the first to know him in this way because God "gave him to be the head over all things to the church" (v. 22). As we seek to know our Lord as God's administrator of redemption and salvation throughout the universe, we will find out what it means to be in Christ.

The phrase "in Christ" is not found in the four Gospels or the book of Acts. We first encounter it in Romans 3:24. Thereafter, Paul's epistles describe our position and allotment in Christ. The books of Hebrews, James, and Jude do not contain this idea. The epistles of Peter and John limit it to the Lord's earthly glories (1 Peter 3:16; 5:10, 14; 1 John 5:20).

In Christ there is deliverance (Romans 3:24), justification (Galatians 2:17), no condemnation (Romans 8:1), freedom (Galatians 5:1), holiness (1 Thessalonians 3:13), life (Romans 6:11, 23), a new creation (2 Corinthians 5:17), and all our expectation (1 Corinthians 15:19). But for believers to comprehend such grace, they must become acquainted with the worth and merit of Christ Jesus. It makes no difference if a person is from the West, the East, the South, or the North. All that God lavishes upon us comes not because of what we are in ourselves, but because of our place in Christ. And since it is only of God that we belong to him, let us not tarnish that splendor by thoughts that we deserve to be in him.

No flesh should glory in his presence. But of him are ye in Christ Jesus,
who of God is made unto us wisdom, and righteousness,
and sanctification, and redemption.
1 CORINTHIANS 1:29–30

How blest the man who fears the Lord
And greatly loves God's holy will;
His children share his great reward,
And blessings all their days shall fill.

AUTHOR UNKNOWN
HOW BLEST THE MAN WHO FEARS THE LORD
PARAPHRASE OF PSALM 112

THE PLATFORM, OR DAIS, OF CHRIST

In the midst of the joy and hope of the gospel message, we read, "For all of us must appear before the judgment seat of Christ, so that each may receive recompense for what has been done in the body, whether good or evil. Therefore, knowing the fear of the Lord. . ." (2 Corinthians 5:10–11 NRSV). This doesn't mean that we should be frightened of our Savior. Rather, it is expected that our spirit will express reverence and awe toward the one who foreknew us and chose us to be holy and flawless in his sight (Romans 8:29; Ephesians 1:4).

Tradition has presented us with a so-called judgment seat of Christ. But in each of the ten times the term *judgment seat* appears in scripture, it is used to translate the Greek word *bema*. This word is still used in modern English to designate a simple platform. The church would have greatly benefited if the translators had allowed Christ's bema to be what it actually is: a dais or a platform. These words do not describe a seat or a judgment. Christ will not sit in judgment of believers in the same way he will sit on the great white throne of the world's judgment (Revelation 20:11–12).

Christ bore our judgment for sin on the cross. Therefore, we are now and always will be entirely justified before God concerning sin. The dais of Christ will simply disclose what has been good and valuable in our lives and what has been worthless in the light of God's purpose (1 Corinthians 3:11–13). This inspires us to be sober and faithful to the Lord and his Word.

Therefore do not pronounce judgment before the time, before the Lord comes, who will bring to light the things now hidden in darkness and will disclose the purposes of the heart. Then each one will receive commendation from God.
1 CORINTHIANS 4:5 NRSV

> *The saints of God! their conflict past,*
> *And life's long battle won at last,*
> *No more they need the shield or sword,*
> *They cast them down before their Lord:*
> *O happy saints! forever blest,*
> *At Jesus' feet how safe your rest!*

WILLIAM D. MACLAGAN (1826–1910)
THE SAINTS OF GOD! THEIR CONFLICT PAST

THE BELIEVERS' SAINTHOOD

Despite the traditional image of people with haloed heads and other worldly gazes, saints are simply people who have been sanctified by God's Spirit. Israel was once a holy nation (Exodus 19:6). It had holy places and holy priests. But the word *holy* does not apply to all the individuals of the chosen nation, because holiness was based on conduct or privilege, not on faith. In the present era, all people who are sanctified by faith in the Lord are saints (Acts 26:18).

Paul's epistles use the word *saint* six times as often as the other New Testament books combined. For example, God's love had been poured out in the hearts of the Romans through the Holy Spirit. (Romans 5:5). The Spirit of the one who raised Jesus from the dead was at home in them (8:11). Therefore, the epistle to the Romans was written to the beloved of God, called "saints" (1:7). Some of the Corinthian believers had been fornicators, idolaters, adulterers, male prostitutes, sodomites, thieves, drunkards, revilers, and robbers. But they were washed, sanctified, and justified in the name of the Lord Jesus Christ and in the Spirit of God (1 Corinthians 6:9–11 NRSV). So both Corinthian epistles were written to the saints (1:2; 2 Corinthians 1:1).

Paul makes it plain that sainthood belongs to all who have the Holy Spirit of God. Formerly, Israel was holy because of its physical status in contrast to the other nations. But now our blessings are spiritual (Ephesians 1:3). None are based on our fleshly accomplishments. Since we have received the Spirit by faith, all believers are saints.

Salute every saint in Christ Jesus. The brethren which are with me greet you. All the saints salute you, chiefly they that are of Caesar's household.
PHILIPPIANS 4:21–22

Thy Word, O Lord, thy precious Word alone, can lead me on;
By this, until the darksome night be gone, lead thou me on!
Thy Word is light, thy Word is life and power;
By it, oh, guide me in each trying hour.

ALBERT MIDLANE (1825–1909)
THY WORD, O LORD

THE VALUE OF PERSONAL STUDY

Authors always seek to control the copyright on their books. This enables them to receive payment for their labors and to protect their ideas and expressions from unauthorized use or distortion. Since we consider a person's words so untouchable, how much more should we honor God's words? He has exalted his Word, like his name, above all else (Psalm 138:2). So let us assign to him all rights to his inspired expressions and not distort scriptural vocabulary or wrench God's ideas from their context to support our human viewpoints.

As we honor the pattern of scripture's sound words and resist the hypocrisy of false expressions, we are led to the glorious goal of the ages (1 Timothy 4:2; 2 Timothy 1:13). This is why our hearts are in awe of God's Word as we prayerfully study it (Psalm 119:161). But why should we take the time and trouble to study when there is no end of people and publications that wish to do this for us?

Personal study of God's Word is our one source of true profit and pleasure. It is our way of seeking to work and walk in conformity to God's will. We study because we wish to graduate from milk to solid food, from predigested teachings to revelation of the truth. We wish to exercise our faculties to discriminate between what is good and what is evil (Hebrews 5:12–14). The Word will tear down the strongholds of human imagination and opinion that are exalted above the knowledge of God. We study it because we want our every thought to be captured by the obedience of Christ (2 Corinthians 10:4–5).

> *Study to shew thyself approved unto God, a workman that*
> *needeth not to be ashamed, rightly dividing the word of truth.*
> 2 TIMOTHY 2:15

Thy wondrous testimonies, Lord, My soul will keep and greatly praise;
Thy Word, by faithful lips proclaimed, To simplest minds the truth
conveys.

AUTHOR UNKNOWN
THY WONDROUS TESTIMONIES, LORD
PARAPHRASE OF PSALM 119

A MESSENGER MUST MATCH HIS MESSAGE

The drive to slander Paul and question his apostleship is nothing new.
This began when he was still living (1 Corinthians 8:1–2). The fact is,
Christ Jesus enabled Paul, counted him faithful, and put him into the
ministry (1 Timothy 1:12). No wonder Paul, not once, but four times,
urges us to imitate him (1 Corinthians 4:16; 11:1; Ephesians 5:1 NRSV;
Philippians 3:17). If we do this, we also may proclaim the word with
faithful lips.

Was Paul's life in harmony with the truth he taught? Paul's
personal testimony is especially found in 2 Corinthians 11–12. These
display the height of the truth of the gospel. The word of the cross
concerns the weakness and shame of Christ's death (1 Corinthians
1:18). This is reflected in Paul's humility and vulnerability as seen in
2 Corinthians 11:7–33. The ministry of reconciliation expresses God's
attitude of peace with the world (2 Corinthians 5:18–19). This is seen
in Paul's forbearance and delight in all his circumstances in 12:1–10.
He was right to testify, "The truth of Christ is in me" (11:10). His
behavior, which exactly matched his words, is proof of this.

This topic deserves an entire dissertation. Two examples must
suffice. Paul knew that God's justification of believers is given freely
(Romans 4:24). So he brought the gospel to Corinth with no charge
and was not burdensome to the saints there (2 Corinthians 11:7, 9).
He also knew that our fleshly advantages and differences were stripped
off in the death of Christ (Colossians 2:11). So he determined not to
know anything among the Corinthians except Jesus Christ and him
crucified (1 Corinthians 2:2). Paul's knowledge was translated into
his attitudes and actions. He shows that if the message is true, the
messenger will display the disposition of Christ.

Let this mind be in you, which was also in Christ Jesus.
PHILIPPIANS 2:5

Give thanks to God, for good is he, His grace abideth ever;
To him all praise and glory be, His mercy faileth never.
His wondrous works with praise record, His grace abideth ever.

AUTHOR UNKNOWN
GIVE THANKS TO GOD, FOR GOOD IS HE
PARAPHRASE OF PSALM 136

BLESSING THE GOD OF HEAVEN

We live in an evil age (Galatians 1:4). A veneer of human politics, religion, and culture barely disguises its confusion and vanity. We are blessed, however, if in the midst of this we can bless God, because the realization of God's goodness and grace saves us from the doubts provoked by the meaninglessness of the world around us.

This is nothing new. The prophet Daniel lived in the evil time of Israel's captivity in Babylon. Because of his character and intelligence, he was chosen to be an adviser to King Nebuchadnezzar. But this did not protect him. When the king had a troubling dream, he demanded that his advisers tell the dream and interpret it. If they could not do this, they would all die (Daniel 2:5). This was utterly unfair to Daniel. He hadn't been given an opportunity to solve the problem yet was to be executed for the failure of others.

Most of us would be indignant and seek to exonerate ourselves from blame. Not Daniel. He knew there is a God in heaven (v. 28). Therefore, when the dream was revealed to him in a vision, he didn't first tell the king or his advisers. Instead, he blessed the God of heaven (v. 19). Surely the hearts of Daniel's companions were filled with praise, as well. Eventually Nebuchadnezzar himself exulted in God (v. 47). And what of the king's hapless advisers? They must have given thanks that their lives were saved. Countless saints have read of the deliverance of Daniel and praised God for it.

Long after Nebuchadnezzar's dream is fulfilled, when God's harvest is ripened and gathered, all his creatures will follow Daniel's example and bless the God of heaven (Philippians 2:11).

Blessed be the God and Father of our Lord Jesus Christ.
EPHESIANS 1:3

We walk by faith, and not by sight;
No gracious words we hear
From him who spake as man ne'er spake;
But we believe him near.

HENRY ALFORD (1810–1871)
WE WALK BY FAITH

THE SPIRIT'S GUARANTEE

Unlike those who walked with Jesus Christ in Galilee, we have not physically heard the Lord's voice. We do, however, possess something they did not have. We walk by faith with the Spirit of God. This Spirit is described in the scriptures by various figures of speech. In 2 Corinthians, we find three of these: the anointing, the seal, and the earnest, or guarantee (1:21–22).

The priests and kings of Israel were anointed with oil when they took up their work for God (1 Samuel 10:1). We are also anointed, not with oil but with the Spirit. This Spirit qualifies us for service to God. We are also sealed with the Spirit as a sign of possession. Just as ranchers brand their cattle to show ownership, the Spirit is the mark upon us that declares we belong to God. Although Henry Alford's hymn says, "We believe him near," God is more than near to us; his Spirit is upon us like anointing oil and pressed into us like an embossed seal.

The earnest is the most experiential of the figures that describe the Spirit. It is that small installment of the Spirit within us—the guarantee that we will receive our celestial allotment in the day of redemption (Ephesians 1:13–14). With this guarantee, we walk by faith while we are absent from the Lord.

God. . .hath given unto us the earnest of the Spirit. Therefore we are always confident, knowing that, whilst we are at home in the body, we are absent from the Lord: (For we walk by faith, not by sight).
2 CORINTHIANS 5:5–7

On a hill far away stood an old rugged cross,
The emblem of suffering and shame;
And I love that old cross where the dearest and best
For a world of lost sinners was slain.

GEORGE BENNARD (1873–1958)
THE OLD RUGGED CROSS

THE LIGHT OF THE KNOWLEDGE
OF THE GLORY OF GOD

How did the world of lost sinners react to the sight of its dying Savior?

Israel, Greece, and Rome represented all humanity on history's most momentous day. The Jews were obsessed with their religion. To them the cross was a stumbling block because they could find no place for it in their teachings. The Greeks were seeking wisdom from their philosophers. The cross was complete foolishness to them (1 Corinthians 1:23). To the Romans, drunk with power, it displayed impotence (v. 25). As a flash of lightning at night exposes the landscape, the cross uncovers the true heart of man. On that day, humanity as a whole was found wanting. We who live today are no different from those living then.

An inscription written in three languages Hebrew, Greek, and Latin—was tacked to Christ's cross (John 19:20). It announced to each culture the identity of the man hanging there: "JESUS OF NAZARETH THE KING OF THE JEWS" (v. 19). He was the King of the nation that God had chosen to bring blessing to all nations (Isaiah 49:6–7). Yet he was also reproachfully branded "Jesus the Nazarene" (Mark 14:67 NASB). There he hung, despised and rejected by all humanity. He is likewise despised today.

The Jews' snare, the Greeks' stupidity, and the Romans' weakness are the power of God and the wisdom of God to us (1 Corinthians 1:23–25). They bring salvation to humanity and reconciliation to the universe (1 Timothy 2:4; Colossians 1:20). Despite the passing glory of religion, philosophy, politics, and all that is to the credit of humanity, light has shined in our hearts to illuminate the knowledge of the glory of God in the face of Jesus Christ (2 Corinthians 4:6).

God forbid that I should glory, save in the cross of our Lord Jesus Christ.
GALATIANS 6:14

Love shall be our token,
Love shall be yours and love be mine,
Love to God and to all men,
Love for plea and gift and sign.

CHRISTINA G. ROSSETTI (1830–1894)
LOVE CAME DOWN AT CHRISTMAS

THE MODEL OF LOVE

One of the earliest impulses of a believer's new life is to love his fellow saints. The young believers in Thessalonica must have been encouraged to read, "As touching brotherly love ye need not that I write unto you: for ye yourselves are taught of God to love one another" (1 Thessalonians 4:9). Brotherly love is instinctive, taught of God. Let us not allow differences in details to cause rifts between those who have the same life and harbor the same love as we.

The conduct of God's saints is based on God's method of working in their particular era. When the law came by Moses, God required conduct matching the law. But now grace has come through Jesus Christ and calls for loving behavior even under the most trying circumstances. The law allowed people to hate their enemies and to exact an equivalent in payment, like an eye for an eye (Matthew 5:38, 43). They could take action toward one another in the same way God dealt with them.

For us, God's grace is the model by which we pattern our conduct (Ephesians 5:1–2). God teaches us to "be kindly affectioned one to another with brotherly love" (Romans 12:10). His grace even extends to our enemies. So we are told:

Therefore if thine enemy hunger, feed him; if he thirst, give him drink: for in so doing thou shalt heap coals of fire on his head. Be not overcome of evil, but overcome evil with good.
ROMANS 12:20–21

Asleep in Jesus! Blessed sleep, From which none ever wakes to weep;
A calm and undisturbed repose, Unbroken by the last of foes.

MARGARET MACKAY (1802–1887)
ASLEEP IN JESUS

SLEEP AS A FIGURE OF DEATH

The scriptures frequently use figures of speech to aid our understanding. For example, the Lamb of God is a figure that helps us understand Jesus Christ as the sin offering. But only in that way is he like a lamb. Margaret Mackay imports the scriptural figure of sleep into her hymn to indicate death. But, to be sure, death is not like sleep in every way. When the Lord told his disciples he was going to awaken Lazarus, they took this literally (John 11:11–13). But Lazarus was not actually reposing in sleep, so the Lord Jesus told the disciples his friend was dead. In doing this, he presented the idea that death is in some ways like sleep.

The word *sleep* is used as a figure for death twelve times in the Greek scriptures. Both Stephen's and David's deaths are called sleep (Acts 7:59–60; 13:36). The death of some believers in the Corinthian church is also called sleep, as are the deaths of some of the witnesses to the Lord's resurrection (1 Corinthians 11:30; 15:6). Death, however, is not literally sleep. Involuntary bodily functions like digestion and breathing continue to operate in sleep. The body is built up by sleep, but in death, it disintegrates.

On the other hand, both the sleeper and the corpse are oblivious to all around them, and the passage of time for them does not exist. With dreamless sleep, the moment of falling asleep seems to be followed immediately by awakening. Then a person is refreshed and ready for a new day. So sleep as a figure of death reminds us of the resurrection, when we will be raised from death with a body fitted for service in the coming age (vv. 42–44).

For if we believe that Jesus died and rose again, even so them also which
sleep in Jesus will God bring with him.
1 THESSALONIANS 4:14

Asleep in Jesus! Oh, how sweet,
To be for such a slumber meet,
With holy confidence to sing
That death has lost his venomed sting!

MARGARET MACKAY (1802–1887)
ASLEEP IN JESUS

THE FACE OF DEATH IN THE WORD OF GOD

Death doesn't wear a friendly face in the Word of God. It is compared to a scorpion or similar creature that has a sting (1 Corinthians 15:55–56). It is considered defeat, because we are told that it will be swallowed up in victory (v. 54). Death reigns like a tyrant in the realm of sin (Romans 5:14, 17; 6:9). It is also a fearful horseman riding on a pale, greenish horse, killing with the sword, with famine and pestilence, and with wild beasts (Revelation 6:8).

The scriptures use several figures of speech to explain death; these clash with popular ideas. We sometimes hear of an angel of death, but scripture calls death an enemy, not an angel (1 Corinthians 15:26). People say death is a doorway to bright, heavenly mansions, but it really casts a dark shadow (Matthew 4:16; Luke 1:79). When our Lord was resurrected, he loosed the pains of death (Acts 2:24). Therefore, bliss is not found in death, no matter how saintly one may be. Even Jesus Christ depended on resurrection to loose him from death; therefore, no one else can expect to be free of death apart from the power of God in resurrection.

Scripture is silent about the period between the moment of death and the resurrection. Lazarus came back after a four-day stay in death, but we have no report of what he had to say about it. It seems Paul might tell us something when he writes, "I would not have you to be ignorant, brethren, concerning them which are asleep" (1 Thessalonians 4:13). But he reveals nothing about the present state of the dead. Instead, he directs us forward to resurrection. In other words, he gives us a glorious hope, not a golden harp.

Knowing that Christ being raised from the dead dieth no more; death hath no more dominion over him.
ROMANS 6:9

As with gladness, men of old
Did the guiding star behold
As with joy they hailed its light
Leading onward, beaming bright
So, most glorious Lord, may we
Evermore be led to thee.

WILLIAM C. DIX (1837–1898)
AS WITH GLADNESS, MEN OF OLD

GROPING FOR GOD

All of humanity emerged from one source and was given life and breath by the Almighty, who set the times and seasons of our existence and laid out the boundaries of the lands in which we dwell. This record of divine providence is intended to cause all people to seek after God (Acts 17:25–27). The magi, mentioned in the Gospel of Matthew, were such seekers. Their long journey from the East in search of the Jewish king is a sublime example of people groping for God.

Though they were guided across the deserts by a star, their searching hearts had been prepared to see that star by their studies of the night skies. So it is with all people. God is God, and he can use any human course of study, occupation, or interest to lead people to Christ. He created us to grope for, or "feel after," God (v. 27).

God is not far away from any of us. Knowing this, let's pray for our friends and loved ones that they will grope for God, who will give them a spirit of revelation in the full knowledge of him (Ephesians 1:17).

[God] hath made of one blood all nations of men for to dwell on all the face
of the earth, and hath determined the times before appointed, and the bounds
of their habitation; that they should seek the Lord, if haply they might feel
after him, and find him, though he be not far from every one of us.
ACTS 17:26–27

God gives his mercies to be spent;
Your hoard will do your soul no good.
Gold is a blessing only lent,
Repaid by giving others food.

WILLIAM COWPER (1731–1800)
GOD GIVES HIS MERCIES TO BE SPENT

THE GIFTS OF THE HAPPY GOD, PART 1

Only Acts 20:35 records these words of the Lord Jesus: "It is more blessed to give than to receive." Their meaning is profound. Happiness is not found in our own blessings, but in those blessings we bring to others. A high point of such happiness will come when the sons of God are unveiled and the whole creation is freed from the slavery of corruption (Romans 8:20–21). Then we will be the means of blessing to God's entire creation. How happy we will be when we deliver that blessing!

All believers, especially church leaders, should review Paul's closing words to the elders at Ephesus. We know the apostle preached grace to the Ephesians, because the word *grace* appears thirteen times in the epistle he wrote to them. But he did far more than preach grace—he practiced it. It was no boast when he said, "These hands have ministered unto my necessities, and to them that were with me" (Acts 20:34). Paul not only told the saints of the grace of Christ in their salvation; his generous behavior opened their eyes and hearts to receive it.

The apostle showed the believers not only how to work to supply their own needs but also to support the weak (v. 35). By doing this, they learned how grace operates, how giving brings more happiness than getting does. When we give to others who cannot give in return, we taste a little of the happiness that God enjoys as the fruit of his grace. Certainly we are made happy by his gifts, but we are not as happy as he is. In fact, we cannot give God anything except the happiness that comes to him when we accept his grace with thankful hearts.

Thanks be unto God for his unspeakable gift.
2 CORINTHIANS 9:15

Lord, thou lov'st the cheerful giver,
Who with open heart and hand
Blesses freely, as a river
That refreshes all the land.
Grant us then the grace of giving
With a spirit large and free,
That our life and all our living
We may consecrate to thee.

ROBERT MURRAY (1832–1910)
LORD, THOU LOV'ST THE CHEERFUL GIVER

THE GIFTS OF THE HAPPY GOD, PART 2

The apostle asks us to imitate God, and we see such imitation in Paul's own graceful, giving ways (Ephesians 5:1–2 NRSV).

Even though he advised that "they which preach the gospel should live of the gospel," Paul took nothing from the saints "lest we should hinder the gospel of Christ" (1 Corinthians 9:14, 12). In this way, he followed the prophet Samuel who, at the end of his career, spoke to the people: "Witness against me before the Lord," he said. "Whose ox have I taken? or whose ass have I taken? or whom have I defrauded? whom have I oppressed?" (1 Samuel 12:3). Moses said something similar during the rebellion of Korah, Dathan, and Abiram: "I have not taken one ass from them" (Numbers 16:15).

The ox and the donkey were the most valuable property of herdsmen and farmers like the Israelites (Exodus 20:17). By Paul's day things had changed, so he told the Ephesian elders, "I have coveted no man's silver, or gold, or apparel" (Acts 20:33). Everyone knew that Paul worked with his hands to support himself (18:3; 1 Corinthians 4:11–12). But unlike Moses and Samuel, Paul served during this era of God's grace. So when he reminded the saints "that these hands have ministered unto my necessities," he added, "and to them that were with me" (Acts 20:34). The second phrase shows that the apostle, like God, was occupied with giving. And so, as if to display how much he enjoys this, grace dominates God's operations.

He that spared not his own Son, but delivered him up for us all, how shall
he not with him also freely give us all things?
ROMANS 8:32

Ere you left your room this morning, did you think to pray?
In the name of Christ our Savior did you sue for loving favor
As a shield today?

MARY ANN KIDDER (1820–1905)
DID YOU THINK TO PRAY?

THE PURPOSE OF PRAYER, PART 1

John tells us that God hears our prayers if we ask according to his will (1 John 5:14). Some people may say, "Since that's the case, why pray at all? It won't change anything." Logically, reasonably, prayer seems to be a mere formality and a fruitless effort. But the fruitless thing is reasoning about the ways of God, which are foolishness to the natural man (1 Corinthians 2:14). We are people of faith, however, so we believe the scriptures. They provide many examples of prayer, requests for prayer, and instructions to pray. We cannot ignore these.

Through the prophet Ezekiel, God describes the restoration of the holy land in the day of the Lord. In the midst of this, he says, "I will also let the house of Israel ask me to do this for them" (Ezekiel 36:37 NRSV). This shows that God determines the answer to prayer, and that the prayer itself is also a part of his plan. The house of Israel will pray because God puts it into their hearts to do so.

Still, the questions come: Why does prayer have any usefulness when God has planned the course of the ages to the last detail? Since prayer cannot change this plan, why bother? These thoughts are from the human side, and they express ignorance of God's purpose. Still, there is a simple answer: Presently God is somewhat important to some people. As we pray, he reveals himself more and more to us and to others. He will continue to do this until the day when he is all in all creation and his purpose is consummated (1 Corinthians 15:28).

For this reason I bow my knees before the Father, from whom every family
in heaven and on earth takes its name.
EPHESIANS 3:14–15 NRSV

When your heart was filled with anger, did you think to pray?
Did you plead for grace, my brother, that you might forgive another
Who had crossed your way?

MARY ANN KIDDER (1820–1905)
DID YOU THINK TO PRAY?

THE PURPOSE OF PRAYER, PART 2

God uses various means to draw us to himself. One of the most effective of these is prayer.

The purpose of prayer is not to tell God what to do. Nor can we convince him to change his plan to match our desires. Imagine the confusion that would cause! President Lincoln noted that each side in America's Civil War "read the same Bible, and pray to the same God; and each invokes his aid against the other. . . . The prayer of both could not be answered; that of neither has [been]." Both sides in that conflict prayed for a quick, easy victory. Both were refused. I wonder if any of those who prayed in those bloody days closed their prayers like Jesus Christ did: "Not my will, but thine be done."

We believers feel the need to fellowship with God. We are privileged to pour our hearts out to him. Over time, as we pray and remain in the Word, we gain a realization of God and his will. This is humbling because it is then we learn that all things work together to *God's* good (Romans 8:28). We pray and God gains. He becomes more and more to us. Our fellowship with him advances his great purpose to draw all to himself, because in those moments he attracts us. Our prayer may or may not be in accord with his will, but still it is a vital part of his plan.

For this cause we. . .do not cease to pray for you, and to desire that ye
might be filled with the knowledge of his will in all wisdom and spiritual
understanding; that ye might walk worthy of the Lord unto all pleasing,
being fruitful in every good work, and increasing in the knowledge of God.
COLOSSIANS 1:9–10

Joys are flowing like a river,
Since the comforter has come;
He abides with us forever,
Makes the trusting heart his home.

MANIE P. FERGUSON (1850–1932)
BLESSED QUIETNESS

THE COMING OF THE COMFORTER

As the shadows of the cross begin to darken his life, Jesus is not concerned for himself but for his beloved disciples. He has always guided and comforted them, but a special measure of consolation will be necessary in his absence. Earlier, Jesus promised to give the Spirit like a living spring to a thirsty world (John 7:39). But in view of the sorrow that will soon engulf his followers, Jesus now gives the name *Comforter* to the Holy Spirit. The Spirit first must console the disciples; later it will refresh them.

After the Crucifixion, the fearful disciples take refuge in a locked room. Then the Comforter comes to them (20:19–23). The resurrected Christ physically enters the room and says, "Peace be unto you" (v. 21). We cannot imagine how encouraging those words are to the men who had recently witnessed the abduction and death of their beloved teacher. But beyond the joy of his presence, Jesus breathes into them and says, "Receive ye the Holy Ghost" (v. 22).

Adam became a living soul when the Creator's breath entered his body (Genesis 2:7). Here the Son of God imparts the promised vital Holy Spirit to his followers simply by breathing. At this moment, the last Adam is revealed as being a life-giving Spirit (1 Corinthians 15:45).

But the Comforter, which is the Holy Ghost, whom the Father will send in my name, he shall teach you all things, and bring all things to your remembrance, whatsoever I have said unto you. Peace I leave with you, my peace I give unto you: not as the world giveth, give I unto you. Let not your heart be troubled, neither let it be afraid.
JOHN 14:26–27

The Lord will come and not be slow, his footsteps cannot err;
Before him righteousness shall go, his royal harbinger.
Truth from the earth, like to a flower, shall bud and blossom then,
And justice, from her heavenly bower, look down on mortal men.

JOHN MILTON (1608–1674)
THE LORD WILL COME AND NOT BE SLOW

THE FIRST AND SECOND COMING OF CHRIST

When Jesus Christ first presented himself as king of Israel, he didn't have a sword or a horse. Instead, he rode into Jerusalem empty-handed on a borrowed donkey. No triumphant army followed him, although some folks were there to cheer him on his way (John 12:12–15). Jesus appeared to be lowly that day, although he was entirely a king. As the prophet said: "Rejoice greatly, O daughter of Jerusalem: behold, thy King cometh unto thee: he is just, and having salvation; lowly, and riding upon an ass, and upon a colt the foal of an ass" (Zechariah 9:9). The citizens of Jerusalem, ignorant of this prophecy, asked, "Who is this?" All they saw was a dusty, despised, Nazarene prophet (Matthew 21:10–11).

When Christ Jesus comes the second time for Israel, he will not ride on a lowly, borrowed donkey. Only a white horse will do to carry him in pursuit of his enemies followed by the armies of heaven astride a whole host of white horses (Revelation 19:14). The uncrowned head that long ago passed through Jerusalem's gate will wear many crowns. The gracious eyes that sadly viewed earthly Jerusalem will then be like a flame of fire (v. 12). He was once weaponless, helpless, crucified. Then his mouth will send forth a saber, and his hands will hold the millennial Shepherd's iron rod (v. 15). Then he was derided as the Nazarene. Soon he will be called Faithful and True (v. 11).

Surely I come quickly.
REVELATION 22:20

Holy Spirit, Truth divine,
Dawn upon this soul of mine;
Word of God and inward light
Wake my spirit, clear my sight.

SAMUEL LONGFELLOW (1819–1892)
HOLY SPIRIT, TRUTH DIVINE

THE OPPOSING SPIRITS

The Comforter is the Spirit of truth (John 16:13). John contrasts this Spirit with the spirit of deception that is now sweeping the world into worship of the Antichrist (1 John 4:3–6). The world finds a sort of comfort in its false philosophies, whereas the saints are consoled by truth. So we must be sure to "believe not every spirit, but try the spirits whether they are of God" (v. 1). This instruction refers to the spirits of the people who intend to teach us the truth.

The standard for testing these spirits is the written revelation, scripture, that testifies to God's living revelation—Jesus Christ. John gives us two examples: A spirit that is of God confirms Jesus Christ came in the flesh (v. 2). This refers to his coming in the past—his birth and life. John's second epistle warns against deceivers who don't acknowledge Christ's future, physical return (2 John 7). In both cases, those who make Christ a mere spirit are associated with the spirit of Antichrist.

These examples show that the spirit of Antichrist is the spirit of the secular world. The world does not want the Christ of scripture but prefers a variety of substitutes suited to its taste. This spirit pervades the religious world, as well. There, rites and ceremonies substitute for faith in Jesus Christ, fleshly energy replaces the Spirit's power, and philosophical, human wisdom displaces the wisdom of God.

For it is written, I will destroy the wisdom of the wise, and will bring to nothing the understanding of the prudent. Where is the wise? where is the scribe? where is the disputer of this world? hath not God made foolish the wisdom of this world?
1 CORINTHIANS 1:19–20

October 5

God's faithful word shall be performed,
Thy brow with many crowns adorned;
All knees shall bow in thy bless'd name
And Jesus Christ as Lord acclaim.

AUTHOR UNKNOWN
OH WONDROUS GOD OF WONDROUS GRACE

THE REVERSAL OF HUMAN HISTORY

In this age, Christ not only humbled himself but was also humiliated by Israel's high priest, the religious authority, and Herod, the political ruler. In the coming age, this will be reversed. "The lofty looks of man shall be humbled, and the haughtiness of men shall be bowed down, and the Lord alone shall be exalted" (Isaiah 2:11). The Crucified One will be crowned with many diadems, and the earth will be filled with blessing. But this blessing will be the portion of the meek and humble, not the high and mighty (Matthew 5:3–12).

Isaiah 2 describes this final scene: "They shall go into the holes of the rocks, and into the caves of the earth, for fear of the Lord, and for the glory of his majesty, when he ariseth to shake terribly the earth" (v. 19). Elsewhere we read of this time: "And the kings of the earth, and the great men, and the rich men, and the chief captains, and the mighty men, and every bondman, and every free man, hid themselves. . . . And said to the mountains and rocks, Fall on us, and hide us from the face of him that sitteth on the throne, and from the wrath of the Lamb" (Revelation 6:15–16).

This frightful destruction during the brief era at the end of this age is not the end at all. It makes way for the long-awaited reign of the Prince of Peace when "he shall judge among the nations, and shall rebuke many people: and they shall beat their swords into plowshares, and their spears into pruninghooks: nation shall not lift up sword against nation, neither shall they learn war any more" (Isaiah 2:4).

His eyes were as a flame of fire, and on his head were many crowns;
and he had a name written, that no man knew, but he himself.
REVELATION 19:12

*Bring a torch, Jeanette, Isabella
Bring a torch, come swiftly and run.
Christ is born, tell the folk of the village,
Jesus is sleeping in his cradle,
Ah, ah, beautiful is the mother,
Ah, ah, beautiful is her Son.*

AUTHOR UNKNOWN (FRENCH RENAISSANCE CAROL)
BRING A TORCH, JEANETTE ISABELLA
TRANSLATED BY E. CUTHBERT NUNN (1868–1914)

GOD'S FOREKNOWLEDGE OF OUR REDEMPTION

Our Redeemer was foreknown before the foundation of the world (1 Peter 1:20). In other words, man's redemption was not an afterthought; it was not God's reaction to an unforeseen event.

It is well known that Satan entered the Garden of Eden. He waylaid the woman, wheedled his way into her sympathies, and persuaded her to eat from the forbidden tree. She gave her husband some of the fruit, and Adam violated the divine command. Yet, God is God. Nothing takes him by surprise. He had mapped out his plans in view of these events. Before Adam's disobedience, prior to the Creation and the work of the six days, the sacrificial Lamb of God was prepared.

God knew his creation would need a redeemer, and so he created the material universe in anticipation of his Son's incarnation. Even the many chemical elements of the human body were prepared in anticipation of the fullness of the time when God sent forth his Son, born of a woman (Galatians 4:4). When, at the dawn of this world, God said, "Let there be light," he set in motion the chain of events that culminated in the incarnation and resurrection of the Son of Man. These thoughts are almost too wonderful for us to consider. But we have been given a prophet whose speaking for the Son to the Father confirm them:

My frame was not hidden from you, when I was being made in secret, intricately woven in the depths of the earth. Your eyes beheld my unformed substance. In your book were written all the days that were formed for me, when none of them as yet existed.
PSALM 139:15–16 NRSV

Go, tell it on the mountain,
Over the hills and everywhere
Go, tell it on the mountain
That Jesus Christ is born.

JOHN WESLEY WORK, JR. (1872–1925)
GO, TELL IT ON THE MOUNTAIN

THE MEDIATOR OF GOD AND MANKIND

The apostle Paul was "separated unto the gospel of God" which "[concerns] his Son Jesus Christ" (Romans 1:1–3). This gospel is not a mere message in words or a code of rules and regulations like the Jewish law. The gospel of God concerns Jesus Christ, God's presentation of himself in the Son. Contrast this with the gospels of men. They are methods—methods of behavior, methods of ethics, methods of thought. But God's gospel is far from a method; it is himself in the Son.

If we were to declare our Lord's birth from a mountaintop, only two phrases would be needed: He comes out of the seed of David, and he is designated the Son of God. One is according to the flesh and the other is according to the spirit of holiness (vv. 3–4). In the flesh he is related to David, Israel's great king, whereas in the spirit he is related to Almighty God. According to the flesh, he belonged to the fathers (9:5). According to the spirit, he was the Son of God. So he is a mediator of God and humankind, because in him God and people find a meeting place (1 Timothy 2:5).

This man Jesus Christ did not simply become the Son of God. Rather, he was declared God's Son with power. His unique holiness and the resurrection from the dead powerfully marked him as God's Son (Romans 1:4). Jesus Christ took part in the same flesh and blood as the children of men. Yet, unlike us, he was begotten by the Holy Spirit (Hebrews 2:14; Luke 1:34–35). We inherited filthiness of the flesh and spirit (2 Corinthians 7:1). But his spirit of holiness labeled him the Son of God.

> *And so it is written, The first man Adam was made a living soul;*
> *the last Adam was made a [life-giving] spirit.*
> 1 CORINTHIANS 15:45

The only Son from heaven, Foretold by ancient seers,
By God, the Father, given, In human shape appears.

ELISABETHE VON MESERITZ CRUCIGER (1500–1535)
THE ONLY SON FROM HEAVEN
TRANSLATED BY ARTHUR T. RUSSELL (1806–1874)

THY KINGDOM COME

Our news reports tell of the constant uproar over the question of who will rule the world. Yet as each century passes into history, it testifies that humankind is incompetent for this task. We have recently left behind the bloodiest century in human history in which man's best efforts again ended in failure. Now, in a new century, let us continue to pray as saints have always prayed, "Thy kingdom come."

God has given all things into the hands of the only one capable of ruling the world (John 13:3). This one brought light to this darkness, and try as it will, the darkness cannot overcome it (1:5). He was offered a satanic rule over the world's kingdoms and refused it (Luke 4:7). This one answered the question of sin in the only effective way by his death (Hebrews 2:14). In his sacrifice, the needs of the righteous God and ungodly sinners were perfectly satisfied. That sacrifice is so perfect that, based upon it, God recommends his love to sinners, does not take account of their offenses, and beseeches them to be reconciled to him (Romans 5:8; 2 Corinthians 5:19–21).

He was "delivered for our offences, and was raised again for our justification" (Romans 4:25). His resurrection assures us of salvation and guarantees his future rule of the world. Although we do not yet see all things put under him, we see Jesus crowned with glory and honor far above all principalities and powers, might and dominion, and every name that is named (Hebrews 2:7–9; Ephesians 1:21). At the consummation, he will hand back to God a perfect universe with all enemies abolished and all the works of the devil destroyed (1 Corinthians 15:25–28; 1 John 3:8).

And he hath on his vesture and on his thigh a name written,
KING OF KINGS, AND LORD OF LORDS.
REVELATION 19:16

My heart has no desire to stay
Where doubts arise and fears dismay;
Though some may dwell where those abound,
My prayer, my aim, is higher ground.

JOHNSON OATMAN, JR. (1856–1922)
HIGHER GROUND

CHRIST IS OUR TEXTBOOK

Scripture calls the laws and ordinances of the Jewish religion "the elements of the world," that is, elementary principals (Galatians 4:3; Colossians 2:20). God's instructions to his believers began with elementary object lessons that used rules and physical things to explain the spiritual realm. For example, physical defilement in Israel was taken away by washing in water. This illustrates the cleansing from spiritual uncleanness by means of the Word (Exodus 29:4; Ephesians 5:26).

The tabernacle made of gold, silver, and other materials is a physical illustration of God's dwelling place and the way of approaching it through Christ (Exodus 25–27; Hebrews 7:1–2). God dealt with Israel like a child in this way. From Moses to Christ, God's people were in elementary school and the law was their teacher. Their textbook was illustrated by the rudimentary elements of Judaism (Hebrews 5:12).

In the ancient Roman Empire, the boys of wealthy families were either escorted to and from school or provided instruction at home by a tutor. This shows the function of the law (Galatians 3:23–24: 4:1–3). We who believe in Jesus Christ are like mature Roman sons who would never tolerate their childhood escorts. Mature believers refuse the bondage of law. It is both unnecessary and humiliating.

Johnson Oatman's prayer for maturity speaks for the hearts of all believers. God has mapped out the way to this higher ground: Jesus Christ revealed his Father's heart entirely and perfectly at the cross, and Paul completed the Word of God (Colossians 1:25). Therefore, we have a comprehensive course in God's salvation. Christ is our textbook, and we are complete in him (2:10).

But when the fulness of the time was come, God sent forth his Son,
made of a woman, made under the law, to redeem them that
were under the law, that we might receive the adoption of sons.
GALATIANS 4:4–5

When upon life's billows you are tempest tossed,
When you are discouraged, thinking all is lost,
Count your many blessings, name them one by one,
And it will surprise you what the Lord hath done.

JOHNSON OATMAN, JR. (1856–1922)
COUNT YOUR BLESSINGS

OUR SPIRITUAL BLESSINGS IN CHRIST, PART 1

Each of Paul's epistles begins with a wonderful salutation of grace that goes something like this: "Grace be to you, and peace" (Ephesians 1:2). The apostle does not simply wish that we have grace; he actually presents it to us. The epistle to the Ephesians richly illustrates this. Grace greets us at the start and enriches us to the very end. Our hearts are immediately bathed with grace: "Blessed be the God and Father of our Lord Jesus Christ, who hath blessed us with all spiritual blessings in heavenly places in Christ" (v. 3). The writer's whole message is condensed in these two phrases: "all spiritual blessings" and "in heavenly places."

These statements are given such a prominent place because they are foundational facts. Ephesians begins with the remarkable declaration that our blessings are spiritual and confirms this all the way through. For example, the seal of the Holy Spirit guarantees our inheritance in the coming ages (1:13–14). In flesh we were apart from Christ, but we now have access to the Father in spirit (2:12, 18). If we wish to count our blessings, the book of Ephesians is the place to start.

The fact that our blessings are in the heavenlies contrasts them with earthly, material things. They are spiritual, not physical. Yes, we must thank God for the material goodness that surrounds us. But our spiritual blessings in Christ are like gold that devalues silver and copper. Count these blessings one by one, and see how material possessions lose their charm.

Blessed be the God and Father of our Lord Jesus Christ, who hath blessed us with all spiritual blessings in heavenly places in Christ.
EPHESIANS 1:3

Count your blessings, name them one by one,
Count your blessings, see what God hath done!
Count your blessings, name them one by one,
And it will surprise you what the Lord hath done.

JOHNSON OATMAN, JR. (1856–1922)
COUNT YOUR BLESSINGS

OUR SPIRITUAL BLESSINGS IN CHRIST, PART 2

Houses, cars, clothes, money, and such are material blessings. Spiritual blessings, however, are intangible and are ours among the heavenlies in Christ (Ephesians 1:3). They are not physical blessings on the earth, and they are not found outside of Christ.

Our body and soul are made to experience material things. For instance, apples are obviously not spiritual because we can see and taste them. Examples of physical blessings are found in Jacob's blessings to his sons (Genesis 49). Note all these are related to the material world. Spiritual things, however, are all of God, who is spirit (John 4:24). One will be enriched in the study of the scriptures to discover all that God has given us in Christ. This includes wisdom, righteousness, holiness, and redemption (1 Corinthians 1:20). These and so much more exist in spirit.

We live in this world by our senses. All we can know is what we perceive. The invisible things are unknown to us until we believe. Then we are given God's Spirit and can at last perceive by faith what is not being observed (Hebrews 11:1). As we explore the realm of the Spirit through prayer and the Word, we find ceaseless delights that are so wonderful that one taste cannot be forgotten.

The first Adam was made a living soul (1 Corinthians 15:45). This means that he was dominated by his soul. Since we are his descendants, our souls are easily occupied with what is visible. But when we prayerfully let our minds delve into just one of the priceless benefits granted to us by God in Christ, we see what spiritual blessing truly is.

But the natural man receiveth not the things of the Spirit of God:
for they are foolishness unto him: neither can he know them,
because they are spiritually discerned.
1 CORINTHIANS 2:14

When you look at others with their lands and gold,
Think that Christ has promised you his wealth untold;
Count your many blessings. Wealth can never buy
Your reward in heaven, nor your home on high.

JOHNSON OATMAN, JR. (1856–1922)
COUNT YOUR BLESSINGS

OUR SPIRITUAL BLESSINGS IN CHRIST, PART 3

Let's consider one of our many spiritual blessings: Isn't it amazing that we are entirely justified from sin in God's sight? This is much better than forgiveness. A forgiven person is guilty of sin yet pardoned by governmental mercy. A justified person is completely innocent by judicial authority.

Romans 3:20 says that "by the deeds of the law there shall no flesh be justified in his sight." As much as we may wish to improve ourselves through rules and laws, these only emphasize our sinfulness (Romans 5:20). So here's the question: How can the righteous God declare that a sinner is not a sinner and still be righteous?

The truth of the gospel is that we are not living anymore; we are united with Christ in death. "Our old man is crucified with him. . .that henceforth we should not serve sin" (6:5–6). Knowing this, Romans 6:7 answers our question: "For he that is dead is freed from sin." This verse echoes Psalm 143:2, which says, "In thy sight shall no man living be justified." Because we have faith in the operation of God, we understand that we are no longer living because we were crucified with Christ (Galatians 2:20). We now stand before God, holy and flawless, complete in Christ (Colossians 2:12). God does not condemn us, because we are alive not in ourselves but in Christ Jesus (Romans 8:1). What a blessing!

Our death and life in Christ is repeatedly emphasized in Paul's epistles. It is the linchpin of the gospel and the only reason we are justified from sin. It also widens and enriches our fellowship as we decide to know nothing among the saints except Jesus Christ and him crucified (1 Corinthians 2:2)

Being justified freely by his grace through the
redemption that is in Christ Jesus.
ROMANS 3:24

October 13

*One holy church of God appears
Through every age and race,
Unwasted by the lapse of years,
Unchanged by changing place.*

SAMUEL LONGFELLOW (1819–1892)
ONE HOLY CHURCH OF GOD APPEARS

THE ORIGIN OF THE CHURCH

The four Gospels tell of a misguided nation that turns against a good king and executes him. Yet Jesus knew that his rejection by Israel and the suffering that resulted were God's will, and he thanked him for them (Matthew 11:25). Indeed, they led to the most glorious accomplishment in God's plan of salvation—the Crucifixion.

Israel's disobedience didn't stop at the cross. In answer to the Son's prayer of forgiveness, the apostles reoffered the kingdom to Israel as recorded in the book of Acts. Again, the chosen nation rejected that gospel. But in God's wisdom, this led to the blessing of all the other nations based on Christ's death. This blessing had previously been a secret, hidden in God from the ages (Ephesians 3:9).

That secret first came to light in Antioch of Pisidia (Acts 13:44–49). Paul spoke in the synagogue there, and the majority of the Jews were filled with jealousy. They contradicted the apostle and even blasphemed. Paul and Barnabas answered them, "It was necessary that the word of God should first have been spoken to you: but seeing ye put it from you, and judge yourselves unworthy of everlasting life, lo, we turn to the Gentiles" (v. 46). This is the first time Israel was set aside and the word of God was delivered directly to Gentiles. The church began there.

It was a sad day when those expatriate Jews denied the gospel because the coming of their kingdom and its Messiah was again delayed. At the same time, God began to raise up the most wonderful building ever seen—the Church, which is his body, the complement of the one who completes the all in all.

[God] hath put all things under his feet, and gave him to be the head over all things to the church, which is his body, the fullness of him that filleth all in all.
EPHESIANS 1:22–23

Arise, the kingdom is at hand, The King is drawing nigh;
Arise with joy, thou faithful band, To meet the Lord most high!

JOHANN RIST (1607–1667)
ARISE, THE KINGDOM IS AT HAND
TRANSLATED BY CATHERINE WINKWORTH (1827–1878)

THE TWO KINGDOMS

What is the difference between the kingdom of God and the kingdom of heaven?

Daniel 2:44 gives the basic meaning of the term *kingdom of heaven.* "The God of heaven [will] set up a kingdom, which shall never be destroyed: and the kingdom shall not be left to other people, but it shall break in pieces and consume all these kingdoms." A study of this verse together with all other references to this kingdom reveals that it is limited to earth, belongs to Israel, and will be established in the future. On the other hand, the kingdom of God is now present in the heavens, and it is not on earth except in his believers. So, our Lord taught his disciples to pray, "Thy will be done on earth, *as it is in heaven*" (Matthew 6:10, emphasis added). Still, the only boundaries of God's kingdom are those of the universe itself, and its subjects are under God's rule.

God's authority in the earthly kingdom of heaven is administered through Israel: "And the kingdom and dominion, and the greatness of the kingdom under the whole heaven, shall be given to the people of the saints of the most High" (Daniel 7:27). In the kingdom of heaven, the twelve apostles will rule the twelve tribes of Israel (Matthew 19:28). There some people have authority over five cities, others over ten (Luke 19:17, 19).

In God's wisdom, the present kingdom of God has been temporarily taken from Israel because they are in unbelief (Matthew 21:43). But Israel has not lost the future kingdom of the heavens. All Israel will be saved and come under God's rule when the fullness of the nations comes in. Then Israel's people will reign as kings and serve as priests for a thousand years (Romans 11:25–26; Revelation 20:6).

For the kingdom of God is. . .righteousness, and peace, and joy in the Holy Ghost.
ROMANS 14:17

I call him my eternal Son,
And raise him from the dead;
I make my holy hill his throne,
And wide his kingdom spread.

ISAAC WATTS (1674–1748)
WHY DID THE NATIONS JOIN TO SLAY?

THE PRESENT KINGDOM AND ITS FUTURE

God's love embraces his Son. Since we have been made citizens of the kingdom of God's beloved Son, his love embraces us, too (Colossians 1:13–14). This kingdom is the expression of the loving relationship of the Father and Son. In spirit, we are seated with God in the heavenlies and have access in one spirit to the Father (Ephesians 2:6, 18). As if that were not enough, we are enjoying the affections of God in the kingdom of the Son of his love.

Compare this with the spiritual kingdom of darkness that is empowered in this world. That darkness controlled us until the Father transferred us into his Son's kingdom of love. Presently, this kingdom only holds spiritual authority. This means we are free from the satanic forces that dominate the affairs and the governments of this earth, yet we are still under the physical authority of those governments (Romans 13:1).

After the resurrection, in the coming age, we will have bodies like Christ's glorious body (Philippians 3:21). At that time, Israel will rule with Christ on earth for a thousand years, and we will have an allotment in the heavens, fully experiencing the affections and blessings of the kingdom of the Son of his love that we now enjoy in spirit. But this is not the end. One day, when the one-thousand-year kingdom ends, a new earth will replace this old one, and the kingdom of God's beloved Son will embrace its inhabitants (Revelation 21:1–4). In that age, Christ will finish his work of subduing every rule, authority, and power. When it ends, at last there will be no need for governments and kingdoms because God will be all in all (1 Corinthians 15:24–28).

He has rescued us from the power of darkness and
transferred us into the kingdom of his beloved Son.
COLOSSIANS 1:13 NRSV

How calm and beautiful the morn
That gilds the sacred tomb,
Where Christ the crucified was borne,
And veiled in midnight gloom!
O weep no more the Savior slain;
The Lord is risen; he lives again.

THOMAS HASTINGS (1784–1872)
HOW CALM AND BEAUTIFUL THE MORN

THE CALMNESS OF RESURRECTION

Death completely mastered Jesus Christ as he hung on the cross (Romans 6:9). He really died; he was paid the wages of sin (v. 23). That death sentence was no less severe just because he was the Son of God. In fact, scripture tells us that when Christ died, he was sin itself (2 Corinthians 5:21). Why is this? It is because someone had to take away God's condemnation of sin by death before humanity could be delivered from the reign of death. So death dominated our Lord just as sin dominated the human race. When Christ died, we were planted together in the likeness of his death and, being dead, we are freed from sin (Romans 6:5–7).

The reality of the cross is not only that we are dead with Christ but that we also will live with him (v. 8). How can we be certain of this? By these words: "Knowing that Christ being raised from the dead dieth no more; death hath no more dominion over him" (v. 9). Our belief is baseless if Christ might die again. The deathlessness of the risen Christ is the basis for our assurance that we, too, will live. He is secured against the assault of sin and death; therefore, so are we. In other words, our assurance of faith is based on the permanence of Christ's life.

Our life together with Christ doesn't depend on the strength of our belief—our self-effort. It depends on the power of his endless life (Hebrews 7:16). The hymn writer describes the resurrection morning as calm and beautiful. Though we live in the turmoil of this world, we can be calm because we are in the likeness of his resurrection and can never be condemned by God (Romans 6:5; 8:1).

Jesus saith unto her, Mary.
JOHN 20:16

Ere yet the dawn has filled the skies,
Behold, my Savior Christ arise;
He chaseth from us sin and night,
And brings us joy and life and light.

JOHANN HEERMAN (1585–1647)
ERE YET THE DAWN HAS FILLED THE SKIES

THE TRUENESS OF RESURRECTION

Some people in the church in Corinth claimed there was no resurrection of the dead, yet Paul didn't condemn them (1 Corinthians 15:12). Instead, he imparted the gracious revelation that all will be made alive (v. 22). It is vital that believers receive this truth, which is the heart of the good news (vv. 1–4). Without it, faith is false and all else is dead.

As if he were in a court of law, the apostle presents the evidence for Christ's resurrection (vv. 5–11). Next, we see our hopelessness without the resurrection (vv. 12–19). Verses 20–28 sketch God's dealings with death that culminates in his becoming all in all. Then verse 29 picks up from verse 19, continuing to describe the negative side of the subject (vv. 29–34). This is followed by an explanation of the process of the resurrection, along with a portrayal of our resurrected bodies (vv. 35–49). Finally, we have the grand climax in which the secret concerning our bodily change is made known. This change will affect all the believers when the Lord descends from heaven, his trumpet sounds, and we are called to him (vv. 50–57; 1 Thessalonians 4:15–18).

Today, like those ancient days, some people consider themselves believers yet do not understand the good news made known in 1 Corinthians 15. This is why the gospel has mutated from the glad message about Christ to a sad message about sin. Brothers and sisters, let us not abandon the fundamental values of our Lord's sacrifice only to be left with our own lifeless endeavors.

For as in Adam all die, even so in Christ shall all be made alive.
But every man in his own order: Christ the firstfruits;
afterward they that are Christ's at his coming.
1 CORINTHIANS 15:22–23

Christ the Lord, the mighty King,
From our sin hath made us free.
Where, O death, is now thy sting?
Where, O grave, thy victory?

HENRY A. BECKER (C. 1880)
CHRIST IS RISEN FROM THE DEAD

THE CONFIRMATION OF RESURRECTION

Christ's resurrection is the focus of all apostolic teaching and the climax of scriptural revelation. When a believer apprehends its truth, he or she finds comfort, assurance, and exultant joy that can be found nowhere else. All who read Romans 4:24–25 can readily understand its meaning: "We believe on him that raised up Jesus our Lord from the dead; who was delivered for our offences, and was raised again for our justification." Though we might explain this with many words, all we really need is faith to believe these six words: "He was raised for our justification."

Jesus Christ died for our sins and was raised from the dead because those sins are truly gone. So we believers are justified, innocent, acquitted, exonerated; that is to say, we didn't do it! Since most believers can benefit from a better understanding of the meaning of the word *justification*, let's again consider this glorious truth.

Justification is not the same as pardon or forgiveness. The sacrifice that God made in Christ on the cross resulted in something much higher than this. The word *justification* is the translation of a Greek word that means "to justify, acquit, or vindicate." A person who is justified is guiltless. A defendant who is acquitted is innocent, exonerated of all accusations. A person who is vindicated is cleared of all blame. Christ Jesus was raised because of our justification. We need no further proof that we are innocent of sin. Christ's blood is the memorial of the permanent effectiveness of his death. We believe that Christ died for us while we were still sinners (Romans 5:8). We rejoice that his resurrection confirms our justification before God.

Therefore just as one man's trespass led to condemnation for all, so one man's act of righteousness leads to justification and life for all.
ROMANS 5:18 NRSV

October 19

How oft, O Lord, thy face hath shone
On doubting souls whose wills were true!
Thou Christ of Cephas and of John,
Thou art the Christ of Thomas, too.

WILLIAM BRIGHT (1824–1901)
HOW OFT, O LORD, THY FACE HATH SHONE

OF DOUBT AND FAITH

Where do doubts concerning the faith come from? They slink in when, distracted from God's grace in Christ, we direct our attention toward ourselves.

In Romans 14, scripture tells of people who were weak in the faith; who imposed dietary restrictions upon themselves thinking this would please God (vv. 1–2). They were either ignorant or sidetracked from the truth that God is completely satisfied with Christ and his death and resurrection. No matter how inadequate we may feel, faith has made Christ our righteousness (2 Corinthians 5:21). A person who hopes to find righteousness outside of Christ doubts the gospel and is weak in the faith.

Abraham is sometimes called the "father of faith." Here's why: When he was told that Sarah would have a son and through him many descendants, Abraham didn't doubt God's promise (Romans 4:20). Likewise, believers today receive the truth that Christ died for their sins (1 Corinthians 15:3). Believing this, let us not harbor doubts about the fullness of our Lord's work and his achievements on our behalf.

God will not condemn any believer, whether weak or strong in the faith (Romans 8:34). Sadly however, those who do not know God's grace or who doubt its power cannot enjoy it. Their habits of thinking have not been trained by the truth, so they suffer under self-imposed condemnation. But let's not forget that Abraham wasn't always confident in God's promises either (Genesis 12:10). We are like him in faith and in doubt. All of us have experienced doubts about God's Word, so let's pray for our brothers and sisters that we all can grow together in faith and faithfulness.

[We] do not cease to pray for you, and to desire that ye might be filled with the knowledge of his will in all wisdom and spiritual understanding.
COLOSSIANS 1:9

Christian, rise and act thy creed;
Let thy prayer be in thy deed;
Seek the right, perform the true,
Raise thy works and life anew.

ROLLO RUSSELL (1849–1914)
CHRISTIAN, RISE AND ACT THY CREED

THE LIFE THAT IS WORTHY OF GOD'S CALLING, PART 1

The teaching of the first three chapters of Ephesians reveals vistas of faith that we could not have imagined had they not been written in God's Word. Believers who learn of the spiritual blessings and the gracious membership in the body of Christ find gratitude and thanksgiving welling up in their hearts. With the eyes of their hearts enlightened by the brightness of these chapters, they will certainly desire to lead a life worthy of the calling described in them (Ephesians 4:1).

This is a grand and glorious calling. In this age, we are to display to the principalities and powers in the heavenly places the manifold wisdom of God (3:10). During the coming ages, we will dwell in those heavenly places, exhibiting "the exceeding riches of [God's] grace in his kindness toward us through Christ Jesus" (2:6–7). Despite the greatness of all this, we are not commanded to live worthily. Instead, we are beseeched, implored, and entreated to bring our lives into harmony with our calling (4:1). This is the language of grace, not law.

What qualities should be found in people who are called by God to so high a calling? Courage, determination, stamina, forcefulness, and zeal come to mind. But these are not even close to what we find in scripture. We carry out our calling in humility and meekness with patience. We bear with one another in love and endeavor to keep the unity of the Spirit in the bond of peace (vv. 2–3). No person can produce these qualities by the efforts of his flesh. They are the fruit of the Spirit.

The fruit of the Spirit is love, joy, peace, longsuffering,
gentleness, goodness, faith, meekness, temperance.
GALATIANS 5:22–23

Teach, O teach us, holy child,
By thy face so meek and mild,
Teach us to resemble thee,
In thy sweet humility.

EDWARD CASWALL (1814–1878)
SEE AMID THE WINTER'S SNOW

THE LIFE THAT IS WORTHY OF GOD'S CALLING, PART 2

The flesh works, but the Spirit bears delicious fruit. We enjoy its taste, and so does God (Galatians 5:19–23). This fruit is not the expression of self-effort, but of spiritual life and growth. A life that is worthy of God's calling is the fruit of the Spirit (Ephesians 4:1–3).

Let's consider two attributes of such a spiritual life. The first is lowliness or humility. A humble person gives credit to God for all things. He recognizes that God operates everything in accord with the counsel of his will (1:11). He knows that we are God's workmanship, that our salvation is not produced by our work but by God's grace (2:9–10). He also regards others as better than he regards himself. Rather than looking to his own interests, he considers the interests of others. He lets the same mind be in him that was in Christ Jesus (Philippians 2:3–5).

Outsiders may see the second attribute, meekness, as weakness. However, we see that Titus, Paul's fellow worker, knew how to be obedient, not to speak evil of anyone, to avoid quarreling, to be gentle, and to display meekness (Titus 3:1–2). This required that he have true strength of character. It seems Titus had formerly passed his days in malice and envy, and was hateful and hated others (v. 3). What brought about the great change in this man? Scripture, in soaring phrases, gives this answer:

The grace of God has appeared, bringing salvation to all, training us to renounce impiety and worldly passions, and in the present age to live lives that are self-controlled, upright, and godly, while we wait for the blessed hope and the manifestation of the glory of our great God and Savior, Jesus Christ.
TITUS 2:11–13 NRSV

Teach me thy patience; still with thee
In closer, dearer, company,
In work that keeps faith sweet and strong,
In trust that triumphs over wrong.

WASHINGTON GLADDEN (1836–1918)
O MASTER, LET ME WALK WITH THEE

THE LIFE THAT IS WORTHY OF GOD'S CALLING, PART 3

Patience is the third quality that marks a person who understands the calling described in the first three chapters of Ephesians (4:2). Such a person is able to wait upon God. However, who has not been impatient to see God bless his life or work? In our zeal, we may try to move things along faster than God intends. This is why we are encouraged to imitate God, the best example of patience (5:1). He has "endured with much longsuffering the vessels of wrath fitted to destruction." While God is patiently delaying his wrath against evildoers, we benefit, because he is now revealing the riches of his glory on us, the vessels of mercy (Romans 9:22–23).

Entire books have been written to answer the complaint, "Why does God allow evil? Why doesn't he intervene?" The key to this is simple: He operates all in accord with the counsel of his will (Ephesians 1:11). He is presently at peace with this world and its inhabitants even though they are for the most part still his enemies (2 Corinthians 5:18–21). As long as this conciliation is in force, he cannot take vengeance on the world. God is exercising patience until the Church, the body of Christ, is complete. We who are trained by God's grace, with an understanding of his will, must likewise have patience with our fellow man.

Christ Jesus exemplifies this for us. What patience he displayed toward Paul, the foremost of sinners. What glorious results followed! The injurious blasphemer and persecutor became a pattern of all those who have since believed (1 Timothy 1:13–16). The joy that this has given our Lord can also be ours as we imitate his patience (Colossians 1:11).

Comfort the [fainthearted], support the weak, be patient toward all.
1 THESSALONIANS 5:14

Truly he taught us to love one another;
His law is love and his gospel is peace.
Chains shall he break for the slave is our brother,
And in his name all oppression shall cease.

PLACIDE CAPPEAU (1808–1877)
O HOLY NIGHT
TRANSLATED BY JOHN S. DWIGHT (1812–1893)

THE LIFE THAT IS WORTHY OF GOD'S CALLING, PART 4

The heart that is enlightened by the transcendent truth of Ephesians is able to bear with others in love (4:2). This is beautifully described by Paul in Philippians 2:1–4 and exemplified by Jesus Christ's matchless love (vv. 5–8). His love for humanity was so passionate, yet he had to suffer so intensively at our hands. Still, in his greatest anguish he cried, "Father, forgive them; for they know not what they do" (Luke 23:34).

The book of Colossians brings our Lord's example into our experience. It says we are to be "forbearing one another, and forgiving one another" (3:13). "Forgiving one another" is more accurately translated with this stronger expression: "dealing graciously among yourselves." To forgive implies that one's heart has already accused someone of committing an offense. To deal graciously with such a person means that we don't charge him with an offense at all.

The results of the dying prayers of Jesus Christ and Stephen explain this difference. Jesus prayed, "Father, forgive them." Still, Peter charged Israel with her crime and urged the people to repent because pardon requires repentance (Acts 2:23, 36–38). However, Stephen prayed, "Lord, lay not this sin to their charge" (7:60). Saul approved of Stephen's murder, yet when he encountered the Lord, he wasn't told to repent. Ananias was sent to Saul, saying simply, "Receive thy sight, and be filled with the Holy Ghost" (9:17). The Lord was gracious to Saul and did not charge him with murder. It is no wonder that years later Paul, the apostle of Christ, exhorted us to be gracious to one another just as the Lord has dealt graciously with us.

[Love] beareth all things, believeth all things,
hopeth all things, endureth all things.
1 CORINTHIANS 13:7

One in the bond of peace,
The service glad and free
Of truth and righteousness,
Of love and equity.

FREDERICK L. HOSMER (1840–1929
THY KINGDOM COME, O LORD

THE LIFE THAT IS WORTHY OF GOD'S CALLING, PART 5

Ephesians beseeches us to walk worthily of the calling with which we are called (4:1). But we must understand that we are not, in ourselves, worthy of such a calling. So how can we walk worthily? This is possible as we accept the message of the cross, which tells us that when we believe we are baptized into Christ's death and in his resurrection, we are walking in newness of life (Romans 6:1–14). We may often fall short of this ideal, but with our understanding enlightened by the truths of Ephesians 1–3, the desire to live worthily is always in our hearts.

In humility, meekness, and patience, such a life endeavors to "keep the unity of the Spirit in the bond of peace" (Ephesians 4:3). Note that we are not asked to *make* the Spirit's unity, but to endeavor to *keep* it— not to break it. The truth is, God's saints are one. We agree to this by refusing anything that mars the spiritual unity made by God. This unity of the Spirit is seen in the unity of the members of the church, which is Christ's body (1:23). It is a spiritual unity, not a fleshly one. In the flesh, we are as different as can be, but in the Spirit we cannot be closer because God makes us one based on our possession of the one Spirit.

We cannot choose the people with whom we are one. That is fleshly. Nor can we reject one single saint whom God is pleased to include in this unity. Differences in doctrine do not destroy our unity, although they mar its expression. Nevertheless, because of our high calling, we lovingly seek to maintain the Spirit's unity.

I press toward the mark for the prize of the high
calling of God in Christ Jesus.
PHILIPPIANS 3:14

Open my eyes, that I may see
Glimpses of truth thou hast for me;
Place in my hands the wonderful key
That shall unclasp and set me free.

CLARA H. SCOTT (1841–1897)
OPEN MY EYES, THAT I MAY SEE

THE LIFE THAT IS WORTHY OF GOD'S CALLING, PART 6

It is impossible for us to live worthily of God's calling in our own strength. To try will only bring discouragement. But the revelation of what God has done in Christ and of what our calling truly is supplies the grace for such a life.

How do we receive this revelation? We pray for it. In Ephesians 1:17–19, the apostle, who was given the wisdom and revelation to write half the New Testament, models our prayer for that same spirit of wisdom and revelation (Ephesians 1:17).

To be sure, everyone who believes is sealed by the Spirit—the foretaste of our future allotment (1:14). But the spirit of wisdom and revelation goes further. It makes God known in his purpose and plan according to the scriptures. This spirit is the portion of those believers who ask for it. It does not impart special, individual revelations that add to the sacred scriptures. That is dreadful. Nor does it give us revelations about other believers. Plus, it is not for only a few, but it is the common property of all the saints. So let us make Ephesians 1:17–19 our daily prayer. God will give us this spirit so we can realize all he has revealed in the scriptures. This will enable us to walk worthily of our calling (4:1).

That the God of our Lord Jesus Christ, the Father of glory, may give unto you the spirit of wisdom and revelation in the knowledge of him: the eyes of your understanding being enlightened; that ye may know what is the hope of his calling, and what the riches of the glory of his inheritance in the saints, and what is the exceeding greatness of his power to us-ward who believe, according to the working of his mighty power.
EPHESIANS 1:17–19

The church of God is one:
As brethren here we meet;
For us salvation's work is done,
In Christ we stand complete.

DANIEL W. WHITTLE (1840–1901)
THE CHURCH OF GOD IS ONE

THE CHURCH OF GOD IS ONE, PART 1

Despite the church's many outward divisions, the first line of Daniel Whittle's hymn is and always will be true. Remember, we walk by faith, not by sight (2 Corinthians 5:7).

The church's unity, spiritual and sevenfold, is briefly outlined in Ephesians 4:4–6. There, the word *one* occurs seven times. This is the number of divine perfection and completeness (Genesis 4:24; Matthew 18:21–22): (1) one body, (2) one Spirit, (3) one expectation of our calling, (4) one Lord, (5) one faith, (6) one baptism, (7) one God and Father of all who is over all and through all and in all.

The one body is energized by the one Spirit and encouraged by the one expectation of its calling. The one Lord, the body's head that directs and motivates all, is the center of the church's oneness. The one faith enables us to take firm hold of the one hope, while the one baptism suggests the work of the cross (Romans 6:3) and leads us to acknowledge the one God and Father of all the members of the body who will eventually embrace the whole creation (1 Corinthians 15:20–28).

The number *one* governs each of these seven items. Let us not permit that number to be increased for any reason, because this denies the unity that God has made. Nowhere but in the Church, the body of Christ, is there such unity except in the unity of the Father and the Son. Also, nowhere more than in the Church does God's adversary Satan struggle to thwart the purpose of God. But neither he nor we can destroy the unity. Its expression may be blurred, but it remains intact because God made it. This will be completely understood when we display God's grace among the celestials in the coming age (Ephesians 2:6–7).

By one Spirit are we all baptized into one body.
1 CORINTHIANS 12:13

The church of God is one,
Is one in faith and love,
Is one in the death by Jesus borne,
One in his life above.

DANIEL W. WHITTLE (1840–1901)
THE CHURCH OF GOD IS ONE

THE CHURCH OF GOD IS ONE, PART 2

Though peace is elusive in the world, it is like a cord that ties Christ's believers lovingly together (Ephesians 4:3). In it we have the unity of the Spirit. This is why peace accompanies grace in every salutation of Paul's epistles: "Grace to you and peace from God our Father, and the Lord Jesus Christ" (Romans 1:7).

When we are inclined toward the Spirit, we have peace (Romans 8:6). That peace has power to keep our hearts and minds in Christ Jesus (Philippians 4:7). This is why "the servant of the Lord must not strive, but be gentle unto all" (2 Timothy 2:24). Peace can govern the hearts and minds of all believers (Colossians 3:15). As we allow it to do so, we practice peace at every opportunity.

However, warfare is continuous on the earth. There are reasons for this brutality and destruction—political, economic, philosophical, and religious. But at their deepest source, these wars rage because humanity is at war with God (Romans 5:10). Therefore, people have no peace, either personally or globally. Nevertheless, God was in Christ conciliating the world to himself, not reckoning their offenses to them (2 Corinthians 5:18–20). This means he is at peace with the world and wishes the world to be at peace with him.

We believers are justified by faith, so we are the first on earth to enjoy peace with God (Romans 5:1). Because we have this peace within us, like God we also are at peace with all humanity. Above all, we share with every member of Christ's body the unity of the Spirit in the bond of peace (Ephesians 4:3).

Now the God of hope fill you with all joy and peace in believing, that ye
may abound in hope, through the power of the Holy Ghost.
ROMANS 15:13

The love of God is greater far
Than tongue or pen can ever tell;
It goes beyond the highest star,
And reaches to the lowest hell;
The guilty pair, bowed down with care,
God gave his Son to win;
His erring child he reconciled,
And pardoned from his sin.

FREDERICK M. LEHMAN (1868–1953)
THE LOVE OF GOD

THE EXTENT OF GOD'S LOVE, PART 1

Although the saying "God is love" sounds trite to some people, it is nevertheless true. God loves you not because of what you are but simply because he is love (1 John 4:8).

God has gone from the heights to the depths of the universe out of love for you. His love "goes beyond the highest star, and reaches to the lowest hell." Christ, who was inherently in the form of God, took the form of a slave in the likeness of humanity, and he descended to the shameful death of the cross (Philippians 2:6–8). You and I could not help but be erring children, as the hymn says, since we are children of Adam. Yet, while we were yet sinners, Christ died for us. As a result, we are more than pardoned—we are justified from sin and reconciled to God for all time (Romans 5:8–10). This is a greater truth than tongue or pen can ever express.

Can you find a hiding place that God cannot locate? Can you escape from his Spirit or flee from his presence? No, and no again! You cannot ascend to a height or dig to a depth where God is not present. Take the wings of the morning to dwell in the uttermost parts of the sea. Surprise! God is there to guide you and hold you. Cover yourself in darkness and gird yourself with the night if you can. Darkness cannot darken God. To him it shines like the light of day (Psalms 139:7–12).

If God be for us, who can be against us? He that spared not his own Son,
but delivered him up for us all, how shall he not with him also freely give
us all things?
ROMANS 8:31–32

*When years of time shall pass away, And earthly thrones
and kingdoms fall, When men, who here refuse to pray,
On rocks and hills and mountains call, God's love so sure,
shall still endure, All measureless and strong;
Redeeming grace to Adam's race— The saints' and angels' song.*

FREDERICK M. LEHMAN (1868–1953)
THE LOVE OF GOD

THE EXTENT OF GOD'S LOVE, PART 2

Does your faith in Christ cause you to feel God's love? It doesn't matter if your answer is no, because "neither death, nor life, nor angels, nor principalities, nor powers, nor things present, nor things to come, nor height, nor depth, nor any other creature, shall be able to separate us from the love of God, which is in Christ Jesus our Lord" (Romans 8:38–39). Somewhere in this list, you may insert, "nor my feelings." Actually, it doesn't matter if you answer no or yes to the opening question, because in Christ, there is only yes. "For all the promises of God in him are yea, and in him Amen, unto the glory of God by us" (2 Corinthians 1:20).

Some first-century believers were deceived into thinking that, although they had begun by simple faith in Christ, they were to somehow perfect themselves by self-effort (Galatians 3:1–3). Like them, you and I began by believing God's message about his Son. The question is, Can that faith keep us blameless until the coming of the Lord Jesus Christ? The gospel says yes, because "faithful is he that calleth you, who also will do it" (1 Thessalonians 5:24).

A well-known hymn supplies a final question:

*How firm a foundation, ye saints of the Lord,
Is laid for your faith in his excellent Word!
What more can he say than to you he hath said,
You, who unto Jesus for refuge have fled?*

And the very God of peace sanctify you wholly; and I pray God your whole spirit and soul and body be preserved blameless unto the coming of our Lord Jesus Christ. Faithful is he that calleth you, who also will do it.
1 THESSALONIANS 5:23–24

Could we with ink the ocean fill,
And were the skies of parchment made,
Were every stalk on earth a quill,
And every man a scribe by trade,
To write the love of God above,
Would drain the ocean dry.
Nor could the scroll contain the whole,
Though stretched from sky to sky.

FREDERICK M. LEHMAN (1868–1953)
THE LOVE OF GOD

THE EXTENT OF GOD'S LOVE, PART 3

Let us relax in the embrace of God's love with those who treasure the apostle's answer to the question, "What can separate us from the love of God in Christ Jesus?" (Romans 8:31–39). His persuasive answer to this question is given in a series of other questions. Each answers the one before it. These include an exhaustive list of all that cannot sever us from God's love: (1) affliction, (2) distress, (3) persecution, (4) famine, (5) nakedness, (6) danger, (7) sword, (8) death, (9) life, (10) angels, (11) sovereignties, (12) powers, (13) the present, (14) what is to come, (15) height, (16) depth, (17) any other creation (vv. 35, 38–39).

This list illustrates the wondrous way God loves us. But he loves the world, as well, and his design includes the well-being of his vast creation (John 3:16). He didn't create it in vain or mean that any part of it should lay waste, unloved (Isaiah 45:18).

Most believers are familiar with the phrase "God so loved the world," but they may not know that the Greek word translated "world" in John 3:16 is *cosmos*. This understanding enlarges our view of God's gospel of grace and glory. This gospel is God's power to those of us who presently believe (Romans 1:16). Yet, in the ages to come, when we make known its grace among the celestials, it will be known and believed in all the cosmos (Ephesians 2:6–7; Philippians 2:9–11).

And the Lord make you to increase and abound in love one toward another,
and toward all men, even as we do toward you.
1 THESSALONIANS 3:12

Tell of the cross where they nailed him, Writhing in anguish and pain.
Tell of the grave where they laid him, Tell how he liveth again.
Love in that story so tender, Clearer than ever I see.
Stay, let me weep while you whisper, Love paid the ransom for me.

FANNY J. CROSBY (1820–1915)
TELL ME THE STORY OF JESUS

THE EXTENT OF GOD'S LOVE, PART 4

Seven terrible things are listed as part of the question, "What shall separate us from the love of Christ?" (Romans 8:35). These are the outcome of our inhumanity to our fellow humans: affliction, distress, persecution, famine, nakedness, danger, and sword. The apostle deals with these with one phrase: "In all these things we are more than conquerors through him that loved us" (v. 37). We must remember that our trials and tribulations aren't evidence of God's anger. On the contrary, the balm of the knowledge of God's love soothes the severity of humankind's heartlessness.

Next, Paul lists nine things that are outside the reach of humankind: death, life, angels, principalities, powers, things present, things to come, height, and depth (vv. 38–39). Then, just in case anything has been omitted, he adds a tenth—any other creation.

In this list, we have all the great forces of the universe. None of them—individually or combined—can come between us and the love of God displayed in Christ Jesus (v. 39). Death will be swallowed up by victory (1 Corinthians 15:54). Life may lead us far from him, but not beyond the reach of his love (Psalm 139:7–10). When we lose sight of that love, the present can be perplexing and the future will be filled with uncertainty. Powers of all kinds, celestial and terrestrial, are subject to him. Nothing high above and nothing deep below has the power to break the bond of love between the weakest believer and the great and glorious God.

If I take the wings of the morning, and dwell in the uttermost parts of the sea; even there shall thy hand lead me, and thy right hand shall hold me.
PSALM 139:9–10

Beneath the cross of Jesus I fain would take my stand,
The shadow of a mighty rock within a weary land;
A home within the wilderness, a rest upon the way,
From the burning of the noontide heat, and the burden of the day.

Elizabeth C. Clephane (1830–1869)
Beneath the Cross of Jesus

They Drank of That Spiritual Rock

This hymn echoes the prophet Isaiah in depicting common difficulties that can blow like the wind and the tempest of evil that rages in the world, rattling the heart's door. It depicts sin as the heat that dries the landscape all around (Isaiah 32:1–2). But in the cross—the death of Jesus Christ—we are sheltered and refreshed. How can this be? It is because we do not glory in the world that generates such danger and discomfort. We have no stake in it, and it can make no claim upon us. "God forbid," says the apostle, "that I should glory, save in the cross of our Lord Jesus Christ, by whom the world is crucified unto me, and I unto the world" (Galatians 6:14).

Christ is symbolically our rock; a great rock in a weary land (1 Corinthians 10:4). Every believer rests in his cool shadow. His cross is not simply an emblem; it certainly is not a talisman or magic charm. It is the place where the Son of God was split open to release blood and water, becoming the one in whom we shelter and from whom, figuratively speaking, we drink of God's grace and truth (John 1:17; 19:34).

Behold, a king shall reign in righteousness, and princes shall rule in judgment. And a man shall be as an hiding place from the wind, and a covert from the tempest; as rivers of water in a dry place, as the shadow of a great rock in a weary land.
Isaiah 32:1–2

I take, O cross, thy shadow for my abiding place;
I ask no other sunshine than the sunshine of his face;
Content to let the world go by to know no gain or loss,
My sinful self my only shame, my glory all the cross.

ELIZABETH C. CLEPHANE (1830–1869)
BENEATH THE CROSS OF JESUS

THE SCHEME OF CROSSLESSNESS

We rest beneath the cross of Jesus Christ. But in the wilderness, God's adversary Satan tempted Jesus Christ to evade that cross. He was offered the world's kingdoms for the price of satanic worship (Matthew 4:8–9). Satan next used Peter in an attempt to prevent Jesus from going to the cross (16:21–23). Finally, when Christ was being crucified, Satan caused the priests to goad him to come down from the cross (27:40–42).

Christ could have come down. But if he had, where would our salvation be? Where would God's purpose be? He could have saved himself, but he wouldn't do it. The nails didn't keep Christ on the cross; his submission to the will of God kept him there (26:39). So, our faith has found a resting place in the cross where the Lord accomplished our death to law, to flesh, to the world, to sin, and to death itself. By not saving himself, he displayed his divine sonship, he saved others, and he fulfilled the mission given to him by God.

Satan first tried to divert the Savior from the cross, and now he is after the believers. He failed to have a Christless cross—now he hopes to have crossless Christians (Matthew 16:24). God rescues us from this scheme through our prayerful attention to the scriptures, which abound with the message of the cross (1 Corinthians 1:18).

Knowing this, that our old man is crucified with him, that the body of sin
might be destroyed, that henceforth we should not serve sin.
ROMANS 6:6

Christ Jesus lay in death's strong bands,
For our offenses given;
But now at God's right hand he stands
And brings us life from heaven.

MARTIN LUTHER (1483–1546)
CHRIST JESUS LAY IN DEATH'S STRONG BANDS

CHRIST OUR LIFE

In this hymn, Martin Luther sketches the two aspects of our salvation: The death of Jesus achieved it; the life of Christ sustains it. In legal terms, the dying Jesus was the testator who bequeathed us our legacy; the living Christ is the executor who distributes it. As Romans 5:10 says, we are reconciled by his death and saved in his life.

We live in a world dominated by God's adversary—the present evil age (Galatians 1:4). Yet, in the midst of this, we believers are saved in Christ's life. In other words, our life is hidden with Christ in God where he intercedes for us (Colossians 3:3; Romans 8:34). It is natural for believers to think they are inadequate, but this thought is not in harmony with the gospel. The truth is, we are complete in Christ (Colossians 2:10). So let us set our affection "on things above, not on things on the earth. For ye are dead, and your life is hid with Christ in God" (3:2–3).

The intercession of our ascended Lord makes it possible for us to live a life of wisdom, righteousness, sanctification, and redemption (1 Corinthians 1:30). Because of Christ's life—his death, burial, and resurrection—we are dead to sin, buried in baptism, made alive, and living to God in newness of life (Romans 6:4–7). One day, Christ our life—the life in which we are now being saved—will be manifested on the earth and we will appear with him in glory (Colossians 3:4).

Christ. . .entered into heaven itself, now to appear
in the presence of God on our behalf.
HEBREWS 9:24 NRSV

November 4

God answers prayer, O do not doubt him;
God answers prayer, believe his Word;
God answers prayer, now venture on him,
His Word the test of time has stood.

<small>GEORGE BENNARD (1873–1958)</small>
<small>GOD ANSWERS PRAYER</small>

THE PRAYERS OF EPHESIANS, PART 1

God is eager to answer the three prayers in the book of Ephesians. This is because no other prayers are as vital to our spiritual well-being. If a believer will read them, meditate upon them, and, most important, pray these words of scripture, God will fulfill them.

The first fourteen verses of Ephesians present the grace that is the culmination of all previous revelation. The apostle was aware, however, that this knowledge was beyond the comprehension and spiritual scope of believers. These riches of Christ are unsearchable (3:8). So he prayed "that the God of our Lord Jesus Christ, the Father of glory, may give unto you the spirit of wisdom and revelation in the knowledge of him" (1:17).

But one might ask, "Hasn't Paul already declared the entire counsel of God to the Ephesians?" (Acts 20:27). Yes, the counsel was complete up to that moment in Miletus. When he got to Rome, the apostle wrote to tell the Ephesians about secrets that had previously been hidden in God (Ephesians 3:3–6, 9). For example, nowhere but in the companion epistles of Ephesians, Philippians, and Colossians do we read of the celestial destiny of the body of Christ (Ephesians 2:6–7; Philippians 3:20; Colossians 1:5). Therefore, like the ancient saints, we must be endowed with the spirit of wisdom and revelation in order to realize such astonishing things.

So let us all pray for a spirit of wisdom and revelation in the knowledge of God:

The eyes of your understanding being enlightened; that ye may know what is the hope of his calling, and what the riches of the glory of his inheritance in the saints, and what is the exceeding greatness of his power to us-ward who believe, according to the working of his mighty power.
<small>EPHESIANS 1:18–19</small>

God answers prayer, O soul, believe him;
God answers prayer, I've proved him true!
God answers prayer, now venture on him;
He answered me, he'll answer you.

GEORGE BENNARD (1873–1958)
GOD ANSWERS PRAYER

THE PRAYERS OF EPHESIANS, PART 2

In Acts, the apostle Paul's message was based on the Hebrew scriptures (Acts 17:2; 18:28). This is why the Bereans were able to consult those scriptures and search out the truth of Paul's message (Acts 17:11). Later he was given grace to bring the unsearchable riches of Christ to the nations (Ephesians 3:8). In other words, if believers were to search the Old Testament, they would not find the secrets, or mysteries, that are brought to light in Ephesians. Those are unsearchable riches because they are not found in prior scriptural writings.

The second prayer in Ephesians begins in 3:1, but it is interrupted by a summary of God's grace and the fellowship, or administration, of the mystery. The prayer picks up again with petitions for inner strength, faith, and love (vv. 14–17). The apostle confidently prays that the Father will make us strong to grasp the breadth, length, depth, and height (v. 18). This means that believers are now able to know all the dimensions of God's plan. Formerly, Paul admitted that his knowledge of the things of God was partial. He looked forward to the time when he would know all (1 Corinthians 13:12). Ephesians records the arrival of that time.

The second prayer in Ephesians is a request for the fortitude of faith that enables us to realize and appreciate the complete revelation of God's grace and love that is ours in Christ Jesus. May we habitually bow our knees to the Father and personalize this prayer:

That he would grant you. . .to be strengthened with might by his Spirit in the inner man; that Christ may dwell in your hearts by faith; that ye, being rooted and grounded in love, may be able to comprehend with all saints what is the breadth, and length, and depth, and height; and to know the love of Christ, which passeth knowledge.
EPHESIANS 3:16–19

November 6

God answers prayer, I dare believe it;
God answers prayer, O praise his name:
God answers prayer, and here this moment,
His love sets all my heart aflame.

GEORGE BENNARD (1873–1958)
GOD ANSWERS PRAYER

THE PRAYERS OF EPHESIANS, PART 3

Ephesians reveals our nearness to God more than any other part of the sacred scriptures. To impress this on our minds, it resorts to striking figures such as a body and its head and a dwelling place with a divine inhabitant. Only here do we see that, in Christ, we are seated among the celestials (2:6). Therefore, unlike his other epistles, the apostle expresses the transcendent truths of Ephesians 1–3 in the form of prayer. This beautifies them and compels us to imitate his prayerful spirit.

Before his arrest and imprisonment, the apostle informed the believers of the whole counsel of God (Acts 20:27). But things have changed. God's ambassador is in chains requesting prayer that he might boldly make known the secret of the gospel (Ephesians 6:20). When Paul was unchained, he fully and freely preached the gospel of the Christ from Jerusalem to Illyricum (Romans 15:19). That job is done. Now he is laboring to make known the secrets newly revealed in Ephesians. He has prayed that we believers will comprehend these things (1:15–23; 3:14–21). But he needs prayer, as well. This is the third prayer of Ephesians (6:18–20). Since Paul is now dead, there is no need to pray for him. But note that he asks we pray for all the saints to have the boldness to make known the secret of the gospel.

As we pray according to Ephesians, God will respond by enlightening the eyes of our hearts, strengthening our inner man and rooting and grounding us in love. Based on this, we pray that others, and we ourselves, will boldly make known the secret of the gospel.

> *Praying always. . .for all saints; and for me, that utterance*
> *may be given unto me, that I may open my mouth boldly,*
> *to make known the mystery of the gospel.*
> EPHESIANS 6:18–19

*Jesus lives! no longer now
Can thy terrors, death, appall us;
Jesus lives! by this we know thou,
Thou, O grave, canst not enthrall us.*

CHRISTIAN F. GELLERT (1715–1769)
JESUS LIVES!
TRANSLATED BY FRANCES E. COX (1812–1897)

THE RESURRECTION OF JESUS CHRIST

Note the difference between Lazarus's rising and the resurrection of our Lord. Lazarus saw corruption; his body was stinking after four days in the tomb (John 11:39). The flesh of Christ saw no corruption (Acts 2:31). Lazarus was raised bound foot and hand in grave clothes, and his face was covered with a cloth—the symbols of mortality and weakness (John 11:44). Christ Jesus was raised in power. His feet were free, hands unbound, and face exposed (2 Corinthians 13:4). Since he had the power to lay down his life and to take it up again (John 10:17–18), it was nothing for him to remove his grave clothes and roll aside the stone blocking the entrance to the tomb. He is not only the Resurrection, he is also the Life (John 11:25).

The first witness to the power of Christ's resurrection was Mary Magdalene, who, though once possessed with seven demons, was among the women who ministered to Jesus (Luke 8:2–3). She was the last to leave the tomb on the day he died, and she returned there early the next morning (Matthew 27:61; 28:1). Unlike Peter and John who merely looked into the tomb and departed, she lingered and became the first to see the risen Christ. Peter and John only saw the grave clothes; let us emulate Mary Magdalene and linger in the scriptures until we see the Lord (John 20:3–18).

But now is Christ risen from the dead, and become the firstfruits of them that slept. For since by man came death, by man came also the resurrection of the dead. For as in Adam all die, even so in Christ shall all be made alive.
1 CORINTHIANS 15:20–22

We walk by faith, and not by sight;
No gracious words we hear
From him who spake as man ne'er spake;
But we believe him near.

HENRY ALFORD (1810–1871)
WE WALK BY FAITH

THE BELIEVER'S TWO HOMES

Henry Alford, the prolific British artist, clergyman, editor, educator, poet, preacher, scholar of New Testament Greek, and writer, here gives us reason to examine the idea that we walk by faith and not by sight.

Second Corinthians 5 begins by comparing our present soulish body with the temporary tent of a nomad. Next, the spiritual body—our habitation from resurrection to the end of the ages—is compared to a building of God that is not made with hands (v. 1).

Two words describe our condition in our present body: "groaning" and "desiring" (v. 2). We groan to be rid of our temporary tabernacle while we desire our celestial body. There is no third option. Contrary to popular thought, scripture views the intermediate condition—death—as an unwelcome enemy (v. 4; 1 Corinthians 15:26). Our expectation is resurrection. Even in his infirmity, the apostle never preferred death, but he longed for the coming of Christ when the mortal will be swallowed up by life (2 Corinthians 5:4).

Thus, we have two homes, two bodies: the tent in which we now live and the house we will be given in the resurrection. By sight, we only know the temporary soulish home in which we presently walk by faith. But we will soon be living in our spiritual body with the Lord (vv. 6–8).

So also is the resurrection of the dead. It is sown in corruption;
it is raised in incorruption: it is sown in dishonour; it is raised in glory:
it is sown in weakness; it is raised in power: it is sown a natural body;
it is raised a spiritual body.
1 CORINTHIANS 15:42–44

O thou once tempted like as we,
Thou knowest our infirmity;
Be thou our helper in the strife,
Be thou our true, our inward life.

JOSEPH F. THRUPP (1827–1867)
AWHILE IN SPIRIT, LORD, TO THEE

THE INNER LIFE, PART 1

Our spiritual life is inward and hidden. Its source and supply are unseen. Outwardly, there is no mark of its existence and no sign of its power. This life springs from the cross of Christ, and our death with him paves the way for it, because "if we be dead with Christ, we believe that we shall also live with him" (Romans 6:8). Although we are dead to the world, we are actually the most living. So, we are told to set our affection on that which is above where our life is hid with Christ in God (Colossians 3:2–3).

Though it is unseen, this wonderful life is founded on all God has done for us in Christ to make us complete in him (2:10). In fact, it is Christ's life, and we are saved in it (Romans 5:10). Eight items in Colossians describe our completed life (2:10–15): We were circumcised with a circumcision not made by hands. That is, we were crucified with Christ (Galatians 2:20). His entombment was our baptism. And when we were given faith to believe in the operation of God, we were raised with Christ, as well. All of this is now our life.

Colossians 2:13–15 continues to describe the effects of Christ's life—his death, burial, and resurrection—upon us: We are dead to all the offenses against God in human history. What a relief. Plus, God has dealt graciously with our personal offenses. The ordinances that were imposed on Gentiles in order to keep peace with Jewish believers have been taken away (Acts 15:20; 16:4). This means no more law-keeping. Add to this the fact that Christ triumphed over all the injurious spiritual powers, and we are perfectly free to enjoy his life.

The life which I now live in the flesh I live by the faith of the Son of God.
GALATIANS 2:20

In doubt and temptation I rest, Lord, in thee;
My hand is in thy hand, thou carest for me;
My soul with thy counsel through life thou wilt guide,
And afterward make me in glory abide.

AUTHOR UNKNOWN
IN DOUBT AND TEMPTATION

THE INNER LIFE, PART 2

God has given his believers unlimited resources. Therefore, in these troubled and faithless times, let us stand firm, nurturing our understanding of the foundational truths of God's Word.

These truths are not conveyed in wisdom of words. If that were so, the cross of Christ would be meaningless. Rather, their testimony comes through human weakness as a demonstration of the Spirit and of power. In this way, our faith does not stand in human wisdom but in the power of God. Therefore, our competency is from God because we are complete in Christ "in whom are hid all the treasures of wisdom and knowledge" (Colossians 2:3).

The following is the truth about our past: We were by nature children of wrath, enemies of God, and children of God's adversary, taken captive by him for his will. We were subjects of the kingdom of darkness, unable to please God, without Christ, without hope, and without God in the world.

Here is the truth about our present: All is new, spiritual, and heavenly. We are in resurrection experiencing a salvation that is of faith and according to grace. We understand that all is in, for, and through Christ Jesus and that we are crucified, raised, and seated with him. God has translated us into the kingdom of his beloved Son; therefore, we are not of the world even as he is not of the world.

This description of our life in Christ is composed from the following verses:
Paragraph 2—1 CORINTHIANS 1:17; 2:1–5, 5; 2 CORINTHIANS 3:5;
COLOSSIANS 2:3, 10
Paragraph 3—EPHESIANS 2:3; COLOSSIANS 1:13, 21; ROMANS 5:10; 8:8;
JOHN 8:44; 2 TIMOTHY 2:26; EPHESIANS 2:11–12
Paragraph 4—2 CORINTHIANS 5:17; EPHESIANS 1:3, 6; 2:4–8; 3:16–21;
COLOSSIANS 1:13; 2:11–13; 3:1; JOHN 1:16–18; 17:14; ROMANS 11:36;
GALATIANS 2:20; 6:14

In glory thou only my portion shall be,
On earth for none other I long for but thee;
My flesh and heart falter, but God is my stay,
The strength of my spirit, my portion for aye.

AUTHOR UNKNOWN
IN DOUBT AND TEMPTATION

THE INNER LIFE, PART 3

As we pursue the knowledge and understanding of scriptural truth, our inner life is enriched and strengthened. In that life, it is not difficult to glory in the cross, because we are enabled to walk worthily of our calling in newness of life, worshipping God in spirit, rejoicing in Christ Jesus, with no confidence in the flesh. Though we are in the world, we are not of, it because the world is crucified to us. Though we honor its human authorities, obey its laws, and pay taxes, our citizenship, our blessings, our position, our warfare, and our very life are all in the heavenlies. Out of them, we await a Savior who will change the body of our humiliation and conform it to the body of his glory.

This world came into being through God's Son, yet he was rejected in it. The apostle Paul was Christ's ambassador, yet the world put him in chains. Truly, everyone who lives godly in Christ Jesus will suffer persecution. Nevertheless, here in the midst of a crooked and perverse generation we are shining as luminaries holding forth the word of life and serving the Lord of heaven and of earth, of the living and the dead. He has triumphed over the power of God's adversary and will be Lord of lords and King of kings, conquering every foe. All will be put under his feet. Therefore, we always triumph in Christ.

The above is composed from the following verses:
Paragraph 1—GALATIANS 6:14; EPHESIANS 1:3; 2:6; 4:1, 17–24; 6:10–18;
ROMANS 6:4; PHILIPPIANS 2:14–16; 3:3, 20–21; JOHN 17:16; ROMANS
13:1–7; TITUS 3:1; COLOSSIANS 3:2–4;
Paragraph 2—JOHN 1:11; 2 CORINTHIANS 2:14; 5:20; EPHESIANS 1:10;
6:20; COLOSSIANS 1:16; 4:18; 2 TIMOTHY 3:12; ACTS 17:24; ROMANS 14:9;
1 TIMOTHY 6:15; PHILIPPIANS 2:9–11; 1 CORINTHIANS 15:24, 28

Clothed in garments of salvation,
At thy table is our place,
We rejoice, and thou rejoicest,
In the riches of thy grace.

JAMES G. DECK (1807–1884)
ABBA, FATHER! WE APPROACH THEE

THE DETERMINATE COUNSEL AND FOREKNOWLEDGE OF GOD

God was not surprised by Adam's failure. His plan of salvation is not a stopgap measure to correct an unexpected event. Christ was delivered to death by the determinate counsel and foreknowledge of God (Acts 2:23). From the foundation of the world, God prepared his Son to be the sacrifice for sin (Revelation 13:8). An illustration of his death is seen in Adam and Eve's garments, which were made from the skin of an animal slain by the Lord God himself (Genesis 3:21).

Skip forward to the flood in Noah's day. "The end of all flesh is come before me," said God. "Make thee an ark" (Genesis 6:13–14). The face of the earth was to be cleared in preparation for a new beginning. Therefore, God gave Noah a detailed design for the ark. This shows that all is perfectly planned in God's operations (Ephesians 1:11). The ark, like a garment, protected those who were to be saved in it.

The original Hebrew language of Genesis 7:1 is best translated like this: "Come thou and all thy house into the ark." Noah wasn't commanded to enter the ark; he was invited into it. This means God was in the ark already. Isn't this much like the gospel's invitation? It is not a legal commandment from afar, but a loving call from the Word who, in God's plan and for his purpose, became flesh (John 1:14). In him, God intimately speaks to us in the likeness of our own nature. This makes it possible for humans to respond to the grace that draws so close as to cover and protect us in our defeat.

> *Who verily was foreordained before the foundation of the world,*
> *but was manifest in these last times for you.*
> 1 PETER 1:20

Here at Bethesda's pool, the poor,
The withered, halt, and blind;
With waiting hearts, expect a cure,
And free admittance find.

JOHN NEWTON (1725–1807)
HERE AT BETHESDA'S POOL

THE HEALING OF ISRAEL

The case of the sick man at the pool of Bethesda is a picture of salvation in Israel before Christ came (John 5:1–9). It describes the utter hopelessness of all law-keeping religions and sects. At the pool a crowd of people waited until an angel stirred up the water. At that moment, the first person who entered the water was supposedly healed (v. 4). That person had to have been the healthiest of all in order to enter the pool first. Apparently, the man whom the Lord healed had been there thirty-eight years, getting weaker and weaker. His healing depended on either his own effort or human help. This shows that, although those who live under religious law are told how to be saved, they are not given the strength to accomplish it.

It is significant that Jesus Christ healed this man on the Sabbath. This means that Israel will be healed of its sickness of legalism and unbelief when the millennial kingdom arrives (Romans 11:26–27). Thus, the man at Bethesda didn't have to repent and wash away his sins in the pool. All he had to do was carry his bedroll and walk (John 5:8–9). That bedroll is the place of rest, another symbol of Israel's kingdom—the true Sabbath.

Later the Lord met this man in the temple and told him, "Sin no more, lest a worse thing come unto thee" (John 5:14). This was the reality of Israel's position before God at that time. They were still under law, and their Messiah hadn't yet been crucified, so God could not forgive his beloved people their sins. However, the words of John 5:14 are not spoken to those who are saved by grace through faith. Such salvation does not spring from our own strength to sin no more. It is God's gift to us (Ephesians 2:8).

And so all Israel shall be saved.
ROMANS 11:26

When Moses wanted water to quench the people's thirst,
He knew that God would then provide a way;
Although his rod was useful he had the power first:
And the pow'r of God is just the same today.

FREDERICK A. GRAVES (1856–1927)
THE POWER OF GOD

THE SPIRITUAL FOOD AND DRINK

Israel was miraculously provided drinking water in the wilderness at the rock of Mount Horeb and the crag in Meribah at Kadesh (Exodus 17:6; Numbers 20:8–13). They also were given a miraculous daily supply of manna for nourishment (Exodus 16:15). If the people had never been hungry or thirsty, they would not have appreciated God's gift of physical water and food. There was also a spiritual message for them in this. We read that they "did all eat the same spiritual meat; and did all drink the same spiritual drink: for they drank of that spiritual Rock that followed them: and that Rock was Christ" (1 Corinthians 10:3–4). Christ accompanied his people in the wilderness to be their spiritual source of refreshment.

Eating and drinking satisfy our physical needs, but unless we are spiritually satisfied, our lives are just an existence in a wilderness. Such spiritual sustenance can never be found apart from the one who is the bread of heaven and who supplies inward rivers of living water (John 6:41; 7:38). When we finally find all our spiritual desires realized in God's Son, our hunger and thirst are truly satisfied.

Today the source of spiritual nourishment is the Word of God, which reveals him. Nothing is lacking in it, so let us nourish ourselves daily with the words of faith and the good teaching as we follow our Lord through the wilderness of this world (1 Timothy 4:6).

From a child thou hast known the holy scriptures, which are able to make thee wise unto salvation through faith which is in Christ Jesus. All scripture is given by inspiration of God, and is profitable for doctrine, for reproof, for correction, for instruction in righteousness.
2 TIMOTHY 3:15–16

For Judah's lion bursts his chains,
Crushing the serpent's head;
And cries aloud through death's domains
To wake the imprisoned dead.

FULBERT OF CHARTRES (952–1028)
YE CHOIRS OF NEW JERUSALEM
TRANSLATED BY ROBERT CAMPBELL (1814–1868)

HOW SATAN IS CRUSHED

Humanity was created by God to have dominion over the other creatures on earth (Genesis 1:26, 28). The serpent disrupted this arrangement, usurped the place of God, and overthrew humanity's authority over it and the other animals. Here is how the Lord responded to the serpent's deed: "I will put enmity between thee and the woman, and between thy seed and her seed; it shall bruise thy head, and thou shalt bruise his heel" (3:15).

How is the serpent's head bruised? This results from the adversary's act of hurting the heel of the woman's seed while attempting to triumph over Christ on the hill of Golgotha. Through death, Jesus Christ destroyed "him that had the power of death, that is, the devil" (Hebrews 2:14). In the end, all enemies including God's adversary will be placed under Christ's feet (1 Corinthians 15:24–25). Then the name of Jesus will be exalted above every name that is named. All of this is the effect of Christ's obedience to the death of the cross (Philippians 2:8–11).

Our Lord's great victory is alluded to in the midst of a warning against discord and snares promoted by those who mislead innocent believers (Romans 16:17–19). We are assured that "the God of peace shall bruise Satan under your feet shortly. The grace of our Lord Jesus Christ be with you" (v. 20). Here we see that the serpent's head is crushed because of grace and peace, which is the gospel, God's power to us who believe (Romans 1:7, 16). This same power will crush the serpent's head in that future day. Then as now, the God of peace will triumph through the operation of the grace of our Lord Jesus Christ.

The Son of God was revealed for this purpose, to destroy the works of the devil.
1 JOHN 3:8 NRSV

Within the churchyard, side by side,
Are many long low graves;
And some have stones set over them,
On some the green grass waves.

CECIL F. ALEXANDER (1818–1895)
WITHIN THE CHURCHYARD, SIDE BY SIDE

THE DEATH OF ADAM

Death is first found in Genesis 2:17: "In the day that thou eatest thereof thou shalt surely die." Some say this warning was not carried out until 930 years later when Adam physically died. But the process of dying began the very day he ate of the tree and ended when he died. This is seen in a more literal translation of this verse: "In the day you eat from it, to die shall you be dying." Because of Adam's transgression, every human is born mortal and eventually goes down to the grave. We have no expectation or possibility of rescue from this except through the promised seed of the woman (3:15).

The death that came upon the human race through Adam is in every way the opposite of the life Christ brings to us. That life is for our bodies in the resurrection, this is true. However, part of the gift of life in Christ Jesus is already ours because our spirit is life because of righteousness (Romans 8:10). The spirit of each believer has been vitalized and justified, perfectly adjusted to God in Christ. But the body is dead because of sin (v. 10). Believers' bodies are still ruled by the death introduced through Adam.

Adam's sin immediately brought mortality to his spirit. Only later did his body die. Similarly, salvation begins in our spirits. In the resurrection, our bodies will also be made alive. Presently, the most important difference between people is that some are in Adam and some are in Christ. An unbeliever has not passed through judgment from death into life, whereas a believer has done so in the death and resurrection of Jesus Christ.

And if Christ be in you, the body is dead because of sin;
but the Spirit is life because of righteousness.
ROMANS 8:10

He comes, the wide world's King, he comes, the true heart's friend,
New gladness to begin, and ancient wrong to end;
He comes, to fill with light the weary waiting eye;
Lift up your heads, rejoice, redemption draweth nigh.

THOMAS T. LYNCH (1818–1871
LIFT UP YOUR HEADS, REJOICE

THE TRANSFIGURATION OF OUR BODIES

The sacred scriptures reveal that every believer has a calling—God's high calling in Christ Jesus (Philippians 3:14). Perhaps the translators used the term "high calling" because to say, "up calling" or "above calling," seemed awkward to them. But these two phrases more closely reflect the meaning of the original Greek text. We are being called up, called from above. No wonder we are urged to set our minds on the things above and are told that our citizenship is in the heavens (Colossians 3:2; Philippians 3:20). Our blessings are among the celestials; we are seated among the celestials; we will display the transcendent riches of God's grace to the celestials; even now God's wisdom is made known to the principalities and powers in heavenly places through the church (Ephesians 1:3, 20; 2:6; 3:10).

In addition to that, we are also awaiting a Savior from above who will change our bodies and conform them to the body of his glory (Philippians 3:20–21). Do we need any more reasons to do as the hymn says and lift up our heads and rejoice?

Our present bodies are weak, mortal, corruptible, and dependent upon the elements of the earth. They are not fit for our heavenly destiny. So our Savior, who has the ability to bring the entire universe beneath his gracious influence, will transfigure them. Our future bodies will be like the glorious body that Paul saw when he met the Lord on the Damascus road. It was a light out of heaven flashing around the apostle, blinding him with its brilliance (Acts 9:3, 8). This indicates what kind of glory will be ours when our bodies are transfigured.

For this corruptible must put on incorruption, and this mortal must put on immortality.
1 CORINTHIANS 15:53

One day there'll be new earth and heaven,
for the first will soon pass away.
And the holy city from heaven will appear in bridal array.
Then with men God will make his dwelling;
they will be his people indeed.
God himself will be with them always and their God will ever be.

SUSAN H. PETERSON (1950–2004)
ONE DAY THERE'LL BE NEW EARTH AND HEAVEN

THE PERMANENCE OF THE NEW CREATION

The simple understanding that the present heaven and earth are transitory enhances a person's spiritual life. The impermanence of all we see is repeatedly mentioned in scripture, but a portion of one verse is sufficient: "I saw a new heaven and a new earth" (Revelation 21:1).

Look about you at the present heaven and earth, keeping in mind that they are stored with fire; that the heavens will pass away with a booming noise and the elements will be dissolved by combustion (2 Peter 3:7, 10). Although it sounds horrific, this is a wonderful event because it makes way for new heavens and a new earth in which righteousness dwells (v. 13).

A striking feature of the new earth is that the sea no longer exists there (Revelation 21:1). The changing character of the present earth is due largely to the abundance of water. Its shifting weather systems are defined by the presence or absence of moisture. Water disintegrates solid rock. In the form of glaciers, it grinds down the landscape. In streams and rivers, it washes soil to the sea. All this is an allegory of the impermanent processes through which humankind is passing. In contrast, when the new earth emerges from the divine alchemist's fiery crucible, its stones will be hardened gems, its gold purified to transparency (vv. 18–21). Like God has always been, it will be permanent, unchanging, and indestructible.

Thou, Lord, in the beginning hast laid the foundation of the earth; and the
heavens are the works of thine hands: they shall perish; but thou remainest;
and they all shall wax old as doth a garment. And as a vesture shalt thou
fold them up, and they shall be changed.
HEBREWS 1:10–12

We bless thee, God and Father, we joy before thy face;
Beyond dark death forever, we share thy Son's blest place.
He lives a man before thee, in cloudless light above,
In thine unbounded favor, thine everlasting love.

ALEXANDER CARRUTHERS (1860–1930)
WE BLESS THEE GOD AND FATHER

THE GOD AND FATHER OF OUR LORD JESUS CHRIST

The essence of God's being is love. It is the depths of God; its measurements are vast, extending from before the foundation of the world to beyond the consummation of the ages (Ephesians 2:4; 1 Corinthians 2:10). Throughout history, God has been known by many names, but in the end he will hold only one title that expresses this love—Father (15:24).

Perhaps the most beautiful and loving description of the Almighty is "God and Father of our Lord Jesus Christ" (see Romans 15:6; see 2 Corinthians 1:3; Ephesians 1:3; see Colossians 1:3). This directs our thoughts to a particular glory of God: He is the Father of our Savior who is the anointed head of the body and Lord of all. This expression also speaks of Jesus Christ's greatest glory: He is Son to the Father. As for us believers, since God is the Father of Jesus Christ and we are in Christ, we share the Son's blessed place (Galatians 4:6). The fact that God is the Father of our Lord Jesus Christ makes his fatherhood infinitely precious to us.

The God and Father of Jesus Christ is the source of all Christ is and all that he has and will accomplish. So let us take our cue from the apostle and bless the one "who hath blessed us with all spiritual blessings in heavenly places in Christ" (Ephesians 1:3), thus insulating our hearts from this world's disdain for the God and Father of our Lord Jesus Christ.

May the God of steadfastness and encouragement grant you to live in harmony with one another, in accordance with Christ Jesus, so that together you may with one voice glorify the God and Father of our Lord Jesus Christ.
ROMANS 15:5–6 NRSV

*His Father and our Father, his God and ours thou art;
And he is thy beloved, the gladness of thy heart.
We're his, in joy he brings us to share his part and place,
To know thy love and favor, the shining of thy face.*

ALEXANDER CARRUTHERS (1860–1930)
WE BLESS THEE GOD AND FATHER

GOD'S NAME IS *FATHER*

A divine purpose lies behind our experiences of sorrow, failure, and frustration. It is that we may come to know God's heart. He is surely power, wisdom, and righteousness. He is Creator, Sustainer, and Savior. Yet, in our life experiences, we are getting to know God as our Father in a relationship marked by love and favor. Believers know the rich benefits of this relationship because we have received the spirit of sonship (Romans 8:15). In this spirit, we know our Father's concern and constant provision. Paul called this the "glorious liberty of the children of God" (v. 21). This freedom is found in that we have nothing to fear; we are not burdened with the frightful, fleshly turmoil described in Romans 7. God gave us this freedom when he "sent forth the Spirit of his Son into [our] hearts, crying, Abba, Father" (Galatians 4:6).

Our problem is that we acknowledge God as our Father without enjoying it, without the confidence of a son with his father. The example of the Son of God can help us grasp the spirit of sonship since he is the firstborn of many brothers (Romans 8:29). His prayer in John 17 expresses his intense awareness and appreciation of his Father (vv. 1, 5, 11, 21, 24–25). There he made it known that God's name is Father and prayed, "Keep through thine own name those whom thou hast given me" (vv. 6, 11). May we all appreciate this name, remain in it despite our sufferings, and thereby know God's love.

*O righteous Father. . .I have declared unto them thy name,
and will declare it: that the love wherewith thou
hast loved me may be in them, and I in them.*
JOHN 17:25–26

Thy love that now enfolds us can ne'er wax cold or dim;
In him that love doth center, and we are loved in him.
In him thy love and glory find their eternal rest;
The many sons his brethren in him, how near, how blest!

ALEXANDER CARRUTHERS (1860–1930)
WE BLESS THEE GOD AND FATHER

THE RICHES THAT ARE IN CHRIST

With four exceptions, the phrase "in Christ" is found only in Paul's epistles. There we find that, by grace, everything is ours in him. The love of God is in Christ Jesus our Lord, and we are loved in him. Such love is expressed in our being justified freely through the redemption that is in Christ. So there is now no condemnation to those in him; nothing can separate us from the love of God that is in Christ. We are sanctified in Christ Jesus and find wisdom, righteousness, and redemption in him.

All around us we see evidence that in Adam all die. The day will come when we see that in Christ all will be made alive. Presently, the God and Father of our Lord Jesus Christ has blessed us with all spiritual blessings in heavenly places in Christ. Knowing this, with the faith and love that is in Christ, and cleaving to the promise of life in him, we press toward the mark for the prize of the high calling of God in Christ Jesus. This makes us strong in the grace that is in Christ looking forward to the salvation that is in him with eternal glory.

These blessings are lavished upon us, not because of what we are in ourselves, but because God has placed us in Christ. We don't deserve them, nor can we sustain them. When tempted to doubt our rich inheritance in him, we must only remember that it is found in Christ. Outside of him, we are poor and miserable. In him, we are rich beyond our wildest dreams.

The first two paragraphs are composed from these verses:
ROMANS 3:24; 8:1; 8:39; 1 CORINTHIANS 1:2; 1:30; 15:22; EPHESIANS 1:3;
PHILIPPIANS 3:14; 1 TIMOTHY 1:1, 14; 2 TIMOTHY 2:1, 10

God, our Father, we adore thee! We, thy children, bless thy name!
Chosen in the Christ before thee, we are "holy without blame."
We adore thee! We adore thee! Abba's praises we proclaim!
We adore thee! We adore thee! Abba's praises we proclaim!

GEORGE W. FRAZER (1830–1896)
GOD OUR FATHER, WE ADORE THEE

THE CHILDREN OF THE FATHER

As we come to know God, our understanding of our privileges as children of God increases, and we delight in all that comes from knowing God's name is Father. Everything about our Father is wonderful. He is love and light. In him is absolutely no darkness. He is faithful, kind, patient, and all-wise. And let's not forget that he is the Almighty. It is amazing that he is mindful of us, let alone that we have been given the place of children, and as children, we are objects of his love.

A human father tries to train his children to be like himself. He tutors them to love what he loves, hate what he hates, and do as he does because he wants them to reflect him and be his expression when they are grown. The perfect Father is God. His children are being trained so that they will ultimately be his perfect expression (Titus 2:11). This training will not be complete until our bodies are delivered from the bondage of flesh. However, he will make progress in our lifetimes as his Spirit bears its fruit in us—love, joy, peace, longsuffering, gentlesness, goodness, faith, meekness, and temperance (Galatians 5:22–23).

Each of these expresses God the Father. So we are urged to be walking in spirit and in love, like beloved children, imitators of God (v. 16; Ephesians 5:1). As this takes place, it is our privilege as children of the Father to become expressions of what he is, displaying his manifold wisdom (3:10).

The Spirit itself beareth witness with our spirit, that we are the children of God: and if children, then heirs; heirs of God, and joint-heirs with Christ.
ROMANS 8:16–17

Thy kingdom come, O Lord,
Wide circling as the sun;
Fulfill of old thy word
And make the nations one.

FREDERICK L. HOSMER (1840–1929)
THY KINGDOM COME, O LORD

ISRAEL'S STUMBLING AND OUR SALVATION

Acts tells of the final years of Israel's privileged position as the chosen nation in God's plan (Romans 9:4–5). It begins with the question, "Lord, wilt thou at this time restore again the kingdom to Israel?" (Acts 1:6). It proceeds to tell the story of the apostles' efforts to spread the gospel of the kingdom in the land of Israel and among Jewish communities elsewhere in the Roman Empire. If Israel had accepted their message, Christ would have come. Instead, by God's choice, the nation stumbled (Romans 9:11, 32). At the end of Acts, the door to the kingdom was closed as the apostle told the Jewish leaders in Rome, "I want you to know that God's salvation has been sent to the Gentiles, and they will listen" (Acts 28:28 NIV).

At the same time, God raised the other nations from their status of complete alienation to that of free access to him (Ephesians 2:13–18). Since Acts is primarily concerned with Israel, this transformation is hidden there. However, Paul's epistles bring it to light. Thus, Acts and the Epistles combine to record the great transition from Israel's privilege based on physical heritage to spiritual blessing for all people (1:3).

God called Israel a "disobedient and gainsaying people," yet he preserves in her a remnant of believers (Romans 10:21; 11:5). While he hasn't abandoned Israel, rejection of the Son of God is virtually national policy there. The reason for this is that God has given them "eyes that they should not see, and ears that they should not hear" (v. 8). This is significant, because it is through God's temporary casting away of the nation of Israel that the world is conciliated to him (v. 15). Thus, Israel's fall brought salvation directly to the nations (vv. 11–12).

Blindness in part is happened to Israel,
until the fulness of the Gentiles be come in.
ROMANS 11:25

Choose for us, God! Nor let our weak preferring
Cheat our poor souls of good thou hast designed;
Choose for us, God! Thy wisdom is unerring,
And we are fools and blind.

WILLIAM H. BURLEIGH (1812–1871)
STILL WILL WE TRUST

THE CALL TO PRAYER

Although we are usually not aware of what we should pray for, God still works all together for good in our lives (Romans 8:26–28). What is the good that God is working toward? It is that we be conformed to the image of his Son (v. 29). If we could see what God is doing in the circumstances of our lives, we would always pray in harmony with God's plan. However, as the hymn says, we are fools and blind, so we need the Spirit's help to pray.

Some people may ask, "Why pray since God will choose anyway?" This is a good example of the folly of human reasoning. It is false to suppose that God's purpose leaves no room for prayer. If this were so, why would scripture repeatedly call on us to pray? Nowhere does it say we should not pray for fear of asking for something God will not give. Rather, we are urged to pray because, though we are weak and unaware, when we do so we are turning to the only source of good. We may pray ignorantly, but this is balanced by the Spirit's pleading (v. 26).

We are not totally ignorant, however. The Word reveals many things for which we should pray. It provides excellent illustrations and patterns of prayer. Take, for example, Paul's prayers for the saints and for all humankind. Plus, our Lord told us to pray for those who persecute and injure us (Matthew 5:44). Scripture urges us to pray; in fact, our every need is a call to prayer.

I exhort therefore, that, first of all, supplications, prayers,
intercessions, and giving of thanks, be made for all men;
for kings, and for all that are in authority; that we may lead
a quiet and peaceable life in all godliness and honesty.
1 TIMOTHY 2:1–2

*Lord, speak to me that I may speak
In living echoes of thy tone;
As thou hast sought, so let me seek
Thine erring children lost and lone.*

FRANCES R. HAVERGAL (1836–1879)
LORD, SPEAK TO ME

THE WAY OF GOD'S SPEAKING

The book of Hebrews was primarily written to the Jews who believed in Jesus Christ as detailed in the first few chapters of Acts. It reminds them that God spoke to their fathers through the prophets (Hebrews 1:1). The record of this speaking is now called the Old Testament. This was not the end of God's speaking, however. The up-to-date speaking of God is in the Son who is "the brightness of [God's] glory, and the express image of his person" (v. 3). This speaking is now recorded in the Gospels, Acts, and Epistles. Therefore, Hebrews 1:1–3 defines and sets the limits of God's speaking.

Elsewhere, we are told that Paul completed, or filled up, the Word of God (Colossians 1:25). Although other scriptural books were written after Colossians, Paul took the divine revelation to its furthest extent: far from Israel to the nations, outside the eons, and beyond the earth (1 Corinthians 2:7; 15:22; Ephesians 2:6; Philippians 3:20). This is how we know that there has been and will be no new revelation of God's purpose for humanity. God has nothing further to say at this time.

This is why, each time we read the scriptures, we can confidently adopt Frances Havergal's prayer, "Lord, speak to me." Only through the scriptures does God speak to humanity because they reveal the Son—the image of the invisible God (Colossians 1:15).

Jesus answered him, saying, It is written, That man shall not live by bread alone, but by every word of God.
LUKE 4:4

*All things bright and beautiful, all creatures great and small,
All things wise and wonderful: the Lord God made them all.
Each little flower that opens, each little bird that sings,
He made their glowing colors, he made their tiny wings.*

CECIL F. ALEXANDER (1818–1895)
ALL THINGS BRIGHT AND BEAUTIFUL

THE SECRET OF CHRIST

The apostle Paul asked for prayer that God would open a door so he could speak the secret of Christ (Colossians 4:3). A part of that secret is expressed in Cecil Alexander's song, "All Things Bright and Beautiful," which brings to mind these words: "The invisible things of him from the creation of the world are clearly seen. . .even his eternal power and Godhead" (Romans 1:20). Creation can teach people about God's power and divinity, yet because God himself is invisible (John 4:24; 1 Timothy 6:16), the creation cannot reveal him. So God sent his Son, who is God's visible, tangible embodiment (Colossians 1:15). Only in him do we see the very God.

In Colossians, Paul tells much about this secret of Christ. There we read, "In him all things in heaven and on earth were created, things visible and invisible, whether thrones or dominions or rulers or powers . . .all things have been created through him and for him" (1:16 NRSV).

Creation was in Christ just as a tree and its fruits are inherent in a seed. In him, the Almighty created the entire universe. This includes the celestial as well as the terrestrial spheres and every spiritual power and nobility. It includes you and me. Through the Son, these not only reveal the power and divinity of the invisible God but also are used by Christ to accomplish God's purpose for the ages.

*No man hath seen God at any time, the only begotten Son,
which is in the bosom of the Father, he hath declared him.*
JOHN 1:18

These doubts and fears that troubled me
Were born of my infirmity;
Though I am weak, God is most high,
And on his goodness I rely.

AUTHOR UNKNOWN
TO GOD WILL I DIRECT MY PRAYER
PARAPHRASE OF PSALM 77

OUR WEAKNESS IN PRAYER

One may have various weaknesses in body and soul, but scripture tells of another infirmity, a spiritual weakness that frustrates prayer (Romans 8:26). This disability is the worst weakness of all because it ruins the harmony that can exist between God and the praying believer. If believers wait until this weakness is removed, they will never pray again.

Our highest privilege and most spiritual activity is prayer; therefore, disability in this exercise is serious. This is why we need the aid of the Spirit. Though we are usually unaware of what we should be praying for, we still must go to God with all our needs and worries. He loves to hear his children's voices call out in prayers of faith. Our weakness does not hamper such prayers or God's answer to them. After all, does a child's ignorance block his mother's nurture?

Jesus Christ once prayed in perplexity: "Now is my soul troubled; and what shall I say? Father, save me from this hour: but for this cause came I unto this hour" (John 12:27). He faced an inconceivable ordeal, yet desired to glorify his Father by doing his will. What a conflict! Then he asked, "Father, glorify thy name," and immediately received an answer that reassured and strengthened him (v. 28).

The apostle Paul prayed three times for his own healing and was not healed. Instead, God's answer instructed him in the all-sufficiency of grace. After that, he gloried in his weaknesses because he had learned that through them he could know Christ's power (2 Corinthians 12:7–10). In the same way, it is better for us to be weak even in prayer, because we do not pray alone; the Holy Spirit always joins in to plead for us (Romans 8:27).

We know not what we should pray for as we ought: but the Spirit itself maketh intercession for us with groanings which cannot be uttered.
ROMANS 8:26

O thou who camest from above,
The pure celestial fire to impart,
Kindle a flame of sacred love
Upon the mean altar of my heart.
There let it for thy glory burn
With inextinguishable blaze;
And trembling to its source return,
In humble prayer and fervent praise.

CHARLES WESLEY (1707–1788)
O THOU WHO CAMEST FROM ABOVE

THE SPIRIT'S GROANING AND PLEADING, PART 1

The celestial fire that Charles Wesley mentions in his hymn is actually the Spirit of God's Son sent into our hearts (Galatians 4:6). If a believer wants to know that Spirit, Romans certifies three spiritual experiences as genuine: (1) The Holy Spirit witnesses in our spirit that we are God's children (Romans 8:16). (2) We have a spirit of sonship to intimately know and love the Father (v. 15). (3) The Spirit joins in our prayers to groan and plead for us (vv. 26–27).

The Spirit pleads for us in the same way one person prays for another. This pleading does not originate with us, though it exists in and through our hearts' prayer. This is why we should always pray. No matter how flawed and selfish they may seem, our prayers are never apart from the Spirit. Rather, they are enhanced, adjusted, refined, and made acceptable to God by the Spirit's groaning and pleading.

Apart from Christ, we can do nothing (John 15:5). This is vividly seen in our prayers. We address God not in our competence but united to the Son and aided by his Spirit. Thank God that he sent the Spirit of his Son into our hearts and, in Wesley's beautiful words, it returns to him in humble prayer and fervent praise.

Likewise the Spirit also helpeth our infirmities: for we know not what we should pray for as we ought: but the Spirit itself maketh intercession for us with groanings which cannot be uttered. And he that searcheth the hearts knoweth what is the mind of the Spirit, because he maketh intercession for the saints according to the will of God.
ROMANS 8:26–27

With us, for us, intercede, And, with voiceless groanings, plead
Our unutterable need, Comforter divine.

GEORGE RAWSON (1807–1889)
COME TO OUR POOR NATURE'S NIGHT

THE SPIRIT'S GROANING AND PLEADING, PART 2

Romans 8 is a high and wide-ranging description of the spiritual life. One would not expect it to describe prayer in terms of pleading and inarticulate groaning (v. 26). This shows that persuasive speech or passionate language does not produce the highest kinds of prayer. Groanings that cannot be uttered are far more profound and spiritual than any articulate expression.

A person whose heart groans in prayer is deeply moved and addresses only God. Nothing in that prayer is insincere or hypocritical. If an idea is to be understood by man, it must be spoken in plain words. God, however, hears what is unintelligible to human ears. In our most spiritual prayers, the Spirit groans, complementing our own inward groans and audible words. In this way, the Spirit enters into fellowship with our suffering, and so can plead for us without being limited by our lack of understanding.

None of our prayers are spoken without the accompaniment of the Spirit's pleading. This harmonizes our shallow and even ignorant appeals with the deepest reality because the Spirit intercedes for the saints according to God (v. 27). True prayer is not a mere groan, however. Our petitions, no matter how weak and inarticulate, are made adequate and effective with the Spirit's aid.

Though our voices may speak eloquently in prayer, the simultaneous yearning groans of our hearts are better than all clarity and expressiveness. In this way we tell God of our fears, worries, and problems; we fellowship with him; we speak of our loved ones and enemies; he lends a willing ear. When confused or unclear, we tell him so. When sorrow, despondency, desire, or aspirations are too much for words, we wait in silence, knowing that he hears the Spirit's plea (Psalm 62:5).

The Spirit itself maketh intercession for us with groanings which cannot be uttered.
ROMANS 8:26

Thou, our God, art wise alone;
Thy counsel doth excel;
Wonderful thy works we own,
Thy ways unsearchable;
Who can sound the mystery,
Thy judgments' deep abyss explain,
Thine, whose eyes in darkness see,
And search the heart of man?

CHARLES WESLEY (1707–1788)
THOU, THE GREAT, ETERNAL GOD

GOD SEARCHES OUR HEARTS

Scripture repeatedly tells us that God searches the human heart. "For man looketh on the outward appearance," it says, "but the Lord looketh on the heart" (1 Samuel 16:7; see 1 Kings 8:39; Proverbs 15:11; Luke 16:15; Acts 1:24; Revelation 2:23). This explains how he can hear prayer no matter if it is spoken or wordless (Romans 8:27). If God did not search our hearts and know our spirits, when it comes to prayer, educated or eloquent people would have an advantage over those who are hesitant or slow of speech. In prayer as in all things, God deals with us in grace where the accomplishments and capabilities of our flesh mean nothing.

We need not fear what God may find while searching our hearts, because he has dealt with our sin on the cross where we were crucified with Christ (Galatians 2:20). In God's eyes, we are dead and therefore justified from sin (Romans 6:7). The law of sin, which is still in our members, cannot bring us under God's condemnation (7:23–25; 8:1). So why not welcome God's scrutiny? Why not emulate David, who desired that God search him and see if he was walking in the ways of the flesh (Psalm 139:23–24)? Then we will no longer see ourselves through human eyes, but as God sees us, and so find much to pray about. In spite of our awareness of failure, we will pray like Peter, "Lord, you know everything; you know that I love you" (John 21:17 NRSV).

He that searcheth the hearts knoweth what is the mind of the Spirit, because he maketh intercession for the saints according to the will of God.
Romans 8:27

Early in the temple meet,
Let us still our Savior greet;
Nightly to the mount repair,
Join our praying pattern there.

CHARLES WESLEY (1707–1788)
HOLY LAMB, WHO THEE CONFESS

HOW TO PRAY WITHOUT CEASING

What are our patterns for prayer? Inarticulate groaning is one of these (Romans 8:26–27). We groan in prayer with the Holy Spirit because we have no idea of how God may work to conform us to the image of his Son (vv. 28–29). Our lives are far too intricate to be completely understood. So we simply lift our hearts to God in a prayer that is like music without words. In this way, we are in tune with God's Spirit and can rest in his peace, knowing that he knows what we need. In such prayer, we are assured that all is well despite appearances. Nothing more than this is needed because the Spirit searches our hearts and intercedes for us in harmony with God (v. 27). Such prayer effortlessly arises as the day passes and the load on our hearts needs lightening.

We also have the privilege of praying the prayers presented in Paul's epistles. Though we benefit immeasurably by their fulfillment, these remove us from our own concerns and turn our hearts to God's purpose and plan. Perhaps the most important of these is the request for a spirit of wisdom and revelation (Ephesians 1:17). By this spirit, given to all believers who ask, we come to understand the mysteries that describe God's work among humankind today (see Romans 11:25; 16:25; 1 Corinthians 2:7; 15:51; Ephesians 1:9; 3:3–4, 9; 5:32; 6:19; Colossians 1:26–27; 2:2; 4:3; and 1 Timothy 3:16).

Our request for the spirit of wisdom and revelation is the prelude to a symphony of prayer recorded in Ephesians 1:18–23. Add to this the strengthening prayer for completion (3:14–19), the prayer for a walk that is worthy of the Lord (Colossians 1:9–12), the prayer for overflowing love (Philippians 4:9–11), and our prayers for all the saints (Ephesians 6:18), and our hearts cannot help but respond to the apostle's charge:

Pray without ceasing.
1 THESSALONIANS 5:17

Whatever passes as a cloud between
The mental eye of faith and things unseen,
Causing that brighter world to disappear,
To seem less lovely and its hopes less clear,
This is our world, our idol, though it bear
Affection's impress or devotion's air.

JANE TAYLOR (1783–1824)
THE WORLD IN THE HEART

A SCRIPTURAL REDEFINITION OF WORLDLINESS

In Christ, we died to everything that opposes us. We died to sin (Romans 6:2), and those under the law died to the law (Galatians 2:19). These are familiar topics. But the poetry of Jane Taylor reminds us we have been crucified to the world and the world to us (6:14). This means we have nothing to do with the "elements of the world" (4:3). Scripture uses the phrase "the elements of the world" to describe religious and philosophical practices and principles of behavior. Taylor says these things impress our affections, give us an air of devotion, yet cloud our eyes of faith.

For example, the Galatian believers received the Spirit of the Son. They, like us, held the position of sons in God's household and were his heirs (v. 7). However, they were deceived into observing weak and beggarly elements (v. 9). These are ritualistically observed religious rites like "days, and months, and times, and years" (v. 10). Meanwhile, the Colossians were warned against the seduction of philosophy and tradition. We can recognize these worldly elements because they are not in accord with Christ (Colossians 2:8). The Colossians knew they had died together with Christ from the elements of the world. Yet they had to be asked, "Why. . .are ye subject to ordinances, (Touch not; taste not; handle not. . .) after the commandments and doctrines of men?" (vv. 20–22).

All these worldly elements—these imitations of wisdom, these commandments and doctrines of men—are of no value (v. 23). They are clouds between the eye of faith and things unseen. So, what are we to do if we do not wish to be worldly? We cleave to scripture and we:

Seek those things which are above, where Christ sitteth on the right hand of God.
COLOSSIANS 3:1

For this alone I live below,
The power of godliness to show,
The wonders wrought by Jesus' name.
O that I may but faithful prove.

CHARLES WESLEY (1707–1788)
O THOU WHO AT THY CREATURE'S BAR

THE SWEET AROMA OF CHRIST

The resurrected Christ told his apostles that they would be his witnesses "among all nations, beginning at Jerusalem" (Luke 24:47). Untold numbers of believers have taken these words as their marching orders for gospel preaching. But when Paul wrote his epistles nearly thirty years later, he didn't mention the idea of witnessing. Instead, he said, "We are unto God a sweet savour of Christ, in them that are saved, and in them that perish" (2 Corinthians 2:15).

People who witness for another are familiar with their subject though separate from him. We are members of Christ's body. Our relationship with him is so intimate that, figuratively speaking, we bear his fragrance. It is possible for our entire living to be Christ by virtue of his death and resurrection (Romans 6:3–4). So every believer can testify, "For to me to live is Christ" (Philippians 1:21; see Galatians 2:20).

In the original Greek language, Philippians 2:16 expresses something similar. There we "appear as luminaries in the world, having on the word of life." The word of life is the living expression of the gospel. This means that the revelation of the truth as found in scripture causes our conduct to match the spirit of the gospel's message. On the other hand, it does not mean that we will not find opportunities to speak the gospel to others. Indeed, Christ's death and resurrection enable us to live wisely among others with speech "always with grace, seasoned with salt (Colossians 4:4–6). Charles Wesley understood this revolutionary idea of evangelism, so through the godliness of his life he showed the wonders wrought by Jesus' name.

Now thanks be unto God, which always causeth us to triumph in Christ, and maketh manifest the savour of his knowledge by us in every place.
2 CORINTHIANS 2:14

All hail the power of Jesus' name!
Let angels prostrate fall;
Bring forth the royal diadem,
And crown him Lord of all.

EDWARD PERRONET (1726–1792)
ALL HAIL THE POWER OF JESUS' NAME

THE HIGHLY EXALTED ONE

People are often successful in making a name for themselves, but only one has the name that is above every name. This belongs to Jesus (Philippians 2:9). How did his become the most illustrious name? It happened like this: He completely humbled himself, and then God exalted him to the highest place in the universe (vv. 6–11). We usually do the opposite. We exalt ourselves, so God humbles us.

Jesus exemplifies true humility because he went from the highest place to the deepest depth. He was the image of God, the visible representation of deity (Hebrews 1:3). Paul saw him on the Damascus road in this celestial glory. Yet that form was laid aside, and in the incarnation, the Son took the form of a slave.

The scripture says he emptied himself (Philippians 2:7). This was not a partial surrender but a total change of form. None of God's glory was found in Jesus, the Son of God who humbled himself, became a man, and was obedient unto death—the degrading death of the cross. Therefore, "God also hath highly exalted him, and given him a name which is above every name" (v. 9). This means that all things, even death, will be put under his feet (1 Corinthians 15:26–27) and the scripture will be fulfilled:

At the name of Jesus every knee should bow, of things in heaven, and things
in earth, and things under the earth; and that every tongue should confess
that Jesus Christ is Lord, to the glory of God the Father.
PHILIPPIANS 2:10–11

There's a wideness in God's mercy,
Like the wideness of the sea;
There's a kindness in his justice,
Which is more than liberty.

FREDRICK W. FABER (1814–1863)
THERE'S A WIDENESS IN GOD'S MERCY

I OBTAINED MERCY

Here is Jesus' story about a man who prayed for mercy (Luke 18:9–14):

A Pharisee and a tax collector—a self-righteous religionist and a self-deprecating sinner—happen to be praying at the same time in the temple. The Pharisee boasts to God of his accomplishments. In the same breath, he criticizes other men. He sees goodness in himself and depravity in others. He thinks God is pleased with his religion.

The tax collector stands apart from the Pharisee. Is he afraid of the religious man's condemnation? He certainly feels his sin acutely, since he will not even raise his eyes to heaven. God has given him insight about his true condition, and this fuels his prayer for God's mercy.

One of these men knows the law; the other knows the tax code. One occupies a prominent place in the temple; the other stands at the fringe of the pious gathering. The one, the Pharisee, lacks what the other, the publican, possesses: self-knowledge. The Pharisee's refined legalism and place of honor mean nothing compared with God's mercy that makes it possible for a person to realize his true condition. The publican is despised in the Pharisee's world, but he is enlightened by God. He confesses his sin, and he experiences the wideness of God's mercy.

I thank Christ Jesus our Lord, who hath enabled me, for that
he counted me faithful, putting me into the ministry; who was
before a blasphemer, and a persecutor, and injurious: but I obtained mercy,
because I did it ignorantly in unbelief.
1 TIMOTHY 1:12–13

There is welcome for the sinner, And more graces for the good;
There is mercy with the Savior; There is healing in his blood.

FREDERICK W. FABER (1814–1863)
THERE'S A WIDENESS IN GOD'S MERCY

GOD'S MERCIFUL CHOICE

As the disciples spread the good news, they encountered a magician
named Simon (Acts 8:9–11). This man wanted to receive the Holy
Spirit, yet he mistakenly thought he could purchase it with money
(v. 20). However, God's gifts are not for sale at any price. Still today,
some people think their monetary gifts to churches or charities buy
them credit with God. In addition to that, many believe their natural
goodness can be traded for divine blessing. To them, Peter would
say, "Your heart is not right before God. Repent therefore of this
wickedness of yours" (vv. 21–22 NRSV).

The gospel is not an investment opportunity. We who believe did
not recognize it as a good deal and then pay the price for salvation.
We were as natural as anyone else; the things of God were foolishness
to us (1 Corinthians 2:14). Nor is the body of Christ like a fraternal
organization. A person does not maintain membership by paying
monthly dues no matter what the currency might be—money, good
works, or even faith, which itself is God's gift (Ephesians 2:8).

Bear in mind the reason why the kindness and love of our Savior
God appeared. It was not because of any works of righteousness that
we have done. He is saving us simply according to his mercy (Titus
3:4–5). God freely chose to be merciful to us, and nothing we do
obligates him. "So then it is not of him that willeth, nor of him that
runneth, but of God that sheweth mercy" (Romans 9:16). Those who
present another gospel than this must not call theirs the gospel of
God (1:1). They preach a human gospel that is not good news at all
(Galatians 1:6–9).

> *[I] will be gracious to whom I will be gracious,*
> *and will shew mercy on whom I will shew mercy.*
> EXODUS 33:19 (SEE ALSO ROMANS 9:15)

But we make his love too narrow
By false limits of our own;
And we magnify his strictness
With a zeal he will not own.

FREDERICK W. FABER (1814–1863)
THERE'S A WIDENESS IN GOD'S MERCY

THE BELIEVER'S AMBASSADORSHIP, PART 1

Elijah once called fire down from heaven that consumed fifty-one threatening soldiers (2 Kings 1:10). James and John, in their zeal, wanted to do the same to Samaritans who didn't welcome Jesus Christ. The Lord rebuked them for this (Luke 9:51–56). Although they had based their suggestion on a scriptural example, it did not complement the spirit of the Lord's work at that time.

Presently, we are Christ's ambassadors. It is vital that we understand the nature of our mission, because relations are strained between this world and our home government. The world is warlike toward God, whereas he desires reconciliation (2 Corinthians 5:19). Therefore, we must accurately exhibit the policies of the power we represent. No matter what has gone before or what will come in the future, right now God isn't angry and is careful not to give or take offense. He is conciliated and desires that the world respond in kind (v. 20). This is the guiding rule of the ministry of reconciliation (v. 18). If we accept our ambassadorship, this will mold every circumstance of our lives. We will draw attention to God's offer of peace by our very attitude and seek opportunities to appeal to the citizens of this world to accept that gracious gift.

A day will come when war is declared between the two realms. Then God will withdraw his ambassadors. This means that before God begins to work in the day of his indignation, he will take us away from this earth (1 Thessalonians 4:17; 5:9; Revelation 6:17). For the moment however, our presence here is a token of God's peace, which we must keep until we are called to the celestials to continue our ministry in a higher sphere.

We are ambassadors for Christ, since God is making his appeal through us;
we entreat you on behalf of Christ, be reconciled to God.
2 CORINTHIANS 5:20 NRSV

December 8

*For the love of God is broader
Than the measure of our mind;
And the heart of the Eternal
Is most wonderfully kind.*

FREDERICK W. FABER (1814–1863)
THERE'S A WIDENESS IN GOD'S MERCY

THE BELIEVER'S AMBASSADORSHIP, PART 2

The word *ambassador* appears in one passage outside of 2 Corinthians 5:18–21. In Ephesians 6:18–20, Paul is seen as an ambassador in chains. What government would maintain a peaceful attitude toward a country that imprisoned its ambassador? Yet God continues to be conciliatory toward this world despite its mistreatment of his ambassador. He is "not counting their trespasses against them" (2 Corinthians 5:19 NRSV).

This doesn't make things any easier for the ambassador, however. So Paul requests the saints' vigilant prayers: "That I may open my mouth boldly, to make known the mystery of the gospel" (Ephesians 6:19). Because it is associated with Paul's ambassadorship, this mystery is the message of God's conciliation with the world. It takes boldness to speak of such peace, because the rulers of the darkness of this world oppose it (v. 12). These principalities and powers do not want anyone to know the God of peace. They prefer that earthlings consider God with dread in their hearts, and so they portray him as an angry avenger of wrongdoing. Opposing this, Frederick Faber is right to sing, "The heart of the Eternal is most wonderfully kind." God's peace is one of the great accomplishments of the blood of the cross, and it is among the spiritual blessings with which we are blessed (Ephesians 1:3; Colossians 1:20;).

Since Paul is no longer living, let us pray for others and for ourselves to know and boldly make known our God who, in Christ, conciliated the world, not counting their offenses against them. Let us pray that we who believe will not restrict the love of God to the measure of our minds, but will enlarge our hearts to contain just a fraction of his vast love.

God was in Christ, reconciling the world unto himself, not imputing their trespasses unto them; and hath committed unto us the word of reconciliation.
2 CORINTHIANS 5:19

If our love were but more simple, We should take him at his word,
And our lives would be all sunshine
In the sweetness of our Lord.

FREDERICK W. FABER (1814–1863)
THERE'S A WIDENESS IN GOD'S MERCY

HOW TO MISHANDLE THE WORD

The ancient serpent who deceives the whole world works through questioning God's Word, denying it, and imposing falsehoods in place of it (Genesis 3:1–5). It has never been necessary for him to develop a new line of attack. This old one works fine.

The original satanic question is, "Did God say, 'You shall not eat from any tree in the garden'?" Eve needed only to rest upon God's Word to resist this seed of unbelief (2:16–17). Instead, doubt caused her to mangle God's words by omitting some of them, adding her own ideas and substituting her thoughts for God's.

God said, "Of every tree of the garden thou mayest freely eat." Eve said, "We may eat of the fruit of the trees of the garden," omitting the word "freely." That word suggests God's generous heart that supplies us according to his riches in glory (Philippians 4:19). Eve could eat and eat freely. Today, as in the primal day, unbelief strips God's grace from his Word.

While God said, "Thou shalt not eat of it," Eve said, "Ye shall not eat of it, neither shall ye touch it." Her addition makes God a tyrant imposing purposeless restrictions upon humankind. God was very specific: "The day that thou eatest thereof thou shalt surely die" (Genesis 2:17). Eve was vague: "Ye shall not eat of it. . .lest ye die." This substitution changes the certainty of the penalty to a mere risk, as though God does not know how to express himself.

To this day, omission, addition, and substitution are the preferred methods of mishandling the Word. These caused Eve's concept of God to fall short of his glory, and that shortfall led to her sin (Romans 3:23).

But I fear, lest by any means, as the serpent beguiled Eve through his subtilty, so your minds should be corrupted from the simplicity that is in Christ.
2 CORINTHIANS 11:3

December 10

My grieving soul revive, O Lord,
According to thy Word;
To thee my ways I have declared
And thou my prayer hast heard.

Author Unknown
My Grieving Soul Revive, O Lord
Paraphrase of Psalm 119

Human Weakness and God's Word

The Psalms are sacred poems addressed to God from his saints, yet they often tell of experiences that are common to all people. Even readers who do not know these poems as God's Word appreciate their greatness. The emotions and circumstances suggested by phrases like "I am a stranger in the earth," "My soul cleaveth unto the dust," and "My soul melteth for heaviness" are universal (Psalm 119:19, 25, 28). Unfortunately, readers who have not yet believed are not likely to view their life struggles in relation to God and his Word as do the authors of the Psalms. These ancient believers were like us in that they were not immune to the insecurity and loneliness, sorrow and pain of this brief life. We are like them in that we delight in God's testimonies and find counsel in his Word (v. 24).

Poetic expressions of human weakness in relation to God's revelation are found in the Greek scriptures, as well. There we find that the illumination of the gospel of the glory of Christ is contained in a weak human vessel (2 Corinthians 4:4–7). That vessel, who was afflicted in everything, perplexed, persecuted, and cast down, was not distressed, despairing, forsaken, or perishing, because he spoke the truth of the gospel in the spirit of faith (vv. 8, 13). His experience echoes the poetry of the psalm to suggest our present human condition and the wideness of heart that results from grasping God's achievements and purpose in his Word.

I cling to your decrees, O Lord; let me not be put to shame.
I run the way of your commandments, for you enlarge my understanding.
Psalm 119:31–32 nrsv

O Thou, in all thy might so far,
In all thy love so near,
Beyond the range of sun and star,
And yet beside us here.

FREDERICK L. HOSMER (1840–1929)
O THOU, IN ALL THY MIGHT SO FAR

GOD'S LOVE UNIVERSAL AND PERSONAL

God's love is not known in the fickle ebb and flow of human emotion but in the believer's inner man that is strengthened by God's Spirit (Ephesians 3:16, 19). In our inner man, we know that God's love is unlike human love, which is inconsistent, prejudiced, and impulsive. In contrast, as the famous verse says, God loves the whole world (John 3:16). He loves it because he made it; because he did not create it in vain, or that any part should be uninhabited by creatures that do not glorify him (Isaiah 45:18). For that reason, when Christ died at Golgotha, he died for all. This is confirmed by faith and God's Word, which tells us that, in God's time and way, all will know the love of Calvary and will glorify God the Father (Philippians 2:10–11). Therefore, the beloved Son, telling of his death, declared, "And I, if I be lifted up from the earth, will draw all men unto me" (John 12:32).

God's love carried his Son through human life to history's darkest moment of death. That love lies behind all the events of our lives, as well. No matter how difficult these are, faith sees them as gifts from God's heart of love. His wisdom and perfect understanding will complete all he desires (Romans 8:31–32). In the interim, while God is operating all things according to the counsel of his will (Ephesians 1:11), we are perfectly guarded from everything that might disconnect us from his love.

What shall we then say to these things? If God be for us, who can be against us? He that spared not his own Son, but delivered him up for us all, how shall he not with him also freely give us all things?
ROMANS 8:31–32

December 12

_Come, divine interpreter, Bring me eyes thy book to read,
Ears the mystic words to hear, Words which did from thee proceed,
Words that endless bliss impart, Kept in an obedient heart._

Charles Wesley (1707–1788)
Come, Divine Interpreter

THE HOPE OF HIS CALLING

Wesley's prayer in this hymn is like the one in scripture that asks for the eyes of our hearts to be enlightened to see the hope of God's calling (Ephesians 1:18–19). This hope, or expectation, is so important that the apostle gave thanks to God that the believers were remaining in it (Colossians 1:3–6). Elsewhere, he established the saints in that same expectation.

The Thessalonian believers had been severely persecuted ever since they had believed. However, they couldn't tell the difference between man's rage and God's wrath. They were shaken in their minds because they had been told their sufferings were proof that the day of the Lord was near (2 Thessalonians 2:2). The apostle responded with a description of the conditions that will exist prior to the Lord's return (vv. 3–12). The dreaded judgments of that day only come upon people like the Thessalonians' persecutors who are unacquainted with God and do not believe the gospel (1:6–10). This argument is based on the first epistle to the Thessalonians, which describes our blessed hope in two aspects. One of these is that the Son will deliver the believers from God's wrath at the end of this age by assembling them together with him in the air (1 Thessalonians 1:10; 4:15–18; 5:9).

The other aspect of our hope came to light because the Thessalonians thought the day of the Lord had come and yet were mourning over their dead loved ones (4:13). They learned that the resurrection of Jesus Christ guarantees that all who belong to him will be raised from the dead when he returns (v. 14).

For the Lord himself shall descend from heaven. . .and the dead in Christ shall rise first: then we which are alive and remain shall be caught up together with them in the clouds, to meet the Lord in the air.
1 Thessalonians 4:16–17

Among the saints on earth
Let mutual love be found,
Heirs of the same inheritance
With mutual blessings crowned.

BENJAMIN BEDDOME (1717–1795)
LET PARTY NAMES NO MORE

THE RICHES OF THE GLORY OF HIS INHERITANCE

The great prayer of Ephesians 1 asks that God will enlighten the eyes of our hearts to see the riches of the glory of his inheritance in the saints (v. 18). To understand the meaning of this wondrous thought, let's examine the word *inheritance*. The literal meaning of the Greek word is "lot-appropriation." Therefore, we better understand this prayer when we use the word *allotment* instead of *inheritance*.

When God allocated the land of Israel each year, the cultivated ground was divided into sections, and the farmers in each village were separated into groups with a man heading each one. Marked pebbles, the lots, were cast in a bag, and a little child drew one out for each group. This determined the allotment of land given to the head of each group. Christ is like the head of a village group who shares his allotment with all who are in his company. This helps us understand the meaning of Ephesians 1:10–11, which is best translated like this: "To head up all in Christ. . .in whom our lot was cast."

God has cast our lot in Christ, who holds the allotment of all the heavens and the earth (v. 10). This knowledge urges us to pray that God will enlighten the eyes of our hearts to see the riches of the glory of the enjoyment of his allotment among the saints. This includes every spiritual blessing in Christ and his choosing the saints in Christ before the foundation of the world (vv. 3–4). They were made alive in Christ. They were raised out of death in him, and they are seated in the celestials in him (2:5–6). Dear God, enlighten us to see the saints' allotment in Christ!

Giving thanks to the Father, who has enabled you to share in the
[allotment] of the saints in the light. . .
COLOSSIANS 1:12 NRSV

Enthroned at God's right hand he sits,
Maintainer of our cause,
Till every vanquished foe submits
To his victorious cross.

CHARLES WESLEY (1707–1788)
COME, LET US RISE WITH CHRIST

THE EXCEEDING GREATNESS OF HIS POWER

Scripture records God's power beginning with his creating the heavens and the earth. But the standard of God's power for believers is in his dealing with death in Christ's resurrection and with enmity in Christ's exaltation (Ephesians 1:19–22).

The raising of Lazarus merely lengthened his life. The raising of Christ took away the sin of the world and resulted in our justification (Romans 4:25). Its complete victory over death will result in the elimination of death from the universe (1 Corinthians 15:22, 26). As we believe God and pray for the spirit of wisdom and revelation, we will know the transcendent greatness of this power (Ephesians 1:17–19).

God's power is entirely positive and constructive: By dealing with death and sin, God brought life and incorruption to light (2 Timothy 1:10), and these will be brought to completion when he is all in all (1 Corinthians 15:28). How beneficial and glorious is the power exhibited in Jesus Christ's resurrection!

In his exaltation, "all principality, and power, and might, and dominion, and every name that is named" is under his feet (Ephesians 1:21). This is not for their destruction, but ultimately for their benefit when they know God as all (1 Corinthians 15:27–28). Presently, believers are privileged to acclaim the lordship of Jesus Christ. Since we know the blessedness of being under his feet, we know something of the power that placed him at God's right hand. By faith, we also know that one day everything will likewise display the power of his exaltation, acclaim Christ's lordship, and so glorify God the Father (Philippians 2:9–11).

And what is the immeasurable greatness of his power for us who believe,
according to the working of his great power. God put this power to work in
Christ when he raised him from the dead and seated him at his right hand
in the heavenly places.
EPHESIANS 1:19–20 NRSV

THE SPIRIT OF FAITH

What can keep us from despondency and cause us to say with the apostle, "Though our outward man perish, yet the inward man is renewed day by day" (2 Corinthians 4:16)? Second Corinthians 4 overflows to tell us this renewal comes through our faith in the Word of God, the truth, the gospel of the glory of Christ, the treasure in our earthen vessels, the dying of the Lord Jesus, and the life of Jesus, as well. It tells us we have the very thing that causes grace to increase, abounding in thanksgiving to the glory of God (v. 15). David the king possessed this, as did Paul the apostle. It is the spirit of faith in which these men drew upon the power of God's Word to lift themselves up in the midst of afflictions: "I believed," Paul declared, "and therefore have I spoken" (v. 13; see Psalm 116:10).

Be encouraged by the love of Christ who died for the sake of all (2 Corinthians 5:14–15). Remember the grace of our Lord Jesus Christ who was rich but because of you became poor so that you, by his poverty, would be rich (8:9). Believe and speak this to others in the spirit of faith. Despite discouraging responses, that spirit is resolute in faithfulness to the truth.

Like Paul, we find encouragement in the resurrection of Christ. Even though few stood with the apostle in his day, he believed and so spoke: "He which raised up the Lord Jesus shall raise up us also by Jesus, and shall present us with you" (4:14). By his example we also believe and say:

Our light affliction, which is but for a moment, worketh for us a far more exceeding and eternal weight of glory.
2 CORINTHIANS 4:17

December 16

The Word of God is sure,
And never can remove;
We shall in heart be pure
And perfected in love.

CHARLES WESLEY (1707–1788)
YE RANSOMED SINNERS, HEAR

HOLD FAST THE PATTERN OF SOUND WORDS

The student of the scriptures does well to heed the advice to "hold fast the form of sound words, which thou hast heard of me" (2 Timothy 1:13). Since Timothy was told to use the apostle Paul's vocabulary, how much more is it necessary that we do the same? The consistent use of scriptural terminology is a great help in understanding and explaining truth. The opposite is also true. Our grasp of the truth is seriously hindered by the use of extrascriptural terms drawn from tradition, theology, philosophy, self-help literature, and poor biblical translation. The good thing that was committed to Timothy (v. 14) is the words of the sacred scriptures (3:15–17). We, too, must guard this treasure, not through fleshly methods but by the indwelling Holy Spirit.

It is important to note that there is a right way to hold fast the pattern of sound words. We do so "in faith and love which is in Christ Jesus" (1:13). Our goal is not mere technical correctness. The pattern of sound words is in harmony with the Lord's work in us, and it is presented to others in a spirit of faith and love. These two qualities are not native in us; they have their source in Christ only.

Surely Timothy understood the importance of the apostle's sound words because he knew that all those in the Roman province of Asia had turned away from Paul (1:15). This calamity happened, at least in part, because of the failure to uphold Paul's pattern of sound words. With this gone from the Asian churches, faith and love probably went by the board, as well. The church's abandonment of the apostle is a sobering lesson that teaches the immeasurable value of the precise words of scripture.

Continue in these things, for in doing this
you will save both yourself and your hearers.
1 TIMOTHY 4:16 NRSV

*I asked the Lord that I might grow
In faith, and love, and every grace;
Might more of his salvation know,
And seek, more earnestly, his face.*

JOHN NEWTON (1725–1807)
I ASKED THE LORD THAT I MIGHT GROW

THE LIFE OF FAITH AND LOVE

The cross of Christ is the hinge on the door of the gospel. That door will not swing open on our strength and virtue. The gospel's message tells us that our deeds and even our beliefs are useless to bring us deliverance in Christ. Only God's grace through faith opens that door (Ephesians 2:8). When we step across its threshold, we find the freedom to grow in faith and love and walk in the good works that God has made ready for us (v. 10).

When we believe the gospel's message, we see that our salvation is a finished work. Then our efforts end. This ending is the starting point of our spiritual growth. All believers have arrived at the finish line we call salvation, because Jesus Christ was obedient to the death of the cross.

Suppose someone is trying to gain entrance into heaven, not by faith in Jesus Christ, but by perfect attendance at church and devotion to the Bible. As good as these are, they will lead to something far from heaven because they are works of the flesh (Galatians 5:19–21). That person is striving to reach the finish line, unaware or unaccepting of the fact that Jesus Christ finished the work of his salvation and that God has already granted citizenship in the heavens to all whom he has called (Philippians 3:20).

We begin our life of faith and love at the cross, which is salvation's finish line. There is no need to struggle for what God has already given us. Rather than nullifying God's grace, let us glory in the cross on which we were crucified with Christ (Galatians 2:20) and allow faith and love to grow in us to the praise of God the Father and our Lord Jesus Christ.

I do not nullify the grace of God.
GALATIANS 2:21 NRSV

Far down the ages now,
Her journey well nigh done,
The pilgrim church pursues her way,
And longs to reach her crown.

HORATIUS BONAR (1808–1889)
FAR DOWN THE AGES NOW

THE PILGRIM CHURCH

Our heritage reaches at least as far back as Abraham, who waited for a heavenly city that has earthly foundations—New Jerusalem (Hebrews 11:10; Revelation 21:2). All of God's believers are like Abraham, sojourners in this world cherishing a glorious expectation. We are, like Moses, strangers in a strange land (Exodus 2:22).

But it was not always so. Formerly, people who were not of the Jewish race could have nothing to do with God. We were "aliens from the commonwealth of Israel, and strangers from the covenants of promise, having no hope, and without God in the world" (Ephesians 2:12). The blood of Christ has solved these problems (v. 13).

Our relationship with the saints of all the past eras is defined in Ephesians 2:19–22. All believers, even those of the far distant past, have three things in common: We are citizens under God's government, we belong to his family, and we are his dwelling place. We today have certain blessings and privileges that are not shared by those who lived before the first coming of Christ. Still we have a rich legacy in the ancient saints; we are being built on the foundation that God laid in them.

We have no visible evidence to prove to the world that these things are true. However, because we believe God's Word, accepting the gospel's pattern of love and grace, we can speak, think, and act in harmony with the truth. In this way, the just shall live by faith (Habakkuk 2:4).

For the vision is yet for an appointed time, but at the end it shall speak, and not lie: though it tarry, wait for it; because it will surely come, it will not tarry.
HABAKKUK 2:3

When life's sun is set, O how blest are the righteous;
They rest from their labors and care,
And when the Lord calls, they'll awake in his likeness;
God's riches of glory to share.

ADLAI LOUDY (1892–1984)
WHEN LIFE'S SUN IS SET

REHEARSALS OF RESURRECTION

Year by year, God illustrates the great truth of life out of death. Seeds lie dormant in the soil through the cold of winter until the summer's warmth transforms them into living plants that flower with a glory that exceeds that of the original seeds (1 Corinthians 15:35–44). This allegorically describes what will happen to all who are dead in Christ when he returns (1 Thessalonians 4:13–18).

One glance at a cemetery confirms the truth that in Adam all die (1 Corinthians 15:22). Since this is undeniable, so also is the second half of 1 Corinthians 15:22: "In Christ shall all be made alive." The confirmation of this is Jesus Christ himself, the firstfruits of resurrection (v. 23). We have the record of his appearances in resurrection and a list of those who saw him (vv. 5–8). Now, we are looking for our Savior from the heavens who, on the day of resurrection, will "transform the body of our humiliation that it may be conformed to the body of his glory" (Philippians 3:21 NRSV).

Every night that we lie down to sleep reminds us that the day will dawn when those who have fallen asleep in Christ will be raised to meet him (1 Corinthians 15:52; 1 Thessalonians 4:14). The sound of an alarm clock raises us from our beds; a trumpet blast will raise the bodies of the dead in Christ to meet him in the air (v. 16; 1 Corinthians 15:52). In all this, we revel to know that our God is rehearsing in this world that which he reveals in his Word—his power and his plan for resurrection.

For since by man came death, by man came also the resurrection of the dead.
For as in Adam all die, even so in Christ shall all be made alive.
1 CORINTHIANS 15:21–22

Then why should we sorrow as having no hope
For loved ones whose journey is o'er?
They peacefully rest till we're called home above,
To be with our Lord evermore.

ADLAI LOUDY (1892–1984)
WHEN LIFE'S SUN IS SET

THE EXPECTATION OF FAITH

An old fisherman and friend explains that when he goes fishing, he hopes he will catch his limit although he knows he may not catch any fish at all. However, my friend fully expects to see the Lord when he returns. This explains why the word *expectation* is preferable over the word *hope* when translating the Greek word *elpis* in scripture. We expect that which is certain, so *expectation* describes the true outlook of faith. Strictly speaking, faith does not hope; it isn't unsure about what is yet to come. Faith relies on the promises of God for the future and expects their fulfillment.

The past is the foundation of faith while the future is its completion. For example, we believe the scriptural record of God's work in creation. We know that he created the heavens and the earth as recorded in Genesis 1:1. Likewise, we love the words of Colossians that reveal all was created in Christ, who is the Son of God's love and his visible image. All that is in the heavens or on the earth, visible or invisible, was created through him and for him (Colossians 1:13–17).

A man's previous record tells us what to expect from him in the future. Therefore, the exalted position of God's Son as the beginning of the creation of God gives us great confidence (Revelation 3:14). We have seen him as the First, so we look forward with assurance to his exaltation in the future. That is, we expect to see him as the Last (1:18).

He has made known to us the mystery of his will, according to his good
pleasure that he set forth in Christ, as a plan for the fullness of time, to
gather up all things in him, things in heaven and things on earth.
EPHESIANS 1:9–10 NRSV

I won't look back. God knows the fruitless efforts,
The wasted hours, the sinning, the regrets,
I leave them all with him who blots the record
And mercifully forgets.

Annie J. Flint (1866–1932)
I Won't Look Back

Behind Is Self, Ahead Is Christ

Our career in Christ is often compared to a race (Hebrews 12:1). We are runners who never look back on our past with regret, but stretch forward toward the goal. Reviewing the ignorance and selfishness that possessed us before Christ became our all does not strengthen our faith. So let us sum up our former lives with the word of the cross: "Our old man is crucified with him, that the body of sin might be destroyed, that henceforth we should not serve sin" (Romans 6:6).

Although we are willing to forget our failures, even our highest achievements are no more than refuse by scriptural standards (Philippians 3:4–8). Paul is a brilliant example of this. He was born into a favored place among humankind. He was "of the stock of Israel, of the tribe of Benjamin, an Hebrew of the Hebrews" (v. 5). His religious achievements gave him the highest place among his own race: "As touching the law, a Pharisee; concerning zeal, persecuting the church; touching the righteousness which is in the law, blameless" (vv. 5–6). But he gave up all this because it interfered with something far superior—his place in Christ (v. 7).

Our Lord humbled himself and became obedient to the death of the cross. Only then was he exalted with the name above every name (2:8–9). Following his path, we are in fellowship with his suffering, seeking conformity with his death and the realization of the power of his resurrection (3:9–10). At the end of the race, we will grasp this completely and receive the prize—our transformation into his glorious likeness (v. 21).

This one thing I do, forgetting those things which are behind, and reaching forth unto those things which are before, I press toward the mark for the prize of the high calling of God in Christ Jesus.
Philippians 3:13–14

I won't look forward. God sees all the future.
The road that's short or long will lead me home,
And he will face with me its every trial, and bear with me
The burdens that may come.

ANNIE J. FLINT (1866–1932)
I WON'T LOOK BACK

THE GLORY OF AFFLICTIONS

Romans 5:1–5 leads us step by step to understand that we will not simply bear the burdens that may come to us, but glory in those afflictions. This path begins with five comforting words: "Therefore being justified by faith" (v. 1). Is there any question that we have been declared innocent in the court of God's righteousness? Certainly not if "we believe on him that raised up Jesus our Lord from the dead; who was delivered for our offences, and was raised again for our justification" (4:24–25). This demolishes the walls of guilt and enmity between God and us. So "we have peace with God through our Lord Jesus Christ" (5:1).

Now that the two steps of justification and reconciliation are accomplished, what shall we do? We should simply stand in God's grace in expectation of the glory of God (v. 2; 8:30). Of course, we don't stand here in a vacuum. We live in the midst of a world that is under the sway of "the prince of the power of the air, the spirit that now worketh in the children of disobedience" (Ephesians 2:2). No wonder we are afflicted. In this we take the final step—we glory in those afflictions (Romans 5:3).

How can this be possible? We see the sufferings of others and worry that we could never cope with them. But scripture pledges that God will not allow us to be tried beyond our ability to bear it (1 Corinthians 10:13). Through afflictions, we gain endurance and experience, and the expectation of our glorification grows (Romans 5:3–4). This proves that there is no shame in sufferings. They do not express God's disapproval, but they guide us into the love that he poured into our hearts (v. 5).

Rejoice in hope, be patient in suffering, persevere in prayer.
ROMANS 12:12 NRSV

*I will look up into the face of Jesus, for there
My weary heart can rest, my fears are stilled,
And there is joy and love and light for darkness,
And perfect peace, and every hope fulfilled.*

ANNIE J. FLINT (1866–1932)
I WON'T LOOK BACK

GLORY IN THE FACE OF JESUS CHRIST

The easiest way to recognize a person is by a glance at his or her face. The hands, feet, or even the entire body will not do so well as the face, which also provides insight into the character behind it. Is it habitually smiling or frowning; gentle, hostile, carefree, or anxious? In the face of Jesus Christ, we see the illumination of the knowledge of the glory of God (2 Corinthians 4:6). Of course, this is not the physical face of Jesus Christ. The face is the figure of speech this verse uses to explain our Lord's character and personality. Can we gain the knowledge of the glory of God elsewhere than in the contemplation of Jesus Christ who is his image (v. 4)? According to scripture, we cannot.

We are currently contending with the rulers of darkness in a dark world (Ephesians 6:12). That anyone can be illuminated by God's glory in Christ is testimony to his power (Colossians 1:13). We shouldn't despair that we cannot see outward evidence of the advance of God's great plan in others, or at times even in ourselves, because his work to establish the believers and bring them to perfection is hidden from view as we walk by faith through this world.

Long ago, by the sound of a still small voice, God comforted a desolate prophet hidden in a lonely cave. Today, a treasure is hidden in our earthen vessels as we gaze at God's glory in the face of Jesus Christ (1 Kings 19:12; 2 Corinthians 4:7).

For God, who commanded the light to shine out of darkness, hath shined in our hearts, to give the light of the knowledge of the glory of God in the face of Jesus Christ.
2 CORINTHIANS 4:6

Alas! and did my Savior bleed
And did my sovereign die?
Would he devote that sacred head
For such a worm as I?

ISAAC WATTS (1674–1748)
ALAS! AND DID MY SAVIOR BLEED?

THE CURE FOR SIN

Are we no better than worms? God truly loves and values us, but in the light of the cross, aren't we even less than this? Weren't we crucified with Christ (Galatians 2:20)? This brings to mind the thieves and criminals who were physically crucified with our Lord. They teach us that, worse than worms, we are dead sinners (Romans 6:6).

Jesus Christ began his ministry to Israel by healing a leper. Leprosy signifies sin. This healing was the Messiah's testimony to the priests that he could heal their sinful nation (Matthew 8:2–4). Leviticus 13 describes the ancient priests' examination of a leper (vv. 12–13). These verses draw an astonishing picture that illustrates how humankind's sin was cured by the cross of Christ. They say, "If the disease breaks out in the skin, so that it covers all the skin of the diseased person from head to foot, so far as the priest can see, then the priest shall make an examination, and if the disease has covered all his body, he shall pronounce him clean of the disease; since it has all turned white, he is clean" (NRSV).

If a man is covered from head to foot in leprosy, he is as good as dead, yet scripture says he is clean. The great truth is that the only cure for the leprosy of sin is death. That is why we treasure the following little phrase: "He that is dead is freed from sin" (Romans 6:7). Our apostle was the foremost of sinners who was declared clean because he was crucified with Christ. So he gives this advice: "You also must consider yourselves dead to sin and alive to God in Christ Jesus" (v. 11 NRSV).

> *It is a faithful saying: For if we be dead with him,*
> *we shall also live with him.*
> 2 TIMOTHY 2:11

Well might the sun in darkness hide
And shut his glories in,
When Christ, the mighty Maker died
For man the creature's sin.

ISAAC WATTS (1674–1748)
ALAS! AND DID MY SAVIOR BLEED?

THE ABANDONMENT OF THE BELOVED

The darkness that came upon the land the day our Lord was crucified shows God's abandonment of his suffering Son (Matthew 27:45). The vicious opposition of Jesus' enemies and the cowardly desertion of his friends could not compare with this calamity. Until the moment that darkness shrouded him, Jesus had always lived in the joyous light of God's countenance. But men hung him on a tree, and he became accursed in God's sight (Galatians 3:13). Though he knew no sin, Christ became sin, and fire from on high entered into his bones (Lamentations 1:13; 2 Corinthians 5:21). In those dark hours, the Almighty bruised him and the question of sin was settled (Isaiah 53:10).

Take a long look at Golgotha's shadowy vista and give thanks for Jesus Christ's faith (Galatians 2:16). Condemned by humankind, forsaken by his allies, abandoned by God; no creature in the universe was more pitiful and desolate than he. When light finally returned to the sky above Jerusalem, he cried, "My God, my God, why hast thou forsaken me?" (Matthew 27:46). This question is unanswerable unless his suffering was for the sins of others. If he had not been made sin for us (2 Corinthians 5:21), God never would have abandoned him. For you, for me, and for the entire world, Jesus Christ not only endured the tremendous physical pain, mental torture, and moral degradation meted out by humans, but he also suffered the enmity and absolute abandonment of almighty God.

He that spared not his own Son, but delivered him up for us all,
how shall he not with him also freely give us all things?
ROMANS 8:32

Praise to the Lord, O let all that is in me adore him!
All that hath life and breath, come now with praises before him.
Let the amen sound from his people again,
Gladly for aye we adore him.

JOACHIM NEANDER (1650–1680)
PRAISE TO THE LORD, THE ALMIGHTY

THE ATTITUDE OF WORSHIP

Scripture provides examples of physical postures that we may adopt as we pray and offer praise to God. Hands were lifted up and knees were bowed (1 Timothy 2:8; Ephesians 3:14). However, we are glad that God reads prayers from our hearts, not from our hands, knees, or lips, because we cannot lift up our hands, bow our knees, or speak aloud everywhere. The workplace, for example, is usually not the place for this, though it is good and even necessary to pray there. While we cannot always assume a typical posture of prayer, we can always take up a prayerful attitude that harmonizes with God's will.

In the past, worship was dependent on physical things. For example, the Samaritan woman pointed out that her people worshipped on Mount Gerizim while the Jews said Jerusalem was the proper place for worship (John 4:20). But those days are long gone. What's more, Gerizim and Jerusalem have not been replaced by other locations. Jesus Christ himself informs us that now "the true worshippers shall worship the Father in spirit and in truth" (v. 23). Therefore, nothing physical is mandatory in our relationship with God.

The overriding requirement today is that we adore the Father in spirit and truth. He is seeking such true worshippers. An attitude of worship in spirit and truth may be conveyed by raised hands or bowed knees. Our feelings can be so intense that we cannot help but express them physically. But the physical is not compulsory. We are free to hold a worshipful posture in our heart toward the Father in every place and at all times.

For God is my witness, whom I serve with my spirit in the gospel of his Son, that without ceasing I make mention of you always in my prayers.
ROMANS 1:9

> Crown him the Son of God,
> Before the worlds began,
> And ye who tread where he hath trod,
> Crown him the Son of Man.

GODFREY THRING (1823–1903)
CROWN HIM WITH MANY CROWNS

THE DOMINION OF THE SON OF MAN

The first appearance of the title "Son of Man" in scripture is found in Psalm 8:4. The subject of this psalm is dominion over the earth: "Thou madest him to have dominion over the works of thy hands; thou hast put all things under his feet" (v. 6). By this we learn why Jesus Christ is called the Son of Man. The first man, Adam, failed to carry out his headship of the human race and dominion over creation, so the Son of Man inherited all that belonged to Adam except sin.

The first time the title Son of Man is seen in the Greek scriptures is in Matthew 8:20. There the Lord contrasts lowly creatures with himself, the highest of all: "Foxes have holes, and birds of the air have nests; but the Son of Man has nowhere to lay his head" (NRSV). Though animals had a place to call home, the Son of Man, their rightful head, was an ostracized wanderer. He came to claim the dominion given him by the Father, but people refused his authority (John 1:11).

The Gospels display the Son of Man's dominion: He has authority on earth to pardon sins (Matthew 9:6). He is the Lord of the Sabbath because the Sabbath was made for people (12:8). He came to seek and to save what Adam lost (Luke 19:10). Finally, all judgment is committed to the Son of Man (John 5:27). Seated on a white cloud, wearing a victor's golden wreath, he thrusts in his sickle, reaps the earth, and sends forth judgment unto victory (Revelation 14:14–16).

For the Son of man shall come in the glory of his Father with his angels; and then he shall reward every man according to his works.
MATTHEW 16:27

Abide with me; fast falls the eventide;
The darkness deepens; Lord with me abide.
When other helpers fail and comforts flee,
Help of the helpless, O abide with me.

HENRY F. LYTE (1793–1847)
ABIDE WITH ME

THE HISTORY OF HELPLESSNESS

Since the day of Adam's transgression, humankind has been seeking happiness independent of God. This goal is enshrined in our Declaration of Independence as an inalienable right. No wonder self-improvement is encouraged and praised. However, those who are impotent to help themselves cannot count on the help of others. God's way is the very opposite of this. When we had proven our utter helplessness, he sent the Savior to help (Romans 5:6).

The ancient Roman republic inspired our form of government, and its laws set the pattern for ours. We hear about the Greeks of long ago and find that the intelligence of those ancients teaches us to this day. The law and literature of ancient Israel describe the unique God-given religion. However, by the time the saving grace of God appeared, all this had been worn to shreds, and humankind was nowhere near its goal of happiness.

The Savior's life, death, and resurrection in the first century laid the foundation of everlasting happiness and launched a renewal. However, this faded as the truth was lost. Humankind again groped in darkness. Then, fifteen centuries later, the Reformation of the Christian religion uplifted the human race by uncovering the light of the Word of God. Whatever blessings we now enjoy have followed in its wake. Still, the helpless human race exhausts itself in the struggle of self-help.

Scripture tells of a coming apostasy that will dwarf the failures of the past. A man of sin will arise and lift himself above all that is godly (2 Thessalonians 2:3–4). As he madly attempts to eradicate all evidence of God's name on this earth and humankind is more helpless than ever before, God will again send Christ with righteousness, peace, and joy, fulfilling every hope of happiness (Haggai 2:7).

For when we were yet without strength,
in due time Christ died for the ungodly.
ROMANS 5:6

Jesus, confirm my heart's desire
To work and speak and think for thee;
Still let me guard the holy fire,
And still stir up thy gift in me.

CHARLES WESLEY (1707–1788)
O THOU WHO CAMEST FROM ABOVE

STIR UP THE GIFT OF GOD

Anyone who has ever tended a fire—a campfire, perhaps, or a fire in a woodstove—can appreciate the apostle's instruction to Timothy: "Stir up the gift of God, which is in thee" (2 Timothy 1:6). But why did a companion of Paul have need of this advice? Wouldn't he always be spiritually invigorated? Timothy had witnessed the apostle chained and imprisoned for at least five years and then released. Apparently, Paul wrote 2 Timothy during a second imprisonment. In those years, evils were creeping into the churches to the extent that all in Asia had turned away from the apostle (1:15). This must have discouraged Timothy.

The apostle encouraged his fellow worker, reminding him that God's calling isn't dependent on what humans do but on the divine purpose and grace. The flood of evil that the apostles encountered—and that increases to this day—cannot hinder this purpose. God's grace was given to us before the ages began (v. 9). We are now living in an evil age (Galatians 1:4). But before the ages, there was no evil, and when they have run their course, evil will no longer be found. God's purpose existed before evil and is above evil. Therefore, we need not be overly concerned by evil's presence. Although death expresses evil's ultimate power, the crucifixion of Jesus Christ was death's furthest limit, and his resurrection was the first step in its eradication (1 Corinthians 15:22–23, 26; 2 Timothy 1:10).

Evil is like cold weather that causes us to draw close to a fire. It gives us reason to stir up the holy fire our spirit the gift of God that is in us. We do this by God's grace in the light of truth, and because:

God did not give us a spirit of cowardice, but rather
a spirit of power and of love and of self-discipline.
2 TIMOTHY 1:7 NRSV

December 30

Fix my heart and eyes on thine! What are other objects worth?
But to see thy glory shine, Is a heav'n begun on earth.

John Newton (1725–1807)
True Happiness

The Believer's Heart of Love

To live in the body, one's heart must be pumping blood. To live in the spirit, one's spiritual heart must pulsate with love. A believer who walks worthily of God's calling, for example, is humble, meek, and patient and loves others (Ephesians 4:1–2). Without love, so-called spirituality is like crashing brass and a clanging cymbal. Without love, a person who possesses gifts, knowledge, understanding, and faith is nothing. The highest forms of service and self-sacrifice are unprofitable without love (1 Corinthians 13:1–3).

A believer possesses the spirit of wisdom and revelation when the eyes of the heart are enlightened (Ephesians 1:17–18). The enlightened heart sees that love fulfills the law, builds up others, and is the place of unity (Romans 13:10; 1 Corinthians 8:1; Colossians 2:2). Such a heart has the faith to see what cannot be observed. Such faith operates through love (Galatians 5:6; Hebrews 11:1). We love the Lord our God because we see him with the enlightened eyes of our heart. We love our neighbors as ourselves because we see them with those same eyes. They, like us and all other men and women, are being drawn to the Savior who, because of God's love, was lifted up on the cross (John 12:32). Let us pray that God will pour his love into their hearts just as he did in ours (Romans 5:5).

Could there be anyone who does not fall short of this quantity of love? Yet none of us is so weak that we cannot, like the apostle Paul, pray according to God's will:

> *That Christ may dwell in your hearts by faith; that ye, being rooted and grounded in love, may be able to comprehend with all saints what is the breadth, and length, and depth, and height; and to know the love of Christ, which passeth knowledge, that ye might be filled with all the fulness of God.*
> Ephesians 3:17–19

His the gold upon the hills, His the light across the sea;
His the purpose that fulfills, His the day that is to be.

J. H. SAXTON
SEE THE GOLD UPON THE HILLS

THE FINAL WORDS

Our God has a purpose for the ages and is operating everything according to the counsel of his will in order to complete his plan (Ephesians 1:11). This sets our faith apart from all others. Central to God's plan is the death, burial, and resurrection of our Lord Jesus Christ (1 Corinthians 15:2–3). We are vitally involved in it, as well. A magnificent scene, described in Ephesians, reveals the Father of glory together with the ascended Christ. There with them among the celestials is the Church, the body of Christ (Ephesians 1:19–23). God, by the might of his strength, raised Christ from the dead and seated him at his right hand in the heavenlies. He subjects all under his feet and gives Christ, as head over all, to the Church. We are the body of Christ in the midst of God's operation as the complement of the one who is completing the all in all.

Although the results of God's plan are everlasting, it is accomplished within the ages, which have a beginning and an ending. Scripture documents that accomplishment, so it records the moment when God's purpose is complete. The journey toward that end began before the ages, when all was in God (2 Timothy 1:9). The divine purpose is to guide the universe through those ages until God is in all (1 Corinthians 15:28). Everything that occurs in the course of the journey is a means to that end (Romans 11:36).

Nearly 800,000 words make up an English translation of the sacred scriptures. These describe the outworking of God's plan from start to finish. Out of them, seven simple words found near the end of one of Paul's epistles describe the success of that plan. We treasure these final words of the divine revelation and long for the day in which they come to pass:

That God may be all in all.
1 CORINTHIANS 15:28

Scripture Index

Author Index

Lyte, Henry F.—12/28
Mackay, Margaret—9/25, 9/26
MacLagan, William D.—9/18
Midlane, Albert—6/14, 9/19
Milton, John—10/3
Monsell, John S. B.—9/13
Montgomery, James—2/17, 4/4
Morris, Leila N.—5/27
Morrison, John—3/30, 4/20
Mote, Edward—4/7
Moule, M. M.—8/14
Murray, Robert—9/29
Neale, John M.—2/11, 6/10, 9/15
Neander, Joachim—12/26
Neumeister, Erdmann—1/26
Newell, William R.—1/10
Newton, John—2/6, 2/14, 3/17, 3/18, 5/13, 5/14, 5/29, 7/30, 11/13, 12/17, 12/30
North, Frank M.—3/7
Nunn, E. Cuthbert—10/6
Oatman, Johnson, Jr.—10/9, 10/10, 10/11, 10/12
Paget, Catesby—6/24, 6/25
Perronet, Edward—12/4
Peters, Mary B.—6/8, 7/8
Peterson, Susan H.—11/18
Pollard, Adelaide A.—7/22

Prentiss, Elizabeth—7/11
Rawson, George—5/8, 5/9, 5/10, 11/29
Richter, E. F.—8/4
Rippon, John—5/11
Rist, Johann—10/14
Robinson, George Wade—5/20
Robinson, Robert—6/27, 6/28
Rossetti, Christina G.—4/2, 9/24
Rowley, Francis H.—2/24
Russell, Arthur T.—1/28, 10/8
Russell, Rollo—10/20
Ryder, T.—7/25
Sandell, Lina—8/15
Saxton, J. H.—12/31
Schaff, Phillip—5/22
Schneesing, Johannes—1/28
Schütz, Johann J.—4/6
Scott, Clara H.—3/22, 10/25
Scriven, Joseph—8/23
Sears, Edmund H.—4/18
Shekleton, Mary—6/17, 6/18
Simpson, A. B.—7/24, 7/26, 7/27, 7/28, 8/9, 8/10, 8/11, 8/17, 8/18, 8/19
Skoog, A. L.—8/15
Small, James G.—3/8
Smith, Walter C.—2/23, 4/24, 4/25, 4/29
Spafford, Horatio—2/2
Tarrant, William G.—8/24
Taylor, Jane—12/2
Theodulph of Orleans—2/11

Thring, Godfrey—12/27
Thrupp, Joseph F.—11/9
Tucker, F. Bland—5/3, 5/4, 9/8
von Zinzendorf, Nikolaus—2/25, 2/26
Walford, William W.—2/21, 8/27, 8/28
Watts, Isaac—2/5, 3/20, 4/8, 4/9, 4/10, 4/27, 4/28, 5/5, 6/5, 6/15, 8/31, 9/1, 10/15, 12/24, 12/25
Wesley, Charles—1/30, 2/16, 2/28, 3/4, 3/5, 3/11, 4/5, 4/12, 4/13, 5/6, 5/7, 6/23, 7/5, 7/20, 9/6, 9/7, 9/10, 11/28, 11/30, 12/1, 12/3, 12/12, 12/14, 12/16, 12/29
Wesley, John—2/25
Wesley, Samuel—2/9, 5/21
West, Robert A.—7/6
Whittle, Daniel W.—6/30, 7/1, 7/2, 10/26, 10/27
Wilkinson, Kate B.—5/16, 8/12, 8/13
Winkworth, Catherine—10/14
Work, John Wesley, Jr.—10/7
Wycliffe, John—8/11

Hymn Title Index